D1174446

Adventures of a Frontier Naturalist

Dr. Gideon Lincecum—photograph made on his eightieth birthday
at a studio in Austin.

Courtesy Barker Texas History Center,
University of Texas, Austin.

Adventures
of a
Frontier Naturalist

•

THE LIFE AND TIMES
OF DR. GIDEON LINCECUM

•

Edited by

Jerry Bryan Lincecum

and

Edward Hake Phillips

Introduction by Jerry Bryan Lincecum

Foreword by A. C. Greene

TEXAS A&M UNIVERSITY PRESS
COLLEGE STATION

Library of Congress Cataloging-in-Publication Data

Lincecum, Gideon, 1793–1874.
  Adventures of a frontier naturalist : the life and times of Dr. Gideon Lincecum / edited by Jerry Bryan Lincecum and Edward Hake Phillips ; introduction by Jerry Bryan Lincecum ; foreword by A.C. Greene.—1st ed.
    p.   cm.
  Includes bibliographical references and index.
    ISBN 0-89096-592-7 (cloth : acid-free paper).—ISBN 0-89096-603-6 (paper : acid-free paper)
    1. Lincecum, Gideon, 1793–1874.   2. Naturalists—Texas—Biography.   3. Frontier and pioneer life—Texas.   I. Lincecum, Jerry Bryan, 1942–   . II. Phillips, Edward Hake.   III. Title.
QH31.L68A3   1994
508.764'092—dc20
[B]   94-11122
                                                                CIP

Free thought!
Oh, yes, holy free thought, I have cherished ye a long lifetime
and I promise myself and the world
that all my efforts, either in word or deed,
shall be on that side of the blanket
so long as this old heart throbs.
—GID

Contents

Foreword

Gideon Lincecum's autobiography, as a parable of the American dream, goes beyond history into sociology. From his boyhood, Gideon was typical of modern Americans—driven, striving, pushing, restless, always seeking something "out there"; something that will help him better himself. But modern, you ask? Gideon Lincecum was born in 1793 and died in 1874, a century or more before most of us regard anything as "modern." Despite the discrepancy in eras, he became what is still considered the ultimate American success: a self-made independent individual, in action and in thought, able—and quite ready—to tell the world to go to hell. Never satisfied, even in success. More than once his career echoes a phrase from his journal that characterized his life: ". . . my spirit was not easy. It wanted a wide[r] field for action."

Gideon Lincecum was probably not an easy person to live with, although his wife, whom he finds "young and pretty" and whose conversational ability matches his own, bore him thirteen children, ten of whom survived into adulthood—and patiently tracked his many changes of home and heart. During his seven-month wilderness sojourn in Texas—a major portion of the autobiography—he never expresses any longing to see his family. Keeping in mind the fact that some of this autobiography is from daily journals, reflecting an immediacy that recollection can't achieve, we may read between the lines for such resentment in passages like this, on marriage and children:

> Regarding marriage . . . Dr. [Ben] Franklin advised early marriage. I did so, and thereby in the course of time, demonstrated the fallacy of the Franklin theory. I was utterly incom-

petent to the duties and responsibilities of domestic life. I, however, made out to worry through with it without calling for help. My ten living children grown, married and settled off on ample homes long ago . . . sustaining themselves pretty well . . . are, in their mental aspect, not above fair to good middling; and the mischief that I have done them by bringing them into a world that is full to the brim with the same sort, and to myself, by placing a clog on the pursuits that nature had fitted me for, is great.

Hardly the notes of a well-adjusted, happy-just-to-be-at-home individual. Like most self-made men, he believed in his own convictions at times a bit too firmly. He did mightily like to win arguments, even with himself. And like so many self-made men, today as then, he tends to blame something outside himself if he feels he has failed his potential, in Gideon's case (unfairly, one feels) his "numerous brood":

When I failed, with the Franklin experiment, to bestow on the world an equivalent for the harm it produced, I do not allude to this matter regretfully, but as a circumstance which continued to check the natural inclination and bent of my capacity up to 1852. At that period, having settled my numerous brood, I found my domestic responsibility ceased. I have since been free and could pursue that which seemed to please me best. But it was no go. The train of philosophic thought had been long since broken. The habit for investigation and experimentation was too long interrupted. The faculties and powers for scientific scrutiny were blunted and no longer capable of producing reliable ultimates.

"Unencumbered" was a favorite word of Gideon Lincecum.

He points out that only after moving to Texas was he free to apply his scientific curiosity toward real achievement. While none of this necessarily creates in the reader a dislike or distaste—Gideon is too boylike to arouse such severe sentiments—the temptation to reach through the page and shake some sense into the stubborn character is almost overwhelming. But to be fair, he did now and then learn his lesson. At one point, looking back on his allopathic medicine career, he says, "But I know now who was the fool then."

Yet, the journal—the autobiography, if you will—is fast and fascinating reading, poetic at times and always willing to express both sides of most questions . . . with the exception of religion. Gideon is, rather proudly stated, an atheist, at best an agnostic. He comments, seeing that he alone had supplied most of the meat during one expedition, "The old preacher in his even[ing] service—and I always thought strange of it—thanked an absent Somebody for the venison and other game."

For twenty years there was no church at Long Point, Texas, which he founded, because he demanded any such building must have an arch over its entrance with FREE DISCUSSION permanently inscribed on its face.

Although it is impossible to repeat a life like the one Gideon lived, his fundamentals of learning are, by one description or another, still in place. "Being early in nature's grand university," he wrote, "my Indian education in all branches of natural science was rapid and delightful." It was from his early experiences that he became a doctor, although he passed through at least three stages before arriving at a point where, "I felt tired of killing people and concluded to quit the mankilling [allopathic medicine] business." From the simple Indian cures ("before I was 15 I had the reputation of a 'sure-cure' Indian doctor"), through the deadly allotropic period, to, finally, what he called a "steam doctor" or, more accurately, his preferred title of a "botanic doctor." In the latter role he could very well fit into some professional organizations today.

The turning point in his life came when he suffered a near-fatal heat stroke while hunting. For nearly four years he was unable to do any kind of heavy work, mainly spending his days alone in the woods. He treated himself with a diet he devised after watching "an abstemious buck" feed: the prescription was one cornmeal waffle with a cup of sassafras tea with a heaping teaspoonful of sugar, three times a day. Gideon drinks little alcohol, and liquor is such a terrible factor so often in the lives around him.

A great deal of the autobiography describes various hunting and fishing trips. Gideon Lincecum is not a conservationist, in today's terms. He liked nothing better than to hit a new territory, the fields full of game and the streams full of fish. But he is farsighted, almost as if he is on the edge of one age and can foresee the next. He knows that game laws must be enacted if America is to have any of the outdoor experiences he has enjoyed.

There is a minor historical digression in his autobiography that also led to an amount of mental advancement on Gideon's part. When he was still a teenager, as a sideline, he kept the library for the Rev. Mason L. Weems, a traveling bookseller and author—the now famous, or infamous, "Parson" Weems, who gave us the Washington cherry tree legend. Regardless of Parson Weems's accuracy, Gideon managed to sell five thousand dollars' worth of books for him during a year of the parson's absence and in gratitude, in addition to 10 percent of sales, the good parson presented Gideon with all the books the youth had set aside to read. Although Gideon had abolished his illiteracy at age fourteen, this gift of books was the basis for his true intellectual achievements—and make no mistake, Gideon Lincecum was true intellectual, not in the academic sense but within the definition of someone who solves life's problems with the mind and not just the hands.

Sometimes we see a Gideon who, even in ordinary pursuits, approaches things in odd ways. Take, for instance, a ninety-three–pound catfish he had caught: "His mouth was so large that I held it open and my wife put the baby's head in it." (The reader's mind conjures up a family group: father, mother, baby, and catfish.) Gideon was also anthropomorphic—that is, he attributes all sorts of human inclinations to birds and animals. He believes his horse Ned could not only think but think well. Ned, for instance, would build up a burnt-out fire (per forefoot) when the gnats were bad. Gideon concludes the freshwater (softshell) tortoise was "universally left-handed" because twelve of thirteen he trapped were caught by the left forefoot. He attributes such agricultural skills as planting crops to one kind of ant and he translates the language of birds and deer. "It is my opinion," he says, "that an ingenious linguist could grammaticize the wild goose language."

In Texas, alone on a wide prairie, cranes by the thousands threatened him after he shot their leader. Couriers flew out, bringing in thousands more so that he and his horse fled for their lives. Whether one believes it or not, it is possibly the most fantastic—and fascinating—episode in the book.

Restless, passionate in his view and dreams, he recognized

his opportunities even though delivered via hardship. Exploring Texas with a trio of young men, Gideon—by then past age forty—discovers none of them can hunt, or will hunt, well enough to furnish meat for their sustenance. Scornfully he reports, "I was born in the woods and lived many a day on my hunt before I was seven years old. These boys slept in feather beds."

And how up-to-the-minute is his lament about his children: "Parties and dancing schools, shopping and 'Charge it to Poppa' was all they seemed to care for." Spoken like a true twentieth-century father.

I am pleased to note I had a hand in the resurrection of old Gideon's autobiography. In 1965 when the late Lois Wood Burkhalter's *Gideon Lincecum: A Biography* was published, as Book Editor of the Dallas *Times Herald,* I wrote an enthusiastic review of the book—a review which caught the eye of Jerry Lincecum and helped create his interest in his until-then unrecognized ancestor, whom Jerry saw as the archetypical American male. Today Jerry Lincecum teaches an adult class at Austin College which not only studies autobiography but affords his students the chance to tell their own stories—Jerry contending there is no such thing as a dull life.

Edward Hake Phillips, Emeritus Professor of History at Austin College, retired in 1983 after twenty-four years with the history department, seven of them heading the department. Dr. Phillips has written two books on the life and career of Speaker Sam Rayburn and has, like his colleague Dr. Lincecum, become fascinated by life stories told by those who lived them.

—a. c. greene

Acknowledgments

We are indebted most of all to the late Lois Wood Burkhalter, as our dedication of the book implies. Another whom we cannot thank in person is the late Mary Harrison Clay, a Lincecum descendant whose Master's thesis on Gideon was very helpful. We are also grateful to Damon Bartlett of San Antonio (a descendant of Gideon's sister, Emily Lincecum Moore), who typed into his word processor (and shared with us) the complete text of two of Gideon's memoirs: "Bully Grandson" and "Personal Reminiscences."

For years of encouragement and assistance, we thank Noel Parsons, editor-in-chief of the Texas A&M University Press. For a generous contribution toward the subvention of publication costs, we are grateful to John Milton Andersen, M.D., and Anne Elaine Kolb Andersen, M.D. For financial support from Austin College's Richardson Endowment and personal encouragement, we thank Pres. Harry Smith and David Jordan, vice-president for academic affairs.

We also wish to thank the following: Dr. Don Carleton, director of the Center for American History of the University of Texas, Austin, and staff members Ralph Elder and Fred Burchsted; Dr. Cheri L. Wolfe, research associate, Institute of Texan Cultures; Dr. Ron Tyler, director, Texas State Historical Association; Choctaw educator and historian Ernest Hooser of Durant, Oklahoma; Dr. Ken Carleton of the Choctaw Nation of Mississippi; Emeritus Professors Edward DeZurko and Kenneth Coleman of the University of Georgia, Athens; Professor Frank B. Vinson of Georgia College, Milledgeville; Charles L. Harper of Warren County, Georgia; Carol Douthit of Macon, Georgia; Dr. Everett C. Wilkie, Jr., head librarian of the Connecticut Historical Society; Melody Specht Kelly, documents librarian, University of North Texas, Denton; independent scholar Robert Weddle of Bonham, Texas; Jacqueline Banfield, reference librarian, Sherman Public Library; Professor Emmet M. Essin III, East Tennessee State University; Rong Wang, librarian, the Historical Society of Pennsylvania; T. K. Griffis, secretary of the Grand Lodge of Mississippi, F. & A.M., Meridian; Fred W. Vaughan, secretary of the Grand Lodge of Alabama, F. & A.M., Montgomery; Dr. Elizabeth A. H. John, independent scholar in history, Austin, Texas; Dr. Michael Lynn Tate, of the University of Nebraska, Omaha; three dedicated local historians of Columbus, Mississippi: Samuel H. Kaye, Rufus Ward, Jr., and Carolyn B. Neault; Austin College reference librarians John West, Dana Williams-Capone, and Cathy Hartman; Gus and Georgie Foerster, Edwin and Edna Kelm, and Walter Seilheimer, all residents of Long Point, Texas; at Washington County, Texas, historian Annie Maud Avis; Star of the Republic Museum Director Houston McGaugh and Curator of Education Ellen Murry; Dr. Douglas Hall, a descendant of Gideon and Lincecum genealogist.

Most important of all has been the unstinting support given by our wives, Peggy A. Redshaw and Patricia Northridge Phillips.

Introduction

WHO WAS GIDEON LINCECUM?

As plans were made for celebrating in grand style the centennial of Texas independence from Mexico in 1936, it was decided that modern-day Texans should pay tribute to the state's early heroes by creating a Lone Star version of Valhalla or Westminster Abbey. Louis W. Kemp, Chairman of the Centennial Advisory Board of Texas Historians, actively promoted the idea of making the State Cemetery in Austin a local equivalent to Arlington National Cemetery, and largely through his efforts a vigorous campaign was launched as part of the "Centennial Tribute" to reinter in this central location the remains of a number of our state's founders and other notables. As a result the graves of thirty-two individuals (including some spouses) were moved to the State Cemetery.[1] Located on a hilltop in east Austin near the former French Legation (now a museum), the State Cemetery is a lovely setting, and the Centennial markers of gray Texas granite, four-and-a-half-feet tall, each one embossed with a bronze wreath and star, make impressive headstones. The idea of creating a "Little Arlington National" was soon forgotten, and today the State Cemetery, though well kept and attractive, is hardly a major tourist attraction. Visitors who wander by Row One of the "Austin Plot" or "Founders Row," so named because it is dominated by the grave and life-sized statue of Stephen F. Austin, are likely to be puzzled when they scan the second marker from the left. It bears the bronze Centennial emblem and the following epitaph, followed by the phrase "Erected by the State of Texas, 1936":

Dr. Gideon Lincecum
A Veteran of the War of 1812
Internationally Famous Botanist
Friend of Darwin
Born in Georgia
April 22, 1793
Died at Long Point
Washington County, Texas
November 28, 1873

Who was this "internationally famous botanist," and why is he buried in "Founders Row," in the shadow of the "Father of Texas" and amidst others whose names are recited by students of Texas history like a litany of saints—Bailey Hardeman, Big Foot Wallace, Empresario Sterling C. Robertson, Judge Abner S. Lipscomb, Gen. Moseley Baker? To answer that question is to begin to explain why the *Autobiography* of Gideon Lincecum deserves to be published and will appeal to a wide audience.

First, an aside to acknowledge a family tie: I am a direct descendant of the man who wrote this autobiography, but for reasons to be explained later, I was unaware of his existence until 1965, when the late Lois Wood Burkhalter published *Gideon Lincecum, 1793–1874: A Biography*. Although my first twenty-one years had been spent in Texas, I was then attending graduate school out-of-state, at Duke University in North Carolina. Three years later, after finishing my Ph.D. in English and returning "home" to begin my teaching career at Austin College, I presented a paper at the South Central Modern Language Association meeting in San Antonio and took the opportunity to call on Mrs. Burkhalter, who was then director of the McNay Art Center, located in that city. We discussed several aspects of her book, including the fact that it incidentally identified George Washington Lincecum, my great-grandfather, as a grandson of Gideon. She had no more information about George but encouraged me to study the Lincecum Papers seriously, as she had found a wealth of material in them which deserved publication. One of the things I remember best about our visit was her warning me that anyone who spends much time studying Gideon's writings is likely to become enamored of his dialect, "Gideonese," which

DR. G. LINCECUM & SON,
BOTANIC PHYSICIANS.

Will continue the practice of Medicine at the village of Long Point, and its vicinity, to any distance. Being well supplied with a full assortment of such Botanic Medicines as are needed in this climate===all fresh===they are ready day or night, to accommodate all those who may call for their professional services. With these advantages and many years experience in the diseases of the South, they flatter themselves, and they know, that they will be able, by close and prompt attention, to give general satisfaction.

Their whole practice will be conducted on purely Botanic principles. They are no half way men. They have the temerity to take a bold and decided stand for progressive Medical reform. Such is their confidence in the supperiority and certainty of their remidies, and their knowledge of disease, that they will make no charge for failure to cure any form of fever, where they are called during the first stage of the disease=== have an efficient nurse, and the patient stricly following their prescription, and continuing to employ them throughout the case.

They feel happy in assuring the community that they have prepared themselves for, and will be able to answer all reasonable expectation. And they are determined to give the public, particularly the friends of medical reform, by their superior skill and managment an opportunity to remove from the Botanic System, the popular charge of ignorance and empyricism.

Long Point, Washington County, Texas.

In 1850 this strongly worded broadside announced to residents of Long Point and Washington County, Texas, "a bold and decided stand for medical progressive reform" on the part of Dr. G. Lincecum and Son, botanic physicians.

Courtesy Barker Texas History Center,
University of Texas, Austin.

in style is vigorous, imaginative, colorful, and often unconventional. She was right about the value of Gideon's papers and the effect of reading him. Perhaps in that spirit the readers of this book will forgive the editors for their unscholarly habit, in the annotation (and this introduction), of referring to the author of the *Autobiography* not as "Lincecum," but rather as "Gideon." We have both come to feel that we know the man intimately, and that the familiar, informal reference is appropriate.

Back to the question of Gideon's identity and significance. The reader of his *Autobiography* will appreciate it more after reading the brief survey of his life with commentary on major themes provided by this essay. Like many tombstone epitaphs, Gideon's inflates somewhat the fame and accomplishments of the deceased. But even with its distortions—and an incorrect death date—this one provides a good starting point. It is correct that he was a veteran of the War of 1812, although when he applied for a pension in 1859, no official records of his service could be found and he had to supply considerable documentation. To say that he was "internationally famous" and a "friend of Darwin" is an exaggeration. The plain, unvarnished facts are remarkable enough: this self-taught naturalist corresponded with a number of the leading scientists of his day (including Charles Darwin), published over two dozen articles about science in scholarly and popular journals, was elected a corresponding member of the Philadelphia Academy of Natural Sciences, and contributed thousands of botanical specimens to world-class museums (including the Smithsonian, the British Museum, and the *Jardin des Plantes* in Paris). Gideon read *Origin of Species* in 1860 (one year after it was first published), embraced the theory of evolution, and wrote Darwin a lengthy letter offering supporting evidence from his observation of the ants of Texas. Moreover, he soon received a cordial reply, wrote a second letter providing more detail about the Texas agricultural ant, and eventually had his letters about the ant read by Darwin before the Linnaean Society (London's scientific elite), published in their learned journal in 1862, and critiqued by a leading Swiss authority on ants. That is a considerable accomplishment for an obscure naturalist from Texas, and it points to the fact that despite his lack of formal training, Gideon had a discerning eye, an analytical mind, and the ability to describe the natural world in ways that make his *Autobiography* a rich source of information about the ecological history of the nineteenth-century South and Texas in particular. When Samuel Wood Geiser considered Gideon's scientific career at length in *Naturalists of the Frontier,* he concluded: "it is cause for wonder not that he did so little, but that he accomplished so much."[2] As our title suggests, despite being raised on the geographical frontiers of America, removed from schools, libraries, and colleagues, this man was motivated by his great curiosity to emulate the *philosophes* of the Enlightenment. He was truly a "frontier intellectual."

Even the listing in Gideon's epitaph of the time and place of his birth suggests a reason why his reminiscences are worth reading, for he was born on the frontiers of Georgia in 1793, only four years after the U.S. Constitution was formally ratified. In his lifetime he witnessed the union grow from fifteen states to thirty-eight. His grandparents came to America from four different European nations, and his father, Hezekiah, loved the bordering life. Thus, Gideon spent his formative years moving from place to place in Georgia and South Carolina as new territories opened, becoming a skilled hunter and woodsman. At the age of fifteen (with only five months of formal schooling), the young man left home after a dispute with his father, spent three years working for two different merchants, then got himself elected tax collector of Eatonton, Georgia, and (in 1812) joined the army. After Gideon and Sarah Bryan were married in Putnam County, Georgia, in 1814 (he was twenty-one, his bride, seventeen), the young couple farmed first with Hezekiah and then on their own nearby for a couple of years.

In 1817, all the Lincecums headed for the newly opened territory of Alabama, but they stopped for a year on the Georgia side of the Ocmulgee River after Hezekiah bought a farm there. Here Gideon taught school briefly (but memorably, as detailed in chap. 2) and his sister Mary married Joseph Bryan (the brother of Gideon's wife). Then the whole extended family (six adults, ten children, and six slaves) set off on a six-week trek into the new territory of Alabama (Gideon recalled it as a joyous expedition). They paused at Tuscaloosa for a few months but decided the atmosphere was sullied by too many settlers, especially the raunchy Tennesseeans. In November, 1818, they traveled westward for twelve days, to an Eden-like setting near Plymouth Crossing on the Tombigbee River, directly opposite the Choctaw Nation in Mississippi. The exact location of Gideon's original homestead near Columbus, Mississippi, was recently identified by Samuel H. Kaye, one of the authors of *By the Flow of the Inland River: A History of the Settlement of Columbus to 1825*. Gideon went on to play a prominent role in the founding of Columbus. In August, 1819, he moved into the town proper, building its first frame structure, in which he opened a store. As its first postmaster, on 1 January 1821, he opened the first batch of mail that came to Columbus, and when the Mississippi legislature recognized Monroe County (which had been considered part of Alabama until the state line was surveyed in 1820) in an act signed by the governor on 9 February 1821, Gideon was named "Chief Justice of the Quorum," a select group of citizens charged with organizing the county. In this capacity one of his duties was to supervise the leasing of lots of school land; thus, he became one of the founders of the Franklin School in Columbus, the oldest free school in Mississippi. He was also one of the organizers of the Masonic Lodge in Columbus (chartered 8 January 1822) and served as its first Worshipful Master.[3]

Entrepreneur as well as civic leader, Gideon remained in Mississippi until 1848 and prospered, supporting his growing family (which eventually numbered thirteen children) as a merchant, an Indian trader popular with both the Choctaws and Chickasaws, and then a physician. Having grown up among the Muskogee Indians in Georgia and worked in an Indian store as a youth, he had empathy for Native Americans as well as experience in business dealings with them. First he operated an Indian store in the Choctaw Nation (near Columbus), learning to speak and write their language from slaves sold to him by Choctaws. Then, moving further north, he ran a store in the Chickasaw Nation at Cotton Gin Port on the Tombigbee. While living among the Choctaws, Gideon was present at the Treaty of Doak's Stand in 1820 and later wrote a detailed account of the eloquent and heated exchanges between Pushmataha, the great Choctaw chief and orator who was his particular friend, and Andrew Jackson. Gideon also made an important contribution to Southeastern American Indian ethnology by making repeated visits over a four-year period to an aged Choctaw sage, Chahta-

Immataha, and writing down (in the Choctaw language) an oral tradition dictated by the sage. Amounting to 650 holograph pages when he eventually translated it into English, Gideon's "*Chahta* Tradition" is the most extensive archive of Southeastern Native American lore collected before 1830. Recognizing its potential value, Gideon prepared it for publication shortly before the Civil War but never found a publisher. Although scholars now disagree about how much of it came straight from Chahta-Immataha and how much from Gideon's embellishment, it has been used as a major source for numerous articles and continues to be studied. A detailed analysis of Gideon's "*Chahta* Tradition" is the subject of a recently completed doctoral dissertation by Cherie L. Wolfe, and she plans to publish an annotated edition of his manuscript.[4] Gideon also wrote an early biography of *Pushmataha* that was based on interviews with the chief and other first-hand knowledge; it proved to be a major source for an important twentieth-century book on this key leader and the politics of Choctaw removal to Oklahoma.[5]

Gideon's friendship with the Choctaws led to one of his notable commercial failures, when he anticipated Buffalo Bill's Wild West Show by half a century. In 1829–30 he toured several states with forty Choctaw ball players (their ball game was similar to lacrosse), putting on exhibition games and performing Indian dances. But he gave up after five months when the enterprise failed to make a profit. The warmth and depth of his feeling for the Choctaws is summed up in a sentence he wrote in 1861: "so long as the life pendulum swings in this old time-shattered bosom, I shall remember their many kindnesses to me and mine, with sentiments of kindest affection and deepest gratitude, and my prayers for their elevation and progress as a people among the enlightened nations of the earth shall not cease."[6]

Gideon's relations with African Americans were more ambivalent. While he believed in the inferiority of the black race and strongly defended the institution of slavery, he nevertheless felt strong affection for several slaves, who are named in the *Autobiography*. One striking fact is that throughout the Lincecum Papers, Gideon rarely used the term "slave," preferring "negro" or "servant" when referring to a slave. On the other hand, in the aftermath of the Civil War, his bitterness over the defeat of the South and the oppressiveness of what he termed "our Yankee masters" was such that he refused to provide jobs for his ex-slaves. James Oakes, in his 1983 scholarly study of slavery in America, *The Ruling Race: A History of American Slaveholders*, summarizes major portions of the previously published version of Gideon's "Autobiography" in order to cite both Hezekiah and Gideon as prototypes of what he calls the "small slaveholder," an important group heretofore neglected in studies of slavery.[7] Thus, the complexity of race relations in the Old South is yet another topic further illuminated by this more complete text of Gideon's memoirs.

Similarly, Gideon's reflections on the genesis and development of his medical career offer insight into a complicated and interesting struggle taking place in the nineteenth-century South between two radically different systems of medical practice. He began studying medical books as early as 1811, at the suggestion of Dr. Henry Branham, a physician in Eatonton, Georgia, who saw in this young man's skill as an "Indian doctor" the basis for a promising medical career. Although he continued to read medical works in the intervening years and worked briefly in a doctor's shop in Tuscaloosa, it was only after he suffered a disabling heat stroke in 1827, resulting in the failure of his mercantile business, that he tried to earn a living as a physician. In 1830, after having tried or considered other money-making ventures (including the abortive tour with Choctaw ball players), he was at length persuaded by two neighbors to begin practicing medicine and to follow the prevailing allopathic system (which relied heavily upon bleeding the patient and administering strong drugs, such as mercury). But in 1832 the deaths of several patients made him question whether the strong drugs might not do more harm than good, and he sought out a Choctaw *Alikchi chito* (doctor of great reputation) to learn more about Indian herbal medicine. Together they spent six weeks in the woods, Gideon having contracted to kill game for their food and to pay the doctor fifty cents a day to teach all he knew about nature's remedies. This venture was successful enough to enable him to resume the practice of medicine with renewed confidence, and it moved him in the direction of allopathy's rival, the botanical system (commonly known as the "steam practice"), which he, like most allopathic practitioners, had initially ridiculed as "tomfoolery."

Reluctantly, Gideon was persuaded by a neighbor to give a fair trial to the botanical system advocated by Samuel Thomson in his *Guide to Health*. In a classic example of fence-sitting, for a time he carried in the two sides of his large saddlebags the drugs for both systems, letting the patient choose. He recalled: "It frequently occurred at houses where two were sick at the same time that one would require the steam practice while the other would say, 'Give me the old school medicines, for I would rather die scientifically than be cured by quackery.'" Then he had an experience that forced him to choose, as he lost a two-year-old child under circumstances leaving him no room to doubt that the death was occasioned by the allopathic remedies. He made a solemn vow to himself: "I would never administer another dose of the poisons of that system." On the way home that day he paused to empty the "old school" medicines from his saddlebags and left them in a pile on the ground. The mixture of drugs produced enough of a chemical reaction to attract attention and became the focus of local gossip for two or three days. Gideon recalled: "The doctors, who by this time were beginning to say a good deal about my apostasy, made a great scandal out of the boiling mass I had thrown out at Malone's gate. But I turned the tables on them by telling the people that it was all old school medicines I had thrown out there, and that, if I kept my senses, I would never kill any more children with it; for I had vowed never to carry a particle of it with me again. After this occurrence I carried none but botanical remedies with me."

Becoming known as a skillful and personable practitioner, he had to build living quarters adjacent to his office in Cotton Gin Port to accommodate the numerous patients who came from afar, and was often called to attend patients fifty miles away. By 1839 his reputation was such that one of the drug stores in Columbus (a much larger town) was advertising that it stocked "Botanical Medicines . . . prepared and manufactured . . . by Doctor Gideon Lincecum." Urged by prominent citizens in Columbus to move his practice there, he did so in 1841 and promptly became embroiled in controversy with the local allopathic physicians. He remained there seven years, growing steadily more prosperous, until in 1847 he felt able to retire to Texas. In 1850, after he moved to Texas, a handbill announcing the practice of "G. Lincecum and Son, Botanical Physicians" clearly indicated his allegiance: "Their whole practice will be conducted on purely Botanic principles. They are no half-way men. They have the temerity to take a bold and decided stand for progressive Medical reform." A statement written near the end of his life included a striking backward glance at his entire medical career: "I practiced the various systems of medicine . . . during a period of 49 years, having all classes and orders of the human genus for my patrons over a range of country extending from Pendleton District in South Carolina to the Valley of the Tuxpan in Mexico." Pat Ireland Nixon, in *The Medical Story of Early Texas*, ranked Gideon as an important and controversial figure,[8] and certainly those curious about the history of nineteenth-century medicine will find much of interest in the *Autobiography.*

But it was Gideon's exploration of Texas in 1835 that he considered the most exciting period of his life, and a substantial part of the *Autobiography* relates that experience. Prior to his move from Cotton Gin Port to Columbus, Gideon took time out to lead a group of six Mississippians to Texas for the purpose of determining whether it was as promising a territory for immigration as they had heard. Although the others went home after two months, Gideon and his intrepid horse Ned remained over six months, traveling as far south as Aransas Bay and west to the Edwards Plateau, where he was captured by Comanche Indians but managed to escape. After returning to Cotton Gin Port, Gideon regaled patients with stories about his exploits in Texas, to the point that his storytelling became known as a form of therapy and probably contributed to the growth of his practice. Since he wrote most of his memoirs when in his eighties, the editors feel sure the stories had improved and expanded somewhat over the years (especially the Texas tales). His reminiscences are often remarkably detailed and precise, with many species of plants and animals given their scientific names (mostly accurate, we found), yet the narrative flow makes them eminently readable. A hint of the appeal Gideon's reminiscences will have for those interested in ecological history comes from his comment on the San Marcos River valley in Texas as he first saw it: "It was then in a perfectly natural condition. Not a hacked tree or other sign of human violence was to be encountered in any direction. The scar of civilization had never marred the beautiful face of that paradise valley."

While on that first visit to Texas, Gideon found in Stephen F. Austin's Colony a choice league of land on Yegua Creek (in today's Washington County) that he liked well enough to reserve for later purchase. On his way home he stopped by San Felipe in May and became so caught up in the revolutionary fervor set off by the threat of invading Mexicans that he enrolled as a volunteer in the company of Capt. Moseley Baker, who held out the promise that he could be named Surgeon General of the Texas Forces West of the Brazos. But three old friends who were present knew his domestic circumstances and argued strenuously that Gideon's wife and ten children back in Mississippi needed him more than did the Texas forces. One of them went so far as to rub Gideon's name off the roster, offending Captain Baker but persuading Gideon to go home. With profoundly mixed feelings, he returned to Mississippi and resumed his medical practice. It is ironic that today Gideon and Gen. Moseley Baker are buried in close proximity to each other, their remains having been removed to the Austin Plot of the State Cemetery in 1936.

Although he remained in Mississippi another dozen years and grew more prosperous each year, Gideon became convinced that he and his family would be better off in Texas. In 1847, he prepared to move to the location in Washington County he had chosen twelve years earlier. A year in advance, he sent two of his older sons with a wagon train of household goods and other items. They arrived in July of that year, and one of them promptly married a local girl. Back in Columbus Gideon closed his medical practice in late 1847, paid his debts, collected on as many accounts as he could, and tore up the rest. He boarded a steamboat with the rest of the family at Columbus on 30 March 1848. They descended the Tombigbee to Mobile, sailed from there to New Orleans and on to Galveston. Then they took a steamboat to Houston, where they were met in wagons by the sons who had come ahead, and the whole family arrived in Washington County on Gideon's birthday, 22 April 1848. He was fifty-five and about to find his freedom.

This small building, which still stands on the old Lincecum place
at Long Point in Washington County, Texas
housed both Gideon's doctor's shop and a blacksmith shop for the
farm.

Photo by Keith Carter.

The choice land on Yegua Creek was still available, and he paid cash for 1,828 acres. Near the community of Long Point he built a house large enough for the extended family, quarters for his blacks, a large barn, a doctor's shop, and other buildings (most of which are still standing). Exercising his penchant for ironic humor, he named his little patriarchy after the home of the gods in Greek mythology, "Mt. Olympus." Then he began to devote the lion's share of his time to matters intellectual. From Mississippi he had brought enough wealth to be secure financially, and most of his children were now old enough to take care of themselves; thus, Gideon at last had the leisure to pursue his interests in ideas generally and the sciences in particular. His youngest daughter, Sarah, became his pupil and assistant on grand expeditions to collect plants, butterflies, and other specimens for various museums. His activities in geology ranged from avidly collecting fossils to attempting (unsuccessfully) to drill an artesian well at Long Point. In entomology his specialty was the Texas agricultural ant (the common red ant), but he also loved honey bees and taught the ones he raised at Mt. Olympus to swim. He became an official weather observer-recorder for the Smithsonian Institution, and the Lincecum Papers include several years' worth of the elaborate meteorological journals for Washington County that he kept. He was also attracted to such pseudosciences as phrenology and graphology, venturing to analyze even the handwriting of Charles Darwin.

Among the local citizenry Gideon cultivated the image of an "infidel," which he defined as "a scoffer and unbeliever in all systems," and in fact he belonged to a loosely organized group of Texas "infidels," who subscribed to the Boston *Investigator* and corresponded with one another. Especially critical of organized religion, he was a thorn in the side of some "religionists," as he called them, in the vicinity of Long Point. In the mid-1850s he stirred up a great deal of controversy when, after giving thought to ways of improving the human race, he advocated emasculation of those convicted of sexual crimes and submitted to members of the Texas legislature a "memorial" calling for a bill to this effect. The "Lincecum Law," as it came to be called, was brought before the Texas House of Representatives in 1855 and 1856 and attracted support from a few prominent citizens, but the legislators did not give it serious consideration.[9] Ironically,

After seven years of drought in Washington County,
in 1860 Gideon attempted unsuccessfully to drill an artesian well
at this site on his farm. His letters indicate he had reached
a depth of 200 feet when early fall rains broke the drought.

Photo by Keith Carter.

as we enter the last decade of the twentieth century, similar bills are regularly introduced in legislatures across the country and debated seriously.

Gideon lived past the age of eighty-one, and during his last twenty-five years he wrote a great deal, on many subjects. The Lincecum Papers (which include typescripts of many of the holograph originals) in the Eugene C. Barker Texas History Center at the University of Texas fill thirteen boxes and occupy four feet, nine inches of shelf space. The majority of this material was written after he arrived in Texas, when Gideon kept voluminous journals, carried on extensive correspondence (much of which was preserved by blotting it in a letter press), and penned two separate and distinct memoirs. He lived until 1874 (not 1873, as the State Historical Commission's epitaph would have it), well past the end of the Civil War, a fact which led to a whole new set of experiences. He and his beloved wife Sarah were both strong supporters of the Confederacy, and the bitter loss of the war, combined with the death of Sarah in 1867, led Gideon at seventy-five to migrate once more, this time with a widowed daughter and her family, and spend six happy years in Tuxpan, Mexico, with the American colony of Confederate expatriates there. Despite a vow never to return, he came back to Texas in 1873, one year before he died at Mt. Olympus on 28 November 1874.

Perhaps the essence of Gideon's character can be illustrated in relation to the fact that he was a talented amateur musician. His biographer records that when he was seventeen years old and clerking in an Indian trading post in Eatonton, Georgia, his employer brought him from Savannah a black English violin as a Christmas present. One of the treasures of his life, it led to the establishment of a family ritual that occurred without fail for sixty-three years. Every Christmas morning, just before the sun came up, Gideon would go out, in nightclothes and barefooted, to play three times a Mississippi version of an old ballad that, like his Bowie ancestors, had come to America from Scotland. The piece was "Killiecrankie," which celebrated a Scottish defeat of English forces in 1689. As Gideon lay on his deathbed in November, 1874, he made a game of calling up memories of the sixty-three Christmases he had saluted the dawn with that old black violin. He chuckled as he recalled the first Christmas after his wife's death; he had been camped out near the home of a very religious man, Mr. Willbourn, who came to his camp later that day to inquire about the unusual daybreak music. Seizing the opportunity to enjoy a joke at the expense of someone else's piety, Gideon explained that he belonged to a new religious sect, and that playing the tune three times at daybreak was part of the devotional. Mr. Willbourn went home puzzled. Now, with Death not far away, Gideon remembered triumphantly his sixty-third playing of the Christmas tune, only eleven months before. As he stepped out of the door barefooted on Christmas morning of 1873, he stubbed his toe on an old white petrified cactus that he had collected years before. In his words (from a letter to his daughter):

> I once again enjoyed the life-giving freshness of the sweet morning; the bright old moon whirling her broad yellow face down behind the western edge of this little bad-fixed world; and at the moment the last thread of her silver light disappeared, the new day was peeping out from the fractured east. Overhead, the great concave dome, bespangled and adorned with glittering constellations of suns and systems of suns, making up the whole brilliant scenery of the glorious morning so grand, so magnificent and transcendently beautiful that my old tired spirit floundered and struggled to get away, to fly upward. Such was the bewildering powers of my splendid surroundings that I could no longer control my feelings, nor at the moment, abstain from yelling out one of my big Indian whoops. For an instant the sound of the whoop reverberated down the branch, and then the world rolled on as good as ever.

Then the night-shirted old man, eighty years of age, barefooted and trembling, stood on his weary legs and completed his Christmas ritual for the last time:

> O Killiecrankie is my song;
> I sing and play it all day long,
> From the heel unto the toe
> Hurrah for Killiecrankie O!
> And ye hae been where I hae been
> Ye wad na be so cantie [light-hearted] O!
> and ye hae seen what I hae seen
> On braes [hills] of Killiecrankie O![10]

In preparing to publish Gideon's *Autobiography*, the editors began with the two memoirs he wrote in the 1870s. One of these resulted when, after his return to Texas from Tuxpan in 1873, he was contacted by an old friend, Wilbur F. Parker, who asked Gideon to write a series of reminiscences about his hunting and fishing exploits to be published serially in Parker's magazine, *The American Sportsman*. "Personal Reminiscences of an Octogenerian" began appearing in the magazine on 12 September 1874, and weekly installments were printed (without interruption) through 16 January 1875. (No manuscripts of "Personal Reminiscences" are known to exist.) Three years earlier, while in Tuxpan, Gideon wrote his first memoir in the form of a lengthy letter, dated 3 November 1871, addressed to a "Bully Grandson" (Frank Lincecum Doran, the son of Gideon's youngest daughter Sallie). A holograph manuscript of this letter is in the Lincecum Papers, but the editors believe it to be a copy, probably in Sallie Doran's handwriting, of the original letter(s) Gideon mailed to her son. Mrs. Doran prepared a heavily edited and expanded version of this memoir which appeared in *Publications of the Mississippi Historical Society* in 1904. Although we had only the printed text of this version to work from (no manuscripts of the *PMHS* memoir have been discovered) and have found no explanation of how it evolved, the added material seems authentic, and much of it could have come only from Gideon himself. A reasonable conjecture is that, since it was in 1874 (after his return to Texas from Tuxpan) that Gideon began writing his second memoir (the "Personal Reminiscences"), Sallie Doran, whose son had received the "Bully Grandson" memoir, seized the opportunity to get her father to expand it as a record of family history, quite different in content from the "Personal Reminiscences." In some cases the additions made in Sallie Doran's published version are such that one can imagine she read back to Gideon portions of the "Bully Grandson" letter and asked him to amplify it.

Thus, the editors of this volume had three principal texts to work from: (1) the holograph "Letter to a Bully Grandson, 3 Nov. 1871"; (2) "The Autobiography of Gideon Lincecum" as it appeared in *PMHS* in 1904; and (3) "Personal Reminiscences of an Octogenerian" as serialized in *The American Sportsman* in

1874–75. Only the "Letter to a Bully Grandson" appears in the Lincecum Papers in manuscript form; the other two texts exist only in their published versions. We chose to draw upon a fourth source for the bulk of one chapter: Gideon's "Life of Apushimataha," which appeared in *PMHS* in 1906, again edited by Sallie Doran. We selected a portion of it which reveals a great deal about Gideon's life during the years he lived in the Choctaw Nation in Mississippi, 1822–25, and his relations with several Choctaw leaders.

These four texts overlap considerably, but they rarely disagree or contradict one another. It seemed most useful to combine the four into one whole, a composite, but to indicate discreetly where the pieces came from. Thus, the beginning of each cutting is designated by a superscript letter indicating its source: [B] for "Bully Grandson"; [P] for "Personal Reminiscences"; [M] for the *PMHS* version of "Autobiography"; and [L] for "Life of Apushimataha." In combining these texts, we faced the problem of lack of technical consistency, as they represented three distinct levels of prior editing, ranging from almost none (we believe the holograph of "Bully Grandson" is a fair copy), to little more than that exercised by a typesetter working from a holograph manuscript ("Personal Reminiscences" contains many obvious errors and one gap), to the much more extensive and careful editing by Sallie Doran and Franklin L. Riley (secretary of the Mississippi Historical Society) of the two pieces published in *PMHS* in 1904 and 1906. While ideally it would have been preferable to get back to Gideon's own manuscripts, we could not. The best compromise seemed to be to achieve uniformity and readability, even if that meant correcting silently some obvious errors and occasionally revising punctuation and syntax for clarity. In keeping with the high Victorian style of his time, Gideon's sentences were often long-winded and his syntax sometimes convoluted. We have tried to convey to the modern reader simply and accurately what Gideon wrote, as best we could determine it. Our annotation identifies as many persons, places, events, and scientific data as we could locate and indicates textual discrepancies and problems. A selected bibliography has been included to enable further research by others.

To close with a poignant question about roots and personal identity, I am left with one unsolved mystery to ponder. In his

Gideon's memorial, erected by the State of Texas in 1936.
The inscription reads in part: "A veteran
of the War of 1812 / internationally famous botanist / friend of
Darwin."

Photo by Peggy A. Redshaw.

letters Gideon makes several references to a grandson, George Washington Lincecum, who was born on Washington's Birthday, 1849. George Washington Lincecum begat Bryan Bowie Lincecum (my grandfather), who begat John Aubon (Jack) Lincecum (my father), who begat Jerry Bryan Lincecum (me), who begat David Bryan Lincecum (my son); and from Bryan Bowie on down, all were first-born males, as was Gideon. The mystery is that we don't know which of Gideon's sons begat George W. (Despite the appeal of symmetry, Gideon's first-born son Lycurgus has proved to be an unlikely candidate.) George was estranged from his family and living two counties away from Mt. Olympus when he died at the age of thirty-nine, 26 October 1888, and all Bryan Bowie knew about his Lincecum ancestors was that his parents rarely mentioned them and had no contact with Lincecum relatives. That is not hard to understand, since one of Gideon's remarks about George W. in a letter reveals a dark, harsher side of the patriarch: "G. W. Lincecum is married. Society, if she knew her rights and had the courage to maintain them, would never permit such conjugal unions as that. What part of your society compact will he and that Seely gal ornament? Who will feed them?"[11] Sue Seely Lincecum was herself an orphan, and her pride must have dictated that after her husband's death she raise three children by herself rather than ask for assistance from the Lincecums. It is striking that George gave his first-born son the maiden names of his Lincecum grandmother (Sarah Bryan) and great-grandmother (Miriam Bowie). That son was only fifteen when his father died. Bryan Bowie remembered that George's mother, Isabella Farquhar, lived with them when he was a young child and died in 1877, when he was only four. Careful searches through the Lincecum Papers, Washington County records, and genealogies compiled by other Lincecums have not cleared up the mystery, and perusal of Washington County census records for 1850, 1860, and 1870 have also failed to provide any help. My best conjecture relates to one of the reasons Gideon gave for moving to Texas, namely, his children were engaging in too much "frolicking" in Columbus. Here he was also adopting the tone of the patriarch: "The boys drank and dressed extravagantly and the girls dressed and danced inimitably. . . . Parties and dancing schools, shopping and charging it to 'Poppa' were all they seemed to care for. The entire community of young people were similar in their habits. . . . So I determined to carry them to a country where the surroundings and conditions would be more promising."[12]

Perhaps George W. Lincecum was the product of some "frolicking" in Washington County and was born out of wedlock (but acknowledged by his grandparents, if not his father). While I do not expect the mystery of my great-grandfather's paternity to be solved, perhaps some of the readers of this book will have pertinent information to share that could fill a gap in my own autobiography.

JERRY BRYAN LINCECUM

Adventures of a Frontier Naturalist

CHAPTER ONE

The Roots of a Botanist

[P]My four grand parents were all Europeans—French, Scotch, English, Dutch. My father[1] resulted from the conjugal union that took place between the French Huguenot, Gideon Lincecum, and the Scotch lassie, Miriam Bowie—own great-aunt to the celebrated desperado, James Bowie, the originator of the Bowie knife. If glory and greatness consist in the amount of throat-cutting performed, the Bowie knife was a greater invention than was Napoleon Bonaparte even.

My mother[2] originated from the union of the Englishman, Willam Hickman and the Dutch lady Marie Ornbeck. It fell my lot to be fathered and mothered by the last born of the two families. My father was raised in the school of rebellion, and graduated on various battle-fields during the American Revolution. He knew nothing of books, being able only to read tolerably. He was possessed of good strong mentality but owing to the unsettled state of the country and the turbulence of affairs generally at the time he was forming his character it had been woefully misdirected. Being matchless in his physical powers and having full confidence in his knowledge of their application and uses, he often repeated the remark that "he had nothing to fear." Delighting in a border life, he reared his numerous progeny on the various boundary lines as they occurred from the frequent little treaties made with the Muskogee Indians on the Western

[Editor's Note: As indicated in the Introduction, this text is a composite of four distinct memoirs. The source of each cutting is designated by a superscript letter: [B] for "Bully Grandson"; [P] for "Personal Reminiscences"; [M] for the *Publications of the Mississippi Historical Society* version of "Autobiography"; and [L] for "Life of Apushimataha."]

borders of the state of Georgia. About my mother, there was nothing remarkable except that she could outrun anybody; was handsome, healthy, energetic, ingenious, industrious, frugal; but entirely illiterate.

ᴮMy father was a large, powerful man, six feet high and weighing in the prime of life 200 pounds. I saw him, when I was a little boy, lift a forge hammer at Byrd's Iron Works that weighed 596 pounds and hold it on his arms until a six-inch rule was set under it. He was the son of Gideon Lincecum, who was born in France and brought to America while he was a nursing infant and raised in Maryland. He was the son of Paschal Lincecum, a Frenchman who was the son of one Linseycomb, an Englishman who was left by the British Army during the terrible wars of that period as an unexchanged prisoner of war. How long he remained in the army was not stated.

It is only known that after peace was made he remained in France as an unexchanged prisoner. He did not return to England, but remaining in France, found and married a wife. They had only one son, whom they named Paschal. Upon him they bestowed all the learning that their means would allow. He grew up to manhood in the literature of his nation and not fancying the English orthography of his father's name changed it to Lincecum. In due time he took a wife. It was a happy union and within the first year of their wedded felicity, a well formed healthy son was born to them. Had it not been for his cherishing the principles of liberty and siding with the Republican party that at that period was beginning to make pretty strong head against the government, they might have been happy. They bestowed upon their new-born son the name of Gideon. But Paschal Lincecum was a Hugenot and was called upon by the government authorities to take the oath of allegiance. Sooner than renounce his religious faith and love of liberty, he gathered up such of his effects as were available, and with his young wife and infant son sailed for America. They settled in Maryland, where they spent the balance of their days. They had three daughters born to them in America but no other male issue.[3]

About the time Paschal Lincecum's son Gideon came to manhood, James Bowie, grandfather of the celebrated desperado Jim Bowie (of Texas notoriety), and his sister Miriam, a beautiful Scotch lass, came from Scotland and settled in the neighborhood of the Lincecums. Very soon the loveliness of this Scotch beauty attracted the attention of the young Frenchman. He paid his addresses, which were not disagreeable to her, and in process of time they entered into a matrimonial contract. But the friends of both parties were violently opposed to their union. The elder Lincecum was a little touched with aristocratic pretentions and did not fancy the idea of his portly, handsome son uniting himself with a stranger from Scotland. On the other side Mr. Bowie said that he could not consent for his beautiful, young and highly accomplished sister to become the wife of a frog-eating Frenchman. While these ugly words and sentiments were passing between the friends of the young lovers, Gideon and Miriam, they concluded not to wait for a termination of the difficulty, instead perpetrating an elopement. And stopping at the first authorized officer on the way, they had themselves lawfully married. To escape from further annoyance and from hearing the bitter words that might emanate from the quarrelsome parties, they continued their journey for many days, until they arrived on the banks of the Saluda river in the state of North Carolina.[4] Finding there a suitable place for a farm, they went bravely to work, fixing a home. This was a new, wilderness country and here the young couple plied their united efforts successfully. At this place they remained fifteen years, until they had several children born to them: two sons, Edward and John; and three daughters, Sally, Dolly and Nancy. Then, in 1769, hearing such good accounts of the territory of Georgia, they sold out their possessions in North Carolina and moved to Warren County, Georgia. Here another son was added to the family in the year of 1770. They named this third and last son Hezekiah.

My grandmother told me that she named him and that her reason for giving him that name was the following circumstance, which she related to me herself: About four months previous to the birth of Hezekiah, she had a very severe attack of fever, in which she was so much reduced that everybody thought she could not recover. She thought so herself, and at the very lowest stage of her disease, when she either slept or was in delirium, she had what seemed to her a dream. She thought that an angel stood by her bedside, looking upon her with a pitying but very bright countenance. She knew it was an angel and she begged of him most fervently to let her recover and live to raise her

children. Her prayer was granted and the angel told her that
her days would be lengthened forty-one years. This incident occurred in 1770, and she lived until 1813.[5] She told this dream
to me when I was quite a small boy, and I was nearly grown
when she died. She was buried a mile and a half north of Eatonton, Georgia. She and Gideon were a very industrious people
and everything went well with them. They were not long in con-
structing comfortable buildings and a good farm upon which
they produced in abundance all the necessaries of subsistence.

Gideon Lincecum, my grandfather and namesake, was Captain of a company of Rangers, one hundred strong, under pay
of the government. They had been organized for protection of
the frontier against the incursions of the Muskogee Indians.
They at that time were very troublesome on the border settlements of Georgia, being hired by the British to kill and scalp the
people of Georgia. From the British government, the Indians
received for each scalp (of man, woman or child) a bottle of Rum
and $8.00 in money.[6] This was about the time that the difficulty
between Great Britain and her American Colonies was taking
form. Captain Lincecum and his Rangers made frequent excursions along the Oconee river, which was at that time the boundary line between the Indians and the white people.

And now came the Declaration of Independence and the
Revolution. Captain Lincecum and his Rangers were all Rebels
and ready for immediate action. His operations were confined
to the border country, where the Tories and Indians were committing depredations continually. Against those savage enemies
he made frequent successful sallies, until Augusta, Ga., fell into
the hands of the English forces.[7] Soon after this discouraging
occurrence, Colonel Nace Few[8] sent an order to Captain Lincecum, directing him to collect his Rangers and meet his forces,
one thousand men, at a certain place on the following Monday.
Captain Lincecum notified his company, ordering them to assemble at the place and time appointed by Colonel Few. When
the appointed day came Captain Lincecum and eight of his
Rangers set out for the rendezvous together. They had progressed about half the day, when at a point a few miles outside of
where Sparta, the county seat of Hancock county Georgia now
stands, they came to a bunch of rawhide ropes that had been
dropped in the path. Here they made a halt and one of the men

dismounted to get the ropes. At that instant the Indians, who were concealed in the switch-cane that covered the ground in that new country, rose up and fired into the crowd. Except Captain Lincecum (who received a shot in the thigh), and Jonathan Hagerthy and Wm. Higginbotham, all fell dead on the spot. (For this part of the history I am indebted to William Higginbotham, who communicated the circumstances to me when I was seventeen years of age.)[9] The Captain and his two surviving companions beat a hasty retreat, the Indians pursuing with awful yelling and firing. They had not proceeded exceeding half a mile, when the Captain, who was bleeding and who seemed to be greatly excited, turned and faced the approaching savages.

His two men begged him not to stop any more and rode on a few hundred yards further, during which time the Captain had again charged his rifle and stopped a second time. His men kept urging him not to stop, for there were at least thirty Indians in sight. He seemed not to heed their earnest admonitions but dismounted from his horse and made ready to fire as the Indians came running and yelling towards him. He fired on them, as did also his two men, who pleaded with him to mount his horse. There was yet time to escape but he seemed busied reloading his rifle, paying no attention to their pleadings. The Indians had now approached sufficiently near, and having opened fire on the little party, the bullets were rattling thickly all around them. The Captain fell mortally wounded, and seeing that there was no possible chance to do anything more, his companions reluctantly left the field. Higginbotham raised a company of men and went the next day to bury the dead. They came to the Captain first. He was pretty badly mutilated, having had five scalps taken from his head. The signs were that he fought to the last, having fallen with his hand full of powder, showing that he was loading his gun when he received the death wound. He had two very large, well-trained dogs that fell with him; and the positions in which they lay, as well as the torn-up ground, bent-down grass and bushes around the blood-stained place, and the fact that both dogs were shot in the mouth, all goes to show that there had been a dire conflict with the dogs before the Indians obtained their scalps from the Captain's head.

Higginbotham and his men found a convenient tree root that had been turned up by the wind; here they placed the Captain and his dogs and punched down the clay from the turned-up roots till they were practically covered. David Criswell,[10] who was one of the party who went to bury them, told me that when they were done, he could see the toe of one of the Captain's shoes still above ground. It was a very dangerous place and but five men in the company. Not being able to find holes in the ground for the other six men, whom they found scalped, stripped of their clothing and all in a heap, Criswell said the best they could do was to cover them with logs and brush. They saw the places of wallowed-down grass and big puddles of blood not far from where the Captain lay, which they supposed had been produced by the shot the Captain fired at the Indians when he dismounted. They reasoned that some of the blood came from Indians who had been wounded by one shot from him and one from each of the men that escaped from the first terrible ambuscade. Thus my grandpa met his death.

Now the situation facing his survivors was grim. Augusta had been taken by the British and Tories. Captain Lincecum, who had been the mainstay and protector of the border country, had with six of his men been killed. Colonel Few had been ordered with his regiment to South Carolina. The remaining population, who were principally women and children, had become alarmed and discouraged. The widow of the late Captain Lincecum did not feel safe in remaining any longer in a country overrun with Tories, who had already abused her by whipping her with an iron ramrod, trying to make her tell where she had concealed her money. The Negroes had all run away and left her in quite a helpless condition. Finally she concluded to move into South Carolina. A number of Georgia people were doing so, and she too gathered up such things as she could carry with her six children and went into Edgefield District, where she remained until peace was made.[11]

In the meantime her sons, Edward and John, had grown up and, finding wives in South Carolina, had both got married. This, however, did not exempt them from army service, for they were both taken prisoner and shot soon after the Battle of Cowpens.[12] Their wives both had children, but as soon as peace was proclaimed, widow Lincecum returned to her home in Georgia, leaving her two daughters-in-law with their parents in South

Carolina and never afterwards heard what went with them. When she got home, having been absent seven years, she found only piles of charred wheat and rye where the barn stood, and all the houses, fences, etc., had long since been consumed by Tory incendiarism. Her stock of cows, hogs, sheep & horses had all been appropriated, so she had nothing but the bare earth that she could call her own. But there were Jonathan Hagerthy, Clabe Nusum,[13] Nace Few and David Criswell, old rebel neighbors, strong, good men, who had passed through the stormy revolution unscathed and were home again, as good friends and neighbors as ever; and they lent a helping hand to the widow and orphans. This timely aid, with what she and her three daughters (Nancy, Dolly, and Sally), now nearly all grown, could do, enabled them to live on till they got houses built and a little farm in operation. [Her one surviving son, Hezekiah, was only 12–13 years of age.]

Another help occurred. Two of her Negroes came back—a man and a woman, Africans, who had concealed themselves eight years in Williamson Swamp, subsisting on pigs, geese, frogs, snakes, fish—anything they could lay their hands on without exposure. They had not been in America but two or three years when the war broke out, and the marauding Tories had frightened them so much they fled into concealment. There they remained until they discovered in their nocturnal excursions that people were returning to their old places again. Seeing all this and hearing no drums or other indications of war, Tom (the name of the male African) took it into his head to creep out in the night and go to his old home and see if Missus had come back too. When he came there and found that they were home again and that it was his people, including "Missus Dolly" and "Ky," his favorites, he could contain himself no longer. He rushed into the little cabin exclaiming, "Gord-a-blessy, Gord-a-blessy, me Tom, Hi-Ki, me glad." He wallowed on the ground, put dirt on his head and put his Missus' foot on it and sobbed heavily. He then rose up and darted out at the door and was gone in an instant. Early next morning he returned with his wife Hannah, both loaded with enormous packs of old pieces of quilts and other bed clothing they had picked up after the runaway. So they got proudly back and, as they were both young, were a great help to the family. And now that peace was assured, the family struggled on in their poverty, striving to increase their stores.

Hezekiah was now a well grown, thirteen-year-old boy who could go to the far-off mill and do most of the errands. Tom and Hannah cultivated the little farm, and the old lady and her grown-up girls spun and wove cloth to clothe the family and produce a little surplus, which they sold for money to purchase other necessaries. In this manner things moved on three or four years until the smoke and shadow of the warcloud had wasted away. The ghastly wounds it had occasioned were mostly healed and the defunct performers on the bloody stage were being forgotten. Quiet was restored and the people, though they were poor, began to wear a cheerful countenance.

About this time came Thomas Roberts, an Englishman who had deserted the British service and had joined and done good service in the Rebel Army during the last three years of the Revolution. He was a highly educated man and notorious for his profane and obscene language. He stopped in the Kelly family and said that he intended to get a wife and raise a family of free-born children. He visited the widow Lincecum's girls, but they did not fancy his bold, balderdash manner. However, Hezekiah pleased him and he used all his powers of fascination to gain the boy's affection, in which he succeeded fully. It was at this time that a bounty was offered to enlist two or three regiments of men to protect the border country against the Muskogee Indians, who were making frequent inroads and committing depredations along the entire line of the frontiers of Georgia.[14] Mr. Roberts enlisted in the state service and also induced his pet, Hezekiah, to take the bounty.[15] It grieved Hezekiah's mother, who had already lost two sons and her husband in the army. Besides all this, Hezekiah was at that time the only male of the name in the known world and on this account particularly, she opposed his enlistment. But he had received the bounty, was already in camp and all her efforts availed nothing.

At the expiration of three years, a treaty of peace was concluded with the Indians and the army disbanded. Hezekiah, now 16, had grown to be a very large and extremely active man, highly educated in all arts, strokes, and punches in the pugilistic science. He returned to the old stamping ground fully able to (and did) whip every man in the settlement who dared to oppose him. He could also hold his hand with any of them in the use of strong drink. Roberts, who had been his teacher in these attainments, was always on hand. Soon after their return Roberts and Miss Elizabeth Kelly were married, and he advised his pupil Hezekiah to do likewise. Hezekiah was not only a large, portly, well-formed man but was also very handsome, with a most musical voice.

At this juncture of time came Abram Brantley, a Baptist preacher,[16] who by his earnest eloquence began to stir sinners up and make them stop and think. It was a new thing and the first religious stirring in that vicinity since the war. Parson Brantley, viewing the irreligious condition of the whole people there, was anxious to see what he could do towards producing a change amongst them. For this purpose he visited every family, praying with them and exercising his bland, persuasive powers in his familiar conversations. In making his rounds in the neighborhood he called at the house of widow Lincecum. Having been a conscientious religionist of the Baptist persuasion all her life, she was thankful for the preacher's attention. Her daughters were now all married and gone, leaving the household to consist only of Hezekiah and herself. The parson sang and prayed with them.

Hezekiah took a full part in the singing, and his firm, manly, melodious voice fairly made the heavenly arches ring. The parson was surprised at the wonderful scope and power of his voice, so much so, that he could not help speaking of it. He told Hezekiah that the Lord had done a great deal for him, for which he should be very thankful. That fine form, handsome face and sweet musical voice abundantly fitted him for a preacher of the Gospel. He should lose no time, but go right to work, studying and improving his mind and praying God to aid him in his preparation for the ministry, for that was surely what the Lord had intended for him. This flattering address waked up a new train of thought in the brain of the handsome young man.

He believed all the preacher had said and, forming a resolution to follow the advice, went to praying forthwith. He attended all the meetings, singings and prayings, and it was but a short time till people noticed and talked of the progress he was making in his religious exercises. Soon he confessed his sins, told his conversion experience and was accepted, not only as a worthy member, but as a bright star and ornament in the fold of God. He was baptized and came out of the water shouting praises and exhorting the people to flee from the wrath to come; to renounce their sins, come to Christ and be baptized.

(For this portion of my narrative I am indebted to Stephen Camp,[17] an old man whom I found dwelling in the hill country on the head waters of New river in Alabama in 1843. I spent six weeks at some mineral springs near his residence, and the old man spent many days at my camp telling me about the life of his old army friend and messmate Hezekiah before I knew him as my father.)

"Kyah," or more frequently "Ky," improved rapidly in singing and praying and it was but a short time till he was closing meetings and making very pretty public exhortations. No one hesitated in expressing themselves openly in reference to what was going to be the result of his unprecedented rapid growth in grace. All said the same thing: He was going to be a big preacher, sure and no mistake. The young ladies all wanted to go to heaven with the good-looking young man. And now he, though very religious and prayerful, could not resist the flattering attentions so frankly bestowed by the young ladies. Out of the many that were being baptized, he selected one—a most beautiful, saintly creature, whose name was Sally Strange.[18] She agreed to walk hand-in-hand with him before the Lord like Zachariah and Elizabeth. They were married, and the nuptial day was one of great religious rejoicing. It was talked everywhere.

Roberts being already married and settled, he too followed the meetings and preachings, and people thought he would soon follow the example of his very popular and promising protege, Hezekiah. Roberts was a very good reader, and the brethren would send for him of Sundays when there was no preaching near and get him to read the Bible for them, a thing he seemed to take pleasure in. This happened often, and Roberts's wife Betsy was converted mostly from listening to the plain, distinct reading and explanations of the scriptures by Roberts himself. A very kind husband, he took pains in giving his wife scripture readings and also encouraged her to seek the Lord. She was baptized. Under the gospel teaching of the kind, good-disposed Abram Brantley, the whole people of that vicinity seemed to be looking heavenward. The church was filling up rapidly and everything seemed to be rolling on finely. By the encouraging lectures on liberty, industry and domestic economy, the people were enlarging their farms, improving their dwellings; thrift and better conditions of affairs were beginning to prevail everywhere. But from some cause unknown, there were some whose worldly and spiritual prospects seemed to be clouded.

It was becoming a noticeable fact that the ardor and spirit of devotion of Hezekiah had considerably cooled down. No one knew, or could say why, but it was certainly so. To his mother, who had hoped so much, the decline of his religious devotions was a source of much concern. She sent for the preacher, who endeavored to cheer him up, but he could say nothing that had any effect. He grew colder and absented himself from attending church. Then Mr. Brantley called to know his reason for absenting himself from meetings. Hezekiah did not explain. Such sad things, however, cannot long be hidden from the public. The eyes and ears of the curious will listen and peep, and they will also talk and whisper about other people's affairs.

It had already leaked out and rumor was busy circulating the precious morsel that there was a difficulty, a deadly split, betwixt Hezekiah and his beautiful and most saintly wife. No one could tell the nature and character of the difficulty, but one thing they could say, it was awful. And sure enough, it terminated as badly as the most malicious could desire, for Hezekiah and his lovely Sally made a final separation of it. Sally went to her parental home and Hezekiah moped about, becoming very religious. He attended all religious gatherings, singing and praying vociferously. It had now become a settled fact among the brethren that he was to be a preacher and a good one too.

Hezekiah began to think so himself and to prepare himself for the sacred service. He practiced the ceremonies, repeating and committing them to memory carefully. Some of the young church boys and Hezekiah being down on Powell's Creek[19] one Sunday, amusing themselves playing in the water, they began talking of Hezekiah's prospects for becoming a preacher. It was proposed that he perform the ceremony of baptism on some of them. This he refused, but consented to baptize a cat that had followed them to the creek. And while he was performing the holy rite on the poor cat, some of the older brethren who were fishing that day happened to be passing at the time and saw him. To their notions of religious propriety, it was very offensive.

They reported the case to the leading members of the society, whereupon it was thought proper to church the presumptuous Hezekiah. While on trial he would make no penitential concessions but remained very still and untractable. His accusers said that recently he had often been seen in company with his old army crony, and they attributed his stubborn conduct to the influence and teachings of Thomas Roberts, whom they now looked upon as one of the emissaries of his Satanic Majesty. They finally concluded that as long as he remained friendly with the said Roberts, he would do no better. The question was read by the clerk: Shall Hezekiah Lincecum be excommunicated from the Baptist church? The vote was counted and found to be unanimous in the affirmative. So they turned him out.

Camp said that as Hezekiah walked down the aisle going out, he turned and remarked to the members, "You have turned me out of your church but you are not able to turn me out of Christ." I should have stated that Thomas Roberts was with him as he walked out of the church. And they went to a liquor shop nearby. You may always notice that wherever you find a church in your life journey, it is not far from it to a liquor shop. They took some refreshments but none to excess. Hezekiah had made a resolution that he would, by a regular course of good behavior and sobriety, falsify the numerous predictions that had been made by the brethren in regard to the course he would pursue now that he was out of the protecting influence of the church.

There was a little log-cabin school started in the settlement and Hezekiah, greatly feeling the need of an education (he was almost entirely illiterate), enrolled. He strove with all his powers to learn the books, but he was a little too far advanced in years and had witnessed too many brain-racking vicissitudes to allow him to be a very apt scholar. And this was not all the brain-disturbing forces by which he was surrounded. The widow Hickman's daughter Sally, a most beautiful girl, fourteen and half years of age, was also entered to the same school. Her power of attraction for him was very great. He felt the want of possessing the fair young creature more than he felt the want of an education. So, from his books he turned his attention wholly to the pretty Sally and they were soon married. Roberts was at the wedding, and on this joyous occasion succeeded in leading Hezekiah so far astray as to get him intoxicated. And now, while his protege was under the excitement of brandy, Roberts told him that he had been greatly wronged and contemptuously treated in the church; and as several of the brethren who took an active part against him during the trial were present, it was a very pretty time to retaliate and get satisfaction. Hezekiah was of the same opinion and went charging into a bunch of five or six of them, knocking them down like children and kicking and cuffing them terribly.

Parson Brantley, who had performed the marriage ceremony, observed that Hezekiah turned his eyes toward him; and to avoid any difficulty with the young inebriate, the parson hurried away in a pretty tall trot. Hezekiah, seeing the hasty departure of the preacher, gave chase, pursuing him two or three hundred yards. The parson, however, made good his escape. Hezekiah returned, vociferating in a very loud voice, and asked if there were any other of the damned rascals who wished to be fed with the same spoon. But he found no one there but the bride and Roberts. The rest of the company had dispersed, so the three of them concluded to go home.

The young couple went to the widow Lincecum's to live and remained until Hezekiah made a house of his own. There he and his very young wife, having comparatively nothing to go upon, bravely labored to mend their condition. They succeeded very well. In the course of twelve months they owned a horse, a cow, had a little start for a stock of hogs, a bed and some other furniture. In addition to all this, as the sun was rising Monday, 22nd day of April 1793, when she was sixteen years and forty-eight days of age, the loving, industrious young wife gave birth to a well-formed and quite large male child. Hezekiah was in ecstacy on the occasion and named the newcomer, which is the writer, for his father Gideon.

Hezekiah remained two seasons at that place. Then, being of a restless spirit, he sold out and moved further out on the border, settling near the Scull Shoals on the Oconee river, Ga.[20] At this place the Indians proved so troublesome that he did not remain but two years. He returned to Hancock County and bought out a man named Byrd Brazil.[21] This was a good home, near the place where he had lived before. On this place he remained three years, accumulating property very rapidly. Here he raised the first crop of cotton that grew in that part of the country. They had a little hand-roller gin, with which and their fingers they picked the seed out of the cotton. They would then tread it into an ordinary meal sack and carry it to market (the nearest store), where they received in silver fifty cents per pound for it.

The greatest trouble was to get the seed out of the cotton and by this problem the inventive genius of the whole community was excited to the highest degree. Various fashions of roller gins were produced. Some went by horse power, having a breast filled with many rollers. They were capable of picking three or four hundred pounds of seed cotton per day. People began to think that these many rollered gins were perfection in that direction, and that there was very little if any improvement to be made in a gin that could clean four hundred pounds of seed cotton per day. It was good enough and it could not be beat.

But this miracle of a cotton gin was destined to be totally eclipsed. It was stated that a Yankee schoolmaster over in Lincoln County, Georgia, by the name of Whitney had invented an iron gin with thirty circular saws. It was driven by horse power and could, it was said (but nobody believed it), clean one thousand pounds of seed cotton in a day. The wonderful report about the saw-gin had excited public curiosity far and wide; numbers were going daily to see it. Among them was Hezekiah, my father, and he took me, a nine-year-old boy, and I saw the man Whitney and the first saw-gin that was made. It had thirty saws, crooked breasting, and was every way like the best form of gins at the present day. The invention was perfect at the start and has not been improved, except perhaps a few alterations in the pullies and running gear, and it has been made larger.[22]

About this time Tyre Kelly, James and John Hickman of Tennessee (three brothers-in-law)[23] wrote my father frequent letters urging him to sell out and go to their rich country. He being naturally of a restless disposition was very willing to try the experiment, and he soon found a purchaser for his rich money-making home. Three years of successful farming had tired him out, and he sold out everything that he could not carry with him, bought a good road wagon and four fine horses, and set out for Tennessee. The amount of freight he had to transport was a big chest, four beds, four white and four Negro children, and his mother, who was at that time eighty-eight years of age and a little unwell. She got worse the first day of our travel. My father thought a great deal of his mother, and the violence of her present paroxysm had frightened him so much that he went to the house nearest to our camp, where lived a Mr. Morris, and got him to agree to let her have shelter with him while her sickness lasted. Her sickness lasted three weeks. My father concluded that the fates were opposed to his removal to Tennessee and, becoming discouraged, rented Mr. Morris's place and moved into his house. Morris was an old man, and had no children with him. He and his wife went to live with one of his sons.

My father worked hard that year, made a heavy crop of corn and cotton, and sold the cotton for five dollars per hundred in the seed. He kept his wagon and horse, and with the money he got for his crop was better prepared for the long journey to Tennessee. So he fixed up again, having for his cargo the same as before, only I had grown to such a big boy and having a splendid bow and arrows, I could not think of riding in the wagon. I preferred walking with my mother and Pat, my black mammy, and shooting at the birds along the woods. I shall never forget the exceeding gladness that filled my boy breast the morning we set out on our journey. I ran far ahead, shooting my arrows at every bird I could see. We rolled on four days and came to Viena, a little dilapidated village on the banks of the Saluda river,[24] just below the mouth of Broad river. There was another company ahead of us, and we could not get our wagon into the flat till near sundown.

Just as the wagon was turning to go down into the ferry boat, a quite handsome young lady came up and, without asking any questions, threw a small budget into the wagon and crossed over with us. After getting over into South Carolina we only had time to get out into the timber before night. Here we camped. While we were collecting wood to make a fire, the young lady came up with a heavier log on her shoulder than a man could carry. Addressing the eldest son of Aunt Sally Kelly, a large man, who had joined us a few days previous, my father said, "Cousin Asa, relieve the lady of her tote."

After he took it and threw it on the fire, the young lady observed to Asa, "Young man, I don't know your name, but I can throw you down." Asa replied, "Neither do I know your name, but I can tell you that is a big banter, for I have not seen the man yet that can throw me down. Further I will say, as you are young and pretty and of an agreeable, jolly temper, I will agree to marry you if you throw me, two best in three falls. On these conditions I accept your challenge."

In reply to this the young lady remarked, "Young man, I consider the proposition you have made as a manifestation of self reliance in your judgement of humanity that pleases me. I have neither house nor home, kith nor kin, nor lover, nor aught of impediment or obstruction to prevent me from doing what suits me best. That I am sound and in good health I will prove to you when we test the question."

Turning to my father she said to him, "Sir, if you will see me fair play, I accept the conditions offered." He assured her most earnestly that she should be fairly dealt with, at the same time manifesting much interest in the young stranger's behalf. The terms being understood and agreed to by both parties, the young lady went into the tent to prepare herself, whilst the men cleared out the ground where the contest was to take place.

Presently she came out with her hair closely bound up, and walking into the ring met my cousin midway. After some little cavil about the manner of taking hold, they locked. Declaring themselves ready for trial, they only waited until my father gave word. Instantly both parties seemed to be striving to lift his antagonist from the ground. This caused one or two turns or facings. The young lady seemed to relax a moment; and then making a sudden whirl, she caught Asa on her hip, and over he went.

Asa got up and remarked to her: "You done that very easy, but I was not on my guard. I did not think you understood gymnastics so well. Try it again. I'll upset you this time." They locked again, declared themselves ready, and the word was given. Asa made a bold effort to get the kneelock on her but she evaded it; and writhing like a tiger in his strong hug, by a sudden and powerful whirl she threw him on the other hip.

Father decided that the thing was fairly done. Asa declared she was as strong as a horse. "I am clearly beaten, but I'll stick to it though I don't even know her name." He went to where she was seated, and making a low bow said, "Madam, will you

honor me so far as to communicate the name of her to whom I
am indebted for the two severe upsettings I received just now?"
She very distinctly, and in a sweet musical voice, replied, "Malinda Nevels. Now sir, will you return the compliment?" "With
pleasure, Miss," he replied. "My name is Asa Lincecum."[25] And
they approached each other and shook hands.

We remained at that camp three days, and Malinda was so
industrious and handy in helping about the camp that Mother
fell in love with her. Father had been gone two days with an old
drunken Irishman, who came to our camp the next day after
we got there. Mother was uneasy and said she didn't understand
it, that it was mighty bad to lose three days of pretty weather in
such a long journey. But father came back on the evening of the
third day and astonished us all by informing us that he had
rented an excellent house and farm on Calhoun Creek, Abbeville District, South Carolina. So we geared up and went there
the very next day, and sure enough found the house a good one
and the land fine.

There were two good sets of houses on the farm. Asa agreed
to crop it with my father, as there was plenty of open land on
the farm. To make everything go more smoothly, Asa informed
Malinda that he was ready to settle up what he had lost with her
in the wrestle at camp. She was ready to receive it and they sent
for Parson Porter,[26] who witnessed the payment and fixed the
papers legally, and they were man and wife. They had nothing
but their health and strength to start the world with, not even a
blanket. But they had courage and went bravely to work, cleaning up and fixing up the other set of houses. Mother lent them
a bed-stick and some blankets, and they made shift to get up
a sufficient bed. Both parties did all they could to mend their
condition. They were very cheerful. Asa made a fine crop of cotton and corn, and Malinda spun and made cloth sufficient for
clothing and rigged up a good bed and furniture. In the course
of a year, they had accumulated a wagonload of property. My
father paid Asa for his share of the large crop they had made,
and it enabled them to supply all their immediate necessities.

My father sold his cotton for a good price, and after getting
the money in hand, he became impressed with the idea that he
must go and see his sister Dolly Durbin, who dwelt in Clarke

County. He was gone two or three weeks, and when he returned he told my mother that he had purchased a tract of land with a good house and farm on it, lying within one mile of Athens, Ga., and twelve miles from his sister's residence. Soon he was on the road again, returning to Ga., and in the course of a week we had reached our new home. Asa and Malinda had remained in South Carolina, where we heard they were doing exceedingly well and had born to them a very fine daughter.[27]

Father exerted every power at his new place. He planted and raised a heavy crop of cotton, and as soon as it began to open, everyone that could pick out five pounds a day was forced into the field. I could pick twenty pounds and father bragged of it to the neighbors. It made me think a great deal more of myself, and I exerted myself to get thirty pounds a day. It was not many days until I succeeded. As a reward father got a blacksmith to make me a nice spike for my arrow, a thing I had long needed to shoot the pike that were found in great numbers in the little creeks and branches of that country.

Sunday came and since I could pick so much cotton, it was the only day I could go out with my bow and arrows. I went out early in the morning with my fine spiked arrows and traveled the branches all day. The weather was getting a little cool, and then is the best time for shooting the pike. You can find them lying perfectly still in the little nooks and by-places in the branches and oh, my good spike! It was so certain to stick them, and being barbed it would not let them drop off. The excitement lasted all day, and no pen can portray the unspeakable delight I experienced on returning home with a string of fish a yard long. It took me until bed-time to tell all about how I slipped up to the sleeping fish and darted my spike into them and how they fluttered but could not get off.

Early Monday morning I pitched into the cotton field again, and keeping myself half-bent all day, picked more cotton than I could carry home. Father said there was forty pounds of it and that I was a brave fellow and he intended to get me a new hat. I would wake before day and lie studying about how I would snatch the fleecy locks from the expanded pods as soon as it was light enough for me to see. We all did our best to get the cotton out by Christmas. We succeeded, and father took it to the gin and got receipts for 4,643 pounds, for which he received 5 cents per pound. He now again became restless, and selling out his place, put his wagon in good repair and set out on his third attempt to get to Tennessee. This time his cargo in the wagon, besides the beds, trunks, etc., consisted of Grandmother and four white and four black children. He had also two white and one Negro child walking. The weather was fine; we made good progress, and I was so glad that we were on the road again. Being in my twelfth year I was an expert with the bow and arrow, and I would run far ahead shooting and killing many birds in the course of a day. I could shoot my arrows with such unerring certainty that it afforded me the highest possible amusement.

I kept a bow all my life, and have a good one now, in 1871. To digress a moment, ^PI was educated by the Muskogee Indians and hunters of a frontier country until I was fifteen, having the Muskogee children for my playmates and the bow and arrows and the blow-gun for my hunting implements. By the time I was five years of age the use of these destructive implements had become a perfect passion with me. I vied with the best marksmen of my age among the Indian boys; could knock the picayune [coin] out of the split stick at ten paces distant as often as any of them; and woe to the luckless snake or rat or lizard that came in my path. Another year and the fish and large birds became the object of my pursuit, and by the time I was ten years old the quantities of fish and fowl, rabbits and squirrels that would come in of an evening from my Indian associates and myself would, to the uninitiated, be a subject of wonder. Talk about the pleasures of the sportsman with dog, shell cartridge and breech-loading guns! Pshaw! Why I tell you that there is a greater amount of real soul-stirring delight and enjoyment, unalloyed pleasure, experienced by the ten or twelve years old boy, with his bow and arrows, on the creeks and branches and in the cane-brakes of a wild, unhacked, echoing wilderness in pursuit of the legitimate bow-and-arrow game, in a single day, than can be had in a whole year of manhood with the breech-loader and setter. The hunting implements of my redskin companions and myself, except the fish-hook, were of purely Indian origin: bows, arrows, blow-gun, fishing spears, snares and many forms of trap, all Indian. My father retired often before the unholy, intrusive tramp of civilization, and my Indian companions were frequently changed. But the new ones I came in contact with at our removes on the borders always seemed proud of me on account of my being able to talk with them, and my sports would be continued with new life.

During my eleventh and twelfth years I had five nice, goodnatured fellows. We were all about the same age; and a better behaved set of boys I have never found in any nation or country. "Would you like that?" would be asked when a doubtful proposition would occur. "No." "Then don't offer it to me." This would be often repeated amongst them, and the sacred principle was as visibly present in their daily intercourse as were their bows and arrows. This prevalence of the basic rule of pure democracy secured the peace and filled our sporting hours with undisturbed delights. All strove manfully to excel; but superior skill of extraordinary success was never alluded to by the performer. This, however, is common with all Indians, previous to their being contaminated with the *is-oon-lush-fil-lok-chee*[28]—the forkedtongue civilities of progressed society.

But that is not what I started to talk about. These boys could, and so could I, imitate the call-notes of all the birds, and we practiced it in our daily sports. The most deadly and murderous deception practiced by us (and the one which was attended with the greatest success) was to take a blow-gun and plenty of arrows. A blow-gun is a middle-sized cane, five-eighths of an inch in the bore, nicely dressed on the inside by forcibly dragging a wet rope covered with sand through it until no inequalities on the inside of it can be seen. It is from eight to twelve feet in length and very straight. I have made them and it requires two or three good days to complete a good one. The arrows are fifteen to eighteen inches long, constructed of splits of the largest cane. The splits are as wide as they are thick; dressed smooth, about one-sixteenth of an inch square. It is then pointed and heated in the embers; and while it is hot and limber, it is twisted until it has the appearance of a coarse screw, and holding it so until it cools, it remains twisted and straight. During the heating process the point is partially charred, and it is as hard as iron. It is now ready for the feather, which is composed of thistle-down, ingeniously wrapped securely on three inches of the hinter end with deer sinews. A good blow-gun and strong, healthy lungs can propel one of these arrows seventy-five yards. Anywhere under forty yards for small game (partridges, rabbits, squirrels), it is certain and fatal as a rifle. I knew an Indian woman who killed her husband with a blow-gun. (Nobody blamed her, for he called her ugly. In Indian etiquette, that is the most unpardonable, offensive word that can be used.) My description of the blow-gun may be superfluous, but with us Indians, it was the most pleasurable, most profitable and effective instrument in our forest sports. I have heard my father brag that no member of the family furnished the table with as great an amount of food as I did, including much fish and all kinds of small game.

Well, as I was saying, with a good blow-gun and plenty of arrows, sneak into a thicket near the edge of a river bottom, and seated at the root of a brushy topped tree, place one of the blow-gun arrows six or eight inches from the hand that holds it under the blabbed out under-lip, giving sufficient upward pressure to spring the arrow gently. Now force the voice at about the flute pitch over the blabbed lip, which will press it downwards but the elastic arrow throws it instantly back, cutting the sound which being continued presses down the lip again; the sound escapes to be checked as before by the upward recoil of the arrow; and so on in a continuous rattle of flute notes: *bub, bub, bub, bub,* which we sometimes continued for several hours. I don't know what the birds think it is or what makes them come to it, but every one of whatever tribe will come close down on the bushes, all the time uttering plaintive notes and cries, like the sounds they make when they all get around a snake.

The blow-gun makes but little noise, and the slow motions of the cautious manipulator are not noticed by the birds who are chirping and shrieking on every bush. I have, previous to starting the attractive music, trimmed and rendered conspicuous a prominent limb by clearing away the brush around it a few feet and then preparing a place for the gun to rest on, with the muzzle eight or ten feet from the conspicuous lighting place I had fixed for them; then taking my seat in the brush at the root of the tree with the breech of the *ooska-thliemfa*[29] (it is a breech-loader) on my knee, I commence the infatuating tune. It would tarnish my reputation amongst modern sportsmen, who deem it an act of cruelty to shoot a bird anywhere but on the wing, were I to narrate the direful fate that befell many hundreds of the feathered race by this method of fascinating them. Our hooks and cane traps and bows and spears were very successful in capturing all kinds of fish. Our snares and curious traps for rabbits, mink, muskrats, opossums, raccoons, foxes and wild turkeys were all more or less successful.

Being daily in nature's grand university, my Indian education in all the branches of natural history was rapid and delightful. Great numbers of the pure, uncontaminated, aboriginal Americans have names for every living thing—vegetable and animal. They teach it while sitting by their fires of long winter nights and during the nooning hours at their camps of summer days. To know the names and uses of everything in forest and stream is to an Indian a subject of great interest. There is where he goes for food when he is hungry; and when he is sick, he goes to the same elaborate drug store for the antidote. It is as natural for him to know it when he finds it, as it is for him to know the articles proper for food. And at their resting spells in the wild wood from the chase, the names and uses of these things make up the subject of conversation with the boys. I knew the name and note of every bird and beast, their manner of propagation and all their little deceptions to hide and protect their young. By the mechanism of the nest, I could tell who made it, and the same by the size, shape and color of their eggs. I knew upon what kind of soil to look for any tree or plant, and before I was fifteen, had the reputation of a "sure-cure" Indian doctor. In short I was "high larnt" in the woods.

[To return to my narrative of the third attempt to journey to Tennessee,] [B]Father did not like to drive a team of horses, and he had hired a straggling old fellow to drive for this trip. We rolled on bravely until we came to the Saluda [Savannah] river. There was a store and smith-shop there, and we stopped until the smith nailed a pair of shoes on the out-riding horse, and until father and the teamster got themselves smartly intoxicated (and bought two bottles of whiskey to carry with them). The river was wide and swift, but shallow. We forded it, and in course of a couple of hours were all safely landed on the border of South Carolina again.

It was an excellent hard, gravelly road, and we had progressed about five miles when father, being most deeply intoxicated, took a notion that he must go back to the store and whip somebody that had insulted him there. Mother and I had stopped, trying to dissuade him from going back. The wagon had gone on and was just out of sight when our ears were greeted with a terrible lumbering noise. It frightened me, and I ran forward with all my might. Soon I came in sight of the teamster lying on the side of the road with the setting sun gleaming on his bald head, and my first impression was that his head was split open. Nearer observation, however, showed me that he lay unhurt, in a sound sleep. At this time the two lead horses came running back with parts of the broken harness on them, and I could hear away off to the right hand in the woods the cries and screams of the wounded children. I made haste to the frightful sounds and found the wagon a perfect wreck; the children scattered all around, some trying to crawl, some lying still, all crying and bleeding from their mouths and swollen lips, and grandmother still in the wagon with her throat cut and bleeding profusely. "Oh! My poor grandmother," I cried, for I loved her more than all the rest of the world. I prayed that she might recover and put my hands on the bloody gash, which was at least three inches in length and so deep that I could see the blue trunk of the great neck veins. I tried to close it up and stop the bleeding and was sitting holding the lips of the wound together when father and mother came up. She took the case in hand and dressed it as soon as possible.

On examination of the children, we found, while they were pretty badly hurt, no bones were broken. Smashed lips and noses and bumped heads was the character of the injuries sustained. They were all soon on foot. When my poor inebriated father came up and surveyed the disastrous scene—his wrecked wagon, wounded children and bleeding mother—he was so deeply smitten that he fell down on the ground and wept like a child. Mother, who in cases of emergency was always equal to two or more hands, went to work as soon as she had completed the dressing of grandmother's wound, and in a comparatively short time had a comfortable bed scaffold set up and a bed on it for grandmother to rest on. Mammy Pat and I, after we had caught the horses and brought them back, helped Mother in her plans for arranging the camp; for she said she would not leave there till grandmother got well enough to travel, which would be two or three weeks. After we had busied ourselves until near midnight, putting things in order and were thinking of retiring for the night, the teamster, who had been sleeping all this time, came up and exclaimed, "Why hello! What is this? What's the matter here!" and he did not seem to know what had happened. Grandmother said, that having his bottle in his pocket, he had repeated his potation until he had become so much intoxicated that he seemed to go to sleep and tumbled off on the wagon tongue, between the horses, which frightened them so they ran off. She supposed he had been killed, as the wagon ran over him. I have often wondered what power it is that protects the poor careless drunkard.

On investigation it was found that the right hand forewheel was all ruined but the hub and the tire. The hounds and axletree were also broken. Father and the teamster carried the broken wagon back to the shop over the river. They told him the work could be completed in a week. So father returned and went about in the settlement in search of provisions. It was a very poor country and provisions were scarce. But the inhabitants were generous and let him have what they could spare freely. We had to stay at that camp three weeks before grandmother could travel.

Curiosity led me one day to trace the route of the horses with the wagon, when they ran away. From where the driver lay, they had run on one side of the road about fifty yards, when they turned to the right into the woods. The trees were numerous but with no undergrowth, and the team continued running amongst the thickest timber for a distance perhaps of three hundred yards, missing all the trees and gradually turning to the right. And had it not been for a large pine log that had been cut for a board tree (but not removed), the end of which projected a few inches into their course, they probably would have succeeded in steering clear of the trees until they had got back into the road. But the log lay in the way, and the right forewheel struck it squarely in the end. The consequence was the instant stoppage of the wagon, which tore the horses loose. As a result the children and some of the freight was instantly thrown forward over the forge gate, and my grandmother came very near having her neck vein severed as she pitched forward, her neck coming in contact with one of the wooden hoops of the frame that supports the cover.

On the day the wagon was to be ready, after dinner father sent his teamster with two horses and the money for it. He had not returned at nine o'clock at night. Father began to show a little uneasiness. Grandmother remarked to him: "You have fixed that poor wretch in pretty good style, two fine horses and money to bear his expenses." He could stand it no longer, but jumped on a horse and galloped away in pursuit of his delinquent teamster. He found the horses geared up and the man in the store very drunk. He beckoned out the store-keeper and inquired if the teamster had paid him the money for the work? The storekeeper said "Yes, but I do not think the fellow would have done so had I not challenged him with having the money." He further advised my father to take his wagon and team in charge and dismiss the teamster, which he did.

At the end of three weeks grandmother said she was able to travel. We started next morning, and made twenty miles that day. After supper father went to a house nearby camp to get some fodder. He stayed late, but after a while returned about half drunk. Speaking to grandmother, he said: "In view of your extreme age and wounded condition I feel that it must be very painful to be dragged about with the rough accommodations I have for you; so I have concluded to stop here and have purchased Hamilton's place up there on the hill." So in the morning Mr. Hamilton cleared out some rooms for us and we moved in. Father paid some money, his wagon and two horses for the place and thus became a free-holder in Pendleton District, S.C.[30] It is proper to state that grandmother recovered entirely from her wound and went to work with her little flax wheel. There was more open land than we could cultivate, and father procured a cropper.

It was a good stand for a tavern, and sales to travelers consumed all the surplus crops at a good price. One day when father was going to Pickensville[31] he told me to take a bag and cut some oats for his fine horse to have when he got back. Near the middle of the field stood a large white oak stump, and I discovered a great many swallows going in and out at the top of it.

Grandmother had told me that this species of swallows constructed their nests of small sticks and glue, and being anxious to see these wonderful nests I climbed to the top of the stump (some twenty feet high). I could see numbers of nests, but could not reach them. So taking the bag, I tried to catch one of the nests, but in the attempt dropped it. In this dilemma I could conceive of no way of recovering it but to go down the hollow; so I turned into the top, and for more than half way down got along very well by humping my back against one side and my hands and knees against the other. Then I came to where the hollow was too large, and not being able to stop, I whirled to the bottom. After several attempts, I concluded that I could not climb out, and sitting down on the bag I halloed and wept. The long horned crickets began to trill their quavering song, and the large black spiders spread their long legs as wide as a man's hand against the black wall of the hollow stump. With increasing darkness came a full sense of utter loneliness. At last I straightened out my bag, lay down upon it and wept myself to sleep. When I awoke next morning the sun was shining in the stump, and I thought I heard the sound of a horn. It came nearer, then I heard the shouts of people. I yelled as loud as I possibly could, for that was a time that I was anxious to be heard, but the fates seemed against me. Finally, a big lazy fellow came and sat down in the shade of the stump. I heard his back scrape against the outside. I knocked against the inside, whereupon he jumped and said, "By golly I've found him!"

They cut a hole for me to get out at. Soon after my adventure in the oat-patch, father concluded to gather his peaches. Near the house were fifty trees said to be forty-four years old. They were certainly the largest peach trees I ever saw. They were full of fruit, and he carried it off to a still and had it made into brandy, which he sold to travelers. All his corn and fodder brought ready money, at a good price. It was an easy place to make money on, and father seemed to be settling down to business. All the family were satisfied and willing to remain. But unfortunately, about this time came Uncle Tyre Kelly, traipsing back from Tennessee, bringing with him his seven motherless children.

Aunt Sally had a carbuncle on the back of her neck that killed her, which was the cause of Uncle Tyre's return to Georgia. He remained with us until the brandy was out, and in the meantime had discouraged father from going to Tennessee.[32] Father became restless after Uncle left and sold out at the first opportunity. Soon we were on the road again. My brother Garland had grown large enough to run ahead of the wagons with me. We made this trip without accident and stopped in a mile of the place we had left the previous year [either Clarke or Hancock County]. The lands beyond the Oconee river had been obtained by the U.S. from the Muskogee Indians.[33] No one had moved on the new purchase, and as father intended to go over as soon as the Indians should complete the twelve months' hunting, which had been a stipulation in the treaty, he took an overseer's place, instead of purchasing land.

[P]A drunken interloper came and prevailed on my father, who was not in favor of too much "larning," to assist him in getting up a school. There was a vacant log cabin three miles from our house, which was nearly central to a district of four or five families of hunters and stock raisers, whose families of healthy uproarious children, were as numerous as the old sow's pigs—dozens. It was finally decided that if Mr. Young Gill[34] the schoolman would teach their children reading, writing and ciphering at sixty cents a month and take it in corn, pork, beef, etc., they would, on their part, agree to furnish the house for him to dwell in and three or four milk cows. Mr. Gill, having a family, agreed, and the next Monday morning the school was opened, causing that portion of the wilderness for the first time, to ring with the A B C's of civilization. [B]Father entered myself, Polly, and Garland[35] as day scholars at the rate of seven dollars per annum. We all started the next day and did not miss a day until father moved to the new purchase, amounting to five months.

I was fourteen years old,[36] and it was the first school house I had ever seen. I began in the alphabet. There were some very small boys, seven years old, who could read. I felt very bad when one of those little fellows would go up and boldly read off his lesson. The teacher finally called me up, asked my name, and if I had been to school. To my answer "No," he said, "Well, Sir, you will begin at the beginning. Here, Sir, begin and say after me," and he began at the letter A, which I repeated until he got down to H. "Now, Sir," said he, "Go and study your first lesson, and when you know it, come and say so to me." Mr. Gill stormed out, "Mind your books" and the scholars struck up a loud blatant confusion of tongues that surpassed anything I had ever heard before. I looked at my book and such was my confusion that I could not remember a word the teacher had said. There I sat in a sea of burning shame, while the clatter and glib clack of tongues rattled on. I did not know how to proceed.

But while I was suffering in woeful silence, a little red-headed fellow sidled up to me and said, "Let me show you," and he pointed out the lesson and said it over two or three times, and then I tried it until I could say it correctly. "Now, go and say it," he said. I went and stood by Mr. Gill and positively I felt like I was seven or eight feet high. All eyes were on me. "Say on," he said, and I repeated down to H, without stopping. There was some snorting and pinching of noses at my expense. He marked another section of the alphabet and told me to go and get it. My little friend again helped me out, and by the closing of the day's exercises I had the alphabet committed to memory. I took my little friend home with me and he helped me learn up to two syllables.

^MI had one of Dillworth's spelling books at first, but there was so much talk about the new spelling book—Webster's—that my father got me one. ^BI continued to go to Mr. Gill, received and recited lessons until one day he said to me, "Now, Gideon, you have catched up with one of the spelling classes and hereafter you will say your lesson with them." The times for saying lessons were so far between that I studied up a plan so as to lose no time. I found no difficulty in committing to memory the lessons, and when we went up to say, the teacher took a book from one of the class and gave out the words. I spelled my word before he had time to give it out to me. He looked at me, but said nothing. When it came my time I spelled my word again. He asked me if I could repeat the whole lesson. I told him I could. Very soon I could repeat Webster's spelling book by heart-brain.

I did not go much further until Mr. Gill told me to get paper and ink. He fixed and ruled off my copy book and set a copy thus: | | | | | |. He made me a pen ^Mand told me that after every lesson I must write two lines. He marked a place on the writing bench that was to be called mine, and said: "Here you are to keep your paper, ink, pens, books, etc., and no one shall interfere with them." I felt very proud of my writing place, though it was nothing more than a wide two inch plank laid on some slanting pins or pegs, driven into two inch auger holes, in one of the pine logs that was a part of the wall of the house. The log above this had been cut out its whole length, leaving a long narrow window immediately above the writing bench. The seat consisted of another two inch plank, placed at the top of some stakes driven in the ground (the house had a dirt floor), and this concludes the inventory of that seminary except some split timbers laid on blocks for seats.

The rule was that he who got to the schoolhouse first said his lesson first; and when the teacher came in, which was never later than an hour by sun, he took his seat and immediately repeated "Come, First." This meant that he who had got there first should come and recite his lesson. The school hours were from an hour by sun in the morning to an hour by sun in the evening. [B]At the end of the five months I could read, the Master said, "very well." Could write a pretty fair hand by a copy and repeat many pieces of poetry which the teacher gave for night lessons. I remember this among many others:

> Ah, few and full of sorrow are the days
> Of miserable man; his life decays
> Like that frail flower which with the sun's uprise
> Her bud unfolds and with the evening dies.
> He like an empty shadow glides away,
> And all his life is but a winter's day.[37]

As far as I am concerned, that verse is erroneous. My days have been neither few nor sorrowful. I have had to fight for subsistence, and when a young man, I took on domestic responsibility and labored for its support fifty-three years. All the conditions surrounding and controlling these eventful years have been shaped by an unerring, irresistible law, the ultimates of which were known to me before entering into them. I knew before leaving my father's house, at fifteen years of age, that I should meet a world of strangers and that the labor and fight of life would have to be done alone. But, where in all these natural results and expected ultimates is there anything to be sorry about, or who will expose his veracity by saying that this long life of mine with so much to love and admire and so few actions to regret, has been like a winter's day? There are nevertheless, many dispositions, whose complaining nature is in unison with that grumbling, mischievous, evil poet.

My father's term of service expired with the year, and the Indians had finished their hunting period and retired from the new purchase, so he prepared himself for the exploration. ᴾHe paid a good eighty-pound shoat to Mr. Gill for my seven months tuition ($4.20), ᴮand taking me with him crossed the Oconee river and traversed the lands for ten or twelve days. He preferred the land on Little river, selected a place, and we returned home and made ready to move. The newly-acquired land belonged to the State, and the Legislature enacted that it should be surveyed into lots of two hundred and two and a half acres each and be drawn for by her citizens in a general lottery.[38] Men having families were entitled to two tickets, single men and women of age and sets of orphaned children one ticket each. My father had been moving and shackling about so much that he was not entitled to a chance in the lottery and so the place he selected was drawn by a man who would not part with it. Father then found a place belonging to Thomas McLellon, with a good cabin on it. For this place he gave all the money he had together with Mammy Pat and her two children. It was situated in the wild woods on a beautiful clear creek, in one mile of where Eatonton now stands.[39]

ᴾHere, in clearing fields and cultivating them for bread, they made me do two summer's pretty hard work. But father had an old army musket that had been left during the Revolution by the French soldiers. With this old kicking gun I killed, during the proper season, plenty of big gobblers to supply the table. I could speak the turkey language good as any turkey. Occasionally I got a shot at a deer, and with that old army gun loaded with two fingers of double F and twenty-one buckshot, at short range (the only condition upon which I would venture to risk a load), I would break nearly every bone in his skin, and get blowed myself.

I must tell you how it happened that I killed my first deer. We let our plow horses feed themselves of nights on the grass and peavine they found in the woods. And while I was hunting them one morning in June, I found and captured a fawn. When I carried it home, my old sensible Scotch grandma told me if I would load up the old gun, and go out and climb a tree near the place where I found the fawn and sit there till its mamma came to suckle it, I could get to kill her. I was soon at the place, but could find no tree near enough except a slim, naked-stem red-oak. It had a sharp fork about fifteen feet from the ground; into this I was, with the old gun, soon lodged. But it was a horrible place to sit, and I twisted and screwed and changed sore corner until I was nearly dead before the hapless old doe came. She came up very cautiously, all the time making a low, clucking sound in her throat. I was all eyes and almost afraid to breathe. I let her come clucking along until she approached the spot where she had left her fawn—it was gone. Her hair all turned up, she looked nearly as big again. I blazed away. I don't know how long it was after this, I found myself wandering in the woods. I did not at first know how or for what I came there. Soon, however, I came to my senses, feeling like I was cracked all over. But remembering the big deer, I hunted up the tree I had been sitting on, found the gun lying ten feet off, three inches of dirt in the muzzle, and the grass wallowed and some blood about the root of the tree. But there lay the big old doe, riddled.

This was big and delightful sport and I enjoyed it very much, but it didn't fill the void that was daily widening in my fifteen-year-old organization. My Indian friends had retired from my vicinity. I saw them but seldom. I had read all the books I could borrow, an old Bible and the Arabian Nights. I didn't know which of these books shocked my reasoning faculties the worst. Nor did I feel there was anything useful in either of them. But I was too young to judge of such matters then. I understand them both now.

[B]Great numbers of people flocked into the new country, and the next year after we came the county seat was laid off and named Eatonton. I was one of the chain carriers to survey the streets and lots. Though I was but fourteen years old at the time, Simon Holt the surveyor[40] said I was more exact in setting the sticks than anyone he had tried. We had cleared and planted ten acres of ground before, and this year we cleared fifteen more. Brother Garland and I grubbed it, and father cut and split the rails to fence it. He was always very ill-natured when he had to work, and wanted everybody to be busy. I was very playful and could throw somersaults and tumble like a show man, and in this exercise had hurt one of my hips. Next morning I was barely able to walk. Father was in a great bluster that morning and seeing me sitting on a stump on the way, for I had started with the rest of them to work, he asked me what ailed me. I told him that I had such a pain in my hip that I could hardly walk. He remarked that it was nothing but laziness, and added several uncomely words, that set awkwardly on the stomach of my pride and in meaning of which I differed widely with him. I remained sitting on the stump till they all had gone to the field. Then I arose and went limping off up the road towards Eatonton. I intended to try to get some kind of work. I had on a coarse home-made shirt and pantaloons and an old wool hat. This completed the inventory of my worldly stores.

It was about a mile to town, and I had progressed about half way when I met Wm. Wilkins, a gentleman merchant in the town,[41] a man with whom I was well acquainted, and who professed to be particularly friendly to me. I had plowed his garden several times and he expressed himself as being well pleased, both with me and my work. As soon as near enough he hailed me in his usual familiar style, "Well, Gideon, whither goest thou this fine morning? I thought you would be busy on the farm." I replied that there was work enough to do there, but I had resolved to quit them. "Quit them?" vociferated he. "Why, what's the matter?" I felt so much aggrieved and full, and his words and looks indicated so much kindness, that I could hold in my wounded feelings no longer; so I put him in possession of my trouble. "Well, well," said he, "I'll tell you, you must go and live with me. I have a good clerk, but need some one to ride errands and attend to outside business. So just go up to my house." He rode on and I limped along until I reached his store. His clerk, whose name was Jeremiah Clark,[42] was three years my senior, and though of very good business capacity, was proud, opinionated, vain and selfish. When I went into the store, without ever saying good morning, he addressed me with, "Well Gid, from the looks of your outfit I should say you were about setting out on a long journey." I made no reply.

Soon Mr. Wilkins returned. He was glad to find me there and said, "Well, Gideon, I will take you for one year, at one hundred dollars, board and clothe you." "What say you to that?" I consented. We went to breakfast and he introduced me to Mrs. Wilkins, who was an excellent body. Mr. Wilkins had a fine horse and he started me that day with some promissory notes to the Magistrate. Next day he sent me with some bagging to a gin twelve miles away. They packed cotton in those days in round bales and the merchants sent bags ready made to the gins to get their customer's cotton. Time passed on and I labored with my books every hour I was not engaged for my employer. Had the head clerk been a good fellow, he could have aided me very much. He was, however, a low-pitched type of humanity, and I never asked him a question. It so happened that two or three days before my time of service expired, John C. Mason, a merchant of the town,[43] came and said he had just bought a wagon load of Tennessee whiskey and wanted Clark to go and gauge it. But he did not care to oblige Mason and pleaded as an excuse that he had forgotten his rule. So I volunteered.

When I returned, Clark sneeringly inquired, "Did you gauge the barrels for Mason?" I replied, "Yes, and I am going to gauge you now! You insulted me the day I came here." "Well, here goes" said he and came very near knocking me down, but I soon got straight and administered a forcible punch in the short ribs, seized him, and whirling towards the door, threw him out. Mr. Wilkins saw us tumble out on the bricks and exclaimed "Hello, boys, are you fighting?" I replied, "Yes, he has been insulting me almost daily ever since I came here. He repeated it today, and as my term is in two or three days of its termination, I thought I would put an end to it. So, if you will come into the house and settle with me, I will seek business elsewhere."

After a moment's reflection, he said, "I would prefer settling with Mr. Clark." So they settled, quarrelled a little, and Clark left very angry and threatening to settle with me at a future period. Mr. Wilkins made me an offer of $300 for the next year, which I accepted and continued to live with him and his kind lady, as one of the family. Through that period I don't think I was idle an hour. [P]Indeed, Mr. Wilkins remarked to a neighboring merchant who came in the store one day, "The business is better attended to now than when I was paying two clerks."

[B]About this time Mason L. Weems,[44] author of the "Life of Washington," "General Marion," "Devil in Petticoats," etc., who had been in the area selling books from his flying library for nearly a year previous, was called home to North Carolina to superintend some important business. He had to depart in such haste that he could not take his library with him, and he solicited Mr. Wilkins to take charge of and sell them for him until his return. Mr. Wilkins said he could not be bothered with them, but if Gideon wanted to, he could take charge of them. [P]My kind-hearted employer permitted me to fit up the lumber-room that was attached to the dry goods store for the purpose, and to retain for my own use the ten per cent Mr. Weems proposed on amount of sales. That was all very well and suited my poverty-stricken condition exactly. But the greatest thing, in my view of the case, was transforming the lumber room, where I had been sleeping with my borrowed books, into a library of $5,000 worth of the best knowledge that the world could boast. Into this—to me, world of books—I plunged with so much earnestness that I thought or cared for nothing outside of it, and I was so much afraid that Mr. Weems would return soon and take them away, that I forwarded the amount of sales as often as it amounted to ten dollars. The thing worked as I desired. He was satisfied with the indications of my management, and did not return until he had fully arranged and settled his business at home—nearly a year. After examining my work and taking account of stock, he was so much pleased that, besides paying me the full amount of our contract, he presented me with the books I had been studying and some others, which he said suited my years and bent of inclination. [B]Mason L. Weems was a very clever gentleman. I have never seen him since, but have often thought of him and always with the greatest respect.

[P]Overall, this had been a glorious year for me. It tore open the windows of my abode of darkness, let in the light of science on my awakening faculties and left me with enough of good books on my shelf to nourish and feed the divine flame another year.[45] Except four or five nights that my employer would have me to go fishing with him, my bow and arrows lay idle, in their case. I continued to do the business in the little dry goods store for my kind-hearted employer another year.

But it was thought, notwithstanding the fact that I discharged all the duties incumbent on me as clerk, salesman, bookkeeper, collector—all things about the establishment—that I read and talked too much about organic life and too little about dollars and cents ever to succeed in the mercantile business. I was advised by those who took an interest in my destiny to read medicine. "You are," said they, "a high order of Indian doctor, thoroughly acquainted with the medical resources of our forests; we have experimental knowledge of that fact," and they contended that a little touch of scientific medicine would make a useful man of me. ^BWhen my time expired with Mr. Wilkins he told me that I was worth more than his business would warrant him in giving. That he had been talking with and recommending me to Mr. Ichabod Thompson,[46] a Yankee merchant who had settled in the place with a heavy stock of goods; and that Thompson would give me $500. So, I went and set in with Thompson. It was a large business. He had an Indian Store out on the Ocmulgee river, which was the boundary line of the U.S., and he loved to stay out there, leaving me frequently alone. My good friend, Dr. Henry Branham,[47] had advised me to read medicine and for the last six months I had been reading all I could.

^PWhen I read medicine, Darwin's "Zoonomia" was the textbook of practice for the United States, and I viewed the work as the finishing stroke on that subject. Medical superstition destroys more life than war! The author of the "Zoonomia," Erasmus Darwin, was still living. His place of residence was on the river Derwent, England, but at that time was Professor, I think (I speak from recollection), of Obstetrics, Guy's Hospital, London.[48] I had possessed myself not only of his medical works but I had his "Botanic Garden" and the "Temple of Nature,"[49] all occupying a plane of thought so far above anything I had before seen, and from which such floods of scientific light and philosophic truths were pouring in upon my uncultivated intellect—soul food—that I felt strongly attracted to, and very much desired to know more about the man. So I got up as good a letter as I could, in which I expressed my sentiments towards him and

his valuable works, gave him a short sketch of my origin, present condition and eager aspirations, addressed to Professor Erasmus Darwin, Guy's Hospital, London. In about three months his very polite, friendly and most interesting reply came.[50] It was a lengthy document, full of philosophic good sense and useful information; exactly such a paper as my blank intellect needed. I looked upon it then, and I think yet, that it was the most holy and useful essay that ever came into my possession. It changed my crude notions in almost everything. The scientific truths and systematic methods of investigating them it contained opened up and withdrew the veil of darkness that had been clouding and fettering my mentality with a considerable amount of intellectual cowardice, checking and forbidding inquiry into any subject that was said to belong to the business of the gods. It showed me also that the sun of science had arisen already, and before its effulgent rays, the witches, ghosts, angry gods, and frightful devils of antiquity would soon have to fly to the mountains or somewhere else for protection. And even now, be my intellectual status on the plane of progressed thought what it may, it is attributable to the impulse given by that letter. I wrote and sent him a letter of thanks and begged of him, if not contrary to his interests, to continue to favor my hungry spirit with his valuable letters. But the war between his country and the United States— the embargo—put an end to our correspondence.

Professor Charles Darwin who, at this moment, occupies the highest plane of intellectual advancement, is the grandson of that Erasmus Darwin, and his world-stirring philosophy and elaborate scientific developments are really the carrying out by an industrious, ingenious, philosophic investigator of the deep-set propositions that had been so happily recorded by his truly renowned progenitor. He made a polite reply to a communication I wrote him in reference to the manners and customs, laws, religion, military regulations and farmer-like action of the agricultural ant (*Myrmica molefaciens*), the propriety of which communication was suggested by my reading of his volume on "Origin of Species."[51] In it he clearly stated that this superior race of emmet had been by a natural selection progressively developed from an unprogressed type still existing here and recognizable. He said it was with much pleasure that he acknowledged the receipt of my communication, and in the most polite possible style thanked me for the flattering manner in which I had alluded to his eminent progenitor. He said other things about me that would not look well here. I wrote again describing another interesting race of ants (*Ecedoma Texana*—Horticultural Ant), but the Confederate war intervened and he did not reply. Isn't it a little singular that my correspondence with the Darwins has always been frustrated by big wars?

[B]On Mr. Thompson's return from a trip to Savannah, he presented me with a fine-toned English violin.[52] I lived out my time with Thompson and had made good progress in my medical books, but now war was approaching. Soon after I became a volunteer. The people of Putnam county had elected me Tax Collector and on that account I could not volunteer for a longer period than five months. [P]I volunteered in a company of dragoons. Full of patriotism and feeling highly incensed at British arrogance, I was anxious for the bloody conflict. [B]The army is a bad place to form character, but I thought it then a great place, and to fight and slay was a great and glorious thing. I entertain a very different opinion on that subject now. [P]We were marched and encamped on the war-path, where we were detained three months. The army becoming demoralized by sickness and tired of inaction, the men began to write home for substitutes, which they effected in great numbers. The face of the army was greatly changed. [M]It was in the month of August when I went into the army.[53] I served until the first of January; then went home, collected the taxes, paid the money into the treasury and married.[54] I served another period of three months after I was married. [P]I stood up to my post and did what they told me until there was no further use for soldiers in that war, and felt myself thoroughly gorged with soldiering. I had come to the conclusion that hereafter I would let those do the fighting who arise the fuss. [M]In the spring of 1815 I went home and gave my father a faithful year's work.

CHAPTER TWO

A Jack-of-All-Trades
on the Road to Mississippi

ᴾRegarding marriage, I had read the works of Dr. Franklin.[1] He advised early marriage. This agreed perfectly with my semi-civilized humanity, and the influence of the controlling animal developments. The advice of the old teacher at that stage of my being seemed quite reasonable and right. I did so, and thereby in course of time, demonstrated the fallacy of the Franklin theory. That is, as far as such an organism as I possess is a test. I was utterly incompetent to the duties and responsibilities of domestic life. I, however, made out to worry through with it without calling for help. My ten living (lost three) children[2] were grown, married and settled off on ample homes long ago, and they are sustaining themselves pretty well. But they are, in their mental aspect, not above fair to good middling; and the mischief that I have done them by bringing them into a world that is full to the brim with the same sort, and to myself, by placing a clog on the pursuits that nature had fitted me for, is great.

While I failed, with the Franklin experiment, to bestow on the world an equivalent for the harm it produced, I do not allude to this matter regretfully, but as a circumstance which continued to check the natural inclination and bent of my capacity up to 1852. At that period, having settled my numerous brood, I found my domestic responsibility ceased. I have since been free and could pursue that which seemed to please me best. But it was no go. The train of philosophic thought had been long since broken. The habit for investigation and experimentation was too long interrupted. The faculties and powers for scientific scrutiny were blunted and no longer capable of producing reliable ultimates. I was in Texas when I obtained my freedom. It was then, scientifically speaking, an unexplored region. Everything was fresh, new and beautiful; and, here I renewed the long neglected inclination for investigating the natural sciences. But before I begin to tell what I did in Texas, I must return to Georgia and commence to narrate some of the most remarkable occurences that turned up, during the period of the Franklin experiment—the thirty-eight years spent in the nursery.

The first year after I was married I dwelt with my brothers[3] and the Negroes to cultivate the farm. [B]I had two years previously bought and sent home a likely young Negro man whose name was Dick, and this is all the record of the poor fellow's name in existence. He worked with me till September, when he hurt himself lifting at a wagon wheel and died soon after. He was a good Negro and was my friend.[4] I hated to lose him.

[P]The farm was not large, the labor strong; I had many days to devote to field sports, which I was beginning to relish very much. It had been many years since I had indulged my aptitude and capabilities for capturing fish and all kinds of game. This was comparatively a new country with plenty of deer, turkey and endless fish. Near my Father's place was a beautiful, clear-running creek, and three miles off a splendid little clear river all full of fish.

It was a matter of astonishment to our neighbors who came from the older, fished-out portions when they saw the amount of fish I took out of the creeks round about with my Indian contrivances. They all wanted fish but said they could catch none. Didn't know what kind of bait nor the good days to fish. Their women were talking about wanting fish; and for the purpose of supplying the craving women with a good mess and to have a little good sport, I, without letting any one of them know that I had spoken to another, had engaged six men, each with three nicely prepared torches of fat pine, to assemble at 4 o'clock p.m. at my Father's home. They had according to my instructions managed the preparations very privately; and now to behold such a company with faggots along on their backs, they looked at each other and said. "We dare not, boys, and were about to break up." But my Father, interfering, said: "No, gentlemen, go on with him, he'll get you plenty of fish if you will hold him a good light long enough." So I, with my bow and two steel-pointed arrows, in advance of my faggot-bearers hurried off, and by the time dark set in we were seven miles off on a nice creek that ran within two miles of Father's house. Our plan was to fish back to that two-mile place.

We rested until it was thoroughly dark, and some of the men remarked it was a dull prospect and that they felt so tired of the wild goose chase I had led them, that they did not feel like dragging any further. I lighted a torch and had not proceeded three steps in the water before I saw and killed a trout twelve inches long. The men who had been sitting all this time were instantly on foot and I heard no more said about the fatigue and briers. The creek had never before been fished with torches. It was full of good fish: trout, pickerel, white suckers and various large perch. Of all the bow and arrow fishing I have ever done in my life, that night was the greatest. I had not waded exceeding five miles up the creek before my torch bearers exclaimed, "It is enough; we can carry no more."

Night fishing with bow and arrow is conducted as follows: two of the company go into the water, one carries the torch, the other has the bow. It takes both hands to shoot the bow and somebody has to carry the light. Though I have carried both and shot many fishes pulling the string with my teeth, I would rather have a torch bearer. When two go in they wade along very gently, holding the light low; both parties search all the still water along both banks and all around the border as far down as you can see. The fish are found fast asleep, and with proper caution there is no necessity for shooting them at a greater distance than two or three inches, except the catfish. You have to shoot him as he flies. I never found one of them napping. In the quiet bays near the seacoast around Tuxpan[5] I shot flounders with a light till it was a shame.

[B]The next year I joined forces and farmed with Judge Strong.[6] [P]He had three hands and sixty acres of open land. I had forty acres of open land and two hands. He was to furnish all the provisions, smithing, etc. I was to superintend the farm and we were to make an equal division of the proceeds of the crop. I planted sixty acres in cotton and forty in corn. I cultivated the ground carefully and both crops were very good. That year cotton was worth 31½ cents a pound, but I became restless and did not feel like staying in that country until the crop could be gathered. ᴮSo I sold everything to Judge Strong.

ᴾThere were at this place plenty of deer and turkey and the fishing was splendid, and I had recovered my passion for the gun, rod and bow; but the immigrants were pouring in with their shot-guns and hounds and it was very plain to be seen that the game would soon be gone. ᴹThe Alabama, Black Warrior, Tombecbee, and Chattahoochee countries had all been acquired by conquest,[7] and I was determined to seek a home in the wilderness. My Father had made up his mind to go to the new country with his large family and he had been insinuating to me the propriety of breaking up to go with him. ᴾHe said to me one day: "My son, we had better fix up and leave this crowded country while times are good."

ᴹThere was another little thing that increased my restlessness. My wife's relations were all wealthy and my wife said they had been mean enough to cast little slurs at her and her poverty. She also persuaded me to sell out and go with my Father to the new country. All these influences confirmed me in the resolution to get ready and bid adieu to my native State. ᴾI immediately sent an order to C. Gump, Lancaster county, Pennsylvania, to make a rifle of certain dimensions and forward it to me by my friend, M. Whitfield, who went to Philadelphia every fall for goods.[8] The gun came, and she was the most completely finished rifle that I had ever seen up to that date, and shot as true as any gun ever did before or since.

ᴹFather and I sold out our possessions and were soon on the road to the new country. We had proceeded about forty-five miles when we came to the Ocmulgee river, which at that time was a dividing line between the Georgians and the Creek Indians. A man by the name of Ferguson came to our camp and, getting a little tight with father, in a kind of frolic sold him his lands and cattle. All along the river the people owned herds of cattle which they kept in the range on the Indian side of it. There was plenty of deer over there, too; and being satisfied that Father would not remain longer than a year, I concluded to do what I never did in my life, idle away the time until he got tired of his bargain and made ready to move again.

I could continue my medical reading, fish in the river, and hunt the deer beyond it; and in this way have a pleasant. The country near the river was densely settled. At a little gathering one day I heard some of the men say that the boys had turned out, ducked and abused White, their schoolmaster, so badly that he had quit the school. Some of the men remarked that their children were so bad that they feared they could never find a man that would be able to manage them. In reply to a remark which I inadvertently made ("Gentlemen, your teachers are of no account"), one of them said, "Could you manage our boys? If you think so we will furnish you forty scholars and give you ten dollars apiece to teach them until the close of the term, and pay you the cash." It struck me that this would be better employment than hunting and fishing; so I told them to make out their articles, and appoint a School committee. The requirements were only to teach reading, writing, and arithmetic. So I signed the articles and appointed the next Monday as the day to commence school at the Mineral Springs, ᴹtwo miles from where I resided.[9] According to appointment ᴮI was there at 8 o'clock and was perfectly astonished at the number of people I found there. Besides the Committee of five men, there were forty-five pupils, fifteen grown men (five of them married), five grown young ladies, and boys and girls of all ages and sizes. ᴹAll entered for the full term. After sitting until I had examined their books and set the lessons, the Committee rose up and the chairman said, "We feel well pleased at your method of setting your classes to work, and sir, what you have before you. We wish and believe you will succeed." They bowed a good day and left.

These children had been born and raised, to the age I found them, among the cows and drunken cow-drivers on the outer borders of the State, and they were positively the coarsest specimens of the human family I had ever seen. I saw very distinctly that no civil or ordinary means would be applicable to their conditions. In the course of the first day they had half a dozen fights in the house; talking and laughing went on incessantly. At play time their conduct was indescribable and intolerable; the cry of "Look what this one or that one is doing to me" rang out from every part of the play ground. Those married and grown men participated in the devilment and seemed to enjoy it hugely. At the expiration of one hour I called them to books, and one of the men, as he came in, said to me: "You give but short play time, Mistofer." I replied as good humoredly as possible, "You must recollect, my young friend, this is my first day with you. I may learn to suit you better after a while." I further remarked to the young man that I intended to make it the most pleasant and profitable school that had ever been instituted in that country, and that I should, when the proper time arrived, call upon him and his companions to aid me in the prosecution of a scheme I had arranged in my mind to make it so.

"Hurrah, for you! Boys, he's the fellow we ought to had here all the time," was his reply. They got their books and carried on a long talk about what I had said. One big, jolly fellow wondered how "Mistofer" could make the school more pleasant than it was.

I was bowed down over my desk writing out my plan for the government of the school, which really consisted of the most outrageous ruffians, rollicking young women, and naughty children I had ever seen. I would occasionally (without looking up) cry out, "Mind your books," to which they did not pay the least attention. I called them up to say their lessons; and to this point in the exercise I paid strict attention, prompting and instructing them in the kindest and friendliest terms possible, and encouraging them to be good and get their lessons well. And so it went on with many curious and disgusting occurrences until 12 o'clock Friday. I had by that time completed a Constitution and set of By-Laws which were intended to teach the poor untutored marauders to govern themselves.

As soon as they had got through with their dinner Friday I called "Books," when they came in a great rush. Before quiet was restored, one of the men impatiently asked, "What's up now, Hoss?" In reply I stated that I wished to read to the school the rules for its government, which I had been engaged in writing all week. They all then took seats and became comparatively quiet. I told them that seeing the school is so large it is necessary that there should be some systematic regulations to insure and control the equal rights of each individual. The Constitution provided for a regularly organized court, with judge, clerk, jury, sheriff and a monitor. It made me the sheriff and also specified the character and degrees of crime, terms of office, etc. The By-Laws regulated the terms of court, duties of officers, modes of drawing jurors, and the manner of conducting trials, punishments, etc., etc.

I read it very distinctly, and when I had finished, inquired:

"Well, gentlemen and ladies, what is your opinion of the documents?" They were almost unanimous in their expression: "It is the best thing in the world." Thus encouraged, I continued: "With your permission, ladies and gentlemen, I will take the vote of the school on the subject." "Yes, go it, Hoss! It's a good thing," exclaimed one of the married men. I put the question, "All you who are in favor of this Constitution and accompanying By-Laws for the government and regulation of this school will make it known by saying 'Aye.'" The vote was taken and the Constitution and By-Laws unanimously adopted.

I expressed my gratification at the result and said that I hoped to be able to convince them thoroughly before the school term had expired that the vote they had given was on the right side of the question. I added, "To certify your approbation it is proper that you all put your names to the Constitution. Let the married men come first." Not more than half of the grown ones could write. They ordered me as sheriff to write their names. In the course of an hour all their names, except those of the little ones who could not understand its nature, were on the paper.

One of the married men, whose name was Elijah Satterwhite,[10] as he handed over the pen to his successor, exultingly exclaimed "I tell you what, folks, this is going to be a big thing. We never had such sort of doings afore in these diggings. What next, old hoss?" I announced the election of officers the next order of business and moved that an election be held for judge, clerk and monitor. After a great deal of telling and directing and much awkwardness, we succeeded in bungling out a set of officers.

I made out the Monitor's list and after explaining it to him, I seated them and read the Constitution and By-Laws to them again. They were all so much pleased that they fairly shouted, saying they had heard how "the great folks done away far off, but none of them have ever come here afore." After telling them that the Constitution and Rules were to be read every day at 12 p.m. and that Friday was the regular court day, I dismissed them and they went off in great glee.

At an hour by sun Monday morning the whole number of pupils was present, and I thought I could discover a considerable change in their behavior. The effect of having put their names to the Constitution was visible. We got through the week without a fight. Friday came and as soon as dinner was over, they came into the house and asked that the Court be organized. The first case on the Monitor's list was that of Stephen Herd,[11] a grown man, charged with the offense of throwing a little girl's bonnet into the branch. I appointed a lawyer for the defense, but being bashful and awkward he said but few words, and the Solicitor followed his good example. The Judge then read the law in such cases and put the case to the Jury. They returned in a few minutes with a verdict of guilty. The Judge sentenced him to three lashes, well laid on with a hickory. I had cut and trimmed a number of nice hickory switches and had them sitting handy. I selected a good one and said, "Come up, Stephen." He came up smiling as though he expected that as he was a grown man, I would only go through the motions with him. I laid my switch against his back to measure the distance, and then with all the force I possessed, inflicted the three lashes, cutting the homespun back of his waistcoat into three ribbands. It surprised him so badly that he burst out crying, and said that he knew of some things which were not on the Monitor's list which he could tell if he was a mind to. I said, "Tell it to the court, Stephen, and whatever the decision of that body may direct me to do, you may rest assured that I will faithfully execute it."

The next case was that of Elijah Satterwhite, one of the jury, and in drawing one to fill his place I slipped in Stephen Herd, hoping that as he had just been punished he would be hard in the case and go for punishment. The crime was willfully running over a little boy. In this trial the lawyers were a little bolder; they understood it better and spoke more to the point. The trial was a little more interesting, and the case being put to the jury, they went out. There being nothing but the wall between the seat I occupied and where they were sitting, I could distinctly hear their deliberations. They were highly elated at the prompt and vigorous manner in which I had discharged the mandate of the court, and were loud for finding Satterwhite guilty of a good deal of offense. They seemed to rejoice at the opportunity and power they possessed, and were in favor of putting it on to their criminal in good style, except Stephen Herd, who had not as yet expressed himself either way. "Well, Steve, what's your verdict in this case?" they asked. "Well, boys," said he, "I have been thinking about the matter very seriously. In the first place I think we have an excellent chance with this man to learn a great deal, if we play our parts correctly. I also think the regulations to which we have all signed our names is the best thing of the kind that could be made. But if we all go for thrashing and punishment for every little offense, we shall soon all get up the spirit of spite among us, and the school will go to nothing as all other schools have in this settlement. I say, let us all try to do better, be more particular with the little ones, more respectful and polite to one another and as lenient in inflicting penalty as the law will allow us. In this case of Satterwhite's it was not clearly proven that the act was willfully committed. The boy was not hurt, but made very angry and his clothes a little soiled. Mind you, I am not in favor of clearing 'Lige, but fine him. My verdict would be find him guilty of running over the boy, without the willful intent, and fine him." Some of them said, "Write out your verdict and let's see how it looks." So Stephen wrote "Guilty, but not willfully." They all agreed and brought it in. The Judge sentenced him to pay three dozen good goose quills for the school. (You will ask what they did with the fines. Well, the Constitution recognized a Treasury and an officer to take charge of and keep a regular book of all the receipts and disbursements. The Treasury belonged to the school, the fines being of a character suitable for school use. Any student could go with a lawful application and draw and receipt for anything he actually needed.)

But Stephen Herd was the first and the last to receive corporal punishment. He was also the first to advocate its abolition. He afterwards became one of the most solid lawyers in my school. Green Wheeler and George Clayton were the other two.[12] All three of them became distinguished lawyers of the state afterward. The school went on increasing in efficiency every day, and the interest that was excited among my employers filled the house every Friday afternoon with spectators. The boys borrowed law books and all of them were filled with the spirit of progress, and before the term was half out they were performing court action finely.

[B]Every Thursday at play time I took the female portion of the school to the play ground and made them select partners from the males and play Cat-Ball[13] one hour. During this game I taught them to practice polite ceremony and society etiquette.

Several holidays occurred, ^Mand at such times a very respectful petition was drawn by a committee appointed for the purpose, specifying its object and praying for a few days vacation for the purpose of recreation. The pupils had all, males and females, become tame and quite polite, and on the last two days of the term had a public examination. At the conclusion of it, my employers declared it to be a complete success. They paid every dollar that was due me and offered me $1000 to teach another session of ten months. I declined most respectfully, for Father had already sold out and was ready to take the road again.

My Father loved a border life, and the place he had purchased on the Ocmulgee, as the people had already commenced settling on the opposite side of the river, was no longer looked upon as a border country. He sold his place and was soon equipped and geared up for the road, and so was I. Having been reared to a belief and faith in the pleasure of frequent change of country, I looked upon the long journey through the wilderness with much pleasure.

^BJoseph Bryan and my sister Mary married at this place, and they also wanted to see the new country. Our company consisted of Father, Mother and eight children with six Negroes; Bryan and his wife and two Negroes; myself and wife, two small sons and two Negroes. We had good horses and wagons and all manner of guns and big dogs. We set out on the 10th of March 1818.[14] ^MI felt as if I was on a big camp hunt. ^BThe journey, the way we traveled, was about five hundred miles, and all a wilderness. We were six weeks on the road ^Mand altogether it was, as I thought and felt, the most delightful time I had ever spent in my life. My brother Garland and I "flanked it" as the wagons rolled along and killed deer, turkeys, wild pigeons. Whenever we camped on any water course, at night (with pine torches) we fished with my bow and arrows and killed a great many. Little creeks were filled with fish in that season.

^POur third camp was in the wilderness, in the Muskogee country. It was an extraordinary dry, pleasant winter; we very seldom had to set up our tents. It had been a fruitful year and the earth was strewn with nuts of many descriptions. Blackhaws (*Viburnum prunifolium*), grapes, persimmons (*Diospyros virginiana*) and berries were plenty on the vines and bushes. Deer and tur-

keys were abundant everywhere. We were in no hurry, and when we found a good camping place we would not leave it for several days. While the women and children and Negroes employed themselves gathering wild fruit, the men would be ranging the wild maiden forests where the unholy ranting and domineering shout of civilization had never before alarmed the birds and beasts.

Except where we crossed the Chattahoochee river (a large stream where they had a ferry boat), we saw no houses in our journey of something over five hundred miles in extent. Our course lay through a hilly, sometimes mountainous country, having many water courses (big creeks and small rivers) dashing their clear, sweet waters over the craggy rocks that floored their gravelly beds. It was on the banks of these rushing streams that we camped. They were all full of fish, and notwithstanding it was pretty cool, almost icy sometimes, my brother Garland and myself would fish them of nights with the bow and arrow. We found in the little eddies about the rocks and near the shore, any place where they could lie still, suckers, small shining trout, and perch as red as the core of a red-meat watermelon. Very plenty they were, fat and well-flavored. At all our camping places we had fine sport. The entire forest was alive with wild pigeons but nobody troubled them.

The greatest camp, and the one at which we tarried the longest, was on the Hightower,[15] a river fifty yards wide and nowhere over knee-deep. We waded for miles in its rushing waters, fishing of nights with torch and gig and bow and arrow. We considered ourselves well paid for wading in its March-cooled waters. The big strings of large white suckers, not-so-large speckled trout and a large red, nearly orbicular perch, weighing six ounces and feeling as firm as a beef-steak, astonished the South Carolina movers who were traveling with us. We remained at this Hightower camp ten days, and my mother had the Negroes to make a scaffold for her and keep a big logheap burning. From it she could obtain a constant supply of live coals to put under the scaffold, which was overlaid with salted venison and fish. By her knowledge of such matters, she kept the temperature adjusted not to cook but to dry the articles so exposed. That was a profitable camp, for we left it with dried meat enough to supply our cooks for two hundred miles.

Our next camp at which we remained a while was on Canoe Creek,[16] a wild, unfrequented country that lay along the foothills of some very lofty mountains. The game was so abundant here, and so easily taken, that I felt like it would be right to make that the end of my journey. My brother and I went into the mountains one evening just at sundown and very silently built a little camp-fire, where we slept till daylight. We left our camp and slipped out on the top of the mountain, intending to go in different directions on its ridge. But before we had separated, the roar of the numerous wild gobblers surprised us so that we both stood and listened. In all directions was to be heard nothing but one continuous roar. My brother sat down saying, "We don't want but one apiece of them, and this is as good a stand as any." We kept ourselves concealed and saw them fighting and chasing each other. Many of them came near enough, and we had fair chances to shoot. But we concluded the amusement was too good to break it up yet, and besides we knew the turkeys would not break up till towards 9 o'clock.

We sat still in our hiding place a while longer, until a pair of old gobblers who had been fighting a long time, not more than fifty yards distant, got their mouths locked and were both pulling back like they were trying to tear each other's jaws off. My brother said "Now is our time, be quick! You take the right, and let's see if we can't both fire at once and cut off their locked heads." I was instantly ready, and "Bang" went the rifle. My brother said he discovered he was a little behind and didn't fire. But the surviving warrior was thrashing away on his headless victim, in the full confident courage that he would conquer, if he had not decapitated the foe himself, which he doubtless thought he had.

I remarked, "They were such equal matches in the fight, I think they are the same weight. Shoot him and we'll see." He shot him, and at that moment, flying from the half-hounds and curs and military guns of our traveling companions, came rushing up the pass through which we had succeeded in gaining the mountain's top, fifteen or twenty deer. They were frightened so badly at meeting us in their only outlet, they didn't know what to do. They were all in amongst us and we amongst them, kicking and striking and halloing, with empty guns in our hands. My brother said, "Well, we've been all our lives in what we thought good hunting countries, but this takes the dilapidated linen."

That country possessed many things besides what delights the industrious lover of sport—bears, panthers, beavers, catamounts, wild-cats, coons, woodchucks, and woodcocks bouncing up everywhere in the thick woods, but what is a very valuable accompaniment to the other fine sport was the great number of bee trees to be found. Indeed, the country being a good one as to water, soil and timber, game of every description was so abundant and the sport so fascinating that it was with effort that I was finally able to tear myself away from it. My brother and I had, during the few days we remained at that camp, several other cases of rare sport with curious and incredible success, from the report of which I shall let you escape.

My handsome young wife, with her two little boys (one two-and-a-half years, the other six-months old), and the Negroes were all healthy and happy. When I made the inquiry as to how would this wild, uninhabited wilderness do for a home, the reply was, "I don't think we shall find a better." The Negroes joined her and said, "Whar all dis good timber is we can soon knock up a nice house close to some o' dose good springs, shoa." But the fates had cast the die. The very next morning we struck our tents and journeyed onward until we reached Tuscaloosa, which we found full of people just landed, mostly from Tennessee, and they were felling timber and hastily building up a town of poles and clapboards. And such people! I had never seen any of that type of the genus before. They were large men generally, full fleshed, and having the appearance of having been well greased with hog's fat. Coarse in conversation they were, and the tenor of their discourse seemed to hang upon one idea—that they were afraid the people might not know, or if they did, they might forget it: namely, that they were not only able, but damned willing, to whip anybody that might be fool enough to come in their way.

ᴹTuscaloosa was at that time a small log cabin village, but people from Tennessee were arriving daily, and in the course of that year it grew to be a considerable town.[17] I concluded to stop there, and Father and Bryan continued their journey to a small improvement eight miles below on the Black Warrior river,[18] where they settled, and, cutting down a canebrake, made corn, and killed bear, venison and fish enough to supply the family. In Tuscaloosa I fished and had as much as we needed of that kind of food, but there were no bear nor deer in reach of the town, and I had to buy provisions at enormous rates: flour, $25 a barrel; corn, $2 ½ a bushel; sugar, 50 cents a pound; coffee, 62 ½ cents a pound; salt, $8 a bushel; bacon, 37 ½ cents a pound. There was no beef to be had. I built a little clapboard house on the river side of the town, which had not yet been surveyed. The land hunters from Georgia found us and continued their friendly calls on us [as fellow Georgians] until what money I had left from the long journey was eaten up. This was a circumstance for which I had made no provision. I felt no uneasiness on that account, for I was as strong as two common men and could do anything from cutting and splitting fence rails to fine cabinet work. In mercantile action I was familiar with all the duties from the lumber room to the counting room. I could mix drugs and practice medicine as far as it was known in the interior of the country in those days. So I felt no alarm at the fact that my money was gone.

I started out one morning with the intention to accept any offer of business that might present itself. I set my face towards Dr. Isbell's shop.[19] It being midsummer, I thought I would try to make some kind of an arrangement with him. But before I reached the doctor's house, I met a very strong man whose name was John Weeks.[20] Having been acquainted with him in Georgia, I asked him where he was going with that whip-saw. He informed me that he had been in partnership with a man that came with him from Tennessee but the fellow was such a drunkard that he had been forced to quit him.

I told him my money was out and I must try to make more some way. I added that I felt capable of performing any kind of work, and that my family was composed of two women and three children, all equally helpless, who must be supported. ᴮ"My friend," said he, "you have never been accustomed to work. The whip-saw and the summer heat will soon upset you." ᴹHe suggested that the surest way for me to support my family would be a partnership with some of the doctors, or a position as salesperson in one of the stores. I replied that I liked the looks of that saw pretty well; and if he had no other objections than

53

those he had named, I would like to go in with him. I inquired where his family was. "Well," said he, "if you go in with me I must go in with you. I left my wife and children in Tennessee and have no home here. Planks are worth four dollars a hundred and we can get the cash for all we can make. But it is heavy work, I tell you." So we went into partnership. He furnished the saw and all the tools and I was to let him live with me as one of my family. We divided the products of our labor equally.

We went to work the very next day. We hewed out stocks enough for 1000 feet of inch planks which we had engaged to saw for Peter Remington, a Yankee, who had brought a heavy stock of goods and was in a great hurry to set them up. We were there to have the planks ready by Saturday evening. We had it done a day sooner. It was for a floor and counter; and he gave us twenty dollars to lay down the floor and make the counter, all rough. We completed the job Saturday, and I helped mark and put the goods all day Sunday, for which I received ten dollars. We continued to saw for about two months—averaging eight dollars a day, except a few days when we went hunting and fishing, and one day when we sawed planks and made a skiff.

[B]There were in the town a set of young men who came out to explore the country, and Tuscaloosa being at that time the only place where provisions could be had, those men made that place the home point, from whence they went out and returned. It was a pretty good game country and they, like myself, all had guns and fishing tackle along. Getting acquainted, for like attracts like, we formed a sportsman's club and were soon ranging the wild canebrakes, which had many bears as well as much other game. Tuscaloosa has wide bottoms, which at that time were densely clothed in the largest cane I ever saw in any country. The old Indian town of *Tush-cah-loo-sa* lay a mile or more below where new Tuscaloosa is situated. The chief whom the place was named for dwelt there previous to the war with the Muskogees. He was a very dark colored Indian, and that fact named him. *Tush-cah* is "a warrior" and *loo-sa* is "black." The white people spell it "Tuscaloosa."

Our sporting club, until the weather became too dry and hot, spent most of the time in the canebrakes. Amongst the immigrants who located on the river were several sets of hounds and big curs, and some half hounds. These people were having bear drives every two or three days. Our club sent a messenger to the bear hunting companies to negotiate with them for the privilege of participating in their hunts. We wanted no part of the game, just the participation in the excitement. Our commission was successful with three or four companies, who engaged to give us notice when and where to meet them, so that we were in a bear drive nearly every day. We had as much of this extremely dangerous sport as we could desire.

There is not much danger in what the bear can do to you, for when the dogs are all around him, baying and snapping at him, he don't seem to regard the approach of man much, but is awful afraid of the dogs. He surveys the approaching man but does not see any way he has to bite him. But the dog, with his wide mouth full of shiny long teeth, the bear understands very well. When the man runs up and stabs him with a knife, he jumps upon and tears up a dog, for he thinks the dog has done it. Except you get tangled up and fall near him, the hunter seldom gets hurt by the bear. The great danger lies in the fact that when the dogs have brought the bear to bay and are making heaven and earth ring with their vociferous threatenings, the eager sportsman, desiring to be first at the dainty performance, dashes up and not seeing or thinking of anything else, bangs away at the bear. Then the complaint of a good dog or somebody else on the opposite side of the grand exciting fracas awakens him from his frantic, unsportsmanlike action to the recollection of the fact that there are others in the hunt besides the bear, and he discovers he has shot—not the bear, but the leader dog or his friend. In this kind of super-excitable character lies the great danger in the bear hunt. When I find one of that sort in the company, I always, if the company refuse to leave their guns at home, make my day's business in some other direction. Not many casualties occur when the company carries knives only. We had many dogs crippled and some killed. A few injuries resulted from fights with large, old experienced he-bears, who had experience in fighting with the little red-mouthed native dog, with yellow eyes and bushy tail—a distinct race of indigenous dogs. The big old fellow knew what to do with his own native, silent, little yellow dog. But when the great big, uproarious, many-colored, crop-eared, bob-tailed American dog undertook the chase, Old Bruin looked upon that new breed in the act of invading his domain as having some belligerent amusement in it, and he would not lead the chase far before he would stop and seat himself for the noisy conflict. And then came the danger to the sportsmen if they had carried their guns into the chase.

All parties dash up to the roaring dogs to find them ranting and raving at a very respectful distance from his forest majesty. Seated in the center of the surrounding circle of his wide-mouthed enemies, sullenly erect, he rolls his gorgon eyes in their red sockets defiantly. There he is, mouth slightly agape, his red tongue lolled a little to one side, among his long, formidable white teeth; his big, strong arms, tipped with iron claws, down by his side. He looked as large as a three-year old cow, but not so amiable.

The yelling sportsmen, drawing near, encourage the dogs, who pitch in. Quick as thought, the foremost dog is mashed by a single stroke of Bruin's iron-clad paw; whilst another is being doubled up in the monster's arms, two or three joints of his backbone torn out, and he is thrown aside, a ruined dog. The balance of the pack become more mannerly, bay at the proper distance and not many more of them get hurt. The sportsmen, in the meantime watching their opportunity, run in and give a stab with the knife, not on the near side, but the opposite. For Bruin is sure to strike where the knife enters, and so first one and then another stab him until the old fellow weakens down, and with a low muttering prayer gives up the ghost.

Towards August the canebrake became too hot for us and we prepared ourselves for cooler sport. About a mile above town is the rapids. This little fall gave the place the name it was then known by—Falls of the Warrior. It consists of a solid flat rock reaching perhaps fifty yards up and down the river, and under-lying both banks with a dip of about twenty feet over this inclin-ing smooth floor. The water at ordinary tide is about eight inches deep and glides swiftly. We did not always keep our feet when wading and fishing with gig and torch of nights. When one slipped and fell, the swift water was strong enough to pre-clude the possibility of recovery until it rolled you and your traps into the foaming eddy below. We were very successful with our gigs both day and night, killing fish on these rapids. They were mostly what the Tennesseans called "drum fish." I had never seen any of them before, nor have I since, though I have often heard of them in the Tombecbee River. There were also some very large blue catfish, some trout, and very plenty of all kinds of the perch family. We very rarely spent an idle day. When not fishing we were out in the woods running and shooting the deer before some of the numerous packs of hounds that filled the country and soon run all the deer off (and me too).

ᴹAbout the last of August a party of Muskogee Indians were passing through on the way to their country west of the Mississippi River, when some foolish Tennesseeans fired upon them. The consequence was the Indians returned the fire and chased them several miles. The Tennesseeans hurried up to town and reported that they had been fired upon by some Indians twenty miles below Tuscaloosa; that there were four or five hundred of them, and that they were heading for Tuscaloosa and killing all who came in their way.

All the efficient men of the place made immediate preparation to go out and meet them. I also got my rifle ready. There were 25 or 30 of us in a doctor's shop loading our guns. We were on the verge of setting off. I had loaded my gun, had laid it on the counter and was priming it from a paper that had two pounds of powder in it. Somebody had been tampering with the triggers, and when, after priming the gun, I shut the pan down, the cock fell, fired off the gun, igniting the powder in my hands. It exploded and burnt me nearly half in two, even with the top of the counter; the explosion blew all the skin and some of the nails off my hands and burnt my face badly. I was badly injured, and was not able to use my hands for three weeks. This misfortune put an end to the whip-saw operation. Weeks hired out to Captain Barker on a keel boat, and I rented a billiard table for one month at $50. I attended to it myself. The billiard table supported my family, but it could not make money like the whipsaw.

ᴾMy Father came up one day and remarked to me, "These Tennesseeans and their dogs are getting too thick; I shall have to leave this country."

"What do you think of doing?" I replied, "for I am like you express yourself to be—tired of these greasy people and their noisy dogs. To tell you the truth, Father, I have never felt like this is the country to stop in."

Said he: "I have just returned from an exploring trip over on the Tombecbee, a very pretty river and country about seventy-five miles west of this place. I think it a very desirable country. Anyhow, no people have got in there yet and that's worth something." I was pleased with his description of the wild, uninhabited district of heavy forests, extensive canebrakes, cypress swamps and pretty river full of fish and beaver and otter. No marks of civilized destructiveness nor clattering bell nor yelping hound disturbed the maiden quietude of that dark forest.

ᴹHe said there was not a house between Tuscaloosa and the Tombecbee. The Choctaws were near the river on the opposite side, but nowhere on the east side was to be found any signs that the country had ever been occupied. The forests were very densely timbered, and the bottomlands were covered with the heaviest kinds of cane. Altogether, it was the wildest, least-trodden and tomahawk-marked country he had ever explored, and the soil was rich enough. His description put me into a perfect transport. I told him that I owed nobody anything. I had nothing to hinder me from starting in two days, if he would be ready by that time. I could take my effects in a boat down the river to his house where my wagon was. He said he was glad to find me so little incumbered, and he could be ready to move in three days. I told him I would be with him before that time.

We had only our beds and wearing apparel to move, except a table and a very nice walnut rocking crib I had made while I was keeping a free hotel in Tuscaloosa. I had thought of leaving the table and crib, but my wife said that she knew how to dispose of them. She brought Mrs. Bird, our nearest neighbor to see them. She was pleased with them, and gave my wife eight dollars in cash for them and a bread waiter I had made of white oak splits.

We had made every arrangement and packed our goods in our little boat by 4 p.m. the next day. We then bade adieu to Tuscaloosa and to a crowd of our newly made young friends, who had followed us down to the river, helping us to pack the boat. About dark we got to my Father's house. They were all delighted to see us, and we were in a perfect ecstacy over the prospect of a wagon journey through a roadless wilderness. We made the preparations and set out on the 1st day of November 1818.[21] We were twelve days *en route*. ᴾOn that first night, we all got together and camped on a little river called *Sipsee* in the Choctaw language, meaning tulip tree. The names of all the water courses from here onward are in the Choctaw language. We had a pretty good working force along. There was no sign of a road, and three or four axemen went in advance. But by picking their way they did not find much chopping to do. ^BIndeed they got along too fast to please me. The woods were burned every year by the Indian hunters. So there were but few logs in our way. ^PIt was my duty to go ahead and steer the course for the choppers to follow, and the deer, bears, wolves, and turkeys were bounding up in front of me every few hundred yards. The country between the Black Warrior and Tombecbee rivers—over which we were then traveling—had been disputed territory between the Muskogees and Choctaws for a long time. Neither party dare be found hunting on that forbidden region, which accounts for the great number of wild beasts seen on our route. It was a delightful autumn—not a drop of rain fell during our entire passage through that dense wilderness, where the wheeled carriage had never before stamped its impress on the face of that virgin soil.

It was pleasant to observe how delighted the women and children were as their scattered ranks strolled along gathering nuts, which the slow moving wagons allowed them plenty of time for. There was much fall fruit, grapes, black-haws (*Viburnum prunifolium*), shellbark hickory (*Carya sulcata*), and all kinds of hickory nuts. But the chestnuts (*Castanea americana* and *C. pumila*) attracted the greatest attention. With these the ground was literally strewed and they were dropping with every little shake of the wind in all directions. A great number of the large forest trees through that region are chestnut trees. They were remarkably fruitful the year we were moving, and they added greatly to the pleasures of our dry autumnal journey in the wilderness. They were plumping down every moment, and when we pitched our camp of an evening we had to look out that we did not locate it under a chestnut tree. We had no use for our tents and did not set one up during the journey. ^MIn the evening it was delightful to observe the women and children wallowing in the dry leaves and gathering such quantities of nuts as to require assistance to get them into camp. Then such cracking and roasting of nuts and loud merry talk till bedtime.

Except when we came to the watercourses, we had but little difficulty. There are three little rivers and several creeks that crossed our path. We were forced to dig down the banks of these streams before crossing them. ᴾOn the seventh day we came to a little river with high banks, which we afterward learned was called *Lua Copesa* (Cold Fire) by the Choctaws. We spent nearly a day hunting a place to cross the pretty stream with the wagons. By cutting a deep narrow channel with the pick that would let the wheels in up to the hubs, we could let the wagons down almost any bank by hand. But we must have a sloping bank to get out on, or dig one, and we would hunt for a natural slope a good while rather than dig one. This we succeeded in at every stream, and after twelve days of the most pleasant time I ever spent in my life, we landed on the Tombecbee river.

At many of our camps *en route* the wolves in great numbers would come near and regale us with their music. At our camp near Cold Fire creek, there certainly must have been half a dozen packs of them around the camp, and they came so near that we could hear them snapping their teeth. They frightened our dogs so that they came and crouched themselves as near the fire as we would permit them. We rigged up the pan and tried to get a shot at them, but they wouldn't stand still long enough for the rifle, and our shotguns were all boxed up in the wagons. We failed getting a wolf, plenty as they were.

Our last camp on the route was on a beautiful little river two miles southeast of Columbus, Miss. Nobody dwelt there then. The name of the little river in Choctaw is *Lookse-ok-pullila*. *"Lookse"* is "a terrapin" and *"ok-pullila"* means "floating on the water." It was full of blue-winged teal, swarming like wild pigeons. We didn't shoot them. Oh, that was a delightful camp: in a thick canebrake, near that little river, where the harsh sounds of obtrusive civilization had never before alarmed the owls or savage beasts. Our camp-fire, rattling chains, growling dogs and popping canes disturbed the wild animals greatly. We heard the panthers scream; the racoons complained; the owls came near and hooted awfully; and the wolves howled all night. The teals swarmed and the beavers slapped their tails delightfully.

We had all been raised in the woods, were all hunters, and the indications presented that night produced a perfect glorification amongst us. We could hardly wait for day. My brother and I slipped off in the cane at the first peep of day and were both back with a good fat turkey each before sunup, having seen hundreds of them. We then made an early start, cut our road through the cane, and made the balance of the trip—four miles—by 12 o'clock. As usual, I led the way, and seeing a big buck with a chairframe [big antlers] on his head, as he was right in my path, I concluded to let him down there where he would be handy to put in the wagon when it came up. The gun did not fire exactly clear, and notwithstanding I cut his lights, it was an inch or so too far back. He ran. I knew he wouldn't go far and set off after him. In those days but few wounded deer could get away from me. I saw that his leaps were getting lower and shorter. I urged my way more vigorously and in half an hour came up with him. He turned to fight but soon found that to be a bad business; for seizing him by the horn with my left hand, I soon dispatched him by cutting his throat. After I had prepared him for transportation, I cut my bloody knife in the bark of an exceeding large pine, at the root of which I had done the deed, to clean it. A year and a half afterwards, when people came in and they built a log cabin hotel, that big pine, with the gashes in the bark where I cleaned the bloody knife, was felled to give place for the Eagle sign-post.[22] But the marks of my knife was the first signs ever made by the white man on that hill where Columbus, Miss. now stands.

^MIn the afternoon we landed on the banks of the Tombecbee river, three miles by land above present-day Columbus. I was delighted with the appearance of the low bluff and the cane-brake that came to a point where the river turned abruptly from the bluff a few steps above where we struck it. Here I made my camp. Father went four hundred yards lower down and pitched his tent. Three or four feet above low water mark, a flat rock that underlay the bluff projected six or eight feet into the river. Here a large sycamore tree had its roots fastened into the bluff immediately on top of the rock, and from beneath these roots gushed a very bold spring of pure clear water. It flowed over the rock, falling into the river from its outer edge with a splashing sound that could be distinctly heard at the camp, which was not more than forty feet away. Everything about the place was beautiful and very convenient.

^PAbout sunset my wife said she heard heavy turkeys flying

up to roost a little distance out there, pointing the direction. I went away from the noise of the children and listening, distinctly heard what I took to be at least forty flying up and alighting on the trees. Before light in the morning I was out under those turkeys and could, by lighting them against the sky, distinctly see many. But there was one on a low limb, not more than thirty feet from the ground, and supposing his reason for setting so low was his weight, I took a seat nearby the side of a tree and waited for daylight. Sure enough he was a very large one. They said they heard him fall quite distinctly at the camp. His weight when dressed was twenty-nine and a half pounds. We looked upon him as the king turkey then, but we saw many such before that year was gone.

[M]I on that day explored the river a few hundred yards above my camp, killed a wild goose, and saw the beginning of a glorious canebrake. There was plenty of bear and deer signs, and the banks of the river were strewn with holes that had been cut and barked by beavers. When I got back to the camp I told my wife what I had discovered. She was a very beautiful young woman then, and she put on one of her sweetest and most satisfied-looking smiles and said, "You have found the right place for us to stop at."[23]

Said she, "Who could look at this fat game, so easily obtained, this beautiful river with its handsome dry bluff and gushing spring water, and think otherwise? And that's not all that pleases me. While you were gone up the river, an hour ago, five very large deer passed lazily along within 30 yards of where Polly[24] and I were standing, and they stared at us with their great black eyes as they passed and held their great chairframe-looking horns so high that we were both frightened and didn't know whether to stand our ground or run to the camp. I have also been down to the spring and examined that beautiful flat rock. It runs under the bluff 30 or 40 yards above the spring, and in one place it is 20 feet wide. Oh! It is so pretty and I think there are plenty of fish. I have saved the turkey's liver for bait. Suppose you try for some after dinner."

I set out three or four hooks before dinner, and after eating dinner, went out into the upland, hunting. I saw a great deal of deer sign, and several deer, but did not get a shot. When I got back in sight of camp my wife saw me, and, in the highest degree of delight, called to me to look what a fine fish she had caught. She had a blue cat weighing 25 ½ pounds.

Suffice it to say, we were all greatly pleased and supplied our table with a superabundance of fish, fowl and venison, and occasionally a glorious fleece [the oily fat] of bear meat. The quantity of game that was found in that dark forest and the canebrakes was a subject of wonder to everybody. My brother Garland and I, after working all day, clearing up ground to plant corn, would go out nights on horseback, taking a big bag of nicely cut, rich pine and a frying pan tied on a stick, to burn the pine in. This pan full of pine, set on fire and carried on the shoulder, produced sufficient light to enable us to see the eyes of a deer 80 to 100 yards away. And with a big old shotgun that we had, we killed plenty of meat for all three of the families.

Three days after we came there I began to prepare for building me a house. I got the clapboards in one day, cut the logs in a day, hauled them together in a day; and the next day, by the aid of my brothers and Jos. Bryan, raised and covered it. The next day I floored it with linwood puncheons, and the day after I made a wooden chimney to it. We then left our camp and moved into it. The weather was getting cool, and with a rousing log fire fed with plenty of rich pine knots, the light was as bright as day, making the whole house, which was lined with newly split board, fairly glitter. Having no bedstead yet, my wife made the bed on the floor. I never shall forget the encouraging remark she made when we lay down. After gazing for a moment on the shining walls of the little cabin, she said: "This is fine and it inspires me with confidence that we are capable of making our way here. The quantity of venison, fish and fowl that we have on hand already and the facility with which it is procured quiets all fears of scarcity." Having no good place to keep our provisions, I then built a little smokehouse. My wife said, while she was placing the meat in it, "This is very convenient, and despite the fact that we are surrounded with this wild impenetrable forest, we have nothing to fear." "No, dat we ha'nt," said Aunt Polly, who was young, too, then.

These little incidents tell the situation we occupied, and how little dread we entertained. We felt ourselves fully competent for the emergency. ᴾI had the dear one and her two boys safe from wet and cold; besides, it was such a nice place, on top of a dry bluff, within thirty feet of the river and right opposite an island containing three or four acres of heavy timber, beyond which passed the largest half of the river. On our side of the island, the river, though swift-running, did not exceed forty feet in width. Just above my house came in a little creek, and here the bluff widened off into the hill country from whence came the creek. At the same place the river bent off northwestwardly for two miles, forming a wide, rich bottom which was heavily clothed in cane and large timber for ten miles. I consider the canebrake the great *sanctum sanctorum;* the inner chamber of the great hunting ground.

Below and opposite the point of the island was deep water, twelve feet. Here was my fishing place. Into this I had all the offal of my game thrown. I also planted two strong forks in the deep water a little way from the bank. Upon these and the bank I laid sills, and on them a dry shelter in which I could sit and fish on rainy days, and since I kept the hole constantly baited, the fish assembled there in great numbers. In that stream that had never been fished, there were many old, full-grown catfish, of which I caught several, including one that weighed ninety-three pounds. His mouth was so large that I held it open and my wife put the baby's head in it. When I skinned and dressed him, his maw, being large and full of something, I cut it open and found nine eels fifteen inches in length in it—but none of the bait I had thrown in. So I concluded that the big cats had come, not to eat the offal I had placed there, but to catch the eels that had gathered after it. On this discovery, I took one of the eels, put it on a good hook, went to my little house and threw it in. Instantly it was seized and run off with much force. It was a very strong fish weighing 81 pounds. It had three eels in it. Both these big cats were quite fat. I took pains and cut them in large pieces, and when they had taken salt sufficiently, I hung them up in our little smokehouse, and they cured very finely. My father said they were better eating than the codfish.

There were no settlers in the country and the corn I had got from the Indians would soon be consumed, so I could see that if I didn't clear me a field and plant corn, no one else would do it. There were six acres of pretty canebrake at the mouth of the little creek already alluded to. I set to work, and at such odd times as I could spare from my hunting excursions in the course of the winter, cut the cane of that six acres all down. It was soon dry and I was about to burn it, but an Indian who happened to be present told me that in March or April big water would come and if the cane was burnt off, it would form a big clean or open space into which much driftwood would come and spoil the field. For being wet and soggy, the driftwood would not burn until the season was too late to plant.

"Well, but will not the dry buoyant cane all wash away?" I inquired. "No, no," he said, "the cane forms a large cake that cannot be separated by the water, and it is made fast by those big trees standing all through it." He convinced me, and sure enough the big river came and lifted the dry cane at least twenty-five feet from the ground. But as the Indian said, it did not float away nor let in the driftwood. I did not burn it until the 5th of May. By then the new crop of young cane was three feet high, and if I had burnt the dry cane off at the time I had intended, this would have been work for the hoe. But now it was consumed with the dry cane and the ground left as clean as a plant bed. On the 6th I planted the corn with a sharp stick. Twice afterward I beat down the young cane ᴹthat sprouted up from the old cane stumps. That was all the work the crop got. The bear and racoons ate and destroyed a good deal of it, and yet I gathered 150 bushels of good corn.

As soon as I got my house done I went over the river to see the Choctaw Indians. They were not exceeding two miles distant. I found there a white man by the name of John Pitchlynn.[25] Sixty-two years of age, he had a large family of half breed children, was very wealthy, possessed a high order of intelligence and was in every point of view a clever gentleman. He was very glad to hear that we were settling so near him and said he would visit the place we had selected, to see if it was above high-water mark. He asked my name, and when I told him, inquired for the name of my Father. I replied, "It is Hezekiah Lincecum."

"Don't they call him 'Ky'"? said he. "His familiar friends do," said I. "Well," said he, "I am second cousin to your mother. I will go right over and see them this day." He was in a perfect ecstacy. He ordered his horse, and then turning to me said, "You were not born when I saw your Father and Mother last. I was on my return from Washington City. I had previously heard from my Father that I had relatives in Georgia, and turning my course down through that state was lucky enough to find them. I sojourned with them a month, and I look upon that time, even now, as the most pleasant period of my life." He went immediately over. I introduced him to my Father and Mother, and they were all overjoyed at meeting again. Twenty-five years had passed and they were all still healthy looking, and exceedingly rejoiced. Pitchlynn was a kind-hearted man and seemed willing to aid us in every way in making our new homes. We lived neighbor to him from 1818 to 1835 and he continued the same kind-hearted gentleman all the time.

ᴾThat is the period my old sporting developments love to recall, when my dilapidated mentality makes a retrograde excursion through the track of the long-gone years. The brightest period it finds is the space that occurred between the 1st of November 1818 and the 15th of July 1819. On memory's register, I find so many exciting and rare hunting events—battles with beasts, long races and swims that could only be performed by full-grown athletic men. I am at a loss to decide which to choose or how to portray some of the most interesting cases in a style for my reader to understand and see the clear picture, without extending my narrative to too great dimensions.

We never seemed to require dog help; still-hunting in the daytime and with the well arranged fire-pan of a night. It is surprising how soon, by constant practice, one can learn to distinguish the eyes of the different animals. Aye more, you can distinguish the fat from the lean deer, and whoever has shined the eyes of a doe with a young fawn can never after mistake the eyes of a mother deer. About the last of November the water-fowls, in great variety, fairly swarmed in the calm, undisturbed river. There were geese, and some swans tarried a few days; brants, snow geese, white fronted and sea geese; ducks of many types: mallards, two species of teal, a black duck with a broad bill.[26] There were two ducks that I have never seen anywhere else, not there either after the first winter. One was a large white, with black and brown spots on him, big as a brant—pretty crown, bill narrow, red.[27] I shot one to examine him. He was too fishy for a food duck and did not look so well in hand as in the distance. The other was no larger than a wild pigeon; colors a little more brilliant, but the form, markings (male and female), precisely

that of a mallard, the two curled green feathers in the tail—
everything the same.[28] On the before-mentioned island the soft-
shelled, fresh water tortoise came out to deposit their eggs. I
could get near enough to them to shoot them from the main
land. I got some very fine ones before they had deposited their
eggs; they were fat and nice and the great number of eggs they
contained (from 60 to 100) added greatly to the delicacy of the
dainty dish. They are superb as an article of food and quite delicious. During the first winter I caught thirteen of them in a
beaver trap, and what I consider remarkable, twelve of them
were caught by the left forefoot, the other by the neck. Which I
recorded as satisfactory evidence that they are universally left-
handed.[29]

They detailed my brother Garland and myself to hunt meat
for the three families. My brother-in-law (Jos. Bryan) being a
poor sportsman, we furnished his family too. There were thirty-
six eaters in the families, and to furnish them venison, fish and
fowl didn't consume half our time, and the work necessary to be
done in my little six-acre field amounted to nothing. We had
time to extend the circle of our exploring expeditions. On one
occasion we made a canoe trip of six or seven miles up the river,
where we found a bee tree and made several pleasing discoveries. Amongst them we found a nest of small islands, beginning
about three miles above where we lived and extending two or
three miles. Among these islands the bed of the river was beautiful white sand and quite shallow. Many places we had to wade
and shove the canoe over it. At play all amongst these islands,
we saw many fine fish. They seemed to be preparing to bed and
deposit their eggs. They were that fine, large boneless sucker,
the red horse [probably the genus *Moxostoma*]. We got home in
time to put handles to our gigs that evening, and had everything
in nice order to return the next day for a big frolic, except the
lock of my brother's rifle was broken, so he took an old-
fashioned British musket that kicked worse than a mule. We
were at the place by a little after ten o'clock, which was too soon;
they had not yet begun to come out to play. We moored our
craft in the shade and waited for them. About eleven o'clock
they surprised us by streaming up from the deep water below.
They seemed to be chasing each other and we kept still until
they had all gone by. We found them in the sand not far above

us; falling in with our gigs, we soon had as many as we wanted. And now, we thought, to keep our fish from spoiling, we would return home.

We were wet all over, as chasing the fish had splashed the water and completely saturated our garments. We towed our now heavier canoe beyond the shallow water and seated ourselves in the sunshine to dry and let the craft float. We got along merrily until the river, at a short bend, bagged out at the elbow of the bend, forming a wide, deep circling pool of water. Here the canoe was making but little headway. Just as we were becoming impatient, we heard the crackling of the dry cane on shore and in came a monster bear. It was a very warm day and from the way he *ha'sed* and *ha'med*, we knew he was enjoying it finely. We both got our guns, and at the distance of forty feet I took aim at the butt of his ear. But the gun missed fire, having had water splash on her flintlock. By this time my brother was up, sighting away with the old musket. Leaning forward to receive and counteract the expected heavy kick, he hauled down the hard trigger. Misfiring also, she didn't kick. Instead, man, gun and all went head-foremost into that deep water. And now the bear, who had not noticed us before, turned and hastily ran away, up the bank, while I kept snapping my flintlock at his broad back until he was out of sight. By this time my brother had come up and was clinging to the gunwale of the boat. I asked, "Where is the gun?" "I left her at the bottom," said he.

There were a great many bears in the cane brake but we had no bear dogs, and it was only once in a while that some rare accident would throw one in our way. We found plenty of honey. One very remarkable bee tree I will try to describe. It was an exceedingly large and very tall swamp pine [or loblolly pine] (*Pinus taeda*), stem about five feet in diameter and seventy feet to the first limbs. About fifty feet from the ground was a round hole three inches in diameter; it had been made by the red head log cocks [woodpeckers]. At this hole the bees passed out and in, and they were so numerous that at the time of day when they were at work the stream of bees gave the idea of the smoke of a cooking stove. We felled the big pine one day, with the hole to one side. We took out a large chip opposite to the hole and found the hollow of the tree as large in width as a flour barrel and perhaps twenty feet in length. It was packed full of honey-comb where we cut in, and after we had got out about five feet, there was at each end a strong partition of dirt and wax, which we thought was the boundary of the honey. And so it was, for that community of bees. On clear examination we discovered leading from the hole two sets of waxen tubes, three in each set, with open ends, just at the inner edge of the hole, one set leading down on the inside of the hollow and passing into the partition of dirt and wax. The other set of tubes passed upwards in the same manner and entered the other partition. We cut away the shell of the log above and below the partition, finding that the tubes had passed through them and into two other cavities or departments of rich honey comb. The upper was about five feet in length, and the lower about six. Both of these cavities of honey were seemingly of a more recent date than the middle section.

In this large hollow pine were three distinct swarms or communities of bees, and as it is a law amongst honey bees that no bee of another tribe shall enter the hive, the construction of those partitions and gangway tubes must have been conventional—done by treaty. The tubes, three in number, were large enough to let the bees pass each other in them; two feet and a half in length. The construction of them amounted to a considerable job of work, which would not have been permitted by the center kingdom, except by some treaty arrangement. The fact that their passage through part of the center hive was only permitted under substantially covered ways is sufficient evidence to substantiate my theory on the subject. After all hands ate as much as they wanted and there was a smart waste besides, we jugged 18 gallons of clear honey. I never saw but one better bee tree—that was a cypress tree (*Cupressus [Chamaecyparis] thyoides*).

All this time—since our arrival on the Tombecbee river in 1818—I have neglected to mention our good friends the Choctaw Indians. Two of them came the third day after we had arrived and with all the indications of familiar friendship introduced themselves. Of course I didn't know a word of their language and our communication was altogether by signs. They admired my new glittering Lancaster rifle greatly and begged me to let them shoot it. They are good marksmen. They invited me to visit them, which I did; and it wasn't long until we were familiar hunting companions. I soon learned the language, so I could exchange thought with them and we found them a high order of good neighbors. They were very kind to us.

[M]In 1819 the government marked or surveyed a road from Nashville, Tenn., to Natchez, Miss. It crossed the Tombecbee River where Columbus, Miss., now stands; this was ten miles by water and three by land from where I had settled.[30] I went down to see what kind of a place it was and found it a beautifully elevated situation, being about the head of navigation. I thought it was an eligible town site, and that it would be a town as soon as the country should settle up. I was so fully impressed with the belief that a big town would some day loom up on that beautiful bluff, that I went home, sawed a thousand boards, put them on a raft and floated them down the river with the intention of building a snug little house on a nice place I had selected, hoping to be able to realize a profit from it, as soon as people should move into the country. [P]The spot I selected for the house was about fifty yards west of the big pine I had gashed with my bloody knife, at the root of which I had killed the big buck ten months before.

[M]I was not the only person that had noticed the eligibility of that locality. When I got down to the place where I intended to land, a man by the name of Caldwell was about landing a keelboat at the same place. [P]It was with difficulty that I got in the mouth of the little creek first. [M]He was from Tuscaloosa,[31] and he had a cargo of Indian goods, which he intended opening on that bluff as soon as he could build a house to put them in. I was acquainted with him while I resided at Tuscaloosa and was glad to see him, thinking I would sell my boards to him.

In the course of our conversation he inquired of me, if, while residing in Tuscaloosa, I had made the acquaintance of one Cornelius Schnider? "I knew him very well," said I. "And what kind of a man did you consider him?" I replied readily that I did not think him a reliable man. "That is my opinion now," said Caldwell. [P]"Schnider was recommended to me as an honest, good man and, understanding the Indian language, he would make an excellent clerk for an Indian store. I believed it and took him in with me, agreeing to give him half the profits. His conduct on the boat the whole trip, drinking, gambling, etc., has been so contrary to what he has been recommended, that I feel entirely discouraged and am at a loss how to proceed." ᴹI remarked to him that had I been apprised of the fact that he had Schnider with him, I should not have been so careless in expressing my sentiments about him.

"My dear friend," said Caldwell, "I am truly obliged to you. I brought him with me to sell these goods for me, and now I don't know what in the world I shall do. He will ruin me if I leave him with them." I replied, "I have a good notion to relieve you by buying out the entire stock, boat and all."

"I wish to the Lord you would," said he. [I said,] "But this raft of 1,000 clap-boards upon which I am standing, except my wagon and horses, is all the available means I possess. It is useless for me to talk about purchasing your goods; but you can give me $10 for these good boards to cover a house to put your goods in, and I'll go home." "But," replied Caldwell, "I can make you able. I will expose my invoices to you. Let you have them at 10 per cent under cost and give you three, six, and twelve months to pay it in; and you can cover your house with the boards you have."

I took the goods, hired his boat hands and went to work with them myself. In three days we had knocked up a pretty good shanty.[32] We soon got the goods into it and commenced opening boxes and taking account of the stock. But the Indians had heard of the arrival of the great supply of nice new goods and plenty of liquors, and they flocked in by hundreds. I began selling to them whiskey and such goods as we had marked; and this prevented us from work in the daytime. Having only night-time to work on the invoices, it took us ten days to get through with them. But I had by that time sold enough to pay the first installment, which I did, and Caldwell went home highly pleased. I sent my boat immediately to Mobile for a cargo of sugar, coffee and whiskey. These were considered staple articles in the Indian trade. In due time the boat returned and the business continued good. I paid the last installment at nine months.

The state line had not been run, and we were supposed to be in Alabama. It was not long until the line dividing the States of Alabama and Mississippi was laid off, and we found ourselves fifteen miles from the line on the Mississippi side, in a strip of country eighty miles long and averaging twenty miles wide, east of the Choctaw and Chickasaw Nations. The Tombecbee River was the line between us and the Indians; we were 200 miles from the other portion of the state. And thus cut off from the law, we were there 18 months before we saw an officer of any kind. At length the Legislature recognised us as a portion of the State, and named that long strip of land Monroe County.[33] They also appointed me Chief Justice, with authority to appoint all the officers necessary to organize the county. The land having been previously surveyed, it was found that Columbus was on a 16th Section—school land. The Legislature also appointed me Chairman of the school commissioners, with power to appoint four associates; also to lay off the town and lease the lots for the term of 99 years, renewable forever. I first appointed four other county justices and a county clerk, called a meeting, organized a county court and proceeded to appoint and commission the rest of the county officers. Everybody wanted office; and I found it a very difficult duty to get through with. I finally succeeded, and then turned my attention to surveying the town, and regulating all the school lands in the county. I had also to superintend the erection of two academies—male and female.[34]

On the first of August, all was ready, and in conformity to my advertisements, which had been published sixty days previous, a very large collection of people came to the leasing of the town lots. In the two days I continued it, I leased not more than half the lots that had been surveyed, but they brought in enough ($4500) to commence building the academies. Holding the courts, appointing the officers, surveying the town lots, appointing and regulating school commissioners at town, and all the other school sections in the county, procuring teachers, engaging workmen for the academies and opening the mail six times a week, consumed so much of my time that my own business was badly neglected.[35] The result of my firm, impartial action in appointing county officers had pleased the people so much that they began to talk of sending me to the Legislature.

To avoid such a dilemma, I immediately went over the river and entered into partnership with John Pitchlynn Jr., a half-breed Choctaw son of the Pitchlynn I mentioned earlier.[36] He was a highly educated man and a very clever fellow, but a most incorrigible drunkard. That, however, made no difference, as according to our contract and the intercourse regulations (which forbade any white man with a white family from dwelling within the nation), Pitchlynn was to have nothing in the management of the business. In the knowledge of all outsiders, I occupied the position of a superintending clerk. Pitchlynn had a pretty good storehouse at the ferry landing opposite Columbus, and four or five thousand dollars' worth of goods. I had about the same amount, and we put them together. I moved my family into a room that was boarded in, of a large two-story building he had commenced, and took possession of the goods and storehouse and ferry. Pitchlynn's residence was two miles from the store, a circumstance favorable to our business; for he was, when drunk, so abusive, and so often drunk, that he was not popular with the Indians.

I was known to almost every Indian in the Nation. My Indian name was *Shappo Tohoba* (White hat). The first time they saw me I had on a white hat. But my most popular name was *Anumpatashula ebisya* (Interpreter's nephew), referring to my kinship with Pitchlynn Sr., the U.S. government interpreter. Sometimes they called me *Hopigeh cheto* (Big leader), because I took the lead and conducted a party of 100 of them out of a condition of starvation on our return from a failure in attempting to get some scalps from a large camp of Ooassashes,[37] west of the Mississippi. All these experiences and the fair, plain manner in which I traded with them, caused them to have full confidence in me, and they crowded my Pitchlynn establishment every day with their produce.

I bartered with them for every kind of produce, consisting of cowhides, deer skins, all kinds of fur and skins; as well as buckhorns, cowhorns; peas, beans, peanuts, pecans, shellbarks, hickory nuts, honey, beeswax; blowguns and blowgun arrows; bacon and venison hams and big gobblers. I made it a rule to purchase (at some price) everything they brought to the store. Every article I have named brought cash at 100 per cent on the cost. I dealt with a supply house—Willcox & Dallas, Philadelphia; and they were glad to get my Indian produce, for which they paid me well. I remember them as clever gentleman. I made frequent trips to Mobile. There I laid in my groceries, sugar, coffee, whiskey, etc., but all my dry goods came from the house of Dallas & Willcox.[38] It was a fine place for business, and in a short time I should have accumulated sufficient wealth to satisfy me, if we could have been healthy there. But one or more of the family was always sick. My wife and I both came very near dying of fever two or three times. The children were sick, and so were our servants. Our domestic affairs were all the time in bad condition. We resided there four years.

CHAPTER THREE

My Life among the Choctaws

[L]During the four years I resided in the *Chahta* country (1822–25), I became acquainted with the chiefs of the three districts into which the nation was divided, and quite a number of their leaders, headmen and warriors.

At that time *Mushulatubi, Apushimataha* and *Apukshinubi*[1] were the chiefs of the three districts which had been established long before my acquaintance with that noble people commenced. Each district was subdivided, with but little system, into *Iksas*, or kindred clans, and each of these *Iksas* had its leader. All the men seemed to be warriors, and they had their captains and generals, which titles they had learned from the white people, for whom they always professed, and indeed manifested, the greatest friendship. I remember now, though the time has long past, with feelings of unfeigned gratitude the many kindnesses bestowed on me and my little family in 1818 and 1819, while we were in their neighborhood, before the country began to fill up with other white people. Some of them would visit us almost every day and seemed quite proud that the white people were about to become their neighbors. Until I had raised a crop of corn we procured all our provisions from our *Chahta* neighbors, on very good terms. I did not then understand their language, but their Negroes whom they had purchased from the white people did, and we used them for interpreters in our business transactions. It affords me pleasure now, after the lapse of near half a century, to recall in memory the many happy days and hours I spent in the days of my young manhood in friendly intercourse with that innocent and unsophisticated people. We met often, hunted together, fished together, swam together, and they were positively, and I have no hesitation in declaring it here, the most truthful, most reliable and best people I have ever dwelt with.

While we resided in their country my wife had a very severe spell of fever that confined her to her bed for several weeks. During her sickness the good, kind-hearted *Chahta* women would come often, bringing with them their nicely prepared tampulo water for her to drink, and remaining by the sick bed for hours at a time, would manifest the deep sympathy they felt by groaning for the afflicted one all the time of their protracted visit.

The time is long gone, and I may never have the pleasure of meeting with any of that most excellent race of people again. But so long as the life pendulum swings in this old time shattered bosom I shall remember their many kindnesses to me and mine, with sentiments of kindest affection and deepest gratitude, and my prayers for their elevation and progress as a people among the enlightened nations of the earth shall not cease.

I might here record many incidents of thrilling interest that occurred during the time of my familiarity with this noble tribe of aboriginal Americans, but as I set out to note a few facts that came under my observation in regard to the history of their war chiefs and a few of their conspicuous headmen, I must forbear saying more on the minor subjects. The chiefs of the three districts were elected every four years. All the time I was acquainted with the political action of the nation, by re-election the same man held the office of chief. Their elections were conducted *viva voce,* or rather by acclamation, and managed by the people, the candidates having no hand in it, or any knowledge of who the candidates were, until the name of the chief-elect was proclaimed by runners among the *Iksas.*

Mushulatubi was the principal chief, and he held that title many years, until the *Chahtas* were removed west of the Mississippi, where he died. He was a handsome man, about six feet in height and quite corpulent. He possessed a lively, cheerful disposition, and as all fat men, was good-natured and would get drunk. He was not much of an orator, and to remedy that deficiency he had selected an orator to speak for him. His name was *Aiahokatubi,* and, except *Apushimataha,* he could deliver himself

76

more gracefully and with more ease than any man I ever heard address an audience.

Mushulatubi was a frequent visitor at my house while I resided in the nation, for it was in his district I had my house, and but eighteen miles from his residence. He was good company, full of agreeable anecdote and witty, inoffensive repartee, until he became too much intoxicated. Then he was nothing but a drunken Indian.

Mushulatubi was not very wealthy, having but a moderate stock of cows and horses and five or six Negroes. He was, however, certainly rich in his family relations. He had a house full of children and two handsome wives, who, like himself, were healthy and somewhat corpulent. They all dwelt together in the same house, and seemed to be very happy. One of his wives was a quarter white blood and had been, in her young days, quite pretty. He was in the habit, when visited by white people, of pointing out his pretty, fair-skinned wife, and bragging a little. But to an accurate observer it was easily seen that his confidence and his affections rested with the full-blooded *Chahta* wife. She, moreover, possessed the strongest and best intellect, and to her management of the household affairs the fair-skinned beauty seemed to yield without hesitation.

Mushulatubi resided on the military road, which (previous to the advent of steamboats on the Mississippi River) was the great thoroughfare upon which returned the hosts of flatboat men from Ohio, Kentucky, Tennessee and Indiana. They were mostly footmen, who, after disposing of their cargo of produce at New Orleans, came up through the *Chahta* country on their way to their respective States. I have often heard those weary footmen while passing my house—I also resided on the military road—speaking of the friendly demeanor and the kind hospitality they had received at the house of *Mushulatubi*.

It sometimes happened that the Ohio traveler would waylay and rob the Kentuckians and Tennesseeans within the limits of *Mushulatubi's* district. On hearing of the robbery he would raise his warriors, rush out in pursuit and never fail to arrest and bring the culprit to Columbus.

Apukshinubi, who was chief of the district westerly from *Mushulatubi's* district, was a very different man. He was a large man, tall and bony, had a down look and was of the religious or superstitious cast of mind. He was, by the people of his district, called a good man, and it was said that he was a man of deep thought and that he was quite intellectual. His studiously maintained taciturnity, however, concealed from my observation that portion of his attributes. But I did not see him often, and my opportunities for making observations in detail on the characteristic traits of the big old ugly chief were not sufficient to enable me to speak decidedly as to the truth or falsehood of his reporters. The people of his district kept him long in the office of chief, and notwithstanding his grim looks and taciturn demeanor, I feel willing to leave him where rumor placed him, an intelligent, good man and a brave, daring warrior. I know nothing of his domestic relations and cannot say whether his couch was or not blessed with one, or a plurality of wives.[2]

The great man of the nation and of the age was the far-famed *Apushimataha*. He was about five feet ten inches in height, stood very erect, full chest, square, broad shoulders and fine front and elevated top head. His mouth was very large, lips rather thick, eyes and nose very good, projecting brow, and cheek bones very prominent. He lacked a great deal of being what the world calls handsome. But he had that inexplicable attribute about him which belongs only to the truly great, that which forced the ejaculation, "Who is that?" from all observant strangers. He died at Washington City in December, 1824 (I speak from recollection), and at his own special request was buried with the honors of war. It was the express opinion of his friends at home when they heard of the respect and distinguished honors manifested by the white people at the funeral of their deceased warrior chief, that his satisfied *shilombish* [spirit] had passed away to the good hunting ground without looking back.

I passed his house soon after the news of his decease had reached the nation; great numbers of families had collected there; had set up and ornamented many poles and were holding a great "cry" [traditional ritual of mourning] for their much-loved chief. Though he had no blood kin that any one knew of, nearly all the people of his district claimed him as a relative; consequently, there were many poles set up at the "cry" they were celebrating for him.

Apushimataha was chief of the district lying south of *Mushula-tubi's,* and he had lived a long way from where I resided. I was never at his place until after his death. But he visited *Mushula-tubi's* district two or three times a year, and while in that region he seldom failed to pay me a visit, and remained with me sometimes as much as two or three weeks.

I may not be a proper judge of such matters, but really I always looked upon him as possessing the strongest and best-balanced intellect of any man I had ever heard speak. I think so yet, although forty years of great men and their written thoughts have passed between that period and the present Sunday night. At their national councils quite a number of white men would attend, and I have seen them, when *Apushimataha* was the speaker, chained to their seats for hours at a time, although they understood not a word of his language. Such was the force of his attitude and expressive gesticulation. His figures and elucidations were sublime beyond comparison. I never shall forget the impression that he made and the change that he produced by one short speech, upon the minds of quite a crowd of reckless boatsmen and other rowdy associates, at a council that was held under a grove of shady oaks near where I lived in the nation.

I had a man by the name of Luther Parker, a yankee, hired, and not having sufficient confidence in him to permit him to sleep in the storehouse, I had attached a little room to the outside of it, where he slept, for the double purpose of guarding the store and being convenient to the ferry, which he kept for me.[3] I had furnished him with a large musket pistol, which he kept over the door of his little bedroom. After he had been there long enough to obtain a smattering of the *Chahta* language he got in the habit of sitting up of nights with the Indians (who were nearly always camped around my place), for the purpose of drinking with them. One night we heard a loud gun down at the store, and very soon the Indians were observed to be rapidly running off from the place. While they were running along the road and passing my dwelling house, a Chickasaw woman, who happened to be there, came to the window and told me that Louie—as the Indians called my ferryman—had got drunk, had been trying to sell a pistol which he said he had in his little house, to *Atoba,* who was the brother to the chief *Mushulatubi.* *Atoba* was also drunk, and said he did not want to buy a pistol, but the drunken Louie would have him to go and look at it. When they came together, talking about the pistol, Louie went in and presently handed the pistol to *Atoba,* who was standing in the bright moonshine, outside of the house. At the instant that *Atoba* took hold of the handle of the pistol, it exploded and instantly killed the white man Louie. On being asked why, if it was an accident, they were all running so, she replied, "Because they are all frightened at the thought of having killed one of your family."

I went immediately down to the store and found the young man lying with his feet at the door and dead, as the Chickasaw woman had said. On further examination I discovered that the contents of the pistol had lodged in his neck, which was broken. Having no other white man about me, and the Indians being all gone, I seated myself on a barrel near the door to wait for the morning. About two hours before day two Indian men came to me and wanted some powder and a ball to fit the pistol. They said *Atoba* had sent them for it, and that he intended to die at 12 o'clock the ensuing day, by the same pistol with which he had in his drunkenness accidentally killed his white friend.

"If it was really an accident," I inquired, "Why will he have himself shot?" They replied, "Life for life is the law, and accidents are not provided for." When I asked, "Who is to do the shooting?" One of the men promptly replied, "That honor falls to my lot." I did not furnish them with the ammunition and they hastened away, telling me that they knew where they could procure it, that *Atoba* was a man and a warrior, not afraid to die, and that I should hear that he did die at the time appointed.

Morning came, and seeing some men who had slept on their boats at the river, I called to them; they came, and while we were washing and shrouding the dead man, the two Indians came again and informed me that *Atoba* had succeeded in procuring powder and lead; that they had hammered out a ball to fit the pistol and *Atoba* would die at the middle of the day. They desired me to be satisfied, for he would be sure to die at the appointed time, and they galloped immediately away, not giving me time to reply.

When I told the boatmen what the Indians said, they seemed to be highly delighted, and they sent one of their number over to the other town to tell the other boatmen and the town people to come over to witness the pleasing affair. By 10 o'clock quite a number of white people had crossed the river and were streaming along the road to the place of the expected execution.

Atoba had his spies out, and when they informed him of the great number of white people that were pressing forward, manifesting so much eagerness to witness his misfortune, he sent a man to tell me that so many of the white people had crossed the river and were hurrying forward to see him die and to laugh at his sorrowful condition, he had concluded to die at another place, and for me not to be uneasy, that he was not trying to evade or escape from justice. He had forfeited his right to live, and that he would be certain to die as soon as he could get far enough from the white people to prevent them from the pleasing gratification they expected to enjoy on seeing it. And so when they came to the place they were greatly mortified to find that *Atoba* was not there. They returned, cursing and foaming, and swearing that they would kill every Indian in the nation, and they went over to Columbus to arm and prepare themselves for the slaughter.

All this time I was busily engaged with the dead. They had all turned to warriors and had left me to make arrangements for the funeral as best I could alone. Soon again the boatmen and such loose characters as they could find about the liquor shops returned, all armed and equipped for the Indian campaign. While I was carrying the dead man over the river to the Columbus graveyard, the army, numbering about fifty men, all half drunk, were passing the river the other way, champing and gnashing their teeth for blood. They marched hurriedly onward, uttering the fierce, horrid yelp of the frantic inebriate and continuing their course to the prairie, about three miles off, where a number of women and children were at that time picking strawberries. On hearing the terrible hooting and yelping of the drunken host, the women and their little ones took fright and fled to the thick forests. The double-sighted, cross-eyed braves of the furious army caught a glimpse of these multitudinous, maneuvering "warriors" [women and children] of the *Chahta* forces as they fled, and firing a few of their guns, beat a retreat. They returned, flushed with their success, the same evening, and crossing back to town, drank and sang war songs through the night. So ended the only war ever waged by the American people against the *Chahtas*.

I had sent *Atoba* word not to die until I could get time to see him. I had, by the time the corpse was ready for the funeral, seen and talked with several of the women who were present when the accident occurred, and finding clearly that there was no intention on the part of *Atoba* of killing the man, I was desirous of saving the unfortunate Indian if I could. And for that reason I had sent him word to suspend the dying until I could see him. Accordingly, on the next morning after the termination of the "war" I received a message, before sunup, instructing me to go down the military road about half a mile, to a large black pine stump and remain there until a signal should be given. I had been at the stump but a short time when the signal for me to turn square off into the thick woods was given. I had not progressed in the tangled thicket exceeding 100 yards until I came in sight of *Atoba*, who was sitting on a log, in company with six other Indians, all armed with rifles and scalping knives. As soon as the unfortunate *Atoba* discovered my approach, he rose from his seat on the log and advanced to meet me, holding the pistol in his hand. When he came near he presented the pistol, breech foremost, and said, "This is the little gun, with which, in my drunkenness, I unfortunately destroyed the life of your man Louie. It is right that I should die for him. Life for life is the law. His unhappy *shilombish* [spirit] will not be satisfied, nor can it pass to the good hunting ground, until I atone with my life for destroying his. I am a man and a warrior, and can die without fear. I am not alive now because I am afraid to die, but because, for reasons of your own, you sent word for me not to die until you could see me. I have obeyed your voice, and have remained until now. You have seen me and I am ready to die. It was your man that I have killed. You are now the avenger. For, inasmuch as you prevented me from dying at the time I had myself appointed, and my friend who was to have performed the last and greatest act of kindness for me has gone away, it devolves on you to do the shooting or appoint some other brave man with a strong heart and steady hand to do it for you. Take the pistol, I am now ready."

I received the pistol and told him to give up his notions about the necessity of dying. I further told him that I had seen and conversed with several persons who were present when the man was killed, from whom I had ascertained that the firing of the pistol was purely accidental, and that I knew of a better way to dispose of the case than for me or any one else to shoot him; that we would go to the United States interpreter and make a paper that would be satisfactory to everybody on the subject. He agreed that such a paper might be made, and that it might relieve and satisfy the minds of the living, but he had done nothing to them, and, besides, it was not the living with whom he had to deal. It was to the wandering, unsatisfied *Shilup* [ghost] of the man that had been killed, that he was to make atonement, and no paper that could be made would answer that purpose. But he would go with me to John Pitchlynn, United States interpreter, who, having been raised among the *Chahtas* from his infancy, was familiar with all their laws and customs, the most particular and best of which was "life for life." Pitchlynn would soon explain it to me, and show me that there is no chance for an honorable escape from death in a case like his. From where we then were to John Pitchlynn's was eight miles over a rough, woodland country, and the weather was quite warm. We had no horses; I, however, did not return home, but set out on foot with them; we found Pitchlynn at home and had quite a council of it. There were three or four steady old Indians at Pitchlynn's when we arrived, who joined the seven I had with me in the argument that ensued against the United States interpreter and myself. They yielded nothing until we read from the journal of the Mississippi Legislature that *Chahtas* had been incorporated as citizens of the State, and that if he got any one to shoot him, whether red or white man, it would lay the shooter liable to trial for murder and for being hung for it. After much discussion the *Chahtas* reluctantly gave up the point on condition that the papers should be so worded as to allow *Atoba,* in case he should be condemned at the trial before a court of white men, the privilege of being shot, in place of being "weighed" like a dog. (They called hanging a man "weighing" him.)[4]

I drew up an ordinary appearance bond, with a penalty of $6,000, including the condition, that if condemned at trial, that he should not be "weighed." And also, that the court should consist of five justices of the peace and, at his special request, that the decision of the court of five magistrates in his case should be final. He also required, for the purpose of giving him time to pay his debts, and settling up his business, that the trial be put off thirty days; at which time he would be ready to meet the white judges at any place in the *Chahta* country I might see proper to designate. So I finished up the bond, delaying the trial one month; it was to take place at the before mentioned grove of oaks, two miles from where the accident occurred. *Atoba* signed it, with John Pitchlynn and several of the Indians who were present for securities.

I had been gone all day; and when I returned at night, I went over to town, and found the whole people laboring under great excitement. There were at that time not exceeding five hundred men in fifty miles around Columbus able to bear arms. Rumor had already in the field an army of a thousand Indians, which was hourly increasing. All could see, now that it was too late, that permitting the drunken boatmen and their grogshop associates to go over the river the day before had been bad management; that the Indians had been imprudently and unnecessarily insulted; that in the weak and sparsely settled condition of the country, it would be an easy matter for the *Chahtas* to raise a sufficient force to cross the river and scalp every man, woman and child in three days. The people were greatly alarmed, and though there was no real ground for it, besides the stories the boatmen had told on their return about the thousands of Indians they had seen and shot at in the prairie, the account had been bandied from mouth to mouth until it had grown into frightful dimensions. Some were talking of gathering up some of their available things, and getting away from the dangerous country as soon as possible. Others were urging the necessity of arming and meeting the Indians in battle. They were hooted at. All were seriously alarmed and no plan that could be offered seemed to suit the emergency.

The chief *Mushulatubi*, who had heard that my wife had become frightened at my absence (not knowing what had become of me and hearing the terrible scalping stories that had been sent over to her), had gone over to town and got some awkward pensman amongst his workmen to write her a letter, telling her not to be frightened, that let what would happen, no *Chahta* was base enough to injure her, or anything belonging to her. This badly indicted letter was passed from hand to hand and interpreted into as many meanings. All agreed, however, that it was an ominous letter and meant a great deal; that it contained concealed intimations and they were certain that it was in some way connected with my unaccountable absence. Plain enough. And as soon as I should come back, if I ever did, I must give a satisfactory explanation, or—they did not say what they would do with me.

In the height of this panic and great trepidation I made my appearance. I could not imagine what was the matter with the people. I was instantly surrounded, and was asked a thousand questions in a minute. Where have you been? What have you been after? How many Indians are embodied over the river, etc., etc., until in my amazement, I told them all to go to—somewhere.

As soon as I could disenthrall myself from the eagerly inquiring crowd, I went to the magistrate's office, told him what I had done, and delivered the bond I had taken from *Atoba,* for his appearance at the time specified in the bond. After he had examined it, he said it was satisfactory and a good deal better way than to arrest him and hold him in prison until the next court. Nevertheless, some of the knowing ones, after the subsidence of the panic, mouthed a good deal about the manner in which the thing had been conducted, and accused their magistrate of having been bribed.

Time passed quickly, and the day for the trial came. As early as 10 a.m. the white people from Columbus had collected at the oak grove in great numbers. It was a beautiful day; the people were lounging in various groups under the shady oaks, seeming to be quite agreeably situated. Having plenty of good water nearby, there was nothing to mar the good feelings inspired by the pleasant grove and fine day, except the presence of forty head of marauding, half-intoxicated boatmen and their drunken associates. They had their bottles hidden out, and they were "browsing" about in the surrounding thickets like so many brutes, as they were.

The balance of the assembly was civil enough, but no Indians had arrived yet, and the white people were becoming restless.

It was in vain that they were told that the hour specified in the bond was twelve o'clock and that it lacked over an hour of that time. They sneeringly replied that it was a "sell," and good enough, as they might have had better sense than to think that *Atoba*, or any one else, would be fool enough to make his appearance, after being set at liberty in the foolish manner he had and for such a crime.

Fifteen minutes of twelve, and no sign of Indians yet. The crowd had become painfully impatient. Some of them were talking about starting back to town and swearing that they never had been so completely entrapped in all their lives. Some were hungry, and others wanted their customary "horn of brandy." They were in a woeful fix. But 12 o'clock would come, in spite of their doubts and impatience; and with the meridian sun, the prisoner rode up, accompanied by about three hundred other Indians, all mounted and well armed. Among them were the three chiefs of the nation. They made their approach in single file, observing good order. It was a long string of warriors, making quite a formidable appearance. *Atoba* was not armed, and he occupied a position near the center of the line; he looked ashamed and not dissatisfied. They came briskly up, right into the grove of oaks, all amongst the scattered groups of unarmed white men.

I looked around on the then-silenced assembly; the vociferous clamor about the faithless Indians, biting hunger, and want of liquor was all hushed. And I thought I saw a good many pale faces.

The Indians, however, broke ranks, went to the bushes and little trees that skirted the grove, and, after hitching their horses, set their guns against the trees. In their usually friendly manner they mixed into the crowd of white people, shaking hands with all they met, at the same time ejaculating the various terms used by them at their friendly greeting. And then the white folks began to smile too.

A table and some benches had been provided, and there were seated around the table five justices of the peace, and as many lawyers. Among the lawyers was the venerable William Cocke.[5] *Atoba* came and took his seat as near to the table as he could get, and said "I am here." The court organized, and the examination of the case commenced.

The chiefs, *Mushulatubi, Apukshinubi* and *Apushimataha,* were invited to take seats among the magistrates, which they did, and seemed to be pleased at it, and to regard it as a proper token of respect. The examination of the witnesses then followed. There were about twenty-five witnesses, mostly women. I was one, and was called and qualified first. My testimony was the same as I have already stated while describing the circumstances connected with the killing and need not be repeated. The next witness was the Chickasaw woman. She manifested signs of considerable embarrassment, but when the nature and penalty of the oath had been explained to her she "blowed the book" [took the oath] and in good style delivered herself, word for word, as she had told me at the window, the same night the man was killed. The balance of the female witnesses, about fifteen, who were seated on a stock of hewn timber near the store at the time the accident occurred, were sworn, one at a time, and they repeated what the Chickasaw woman had testified to almost verbatim. All the testimony went to show very clearly that the killing was accidental, and that *Atoba* was not only innocent, but that he was particularly friendly to the man he had in his drunkenness unfortunately killed.

As soon as the boatmen and rowdies who were on the council grounds discovered that no criminality could be established against *Atoba* and that he would be acquitted, they collected in squads and were trying to get up an excitement for the purpose of mobbing the Indians, and perhaps the council of majesty and lawyers "into the bargain." Some *Chahtas* who understood English overheard their plottings and went and informed *Apushimataha,* who having satisfied himself that the trial was conducted fairly, had left the table. When the Indian that brought news of the contemplated riot came to him, he was seated a little way off from the crowd, on a fence. After hearing what the Indians had to say about the plot, he slid down from the fence, went directly to the council, took up a book, and stamping it on the table, spoke.

"It is to you, my white brothers, that I wish to address myself this fair day. I had kept my seat among the wise and good men who were conducting the investigation of my friend *Atoba's* case until I satisfied myself that the trial is a fair one. And I had, as there was no further use for my presence, gone off a little way,

87

and was seated in a pleasant place, amusing myself with the contemplation of the magnitude of the government and wonderful greatness of the American people, when one of my own countrymen came and informed me that a number of white men, now present [for when *Apushimataha* went to the table all had gathered around to hear him speak], who have no families or anything else that is valuable in the country to detain them when they are guilty of an outrage, are counseling among one another. And their aim is to break up the peace and friendly intercourse that has always obtained between the *Chahtas* and the American white people. It must be prevented. It will be put a stop to—"

At this point the venerable William Cocke, who was familiarly acquainted with the speaker, interrupted him and remarked "Brother Push, you speak too bold and plain; it might occasion the spilling of blood." *Apushimataha* listened, but made no reply at that time. He, however, continued and said: "I would have you, my white brothers, to understand that I have visited the big white house where our father, the President, resides; and locking my five fingers with his five fingers we made a treaty of peace, in the presence of that Being under the shadow of whose far-spreading wings we all exist, whose strong arm extends through all orders of the animal creation and down into the lowest grass and herbs in the forest. It was in the presence of this spirit that we made our peace, swept our paths clean, made them white; and on my part, and I speak for the entire *Chahta* people, there has been no track made in them. If, after a fair investigation, this unfortunate man, *Atoba,* shall be found guilty, we will give him up, cheerfully submit him to his destiny. We came here determined to do that. But on the other hand, if he is not found guilty, we shall sustain him like men, and we will do it at all hazards. I here frankly confess that I feel no misgivings in relation to the wise and very respectable gentlemen who are managing the trial. I know them all personally; I am satisfied with them and shall yield to their decision in the case. But it is to the reckless, loose crowd of irresponsible men to whom I have made allusion; men who are here today and there tomorrow; men who care no more for the white man than for the red man, and who would be willing to sacrifice both for a frolic with a big jug of whiskey. These are the kind of men I speak of. They are here close by; they hear my voice now; and when they have matured their plot and make the attempt to put it into action, if the officers of this well conducted council desire that it shall be suppressed, and are not in sufficient force to acccomplish it, let them call on me and I will instantly bring to their aid at a single whoop all the *Chahtas* who are on the ground. If the court do not see fit to call the red people to their assistance, and suffer a riot to occur here today, I shall take it upon myself to assume the responsibility in suppressing any outrage that may be attempted in this *Chahta* grove of red oaks, either while the council holds its session or after they have adjorned."

Then turning to the venerable Judge Cocke, he said, "*Konka nokni sipokni*" ["old chicken cock," the name Cocke was known by among the *Chahtas*], "Speak not to me of blood. I was raised in blood." He then very quietly seated himself on the bench near the old judge.

The above speech was interpreted into English by John Pitchlynn, who had been United States interpreter for the *Chahta* nation ever since the Hopewell treaty. The rowdy boatsmen were all jammed up as near as they could get and heard every word, for Pitchlynn rendered it in good English, and spoke quite loud and distinct. *Apushimataha's* manner and the bold tone of his voice while speaking had subdued their malicious intentions and they were all perfectly dumb. They looked at each other and said nothing, but when they turned their eyes, which had been riveted upon *Apushimataha* while he was delivering his little speech, and discovered that the Indians' guns, which had been all day leaning against the trees, were all gone, they became alarmed, and as it was getting late in the day, they excused themselves and departed for Columbus.

The examination of the testimony was concluded, and after some short speeches by two or three of the lawyers, *Atoba* was acquitted. But he was not satisfied, and in the course of a month he was found drowned in the river.

During the first year of my residence in the *Chahta* country I finished a large and very excellent building. When it was completed the white people solicited me, for the novelty of having it in the *Chahta* nation, to give them a ball in the new house. I did so and invited all three of the chiefs, the old national interpreter, John Pitchlynn, and a good many of the head men. The party was a very full one, well conducted, and it passed off in good style. ʳThe *mingos* [sub-chiefs] and chiefs had, according to my request, come early and were all seated in their places, dressed in full Choctaw costume, with their broad silver headbands, long series of diminishing crescents hanging on their breasts, armlets and wristbands, all solid silver, and beads ornamented with three white tail feathers of their own big bald eagle. Their moccasins and leggings were of fine dressed deer skins, ornamented with finely cut fringe of the same, and very small white beads sewed on in curious figures. In their native costume and by their modest deportment, they attracted considerable attention from the civil, well-bred participants of the delighted company. ᴸNotwithstanding that they were often invited, none of the *Chahtas,* except a few educated half breeds, participated in the dance. They kept their seats, behaving very orderly, and were doubtless highly amused and deeply interested. To them it was a great performance, or a show, the like of which they had never before witnessed.

Apushimataha, after supper was over, desiring to render himself agreeable and to attract attention (as I then supposed), came to me and asked me to talk a little for him. The party being large, I had a great deal to attend to, and the national interpreter, who was a very lively man, being present, I went to him and got him to go and interpret for the chief. *Apushimataha,* pointing to a group of very finely dressed young ladies, told Pitchlynn that he desired to have a little talk with them. Pitchlynn agreeing, they approached the group of young ladies and the chief said: "My friend, the interpreter, has often read in my presence from a big book which has many strange things. Amongst the rest of the very strange account was one about angels. The book said they looked exactly like people, yet they were so delicate in their formation that the inhabitants of this world could not feel them when they tried to handle them. Now, I have been observing these six bright and most elegantly beautiful beings all night, and I have come to the conclusion that if there are any such beings as angels, a thing I never before credited, these must be some of them. To satisfy my great curiosity on the subject, I solicited my friend to come and talk for me, and to ask the privilege for me to touch the pretty creatures to see if I could feel them." Pitchlynn told them what he said, and they being greatly flattered, readily consented that the chief might satisfy his curiosity by feeling of them. *Apushimataha* then proceeded in a most delicate and polite manner possible, using only his thumb and middle finger to grasp very gently the arm of one of them. After touching the arm in several places until his hand was nearly at the shoulder, he turned to Pitchlynn and said, "It's folks, for I can feel it very distinctly, but without the experiment I should never have believed. It is sure enough somebody, and I must say, a very nice somebody. But perhaps they are not all people; some of them may yet turn out to be *Ubba hatak* (angels); I must touch all of them before I can rest satisfied about it." And he paid them the compliment of taking hold of the arm of each of the six young ladies. When he had got through with it he told the interpreter to say to them that he had convinced himself that they were people, inhabitants of earth, a conclusion he should never have been able to come to except by the experiment of actual contact. Pitchlynn delivered his speech to the young ladies and they acknowledged that they felt themselves highly complimented.

With all his greatness, no one knew or could tell anything about the origin or parentage of *Apushimataha*. And this was a secret of which he seemed to be very proud. I made efforts often, among the people of his district when they came about me, trying to find some scrap of items in relation to the history of his early life. It was an entire failure. I saw that no one knew anything about him until he was about eighteen or nineteen years of age. John Pitchlynn, who was a few years older than *Apushimataha*, was raised in the nation from his fourth year. He was as ignorant of the early history of the great chief as everybody else, although he had, and he told me it himself, sought long and in various ways to unriddle the perplexing secret.[6]

There was a yankee once who visited the *Chahta* people in search of material to compose a book, and being about the missionary establishments—the missionaries were also yankees—the book man attended one *Chahta* council, when he heard *Apushimataha* make one of his flaming speeches. He was so much pleased with the chief and his oratorical ability that he made up his mind to procure the necessary facts and write a history of the great man. He inquired of the missionaries as to his origin and early life. The missionaries knew nothing about it, of course, but they promised the book man that they would procure the information he required the very next day. They told him *Apushimataha* was to make another one of his fine speeches the next day and they would prepare another speaking Indian (who was friendly to the missionary cause) to flatter the old chief a little as soon as he had finished his business speech, and as the old sinner could not resist flattery they would be certain to get the history of his origin. It is true, they said, that his origin is not known to anyone alive, and he professed to be proud of the secret, but as we hold the key that will unlock the mystery, we will work it out of him tomorrow.

Tomorrow came, and after several speeches had been delivered, *Apushimataha* took the stand and continued to speak at least an hour. He was unusually eloquent, his arguments irresistible and his embellishment unique and unsurpassingly beautiful. The book man said that he had never before heard a speech from any man that would compare with it.

As soon as *Apushimataha* had taken his seat, the chief that had been prepared by the missionaries for the purpose arose, and after a few flattering remarks on the subject of the masterly speech he had just heard, furthermore said that the history of the origin of so great a man should no longer be withheld from his own nation at least. He pressed it upon the chief as a right which his people could in justice claim of him, and he asked it of him in all kindness and the name of the nation that he avail himself of the present occasion to rise up and at once relieve the minds of his people on that interesting topic.

Apushimataha immediately responded to this polite request by rising from his seat and taking the speaker's stand. After some few preliminary remarks on the subject of the vanity of aspirants to fame and political egotism, he very gravely delivered himself of the following wonderful account of his origin:

"It was a long time ago; at the season when the glorious sun was pouring down his brightest, balmiest and greatest life-giving influence; when the gay flowers, bedecked in their most gorgeous habiliments, were sweetest, brightest and most numerous; when the joyous birds in full chorus were chanting their gleeful songs of life and love, full of inspiration; when all nature seemed to quiver in rapturous emotion. 'Twas noon. The day was calm and fair and very pleasant. There was a beautiful wide spreading plain, with but few trees on it. One there was of giant size and venerable age. It was a red oak, and its dark waving branches, overshadowing an immense area of the beautiful green plain, had bid defiance and braved unscathed the storms of many winters. There it stood, vast in its proportions, calm in its strength, majestic in its attitude. It had witnessed the rise and fall of many generations of animal life. But everything must have its time, fulfill its destiny. That magnificent red oak, the prominent feature on that far reaching landscape, and had been for centuries, had not accomplished the object for which the great spirit had planted it. There it was in full foliage, casting its dark, widely spreading shadow upon the sunlit plain. All nature was clad in smiles of joy on that bright day. Anon a cloud was rising in the west, a black, angry, threatening cloud, looming upwards and rapidly widening its scowling front. Harshly grumbling as it whirled its black folds onward, nearer and nearer, very soon it overspread the whole heavens, veiling the landscape in utter darkness and appalling uproar. It was a sweeping tornado, fringed with forked lightning, thunders rolling and bellowing; the winds fiercely howled and the solid earth trembled. In the height of this confusion and war of elements, a flash of fire gleamed through the black obscurity. A shattering crash came, followed by a burst of terrific thunder that, heavily rumbling through the surging storm, seemed to shake down the humid contents of the fast rolling cloud in irresistible torrents. Awful sounds assailed the startled senses in all directions as the frightful tornado swiftly swept by in its devastating course. Soon it passed and was all calm again. The sun poured down his beaming rays in their wonted brilliancy; but the vast, time-honored sylvan king, the red oak, had been shivered into fragments; its odd-shapen splinters lay widely scattered on the rain-beaten plain. Not a vestige remained to mark the spot where once stood that towering tree. Not even a snag of the stump remained. The object of its creation was accomplished, and in its place there was a new thing under the sun! Shall I name it? Equipped and ready for battle, holding in his right hand a ponderous club, standing erect on the place of the demolished red oak, was your dauntless chief, *'Apushimataha.'*"

He took his seat without making any further remarks. The missionaries were astounded when they found out that the sagacious chief had scented out their secret design and played them off with so much ingenuity. The book man said his speeches surpassed anything he had ever heard before, and that it was not only a great pity but it was a damaging loss to the literary world that no one had ever taken the pains to preserve them. He regretted very much that he was not prepared for it, that he might have preserved the speeches he had heard him deliver at the present council. He had heard them; they were wonderful, and that was about all he should be able to say on the subject.

Apushimataha attended only one more treaty, which was held in Washington City [in 1824], during which time he died of the croup. His speeches on that occasion were not preserved. On his deathbed he made a speech, and General Jackson and many other United States officers were gathered about the bedside. General Jackson bent over the prostrate form and inquired, "What is the last request of the chief?"

"Bury me with the big guns firing over the grave," was the reply. He was buried at Washington and an artillery salute fired over the grave as requested by the dying warrior. He was buried with all the honors of a brigadier general.

Many years ago I visited the Congressional burying ground to pay my respects to the greatest chief of the Choctaw Nation. A modest monument, erected by the chiefs, marks his resting place, on which are inscribed his last words: "When I am dead let the big guns be fired over me." If, as Paul says, "They that have not the law are a law unto themselves," then will the heaven of the Indian be as bright and beautiful as the paradise of Mahomet, and none will enter therein more worthy of Divine favor than *Apushimataha*.

Meeting with a Choctaw Sage, Hunting with a New Yorker, and Moving into Chickasaw Territory

---

ᴾThere occurred a notable circumstance during my residence in the Choctaw nation that would do to place in this portion of my narrative. From my first hunting excursion in this new country and up to the time I went to live in the nation, I had discovered many earth mounds. They were commonly about forty feet thick at the base, conic in form and seven to eight feet in height. As soon as I could speak the language sufficiently I inquired of the middle-aged men among the Indians who it was that had built up the numerous mounds that embossed the country. The reply was: "They were always here."[1]

But these men told me, and so did everybody else of whom I made inquiries in reference to the monumental remains that occurred so frequently in the land, that on a creek called in Choctaw *Bogue Tuculo*,[2] forty miles distant, there lived the oldest man in the world, a man that knew everything. If I would go and see him he could tell me all about the mounds and everything else I might desire to know about the traditional history of the Choctaw people. So many of them told of this man that I concluded to go and see him. I arranged my business so I could leave it a few days and set out to see the wise old man that all the Indians told me of. Sure enough, I found the intelligent old man residing, as they said, on *Bogue Tuculo*, but such a man as he was, I have never seen before nor since. He dwelt in a very comfortable though small, circular dirt house, with a small hole in the apex through which the smoke from his fire (on the ground in the center below) made its escape. A small, smooth, round pole or handrail extended from its attachment to the facing on one side of the doorway, to his cane bunk, the front side of which rested on two posts that were planted in the earth, while the other side of the bunk rested on fastenings in the dirt wall. The floor or bottom of the bunk or bedplace was neatly filled with selected straight cane, cut to fit the framework. This was his sleeping place and his bedding consisted of a variety of dry skins with the hair still on them—buffalo, bear, panther, deer, wild-cat, and some blankets. The deerskins were most numerous. Here he slept, and by the aid of the handrail he could make his way to the door where, in pleasant weather, he spent most of his time in sitting on a bench that had been prepared for the purpose. There he could look out upon the little village and its surrounding scenery, see the play of the numerous village children, the running to and fro of the women, busy beating meal for bread and dressing the skins which had been supplied to them by the hunters.

Such was the visible aspect and condition of things in the little Indian town at the time I arrived on my first visit, to the door of the dirt house wherein resided the old man *Chahta-Immataha*.[3] There he sat on his time-polished pine bench by the side of the door, his unclad lower extremities extending at full length in front, his feet dry and scaly, toes contracted and crumpled up, and his relaxed muscles swinging in pendent bags of shrivelled skin beneath his bony legs. His long, bony fingers were wrapped around a neat, smooth rod six or seven feet in length, with a hook at one end, which he used to drag up his things that might lie out of reach and also to hook by their garments and pull into captivity the little children when he was playing with them. His upper extremities and his body were covered with an ordinary cotton shirt, which constituted his entire clothing. At the time I rode up he was sitting motionless, with the exception of his brilliant, smiling eyes and large head, which was covered with a heavy coat of not very long, iron gray hair. Every part of his person seemed to be out and powerless.

I spoke to him in his own tongue, inquiring if he was *Chahta-Immataha?* He replied in plain English, "That's my name, sir." Still addressing him in Choctaw, I informed him that I had long desired, and had now come a great way, to see and have a talk with him in relation to the traditional history of the *Chahta* people and the origin of the monumental remains which are found so extensively distributed over the country. He smiled and bid me welcome, remarking that he was not only willing, but that he felt proud of having an opportunity to communicate the traditional history of his people to a man whom he felt sure, after hearing it, would feel sufficient interest to write it on paper and take care of it. He said he based this opinion on the fact that I had traveled so far to hear it. He would not only repeat the traditional account of the origin, progress, manners, customs, wars, etc., of the *Chahtas*, but he would certainly satisfy me as to the cause and by whom the mounds were built.

After a short pause he resumed and said, "If it is to make a book you are seeking this information, I shall be still more highly pleased and will take great pains to narrate the whole of our traditional history."[4] I informed him frankly that to collect material of which to make a book was the object of my visit, having been told by a great number of his people that he was the only man now living that could inform me, and on that account alone I had called on him. "You have," said he, "been correctly informed—I am, and I regret that it is true, the only man left who can repeat correctly the *Shukhah-anumpula* [literally "hog talk"; the Choctaw name for their traditional history], and because you will write my talk in a book that shall speak for me a long time after I have passed away to the good hunting ground, I am proud of you and glad that you have come."

He then rehearsed a part of his own history, concluding with "I have always advocated honesty and fairness. Have never been drunk, have never swallowed a drop of the strong water; have always been sober, speaking to the people in earnest, telling truth." Then for the purpose of starting him on the subject of the traditions, I inquired of him how the notion had originated and obtained with so many of the people, that the *Chahtas* came out of *Nanih-waya* hill? He replied, "They have been drunk ever since the white people came amongst us and they have lost the truth."

"Long time ago, before the white man came, it was a custom with the old men, when they had from age and decrepitude become too inactive to pursue the chase, for them to remain at home with the women and children, assist them in the cultivation of their little farm patches and carefully teach the traditions to the children. Then everyone who had sense enough to learn it knew it and could teach it correctly, and everybody knew it in the same words. But when the white people came and brought with them the maddening drinks—the fire-water—old men as well as the young could get drunk and the traditional teaching ceased. That pure, truthful, sacred account of the origin and progress of the *Chahta* people—the hog talk—was heard no more. And now, there are none, not even the old men amongst them, who can state anything that is reliable on the subject.

"But I have not answered your question in relation to the notion which prevails among the people now, that the first *Chahta* came out of *Nanih-waya* hill.[5] Its origin occurred in this wise: About three hundred winters ago, when the *Chahta* people came to a halt from a journey of forty-three winters in the wilderness, traveling from the direction of the setting sun, they settled and forted themselves in, very near to *Nanih-waya* hill. At this plentiful place they remained and were very happy and thrifty for many winters. For a long time the hunters could readily supply the women and children with plenty of meat, fish and the like. But in process of time the game became scarcer and further off until it was difficult, laborious work to the hunters for them to procure even a moderate supply of food for their families.

"It had been long known to them, that in the extent of country for many days journey around *Nanih-waya*, there was no sign of people of any kind—no enemies or dangers to encounter. And so, the chiefs and leaders, at a council fire that had been enkindled for the purpose of investigating this matter, after mature deliberation decided that inasmuch as there were no enemies or anything to be afraid of in this vastly extensive and exceedingly fruitful country, there could be no impropriety for some of the *iksahs* (clans) to go out, select and settle new homes for themselves where provisions could be obtained with less labor to the hunter.

"With the decision of this council the people were highly pleased. And, soon an *iksah* with their families went out from *Nanih-waya* and settled the town called *Yazoo* by the white people. The *Chahtas* call it *Eah-shah,* and it signifies *went out from here.*

"In a short time many *iksahs* had selected locations and had gone out from *Nanih-waya* and built up towns for themselves to dwell in. In after years, when a stranger would happen at one of these towns, and should chance to inquire of the people, 'Whence they came?', the answer would be 'We came out from *Nanih-waya*,' and not as the drunken, uninformed people have it now, 'out *of Nanih-waya*.' And that is the way in which the foolish falsehood originated. The distinction is, they came out *from* and not out *of Nanih-waya*, when they dispersed and spread over the country.

"They have used the terms 'out of' until they have forgotten its original signification, and it has obtained in the minds of the people as a belief—a traditional fact—that *Nanih-waya*, the little leaning hillock, with a scooped-out hole in one side of it, which had been washed out by the freshets in a considerable creek (which the hill overhangs), is the mother of the *Chahta* people, the place that originated the *Chahta* race. But I have told you, my friend, that it is false. The *Chahtas* had their origin in the far off country, from a very different source, a source wrapped up in many mysteries and singular traditional facts, that will by the time I am through with it, excite the wonder and admiration of the red people themselves, as much as it will in you, my white friend.

"While I am narrating my traditional account of the occurrences, customs of the people, and historical facts belonging to ages long gone, you will find them supported by no testimony except traditional assertion. They sustain themselves in the bounds of probability and the completeness of their connections. You will also find many other facts, incidents and adventures, carrying on their face the evidence of undeniable truthfulness—sufficient to establish their characters as reliable traditional data.

"I shall not, in the beginning of my narrative, however, attempt to establish or defend its account of the origin of red men. But I have heard the strange account of the origin of the race of white men, interpreted by John Pitchlynn, United States interpreter, from a very large book which he held in his lap and from which he said he read while he translated the singular account of the creation of the first white man. It was very curious, and I may here state with much confidence, that our traditional account of the origin of the red man is at least as feasible a story as that is. And I feel assured that when the truthful traditional history which I shall deliver to you, containing the origin of the *Chahta* race, their religion, their laws, societies, customs, journeyings, great leaders and warlike actions, shall be written in a book, it will be like the white man's big book, preserved, esteemed, venerated, as the Sacred *Holisso Holitopa* for the coming generations of enlightened *Chahtas!*"

Let me interject here that *Holisso Holitopa* is the *Chahta* appellation for the Bible, taught them by the missionaries. *Holisso* is "paper, writing or book"; *Holitopa* means "sacred." *Chahta* is the old man's word for Choctaw. *Iksah* is a family connection or clan. *Nanih-waya*—give the "a" the broad sound—is the hill where they planted or deposited the bones of their ancestors. The above is the result of my first visit to the old *Chahta's* house. It is a fair preface to what follows.

During the ensuing four years I visited him about ten times and his narrative, which I took down in Choctaw, amounts to 650 closely written pages on large letter paper. It contains an account of the origin of the *Chahtas,* their increase to a very great multitude, a farming people, building stone houses, immense cities with very large stone temples dedicated to the sun, the perpetual fire, and lazy, wicked priests. Ruled by a great *Inka* and *Ishca,* they were a very numerous and very happy people many ages, till the palefaces came one stormy night in their big canoes, having wings and carrying the thunder, and alighted in the sea at their fishery. The people thought the Great Spirit sent them and they rejoiced, called them *Nahulo* (beloved) and gave them much gold. The palefaces behaved so badly that the Indians killed some of them, [and] that brought on war, which lasted twenty years. The Indians were conquered. Three tribes, the *Chahta, Muscogees* and *Chickeshas,* fled from the murderous palefaces and traveled together but a few days before they were compelled to separate on account of their numbers and the difficulty of procuring food in the wilderness.

The *Chahtas* took the middle route, and the old man's traditional history tells of all their encampments, travels, buffalo hunts, crossing of water courses; how they crossed the Mississippi on cane-rafts; and finally at the end of forty-three winters landed at *Nanih-waya*. They had cleaned and packed the bones of all their dead from the start, until they had accumulated in numbers to more than the living. They planted them at *Nanih-waya* and raised a mound eighty feet high and six hundred feet at the base. I have been on it and measured it. The tradition goes on and tells what they did at *Nanih-waya* for near two hundred years, up to the Hopewell Treaty between the Americans and *Chahtas*,[6] when they buried the war-hatchet and made a treaty of peace forever.

This digression began with me in a store in the Choctaw nation. The intercourse law would not have permitted me to move my family into the nation, but the articles of agreement betwixt my Indian partner [Pitchlynn Jr.] and myself gave me the character of a hireling. He had commenced collecting material for a house at that place. He had a pretty good storehouse. I went over with my stock of Indian goods and finished up a large two-story house with double porches, all made of cedar.

In trading with the Indians I took everything they brought, and was accumulating wealth rapidly for four years. But the object of this narrative is not to describe a mercantile action but to describe some of my fine sporting whilst I resided in that wild, cany bend of the Tombecbee River.

In the canebrake and all around the cypress swamp could be found more turkeys and deer, and some bear, coons, foxes, panthers and catamounts than at any place I ever lived. And because I had to be confined the most of my time to the store and couldn't hunt far off, the Indians had made an ordinance and published to all the people, that if any one were to shoot a deer inside of the White Slue (what the string of ponds and lakes outside of my dwelling place was called)[7] they should pay me a good well-dressed doeskin or half a dollar in money. They all said it was right and no Indian was ever found hunting in that district again as long as I remained in it. The consequence was, that being hunted and shot all round outside of *Shonk Colochenocoby* ("crooked cypress," the name given the White Slue), the deer and other game soon became very numerous in my reserve, as I called it. The river was an excellent river for hook and line fish. Buffalo fish took the bait freely all winter; large cat-fish and soft shell tortoise were abundant on troll-line; innumerable perch of many kinds could be caught all summer with young wasps and pinworms. In the round ponds and the big lakes in the White Slue, the black bass and large goggle-eyed perch were very plenty; minnows, large water spiders, lizards and small frogs would raise them any fair day in the winter time. There never was a fair day the year round that fishing or shooting wasn't good.

The night hunting in the summer season was for old fat bucks, when their antlers were eight or ten inches long, with spikes or snags just forking off, when the outer ends would be as large in some of them as your two fists, covered with velvet and feeling quite soft and tender. The large, tender knobs of the antlers, when nicely roasted and dressed with a little salt, very closely resemble the black marrow of the deer's thigh bone; with good bread it is very good, pleasant food. At the same time of the year the old suckling does are seen. But their eyes are so different from the white paper eyes of a fat buck, there is no danger of shooting the does. I have shined the eyes of thousands, and I never shot a suckling doe in my life. If she has but one fawn, it is sure to be fat, and I have occasionally taken it away from her. It makes nicer pies than chicken, and I have taken them to help the good lady out when she expected company. There is another thing I have often done when we killed our hogs. The night before she ground up her sausage meat, my wife would tell me she would like to have the flesh of one or two good deer to mix and grind with her sausage meat. I'd fix up my flambeau pan and go and get them for her. Sausages made with equal parts of pork and venison are better, less greasy and they will dry nicely, and keep as long as a venison ham. Our smoke house was never clear of venison hams, and sometimes when there was more than we could consume, I would pack and send 50 or 100 to Mobile for sale.

There came a clever looking gentleman, a New Yorker, on his way to New Orleans, who called about noon one day, while we were at dinner. He said he was surprised at the quantity of game upon the table. It was winter, and ducks, geese, turkeys and venison were on the table. When the traveler found out how it came there, he observed that he was a sportsman himself; and his horse was a little jaded. If I would permit him, he would like to tarry with me eight or ten days to rest his horse, and have a little sport with me. I was proud of him, being nearly all the time without company of that kind. I readily made him welcome, and informed him that we would commence the sport that very night. He said he did not know how he would relish coon hunting, but I told him it would be deer hunting. He regretted very much that he did not have his fine lamellated English gun with him. That was during the flint-lock age; and my big fire-hunting gun, inch bore, with four feet barrel, was a snug-finished gun, in good order, and her charge of lead was 49 buck shot. She was a promising looking piece.

I got all ready and when dark came, I mounted the stranger, with a bag of fat pine and the gun on one horse, and myself with the pan on another. He rode along behind, replenishing the pan when the light grew dim. Two or three times as we rode slowly onwards, he said: "I think, sir, the chance to find game in this way must be very poor." My reply was: "From what do you judge?" "Well, sir, I certainly have the advantage of the light all behind here, and I couldn't see a buffalo twenty feet." "Don't talk so loud," I said. I saw a single eye of a buck, and from its motion knew it was feeding. I got down, went back for the gun and speaking very low, told him I saw one deer. He handed me the gun, repeating at the same time, "By Jove, I see nothing!" The distance did not exceed thirty yards. It was still feeding, with but one eye visible. I shot its head and it fell where it stood. The gun was unusually loud, and the stranger said it jarred the trash from the trees. The bold shove she had given me when she fired had a little disordered my attention, and I inquired of my companion, "Did you hear anything run off?" "Run off!" said he, ironically.

I went down to the place. There lay a very large buck; and at the same time, ten or fifteen steps further, I heard a deer cough, as they do when shot in the lungs. I called and told the man to bring the horses. He came slowly up. When he saw the large head of horns, he descended from his horse, exclaiming: "By Jove! I never saw it." We took off the head and legs and bowels, tied the carcass upon my horse, and then I said: "Stand here till I look; I think there is another a little way out there." It was but a few steps, and sure enough there lay another, not so large, but a pretty good buck, with a single shot behind the shoulders. We fixed that one and tied it up on his horse. When he saw I was about to turn homewards, he said anxiously: "See here, stranger, hadn't you better look a few hundred yards further out of the course you shot? There may be more dead out there." I replied, "Quite likely, but don't you think we've got enough?"

I did not reload the gun, and the stranger talked all the way home, inquiring and learning all about how I had discovered and shot the deer so exactly, when he couldn't see it. I informed him all about it; and before his horse had rested enough—three weeks—he had found and shot three by firelight, two of which we got.

All animals have languages and signs by which they communicate to each other all that is necessary for them in their peculiar mode of existence. Some species talk a great deal more than others, and when domesticated, are more intelligent and docile. The big old goose (*Anser canadensis*)[8] is a very talkative, intelligent bird, having many words in his language. I had a blind once by the side of a grassy pond where the geese fed a great deal during the winter season. While hiding in this big pile of brush, waiting for a good range to discharge eight ounces of No. 8's from my big old single-barrel, four-foot-long trumpet muzzle buccaneer (which lay fastened in the stocks like a cannon), I have many times, when they came feeding along near my concealment, heard them in conversation. They use many distinct articulate sounds, the most of which are guttural and nasal and broken into many syllables. I learned some of it and could speak to them, telling them what to do and they would do it. With guttural and nasal voice I would say *onk ha,* which means "look out," and they would instantly stretch up their necks and look and listen for fifteen minutes. This is what I had heard the sentinel say in a low clear voice, when he heard suspicious noises that he could not see the cause of, and the flock would listen in the manner I have described. But when the sentinel actually discovers approaching danger, he repeats with energy, in a loud voice, very distinctly: *onk ha oik,* and the whole flock repeats the same words. Then they spring up from the water shouting *hoi ik, hoi ik,* and are soon out of the reach of danger. It is my opinion that an ingenious linguist could grammaticize the wild goose language.

It was to this pond where I took my new sporting companion the first time we went fowling. We got into the blind without exciting any alarm, and the pond was literally covered with game. My companion at the sight was highly excited, and was fixing to fire instantly. He was agitated and trembling from head to foot. I laid my hand on the gun, and said, "Be still until you come to your senses; wait until you can look at the game; select a good range, sight and hold your piece steady on them until you distinctly hear the crack of my rifle, and then let off at their opening wings." He went through the maneuver elegantly, fired at the right time, and when I saw him with a distorted countenance crawling out from under the side of the brush blind, rubbing his shoulder, I was afraid he was hurt; but before I had time to speak, he had cast his eyes over the pond, where he saw a quarter of an acre of fluttering and floundering geese and mallard. He quit rubbing his shoulder, bounded over the brush with a whoop, and went whirling into the water, and no retriever that ever took water could have manifested the activity and vigilance that he did in catching and killing the crippled ones. I stood calmly admiring, and at the time he was closely engaged securing four broken-winged ones, I saw one creep out on dry land and hide itself under the side of a log. I kept my eye on it, intending to tell him where it was, but he had seen it, and as soon as he had quieted those in the water, he went and got it. He gathered them all and put them in a pile on land. He had twelve geese and three mallard ducks; I had killed but one. With our knives we cut a pole, and tying their necks to the pole carried them a mile home. As we trudged along under the pretty heavy load the man said: "This gun of yours is a rough customer, but when I view the results, I am satisfied she couldn't do it softly." I asked, "Are you hurt?" "Oh, yes, she stiffened my neck a little." Afterwards when we shot from that blind he placed the gun in the frame I shot her from.

Hunting one dry day, between the Big Lake and the river, we came across an alligator traveling towards the river. It was eleven feet long, and the first my friend had ever seen. As soon as it discovered us it turned to make battle. We set our guns against a tree, and commenced teasing him by throwing pine knots at him. He became very much excited, and would strike at the pine knots with his tail with great force; sometimes hit them as they came and sent them back a considerable distance. I said to my friend: "There is danger in that, look out or he'll hurt you." He remarked: "Not much danger, but a heap of fun." Presently he came along with a big pine knot, so large that he had to go close so as to heave it on the alligator. As he pitched it, the alligator swept his tail around with violent force, and striking the pine knot squarely sent it whizzing back, narrowly missing my friend's head, thirty-five yards. He was then satisfied with his play with the big lizard, and with the rifle shot it close up behind the arm, which paralyzed him instantly. After measuring him and otherwise examining the creature, we left him for the vultures to fight over.

The traveler's name was Andrews, and he was a dweller among the lakes of New York; a good shot, and an industrious hunter. He was an educated man, about twenty-seven years of age, and was bound to New Orleans on some big speculation in the year 1828. He was an excellent sporting companion, good-natured, and full of fun. When he left I was lonesome. I did not go out with my gun in a couple of weeks after the traveler went away. It was in the prime season for buffalo fishing, and with a trot line of 200 hooks I had fine sport till the river rose and became muddy with the rains. I don't know what science calls the Buffalo Fish.[9] It is the hump on his back that gave him the name with the populace. A stiff mush made of corn meal, with sufficient cotton worked into it to make it hang together, is a good bait for them and the Red Horse. I have caught the buffalo fish that would weigh twelve pounds. Six to eight pounds are the best sizes for food, and when they are fat they are a delicious fish.

I had a Kentucky partner in the trot line, and while he would be taking off the fish of a morning, I would be sitting on the bank of the river engaged with buffalo. He advertised "Fish Market in the ferry boat every morning," and for the cat-fish, soft shell tortoise, and the fish I caught, would take in from three to five dollars in cash every morning. He paid all our sporting expenses, and for the new boat we had built before the high water came. It took two or three ducks to bait the trot line, but deer's liver was the most successful bait for the soft shells. The Indians are poor fishermen. They have no methods that fish them out and destroy them like we do. Hence, in all the Indian countries I have stopped in, I have found the fish very abundant. In moving through different nations of wild Indians, I have often, when camped on a small creek, a mere rivulet, gone with a torch and the bow and arrow, any time of the year if the weather was clear, and in a short time got as many fish as we could all eat. It is astonishing, in a country where civilization has never set her poison foot, to see how full of life every creek and even little rills are. (In wild countries I have taken good panfuls of fish from the little puddles in running branches so small that I could stop the flow with my foot.)

The enjoyment of field sports, such as shooting larks, bob-whites, pigeons and snipes, when compared with the game found in the far West—in the Rocky Mountains—must be very poor. I never resided where the people cared enough for small game to hunt it. I have shot a few prairie chickens (the cocks) here in Texas, in the fall of the year, where I would find them in the post-oak trees gathering acorns. I would with any rifle pick the cocks out of the tree tops when I first came to the country, but here I have skipped over thirty years. I will go back to the Choctaw Nation, to the White Slue, and tell you what happened there before I left the nation.

Inside of my hunting reserve had come a very large buck. He was known to a good many of the Indians for three or four years. Several of them told me they had shot at him, but could never hit him. They called him the *Isse Mingo* (king deer), and the belief was prevalent amongst them that he was a charmed deer and could not be hit. They said he was known to many hunters, and that there were few men now, in a region of ten or twelve miles around, that would be fools enough to waste their ammunition in shooting at him. Several of them told me that he had taken to my reserve, and that although I would see him often, it would be useless for me to shoot at him, as my bullet could not get to him. It was not many days before I went out with my rifle. I proceeded in the direction in which he had been seen most frequently. I had not walked half a mile before I discovered him. He was much the largest deer I had ever seen, and the most conspicuous thing about him was his tremendous antlers. I was so anxious to get the charmed king deer that I almost had a fit of buck-fever. He was browsing on the green briers and did not seem to be on the alert at all. I wondered at that, but moved very cautiously, so as to be sure that he would not see me. I consumed nearly half an hour creeping, and when I had got to the big pine where I intended to shoot from, and was resting a little for my nerves to get steady, off about forty or fifty yards to one side I heard the alarm snort, and away bounded the *Isse Mingo*. He had five or six little bucks scattered around him as his guards; but I had kept my attention so steadily fixed on the big one that I saw but little else. I knew long ago that big old bucks keep a platoon of little ones to watch for them, but this time my attention was so thoroughly engrossed that I did not think of it.

I saw him on several other occasions. Once I had slipped on to the island in the cypress swamp a while before day, and had laid down in the leaves and slept for a while. When I awoke I discovered plenty of turkeys in the trees, and it was nearly light enough to shoot; but I was smelling a deer very strong. I slowly turned on my right side, for that was the course the scent seemed to come from, and not exceeding twenty yards from me I discovered the antlers of the king deer. I thought to myself, "Well, old fellow, the fates have sealed your doom at last." I intended to shoot him in the bur of the ear, and setting my trigger and fixing my rifle all right, I looked around for his guards, but there were none on my side of him. I raised myself as slowly as a snail crawls, and as I elevated my gun to shoot, the alarm was given within one yard of where I lay, by a little rascal that I think had been creeping up to see what I was, lying there in the leaves. I shot a brace of turkeys and went home.

Not many days more had passed until an Indian came to get some goods from my store, and he told me that he saw the *Isse Mingo* a little way down the road. I asked why he didn't shoot him. Well, he said, he had such a gang of little bucks about him. He was gone but a little while, when he came back and said, this time when he saw the king deer he went no nearer, but laid up against a tree, and taking steady sight, aimed to break his back over the kidneys, but the bullet went below the bone and cut the big artery. The buck instantly dropped down, "baaing," and by the time he reloaded the gun and got to him he was dead. He was quite poor, and had several wounds, some of them recent. I made them get the cart and haul him home for the hogs. His horns were large, one had 17 and the other 15 points, plus many more snags, not more than an inch or two long. The antlers were regular and not larger than some I had purchased from the natives. His old poor frame, by far the largest I ever saw, was marked with many scars. Had it not been for his horns and hoofs, he might have produced a question as to what species he belonged. He was, however, unmistakably a genuine *Cervida virginianus*. I resided at that place four years, and while there killed three or four hundred deer. Their hams (when dry) were readily sold to the boats, and at Mobile, at 50 cents, and during the proper season for it, I killed all I could, and bartered for all the hams the Indians brought to the store, dried them in my smoke house and in the spring sent them to market.

This was a profitable, easy place to live at and, for the very best abundant, big, manly sport, there were few places on the continent that could equal it. But those back swamps were very unhealthy, and myself and my whole family suffered severely with malarial fever every autumn. The ill-health of my family, and the fact that the transactions of my Indian partner Pitchlynn with the Yankee clerk, in their Chickasaw store, were about to involve my business in great financial losses, made it necessary for me to take hold of the Chickasaw store and make the best I could of the already greatly wasted stock.

ᴹPitchlynn, Jr., without my knowledge, had gone up to Cotton Gin Port, rented a house, and ordering his goods on the reputation of our Choctaw establishment, had set up a $5,000 stock of goods and engaged a drunken fellow by the name of Andrew Morrison to superintend the selling of them to the Chickasaw people. The Chickasaws dwelt opposite to that place and received $35,000 annually, in the form of an annuity paid them by the Government of the United States. Pitchlynn spent most of his time at Cotton Gin, where he could drink free of my interference. It, however, suited the drunken Morrison and they had a grand time of it, both drunk and often leaving the doors open all night. After a little while, Pitchlynn came and told me that Morrison had made way with the greater part of the Cotton Gin goods, and that he wanted me to go up there, take possession and save what I could of them. At first thought, I was determined not to go. But on reflection, I knew that the whole amount of the loss would fall on my own Choctaw account, and as I intended to abandon the place I then occupied, I finally consented. Pitchlynn was greatly pleased and promised me that he would not drink anything at that place as long as we continued in partnership,[10] and he kept his word, though he did not often visit the place. Upon my arrival I found about $2,000 worth of badly abused remnants and an equal amount of unavailable accounts. It was entirely an Indian business, and many of the names were so badly spelled that I could not make out who they were. PMorrison was an incorrigible drunkard, and in his spiritualized liberality he had let out more than half of the goods on credit to the Indians without keeping any account of it. I tried to sober him up and get him to point out his customers when they came to the store. It was, however, no use and I was forced to get clear of him. I did the best I could with it.

My bargain with Pitchlynn Jr. excluded him from interfering with anything about the store. I did all, and he received his share of the profits quarterly. As I did not drink myself, I was an unfit associate for those who did; consequently my partner spent but little time about the store. After I took possession of it he was seldom seen at it. Our business, on account of his confidence in the Yankee, sustained a loss of over $5000, and the Yankee made nothing but one long drunk. MMany of the Chickasaws who had dealt with me at the Choctaw store came to Cotton Gin, expressing joy at my having come so near to them.

PAlthough the white people called it Cotton Gin Port, *Tanuptokche* was the Chickasaw name of the place. It was a small town on the south bank of the Tombecbee river. At the time the U.S. Government sent their first agent to the Chickasaws, they sent also a cotton gin and had it put up at *Tanuptokche*. But the Indians thought it was an indication that the United States intended to make Negroes of them, and they burnt it up. The Government had proposed to make farmers of the Indians, and sent them cotton seed and a gin. The Indians didn't believe in it. The opposition no doubt had originated from the few runaway Negroes that had got amongst them, and very probably the Negroes burnt the gin. Be that as it may, when the white people obtained the country, they commenced a town at *Tanuptokche* and called it Cotton Gin Port.[11]

Tanuptokche has a very different signification: simply, "strung our bows." About eighty years previous to the introduction of the cotton gin, a French colony had forced their way up the river, to a point on the left hand prong of the river two miles above *Tanuptokche* and built a strong fortification on the west of that river. For this account I am indebted to *Itewaumba*,[12] the principal chief of the Chickasaws. He was born twenty years after the French fort was massacred, and remembers the traditional history of it well.[13] The Chickasaw *Mingo* [sub-chief] had warned the palefaces not to build a fort there. The intruders did not respect the warnings of the chief, and finished a strongwork there. The Indians gathered their forces, and when they came within two miles of the fort, to the place where Cotton Gin Port now is, they strung their bows preparatory to the attack, and that gave a name for the place: *Tanuptokche*, "where we tied our bows." By the assistance of my old friend *Itewaumba*, I found the site of the old fortification. There were sufficient signs yet remaining to show that there had been a defense made there— pits and embankments and rank weeds, etc. My guide informed me that when he was a boy hunting with the blow gun, he frequently visited the place, finding bullets, scraps of iron, and scales and splinters of burnt bone on the surface of the ground where the fort stood. His mother's father told him that when they destroyed the fort, they took all the cannon they could carry and rolled the big heavy brass guns into the river, within thirty feet of which, on a low bluff, the fort was placed. Some things thought to be useful were buried by the claimants at various points on the banks of the river, such as spades, big chains and much lead, some boxes full of musket balls, etc. A great number of the Indian warriors had been killed in the siege, and they had been deposited in a mound two miles above the fort, on the bank of the river.

After the time of my arrival at Cotton Gin, the old chief hired a Virginian to build a water-mill for him, and the fall of the river (the place where the dam had to be put in) was near the burial mound. After the dam had been planked, they threw in from both sides a quantity of earth; thus the mound was entirely removed and wheeled onto the dam. It was a dry, sandy soil, and the bones, which were in a high state of preservation, were wheeled in with the clay, and no Indian—and the old ones all knew whose bones they were—said or seemed to care anything about the use they were put to. Part of the mound had been carried away before I saw it, so a correct estimate of the number of skeletons could not be had. From the account given by the workmen and what I saw in what was left of the mound, there must have been near two thousand. The mound was twenty feet high, circular, and about fifty feet thick at the base. The dead had been placed in circular layers, in double rows on the five lower tiers. Many of the bones were broken, some shattered into splinters. Many of the skulls had regular bullet holes in them. There were also many sound, well-preserved crania, and although I had heard nothing about craniognomy in those days [1825],[14] my attention was strongly attracted to the great variety of forms that was presented by the multitude of skulls as they were being rolled out with the sand. The Choctaws, with whom I had resided so long, had long ago related to me the history of the destruction of the French fort up near *Tanuptokche*. Their account was that after the Chickasaws had been twice repulsed, they called on the Choctaws, who went to their assistance in great numbers. Then, with much difficulty and loss of men, the Indians succeeded in destroying every living creature in the fort and burning all the property they couldn't carry away. The contents of the excavated mound showed that more Choctaws than Chickasaws had been killed, which *Itewaumba* said was easily accounted for. The traditional account of the affair is that there were four Choctaws to three Chickasaws engaged at the last effort—when the fort fell. I selected some fairly typical skulls of the two nations, and preserved them in my cabinet many years. The Choctaw cranium of that period, was flattened on top.[15] The Chickasaw head had not been distorted. To separate the skulls of the two nations was very readily done.

During the year 1826, a man by the name of John Bickerstaff[16] launched a flat boat, half a mile above Cotton Gin Port, and in preparing the way for the purpose, he removed to a considerable depth a portion of the river bank. While prosecuting the work, he came to a deposit of musket balls, amounting to 500 pounds. The shape of the hole they were found in was square, showing that when placed there, they were in a box. I procured a spike pole, and in my boat went up to the fort, intending to make a search for the brass cannons the chief told me had been rolled into the river at that place. But on a careful examination of the premises I found that the river had moved westwardly a little more than its entire width, and that what was then the bed of the river now underlay a bank of sand overgrown with birch and willow. So I didn't sound for the guns.

That is the traditional history of this attempt of the French to establish a colony on the Tombecbee River, three hundred and fifty miles above Mobile, long before any Americans had ever seen that portion of the country. It is very probable that (unless it can be found in France) this is the only account of the fate of that unfortunate experiment. That the old chief's statement is true is abundantly proven by the number of small cannon found in the Chickasaw country after they had sold their lands—their country—to the United States. I saw seven of their guns, with plenty of balls and some twelve pound shot, which was the cause of my attempt to search for the brass guns said to be rolled into the river. The 500 pounds of musket balls found buried in the bank of the river just below the fort is additional testimony in favor of the statement of the chief. That the colony was numerous is, I think, satisfactorily demonstrated by the great number of skeletons found in the monumental grave of the slain Indian warriors. The number of cannon found, and balls suited to larger guns not found, and the amount of surplus musket balls, with pits, embankments, and other signs of heavy works that were still to be seen in 1825, all go to establish the authenticity of the account given by the Chief *Itewaumba*.

CHAPTER FIVE

First the Patient, Then the Doctor

^PI had four children then [c. 1825],¹ and ^MI rented some houses at Cotton Gin for my family to dwell in. The houses were good and comfortable enough, but the family continued unhealthy. I soon discovered that it would not do to try to keep them there. So I went out into the hill country and selected a quarter section of public land ^Pwith a cold spring of freestone water, eleven miles above Cotton Gin, on the dry line between the Chickasaw lands and the United States. The river was the line between the Indians and white people, to a few hundred yards above Cotton Gin. At that point General Coffee, returning from the Battle of New Orleans, had crossed the river, cutting his way through the wilderness towards Nashville, Tennessee. This trace was afterwards made a dividing line [the "dry line"] betwixt the two peoples.² It was on this trace where I settled my family, and ^Mhere among the clean, uncropped grass, in high, dry and open woods, timbered with oak, hickory, chestnut and tall pines, with a gushing spring of pure, good, cool water, the children soon recovered their health. This was altogether a lovely situation. We resided there eight years. And—Oh! while I write, the crowding reminiscences that cluster around memory's aged dome, good and bad, swell this old heart with oppressive emotions.

^PThe trace had diverged from the river eight miles at the point where I settled. Neither Indians nor whites dwelt between the trace and the river bottom. A heavy canebrake and beech timber clothed the low grounds, which was two miles wide, and at least fifteen miles in extent upwards. Among the settlers along the trace there were but few hunters, and this grand unoccupied space of two hundred square miles was my hunting ground for

fifteen years. Game of all kinds that inhabit that latitude were plentiful there. And that prong of the river, which, though it was the main branch of the Tombecbee, did not (on an average) exceed fifty yards in width, seemed to work its passage through that dense canebrake and overlapping beech trees laboriously. Having never been fished any, it was well stocked with a great variety of good fish.

And there were found in that extensive, unfrequented dark bottom many beavers and otters. I have many times, when camped in the thick cane of a frosty night, heard the beavers in low conversation, swimming near the shore as they passed my camp. The first time I heard a beaver come talking along, I was certain it was a human voice until they came very near, and I found they were in the water, and then one of them slapped his tail close by my place. I have, when camping on the banks of the undisturbed water courses in all new countries, occasionally heard them, but only in clear, frosty weather and at night. Beavers who inhabit the rivers do not build houses to dwell in. Instead, they select a high bank, bore a hole at low water mark, and working in the bank eight or ten feet above the level of the river, there widen out a den until the cavity is large enough to accommodate the family. They make themselves very comfortable beds by carrying plenty of dry leaves into their sleeping apartments.

But when they choose a pond, either natural or artificial, to reside in, they construct a house in the shallow water towards the shore. In size it is eight or ten feet in diameter, circular and conic, twenty inches to two feet above water. It has two floors, one in the water the other just above. To the lower apartment there is a circular floor, half of which is visible above water. There is also another outlet at the back part of this room, opening in the water two feet beneath the surface. The upper story is a comfortable little apartment, having a full bed of dry leaves, with a hole through one side of the floor, immediately over the submerged passage. The entire fabric is composed of mud, leaves and trash, which seems to have been collected from the bottom of the pond in which it is located. I have demolished several of these beaver houses, but never at the proper time to find a young one; nor have I ever found anything laid up for food. As to their young, I think it quite probable that the beaver, who possess so much sagacity and cautiousness, would not risk their young in an exposed mud house; but would construct their lying-in apartments in some safe bank.

Here the Tombecbee River had many nice deep places in it, containing blue catfish, buffalo, red-horse, very large black bass, and many species of perch. In this country we call all the small flat fish perch—white, red, yellow, black, or ringed like a coon's tail. Opposite my place of abode, and eight miles distant, a large cypress (*Cupressus [Chamaecyparis] thyoides*) log had fallen across the river, forming a very convenient bridge to pass to the other side upon. This was my fishing place, and was known and called the "cypress log." I have had many rich scaffolds of dried fish and venison, turkeys and honey at the cypress log. Five miles above the cypress log was a shallow, shoaly place, and immediately above this shoal there set in deep, still water, which continued seven or eight miles. The year 1828 was exceedingly dry, and the river became very low—favorable for the Indian method of fishing, which I will now describe.

It was about the middle of August, when *Itewaumba,* the old chief, sent me an invitation to attend the grand national picnic, for which purpose the Chickasaws were already beginning to assemble at the deep river, above the Paineyigabee shoal.[3] Two or three days after the invitation came, I went to the appointed place and was surprised to find such a multitude of men, women and children. My old friend *Itewaumba* was there, having his three wives and their thirty children with him. Many of them were grown young men and women, including three married ones. With this big family I tarried during the feast. They were a clever people with whom I had been long familiar.

It was to be a national feast, and every one came who was able to travel. They told me that there were on the ground four thousand and four people, all Chickasaws. They were camped along the shore the whole length of the deep water; and those who were not out in the woods digging and preparing the buckeye root (*Aesculus rubra*)[4] were making wide, low scaffolds to barbecue fish on. Except the old men and boys under sixteen years, every male had to furnish a basket of finely beat up buckeye root. The basket contained about fifty-five pounds. Some females having no husband also brought baskets full. Soon after my arrival it was stated that the buckeye was all there, and the *castihulos* (medicine men or priests) sent out word that the medicine had worked very favorably, and the buckeye root must be put into the river at an hour before sunset. The time came, and in they went with their baskets full of fish poison, and plunging, or rather churning these baskets violently as they moved along, distributed the pulverized root everywhere the whole length of the deep hole. Now they waited for the medicine to work.

The Indians danced nearly all night, so they might know when to begin to take out the fish. Fires were kindled under all the scaffolds before sunrise, and everything was ready to cook the fish, which were visible everywhere on the surface of the water, not dead but feebly moving about on their backs. No one attempted to touch a fish until the medicine men proclaimed that the time had come. It was quite perceptible that the young people were becoming impatient, and the whole ground was beginning to work with many curious water bugs and small terrapins, and things I had never seen before. At 8 o'clock, the signal came for the work to begin, and into the river plunged the young people, male and female, who had long been holding themselves ready for it.

In a very short time every scaffold was covered with all sorts of fish. The elderly people were attending to the cooking, whilst the young folks took them out of the river. When enough had been cooked for breakfast, a signal whoop came from the camp of the medicine men, which meant that everyone must come out of the water and commence the feast. Instantly the river was evacuated, the scaffolds surrounded, and the "fiesta" began. By this time the entire ground along the river bank was covered with scale fish of all the kinds belonging to the river, in amazing quantities. My friend had told his eldest unmarried daughter to cook some of the perch after the American fashion for his friend here, who did not like Indian cooking. She prepared a panful very well, brought them to me with some bread and coffee, and then told me that in a few minutes orders would come for them to use their spears and bows to take the strong fish with. She continued, "As you will not want to go into the muddy water, let me have your nice bow and arrow to fish with." Of course I let her have it. She went off delighted, showing it to all she met. In less than twenty minutes after, there was a great shout a hundred yards down the river, in which I could hear the words *suu-*

neh mingo (king fish), and soon a shouting crowd of youngsters came in sight, vociferating the praise of the young woman who had my bow and arrow. She, in the midst of the noisy gang, was hurrying onward, carrying the king fish still transfixed with the arrow. Everybody who saw her with it shouted flattering praises. She brought it to me, highly pleased.

Soon the signal came for them to use their spears and arrows, with orders to finish taking out the fish as soon as possible, and for the cooking and drying of them to be hurried, for tomorrow they would start home and the fish must be ready to pack. All that day and till late at night the scaffolds were kept full of fish. The fish were not scaled, only disembowelled, and placed immediately over the fire. There were some or another of them eating all day. They did not get all the fish out till near night. It was a little curious to observe the different degrees of power amongst the fish to resist the deleterious effects of the poison. The perch and small scale fish came first, then the trout family, suckers, all the scale fish. Then the blue cats, then the big, fat yellow cats, then the mud cats and eels, and lastly the soft-shell turtles and loggerheads. Of these last there were many, and the Indians were very proud of them.

I did not know before that a deep hole in the river could be so densely populated. When they had cleaned the river of the fish, all hands attended to the fires, and they ate and danced and cooked and made up packs of dried fish until midnight, when the fish were all dried and bundled, ready for an early start in the morning. It never can be known how much those 4,000 Indians ate. Every family carried off a pretty fair pony-load of dried fish, and the ground for some distance was working with small terrapins and creeping insects that had crawled out of the suffocating water.

ᴾA few days after the big fish feast, the white people had appointed a big bear hunt to take place in the same portion of the Tombecbee beach and canebrake bottom. There ten or twelve men and a big train of dogs of all sizes and shapes and breeds, from the great sheep-killing cur through all races of dogs—except the good one—down to the ill-treated suck-egg hound. Of course I went, and we had not been placed at our stands but a little while, until the row amongst the dogs began.

Soon the rifles began to crack and the whole bottom was filled with an awful uproar. The bottom was filled with foxes, rabbits and deer, and every dog seemed to be in full chase after his own game, and they were roaring through the densely-set canebrake in all directions.

It was a remarkably warm day, and I was sorry that I had consented to expose myself in that close cane, with such a pack of howling, untrained dogs, and a set of men that were blazing away at the deer, or even a fox if it ran by them. In a bear hunt the rule is to shoot nothing but bear. There was, however, an old man in the crowd who had two trained bear dogs, and they paid no attention to foxes nor deer either; and in the course of an hour had scented up the big old hog-killing bear, who by his frequent depredations on their swine, had caused this large turn-out of men and dogs. They jumped him half a mile from my stand, and seemed to be going up the river. Presently they turned towards me and came near me, then they turned again up the river. Now thought I, if I can reach the Paneigby [sic] crossing in time, I can get a chance at the monster. I was already quite warm. It was about one o'clock, and a mile and a half to the crossing. I ran violently through the thick canes and little tough rope vines that thwarted my path. The dogs were in full cry, not far to my left all the way up. I could see I was gaining ground, which encouraged me to let on a little more steam; and I reached the river bank within a few steps of the ford and still heard the cry of the dogs.

I did not suffer any severe inconvenience while I was running; but I had not stopped five seconds until I found there was no air in the world, not enough for a single breath. I felt like I was immersed in flame. I was standing on the very brink of the river bank and had already cast aside my gun and shot pouch. Turning my face toward the opening of the river to see if there was any wind in that direction, I saw the water, and being about the dying point, half conscious and half fainting, I tumbled into it. The water was three feet deep, and the effort that was required to keep my head out of it for some minutes put my physical force up to the last notch.

It wasn't long till I found my strength increasing so far that I made shift to get hold of the branch of a river-bank shrub that hung down to the water, and my surroundings did not seem so hot. But my heart was wallowing and struggling so heavily that it shook my whole frame, and from the sound in my ears it seemed like the blood was forcibly squirting out of them. I was sensible that I needed help but could make no noise with my voice, and I was beginning to feel pretty lonesome. When I could stir about a little and move the heated water from around my body, I would for a little while feel better. But the laboring heart, which I could distinctly hear, did not abate the violence of its motion in the least, and I began to realize the fact that I was permanently injured. For such a powerful man as I was but half an hour before, it was a sad reflection, and I was thinking of the propriety of letting the pendent limb go. Then two of the straggling hunters coming along up the river found my hat and gun and shot-bag scattered around, and they called. My throat was out of fix when I tried to answer. My voice was gone! But I made out to agitate the water a little, and they found me.

I couldn't get up, and they had to get into the river and carry me, or rather floated me along up to the ford and across to my own side of the river, where they made me a thick bed of the beech branches and laid me on it. It relieved my limbs very much when I could straighten them out and rest in the horizontal position. But my heart continued to wallow and labor, and there was coming on a disagreeable, tired ache in that region. I had remained submerged over an hour, and my skin was getting a little too cool. After being taken out and my clothes getting nearly dry, however, a reaction took place, a high fever supervened, and the man that remained with me said, "I think your heart is about to break its bounds now."

They carried me home the next day, and I was utterly helpless. My condition was made worse daily by the kind attentions of my medical friends who flocked around me from some distance. ᴹThere I lay and fretted at the hard fortune. The doctors were all my friends and they came often to see me and to note the progress of the case. Their opinions and prescriptions were as varied as their faces. Some were of the opinion that it was enlargement of one of the oracles [auricles]; others, that the symptoms indicated aneurism of the arch of the aorta; others, that it was enlargement of the heart itself. One thought that it was a softening of the substance of the heart. So one and another of them, first and last, suggested treatment for all the heart complaints known to the faculty.[5] Bleeding was the remedy most universally believed in by them. And I also had more faith in it, so I bled myself every day. In 20 days I had taken 22 ½ pounds of blood; and hoping to salivate myself had taken 10 gr. doses of calomel daily and rubbed on myself 1 ½ pounds of strong blue ointment. It did not salivate me; but the depletion of the lancet and mercury had laid me pretty low.

The doctors all continued their visits and advice. It was an interesting case they said, and they wanted to watch it through all its changes and variations. Nothing they prescribed seemed to act on my side of the question. I lay on the floor, and became weaker, worse and worse, for the term of three years. At this period my wife began to grumble at the doctors. She declared that they were doing me no good; indeed, she said, they were killing me, and besides, they and their horses were eating us up. She said I ought to try to get rid of them some way.

"Well, how am I to get rid of them?" I calmly asked.

"Run away from them. Go to Columbus and see Dr. Hand.[6] Let him class your complaint," she replied. I told her to fix me up and go part of the way with me, and I would go.

We set out the next day, and I reached Columbus in three days of painful travel. My wife returned on the third morning, leaving me but ten miles more to travel, and my brother Garland accompanied me that distance.

I called on Dr. Hand, and after he had made a careful examination of my case, he asked me what all those doctors said about my complaint. I told him that no two of them, when alone with me, expressed the same opinion. He then inquired what I thought of it myself.

I replied that I was certain that it came from excessive overheat; that from the heavy palpitation and floundering sensation at the time I was overheated, I thought it quite probable that some of the blood vessels about the heart, or the heart itself, had been considerably strained, if not somewhat distended, which strain and distention had caused the irregular pulsation and pain I experienced at the time, and which I felt more or less even now. "Some of the painful symptoms I experience now, may be attributed to the heart's sympathy with the stomach, which has been greatly injured by the excessive use of mercury and cathartics. And now," said I, "You have heard the various opinions of the other physicians, with my opinion, and you have carefully examined the indications yourself; and as yet have expressed no opinion. Let me hear what you think of it."

"Well," said he, "I think that you know more about the case than any one else can know. Here is the key of my shop, in which you will find a choice selection of fresh medicines. Go there and help yourself to such of them as you may think your case requires, and welcome. I may at any time counsel with you and suggest remedies, but do you follow the dictates of your own impressions in the case, for they are better than any other." I accepted the kind offer of my good friend, Dr. Hand, and boarded at a hotel near his shop. I remained at Columbus five months, after which I had improved somewhat.[7] I returned home, but was not able to do any kind of business. ᴾBy the time I was able to examine the books of my mercantile establishment, my partner Pitchlynn Jr. had been murdered, the accounts all run out of date, and the store had been plundered.[8] After I auctioned off the remnants of my goods and the good house, I was penniless and owed $5,000 to my suppliers in Mobile.

ᴹMy family was suffering for want of proper substance, yet on my books I had $20,000 due me, by perhaps five hundred different men. But it had been three years and a half since these accounts had been made. They were nearly all on solvent men, so I sent a boy around to try to get some money from them. He returned with a dollar. I then made a contract with a magistrate, for experiment, to sue some of them, and if he made no collections, he was to charge no costs. So I selected forty of the best of the accounts and sued on them. Processes were issued, and the day of trial came. The law of limitation in Mississippi is or was two years, and these forty men, that I had selected for the best in the country, pled the limitation act, to a man.

This experiment proved to me that I needn't try any more of them. I let that twenty thousand dollars—the labor of seven years of the prime of my life—go for naught. Many of these people were my near neighbors, and knew how poor and destitute my condition was. I did not possess the means to procure even sugar to put in my sassafras tea, and they knew it. They acted towards me as if I had done something to offend them.

They quit coming to see me. I needed everything, and I thought if I had a piece of venison it would strengthen me. So I made shift to creep out to a water hole in the woods, a mile and a half from home, where I lay and watched till night, and, feeling too feeble to try to walk home, I remained and slept some at the root of a big red oak. Morning came, and I felt better and stronger than I had felt since I was diseased. I concluded that I felt so well, I would watch the water hole another day and in the calm, uninterrupted stillness of the forest (it was on the Indian side of the line) try to study out the cause of my improvement. I had eaten nothing since breakfast the day before, and my mind had begun to lay my sluggish condition and the tardy progress of my recovery to too much or improper food.

While I was sagely investigating this proposition, I discovered in the distance and coming towards the waterhole, a very large deer. From the appearance of his horns, he was a very old one. Instantly I was all anxiety and vigilance. But when he came nearer, I could see that he limped pretty badly and that he was very poor. I did not shoot him, but suffered him to come to the water unmolested. I supposed that in his crippled condition, he had done without water as long as he could, and that he would drink heartily. But I was mistaken. He sipped of it very lightly. I wondered at that, and my wonder was increased, when he ate but two or three of the green brier leaves, which is the natural food of the deer and which grew abundantly on the bank of the water hole. I knew he must be hungry and thirsty and yet he partook very sparingly of both food and water. He hobbled away on three legs to a little copse of brushwood, where he had concealed himself and lay down, to ruminate the scant amount of brier leaves he had taken.

Whether this poor wounded stag knew what he was so abstemious for or not was a thing I was not able to ascertain. But it excited in my mind a new train of thought. Before I left my hiding place, I supposed I had penetrated the secret of the old buck's abstemious conduct and had formed a resolution to feed equally light and sparingly.

So I set out for home and, notwithstanding the fact that I had taken no food during the past thirty hours, I made the trip with much more ease than when I went out. I reached home about dinner time and found them greatly alarmed at my unaccountable absence, and several of the neighbors, whom my wife had called in, were already out in search of me.

I fired off my gun twice in quick succession, and told my wife that I was hungry. She replied, "Dinner is ready, come in and eat." I said, "No, I have had instructions on a new method of dieting, and I intend to commence it this day." She inquired what it was to consist of. In reply, I told her it was to consist of one corn meal waffle and a cup of sassafras tea, with a heaping teaspoonful of sugar, three times a day. She was very much opposed to the new dietetic rule, declaring that it would thin my blood and starve me to death. She prepared the waffle and tea, and I made my dinner on it. I then slept till nearly night, for I was greatly fatigued, and the gnats had prevented me from sleeping quietly the night before. Supper time came, and with it the corn waffle and sassafras tea. I arose the ensuing morning in a rage of hunger. But feeling stronger and much improved, I had the waffle and tea for breakfast, and immediately took my gun and set out for the water hole again, leaving instructions not to alarm the neighbors again, if I should fail to return at night.

I was more successful this time. I found a bee tree, and killed a very good doe. I could not get the honey nor carry the venison home. I had made shift to dress the deer, and to hang the quarters on the bushes around. Night had by this time set in, and I was extremely hungry. I kindled a fire, and was roasting the deer's milt, when I heard some person whoop, and I answered and soon my oldest son Lycurgus and a young man who was living with us rode up to my camp. I told them before I left home where I intended to hunt, and they knew the place. But I would not go with them until my deer's milt was done. It got done presently, and, although I had neither bread nor salt to eat with it, I thought then and it seems so yet, that it was the most palatable piece of meat I had ever tasted. I was afraid to eat the whole milt, and I wrapped what I had left in some brier leaves and took it home with me. On the ensuing morning I was still improving, and I took my waffle and tea, but none of the venison.

For two or three months I continued to go about in the woods alone. To be alone suited me best, for I could uninterruptedly think over and weigh and measure the forlorn poverty-stricken condition that had possession of me. What my mind was working at was to think of some feasible shift for the support of my family of nine small children.

I had, during my whole life, done all my reading in medical works, and knew all that had been published on that subject; and, had felt seriously inclined to set up shop and try to make a living in that way. But I had no medicine nor the means to procure it. I continued to poke about in the woods, finding bee trees and killing as many deer as were needed to supply our table. It was on the Chickasaw side of the line where I hunted, a wild swampy country, on the Bull Mountain fork of the Tombecbee River, and it was full of deer, bear and turkeys.

It often happened, when I had wandered too far that I did not return home, but selecting a dry place by the side of a log, or at the foot of some large tree, slept there. If I had a deer I would cut it up and hang the good pieces on the bushes, and let the wolves fight for the rest of it. In that wilderness country the wolves were very numerous. I have many times heard them fighting over the fragments of my venison, snapping their teeth, howling and making so much noise that I could not sleep well. I could sometimes creep near enough to their frantic revels to get a shot at them, and in that way silenced several of them.

Some people said I was going deranged. Others that I was badly hypoed [suffering from hypochondria]. They were all indebted to me and would not pay me, and as they were ashamed to come about me, I was not much pestered by them. At length I matured a plan that I thought would make money, if I could succeed in getting it into action. The project was to raise a company of ball players in the Choctaw Nation, travel with them and exhibit them in their ball plays and war dances.[9] The Choctaw chiefs had recently sold their country and the common people were very much dissatisfied. I thought it was a good time to raise a company of ball players, and to find out all about it I wrote to my good friend John Pitchlynn Sr., desiring him to feel of the Choctaws on the subject, and to communicate to me the result of his efforts.

In the meantime, the neighbors solicited me to take a school. Fearing that my Indian project might prove a failure, I agreed to take a school for them; and they immediately went to work, building a house for the purpose. They had made up the number of pupils I had required and I was to open school the ensuing Monday. On the previous Saturday I received a letter from my friend Pitchlynn, that *Fulahooma*,[10] the bearer of the letter, had made up a company of forty choice ball players who would assemble at the Oakslush spring[11] the ensuing Monday, 28 November, 1829, and that *Fulahooma* would carry me down to the place where the intended meeting was to be held.

It was forty miles distant. I was anxious that no failure should take place, and, having nothing to arrange, I was on the road in an hour. As we journeyed, *Fulahooma* told me that the Choctaws were mad with their chiefs, that in their present discontented state he found them all willing to go with me. He said the difficulty would be in getting rid of the surplus.

We were on the ground in due time; and by 12 o'clock there were upwards of four hundred ball players assembled. We built up the council fire and held a big talk. They were all familiarly acquainted with me; and they told me that their headmen had sold their homes and made them very poor; that they were willing to travel with me any length of time, just for their victuals and clothes. They thought that four hundred was not too many, and begged me to let them all go. Poor fellows, I didn't know what to do, or how to escape from the dilemma so as not to give offense.

They were all hungry, and I got my friend Pitchlynn to have three large beeves driven to the place and slaughtered for them to eat. I next proposed a draft. I would take every tenth man. *Fulahooma* had privately engaged forty brag players and had given me their names. These names were put into a hat, a little boy called up, and instructed how to draw. Then Pitchlynn explained to them that the draft would take only every tenth man, and, to make it fair, the little boy had been selected to draw out the names. There were 365 blank tickets put in the hat. The drawing commenced and perhaps twenty blanks came first. Then came one with a name, which I wrote down. The Indians could not see into the deception, but, calling it a lottery, directed by the Great Spirit, thought it was the fairest thing in the world. They were all satisfied with the result, and went to cooking and eating the fat beef I had procured for them.

By light the next morning I set my face towards the east and, passing through Columbus, Miss., went up the military road with my forty Choctaw ball players. Well, I traveled and exhibited those Indians eight months, but made only money enough to feed and clothe the company decently. I started without money, and me so weak and feeble that the Indians would lift me and set me on my pony every morning. I camped out all the time, and though it was a very severe winter, my health and strength improved every day. I could scarcely walk when I started, but on our return, one of the Indians having crippled himself, I let him ride my horse and I walked 500 miles.

I took all the Indians back to their own country, got them five pounds of bacon each and discharged them, well satisfied with me and our long journey. They dubbed me *Hopigeh cheto* (Big leader),[12] and we separated forever. During our travels through the States, they often said that if I was to die, they would not be able to find the way home through all the fields and fences, and they watched and treated me with great care and tenderness. That I got them back home was to them a wonder.

I made no money to carry home by the experiment, but the improvement in my health and activity was ample remuneration for the hardships I underwent and the eight months' absence from home. I found my wife working and scuffling and fighting poverty as well as she could. She had been spinning and weaving and had the children well clothed, and they had not consumed the corn and hogs I had provided for them before I went off with the Indians.

I was strong enough to work some, but the time for planting a crop had passed, and I could think of nothing to do that would pay. In fact, the long eight months' worrying with those drunken Indians had to a degree blunted my energies, and I felt no inclination to work. Indeed I felt more like I needed quiet rest. Accordingly I took my rifle and retired to the canebrake and the dark, lonely forests.

I would go out by light, or even earlier of a morning, and generally get in by dark, with as much meat of some kind as I could pack. If I got more than I could carry home on my back, I would hang it up, and next morning make Lycurgus go out with the pony and bring it home. I killed more meat and found more honey than the family could consume. And, in that solitary manner I spent my days; the nights I spent at home with my family, as cheerfully as I could. But my spirit was not easy. It wanted a wide field for action, and during all the lonely days spent in these dark woods, my mind was carrying on a sharp investigation, discussing all possible subjects for a livelihood. I thought of many things to do, but none suited.

I was not now, as at Tuscaloosa, able to take hold of the whip-saw or any other heavy work. There were but few things that my strength would allow me to undertake. Some people suggested that peddling in drygoods would suit my condition best. But I did not possess the means to make the outfit, much less pay for a stock of goods to start with. I continued to hunt and spend my time in the woods, until about the first of August, 1830, when my nearest neighbor, William Wall,[13] an elderly gentleman who indulged considerably in the use of ardent spirits, sent for me to tell him what to do. He was very sick, and also considerably alarmed.

He had some remnants of medicine in his old medicine chest. I hunted amongst them and, finding some that suited his case, relieved him. He was very highly pleased, for he thought his time had come. He begged me to remain all night with him for fear of another attack. In the course of the night he remarked to me, "You know more about this disease and its antidote than any of the doctors in this country, and I am surprised that you don't get you some medicine and set up shop. You are needy enough, and you are capable and would soon get a good practice."

I told him I had been thinking of that, but it required money to set up shop, as he called it, and that was an article I did not possess. "Well," said he, "You are too modest. I have been waiting for you to ask me to lend you some." My reply was, "I can't do that. It seems to me to be too precarious a prospect to borrow money to prepare for the practice of medicine in a community where nearly all the people are indebted to me, and because I didn't sue and collect it of them before the law of limitation had expired, they refused to pay. Furthermore, in a country already overstocked with poor doctors, there are too many chances against the probability for me ever to be able to pay it back."

"I'll risk that," said he. "So here is $100 to begin with. Take my horse tomorrow or next day; go up to Tuscumbia and get you some medicine and go to work with it."

Robert Gordon,[14] a Scotchman, merchant in Cotton Gin, a man I had privately relieved several times from a pretty bad condition, heard what Captain Wall was urging me to do, and he, being acquainted with the druggist at Tuscumbia, wrote a letter of introduction in which he stated to the druggist that if I needed more medicine than what money I had would pay for, to put it up and charge the same to him. Several other people encouraged me by assuring me that I should have their practice.

Under these circumstances, which I looked upon as favorable indications, I concluded to try it, and taking my friend Wall's fine horse and his money, set out on the 10th of August. I laid in $80 worth of drugs and furniture; and it looked like a poor chance to make support for my family on. But when I had set up, I was surprised at its being so much more than any doctor's shop anywhere around. It showed me that they were poorer and were doing business on a smaller scale than I had ever supposed it possible. The neighbors all flocked in to see the grand drug store, as they styled it, and they looked upon it as a perfect wonder. They said it was no stingy affair and promised safety and that they should feel easier hereafter when the sickly season came.

I soon had calls. But the only horse I owned was a small black Indian pony, worth $15. He was an excellent hunting horse, for he would track a deer equal to the best trained dog. Besides he was a very rapid pacer. Still he was a poor thing to practice on. Riding on a borrowed horse, my wife went on a visit to Columbus, with Lycurgus on the pony. At that time races were going on at Columbus, and one of the racers, having lost a heavy sum on one of his horses, was offended with him. Seeing Lycurgus pacing around on the pony, he took a liking to him and offered to trade the delinquent race horse for him. Lycurgus informed Mrs. Lincecum of the proposition, whereupon she sent for the man and made the swap. His horse Ned was a fine one. I kept him seven years, and rode him until my legs had grown to fit his back. Everybody finally knew "Old Ned." He was ten years old when I got him, and in his seventeenth year I rode him to Texas, and explored the country west of the Brazos six months. He carried me safely back home and, feeling that he had done enough for me, I set him free. He had helped me to make many thousands of dollars.

With my new, good horse, Ned, I attended cases almost every day, and when Christmas came I had a pretty good crib of corn, plenty of pork in my smokehouse, had paid my friend Wall the $100 he had loaned me to start with, and had upwards of $300 of good accounts on my books. I went round telling the people that for me to have power to serve them scientifically, I must have more medicine. They were all highly pleased, and paid me every cent they owed me. Some of them offered to lend me money, if I had not enough. My wife, when I got home with the money I had collected, put on her prettiest, blandest smile, and declared that we were no longer inhabitants of the dreary vale of poverty, that we were still young, and should ere long enjoy the comforts we had been so long and so unjustly deprived of.

"But what shall we do about the $5,000 debt that is hanging over us?" I asked. "Why pay it the first thing you do," said she. "You are my own dear wife," said I, "And as fast as I get money into my hands, I intend to pay it over to my creditors until I am a free man again." The men to whom I was indebted all resided in Mobile. I took what money I had and went down to see them. There were three of them. I got them all together and made a clear, correct statement of the cause of my delinquency, told them that I had started to work again, what it was I had done, and showed the money that I had made and proposed to divide amongst them. I also proposed to renew my notes, which had already run out of date, for the balance due. They all looked at me for a moment, and then arose from their seats and passed into another room, saying as they retired, they would be back directly.

They remained away a half hour perhaps, and as they were entering the room where I was sitting again, one of them inquired, "How many children have you, Lincecum?" I replied, "Nine, all small." "Have they got on hand plenty to eat and wear," he asked. "I have," said I, "provided corn and pork enough to do them five or six months. We have a few cows to give us milk, and their mother, with her wheel and loom has succeeded in clothing them during my period of affliction."

"We have had your case under consultation, and for reasons

which we shall not divulge to you, we have arrived at the following conclusions:

"First, to make all safe, we propose that you renew your notes."

"Write them out," said I, "I would pay them if I could."

They drew out the old notes and one of them began to cast up the interest, but the other rebuked him and said, "Let the new notes call for no more than the original amount." And in that way they were drawn, and I signed them immediately, thanking them at the same time for their leniency.

"Now," said they, "we propose introducing you to our favorite druggist. Order him to put a bill of such articles as your business requires, vouch for the payment and let you take your little scrap of cash back with you to supply your family with such articles of food and raiment as they were formerly accustomed to, and if you need any goods for family use, one or another of us can supply you on as good terms as anybody else; and we can wait till it suits your convenience to pay for them."

The allopathic system[15] needs no great amount of medicines. I got $100 worth of the crude concentrated poisons, $150 worth of nice furniture for a practice shop, 3 dozen gallon bottles and all the smaller vessels in proportionate quantities down to pints, with an equal number of glass jars of the same sizes and sufficient instruments for a country practice. I showed the bill to my three friends. They observed, "You are quite cautious, Sir."

I got it all home safely and worked diligently every day until I got them all labeled, filled with superior preparations and set up. My customers came to see the wonder, and said that it looked like I should be able to encounter disease in any and all its forms. I could discover from their remarks that I had pursued the proper course, that the money I had expended would soon come back to me. It was soon widespread that I had more medicine than all the doctors in the county, and that the man who understood the profession well enough to apply all the remedies in that shop was no ordinary doctor. In accordance with their exalted opinions of my preparations for their necessities, they came for me, and it was but a short time till I was riding day and night and my circle widening till I went often forty to fifty miles. Many cases of chronic disease came to stay with me. For want of house room I could take only one or two at a time.

A year had passed since I left Mobile. I had made and collected over $2000. I went to Mobile again, paid my friends $1000, also my medicine debt, and cashed a considerable bill for such drugs as I needed for another season. I also bought dry goods for family use. In that sparsely settled hill country there were no schools, and my children, six of them,[16] were getting to be the proper age for the seminary. As there was no chance where I resided to send them to school, I conceived the idea of taking them and their mother down to Columbus and getting them into a house, where she could board them, while I would remain with my shop and supply them with provisions. In accordance with this plan, I went to Columbus, bought a lot and a sufficient amount of lumber to build a good single-story house with a parlor and two rooms, all amply large for the family.

I then carried them down and entered six of them at school the first day. My success in this enterprise had made me quite happy. Everybody in Columbus assured me that the male and female seminaries were conducted in the very best style. I returned to my shop with a redoubled resolution to exert all my resources to supply in full quantities everything for their support. When I got back, my friend Capt. Wall had built a house near his gate, in his yard, and invited me to put my medicine in it, and to come and live with him during the absence of my family.

I very cheerfully accepted his kind offer, and he gave me a room in his dwelling which I was to call my home. Being situated on the great thoroughfare from Tuscumbia to Cotton Gin Port, this was a much more convenient and easy place for my patrons to find than the one I had left. My practice increased daily. I would tell the people to pay a little flour or a little corn, and when the time came I would take three or four thousands of pork, and that, if in this way I should be able to keep my family supplied at Columbus, I would remain with them till the children were educated. They assured me that they would keep their supplies up; that one or another of them went down almost once a week and it would be no trouble to carry down supplies of flour, corn meal, bacon, etc., get my wife's receipt for the amount, and when they returned hand over such receipt to be placed to their credit.

By these means I was able to keep my family well supplied constantly. It was an unusually sickly season, and almost everybody became indebted to me. As their ill health had retarded the progress of the cotton crops, it obliged them for me to take a portion of their produce. After the family had gone down to Columbus, I sold my home place for $200[17] and remitted the same to my Mobile masters.

In November I concluded to go down and see how much the children had improved at the highly lauded seminary. I was so rejoiced at the success I had met with in my little plan for providing the means of educating my offspring that I rode down in a perfect glee of delight. I pictured to myself the pleasure I should experience on hearing their polished answers to the questions I should put to them that night. I grew more and more anxious as I neared the place to see and hear their manifestations of progress. I knew they were all sprightly minded children and I knew at such a grand institution they would be greatly improved.

At length I reached the house they resided in. They were all glad and so was I, and they were so full of narrative, telling of what they had seen there, the shows, races, fights, shooting encounters, etc., etc., that I concluded not to interrupt their historical accounts by an examination that night. Being anxious to ascertain how much they had learned, I did not wait long the next day before I began to interrogate them. I began by asking what they were studying. They answered, "Geography and history."

"What kind of history?" I inquired. "Well, it's just history," they said. "History of what?" I asked. "It's just history," was the reply.

"You say you are studying geography. Name the principal rivers in this State." They replied, "Oh, we don't study that. We study geography."

"Well, then, tell me the names of the largest river in the United States, and tell me also where the United States is located." They answered, "We don't study that. We just study geography and history."

I had strained every financial nerve I possessed in getting up a good house at Columbus for them to live in, and had exerted myself almost to the utmost to furnish provisions, clothing, etc., to keep them comfortable. And from the oft-repeated high reputation given the teachers in the newspapers, I had hoped much that I should experience the gratification of seeing some of the signs of it manifested in the progress of my children. But from their utter ignorance of the questions I put to them, I began to fear that all my hopes would end in disappointment. As I could find nothing out from them by my questions, I directed them to question each other as they did in school.

At this proposition they brightened up, and said they would show me now that they had learned something. After deciding who should ask the questions, they began:

Q. "Who was the first man?" A. "Adam."
Q. "Who slew his brother?" A. "Cain."
Q. "Who was the hairy man?" A. "Esau."

A great many other questions equally as foolish were asked. I was overwhelmed with disappointment. I felt that the whole world was a sham. My children, after six months' constant attendance on that highly praised institution, could answer no question of use. But they had been put on the road to salvation, and could tell who was "the hairy man."

Now, I never cared who was "hairy," nor did I believe that it would benefit my children to learn such infernal foolishness. I was deeply wounded in my feelings and expectations and I decided at once to take them away from the hypocritical place. Before night of that same day, I had engaged a carriage and two wagons. Having loaded the wagons before I slept, I was on the road before nine o'clock the next morning. I carried them back to the old settlement where my shop was. My friend Capt. Wall took eight or ten of his hands into the woods, cut and hewed out the timbers, and in the course of a month, with the assistance of the neighbors constructed a double log cabin, shop, smokehouse, kitchen and a stable on a forty acre tract of land he owned, in half a mile of his dwelling and made me a present of it. It was a good, healthy home.[18] I was proud of it, and went to work to improve it. I planted fruit trees, and made a three-acre garden which in a short time yielded fine supplies for our table.

About this time the alarm of the cholera reached the United States, and a very fatal type of dysentery pervaded the region of country we occupied.[19] They called it bloody flux, and it killed two to the hundred of the population. I was very successful in the treatment of this fatal complaint. I did not lose a case and they sent for me in a wide circle. Following this flux was a stubborn fever. A great many people died. I lost several important cases. In fact, I did not believe that any of it had been cured by any of the practitioners. Our remedies did not answer the indications.

The physicians were trying to make out to the people that it was a kind of plague that had got into the country. They lost a great many cases. I lost several. I began to suspect the treatment that was practiced, and watched the effects of our remedies very carefully. At length a large, muscular and very strong man, about thirty years of age, fell into my hands, and feeling a strong desire to restore him, I stayed with him and did my very best for him. He died under circumstances that left me but little grounds to doubt the fact that the calomel and other poisons I gave him hastened his dissolution. I was greatly discouraged. This strong man, with three others that fell under my treatment that season and the hundreds that were dying all around me in the hands of other physicians, convinced me that our remedies were impotent, or that they were even worse than that, for they seemed to increase the force of the disease. I felt tired of killing people, and concluded to quit the man-killing practice and try to procure a living by some other method. But when I came to reflect about the matter, I found I was not able to perform manual labor and that somehow or other my houseful of small children must be supported. I did not intend to practice the allopathic system any more, and I was at a loss to know how to proceed.

People came for me, but I refused to go, and I moped about two or three weeks till my mind finally settled on a plan. I had long felt the need of good medical works written by Southern practitioners. All our medical books had been composed by Northern practitioners, and their prescriptions really did not suit Southern complaints. So the plan I had conceived was to visit an Indian doctor of great reputation, who resided in the Six Towns, Choctaw Nation,[20] and try to get him to show me what he knew of medicine and disease. I knew that there were very few men among the Indians who pretended to any conclusive knowledge of the use of their remedial agents. The Indians all knew them, and it is just as natural for one of them, when he is sick, to go to the woods and get medicine to cure himself, as it is for him to go there when he is hungry to get something to eat. Yet there is occasionally a highly developed, philosophic intellect among them that collects and stores up all the useful knowledge he can get hold of, medicine and everything else. I had been raised and had spent the greater part of my life with the Indians, and I knew all about them.

I had, however, never seen the *Eliccha chito*[21] of the Six Towns, and I wrote a letter to P. Jurzong,[22] a half-breed, instructing him to see the doctor, and inquire of him if he would be willing to meet me somewhere in the woods, and stay with me until he had taught me his system of medical practice. If so, for him to say where he would meet me and what would be his terms; and report the same to me at his earliest convenience.

It was 200 miles from where I lived. However, in a month I received from friend Jurzong a very satisfactory letter. He informed me that the great Six Towns *Eliccha* would be extremely willing to teach what he knew about medicine before he died to somebody, and to a white man in preference to one of his own people, because the white man would place it on paper and preserve it. He would meet me at the middle of the day after twelve sleeps, at the black rock bluff on Noxuby river.[23] He also informed me that he would stay in the woods as long as I desired and that I must pay him 50 cents a day and find provisions for him.

It was seventy miles to the black rock bluff on Noxuby. I took my gun, some fish hooks and lines, a bushel of crackers and so arranged it as to be riding up to the appointed place precisely at 12 o'clock, and I fully expected to see the doctor come riding up on the opposite side of the river at the same time. Sure enough, there he came.

As soon as he discovered me, he hailed and said, "I know who you are, and what a pity it is you are a white man." "Why?" said I. "Because you would have made such a good Indian," he replied. At his request I crossed to his side, where we staked our horses, lay down in the shade, made up our acquaintance, and planned the course to pursue. We then dined on some scraps of cold victuals I had in a little wallet; saddled up and set out for a place five or six miles distant where there was good water and where we should sleep that night. As we rode off from the river, he observed to me, "You have a good looking gun, and the deer are very plentiful in this region. Turn off to the left there, travel in that direction about two miles, then turn to the right going directly north about four miles and you will come to a pretty little creek. I'll meet you there, and if you are a good hunter, you will bring me a piece of fresh meat for my supper."

I left him, and set out in accordance with his instructions, but had not progressed exceeding a mile before I shot a very fat buck, and saw many more. As soon as possible I cut out the back straps, and with the two hams packed up and went towards the designated camping place as fast as I could. In two hours and a half from the time we had parted I had found the pretty little running creek. I made a little scaffold and soon had the venison cooking. It was nearly dark when the old man rode up and re-marked, "It was by the delicious odor of your roasting meat that I found your camp. You are a mile higher up than I expected to find you." He staked out his horse, and I expected to see him go to the meat scaffold; but instead, he unrolled his specimens of medical plants and laid them in order on his right where he was sitting. He then took them up, one by one, described the kind of soil they were found in, their uses, the season to collect them and what other plants they were sometimes combined with. He would then lay it on his left; and so on until he got through with that day's collection. On my part, I wrote down all he said and preserved small specimens of each plant. As soon as this was completed, he went and ate a dog's bait of the venison without speaking a word. I also ate my supper of it, and I discovered that to find him plenty of meat could only be done where game was very abundant.

Every night he would have some specimens, and would at-tend to nothing else until he got through with his lecture. Then he would eat heartily if I had anything; if not, he did not com-plain or make any remarks. If I had nothing for our supper he knew the reason of it; and his mind had not been forced into the habit of making unreasonable demands. The nearest he came complaining during the six weeks we were out was once when we had been two days without anything to eat. As we rode along,

I asked him the name and uses of a plant he was getting. He replied, "Go and kill something to eat. You will be talking about your slack belt again to-night."

He seemed to be familiar with every branch and creek in the whole country. He directed me to go to the right a little, and in about four miles I would find a swampy little creek. He said, "Get a deer there for they are plentiful and come back to this little branch. I shall sleep here, the grass is good for the horses."

I went and found the creek and the swamp, but saw no deer. I heard a dog bark, and going to it, I found a hunter's camp and plenty of meat, dry and fresh. He also had some sweet potatoes. I told him what I was doing, and that the old *Eliccha chito* went through such a poor country that I could find no game. He replied, "It is just like the old doctor, for he don't care about eating anything." So I filled my wallet with potatoes, packed up a lot of nice dry venison, took a good fresh ham, gave the hunter (who took it very reluctantly) a dollar and returned to the camping place on the grassy branch.

The old man came before dark. I had been broiling some of the dry meat, and before he got near enough to see my fire, he inquired, "How did you kill the dry venison?" I asked how he knew it was dry.

"Oh," said he, "I smelt it a mile off."

We had a sumptuous supper and a pleasant night. After this manner we lived constantly in the woods until the old man had got through with his catalogue of medical plants.

He would not go to any house nor suffer me to do so. He said it would spoil the knowledge he was teaching, and make me forgetful. At the expiration of six weeks the old doctor told me there were no more medical plants this side of the Mississippi river for me to study; and that as soon as I would read and let him hear what I had put on the paper about what he had told me he would let me go to my own country.

I procured some fat pine and read a good deal that night. He corrected some errors—it was written in Choctaw—and added many things. We got through with the examination the next day at 10 p.m. He was greatly pleased. He took the manuscript and seemed to weigh it in his hands. "How strange it is," said he, "but it is true that this small bundle of *holisso* (paper) contains all the knowledge I ever possessed that is really of any account. Oh! if I had only the power to do that, I should have been one of the renowned men of the world. Will you keep it and take care of it?" he eagerly inquired.

"Oh, yes," said I, "I shall soon translate it into English. It will then be printed on a great number of papers and made so plain that everybody can understand it. I shall also state that *Eliccha chito* of *Okla hunale* taught it to me and everybody will read that too."[24]

"Well, well," said he, "that is wonderful. I am truly gratified. My old wasted heart is glad." I told him further that when the book should be completed, I would send him one, and he could get his friend Pierre Jurzong to read it for him, when he would see that the same words had been faithfully preserved.

"Then the time for me to go to the good hunting ground will be come," said he. Morning came. I paid him $21. He looked steadily at the money a few moments and then handed $10 of it back, saying, "You are a young man and will need this more than I shall. I would not have any of it, but at a little store on my road home are two very good blankets that I laid aside as I came up. I must pay for them." It was in vain that I urged him to keep all the money. He persisted in saying that he didn't need it.

So on that little branch, not far from the *Yak nubbe* old fields,[25] we shook hands most affectionately and parted forever. I went home and found a great many people had been complaining about my absenting myself from my shop. I told them that I was tired of a sham practice, that our medical system was too uncertain, and that it failed too often. It is defective, I told them. "Oh, pshaw!" exclaimed they, "people must die. You will never find a system that will cure all your cases. Go to work again, we are satisfied with your practice, and some of us need your services every day."

About this time Samuel Thomson's *Guide to Health*[26] was being widely distributed at $20 a copy; and the people were felicitating themselves at their good fortune, for now, with their lobelias, cayenne, nervine and No. 6,[27] they were able to cope with disease in any form, they maintained. I listened at the bragging and prating amongst the steam doctors,[28] as all those who had purchased Thomson's patent were called, and I verily thought it to be the most perfect tomfoolery I had ever heard in all my life. I considered that the medical science was invaded. I resumed practice and went to work again. People rejoiced that I did so and sent for me more than ever. Some of the steam doctors sent for me to go and see some cases where they had administered the lobelia a little too freely and had got their patient into what is termed amongst them the Alarm.

I would remain with them, administering gentle stimulants until the alarm would go off, and then, thinking I had cured the case, would talk and tell what I had done for the steam doctors. I would often quiz those steam doctors with questions in anatomy and physiology, and confuse them till they would almost weep for vexation. I thought it was right and a little smart to devil the poor fellows. But I know now who was the fool then.

There was a very wealthy connection of people in that country by the name of Pruett.[29] There were a dozen families of them, all owning many Negroes. The old man, Samuel Pruett, father and director of the clan, came to me and told me that he and all his boys were going, as soon as the Chickasaw lands were surveyed, to engage in buying the Indian reservations; and that they would for a year or two, be absent from home a great portion of the time, consequently would not be able to attend to their cases of sickness. They all had made themselves sufficiently acquainted with the Thomsonian System to feel entirely independent of the old school doctors. They had had two years' practice with Thomson's remedies, and they felt assured that they were able to cure any of the climatic complaints. Their women could attend to all minor cases, but once in a while bad cases in so great a number would occur, particularly amongst their Negroes.

"This kind of cases," said they, "we do not intend to impose the labor of treating upon our women, and we want to engage someone in whom we can place confidence to attend to the bad cases during our absence. We have had a family council on the subject in which we have discussed the merits and character of all our doctor acquaintances. We know all the fool talk and ugly words you have displayed in your game-making about the steam doctors. We don't care for that. We have confidence that you will not fail to do anything you say you will. And now let me say to you, that the object of my visit is to try to get you to say that you will study the Thomsonian System and practice it in our families during the time we are engaged in the land speculations. We don't ask you to practice it except in our families, but we demand that you employ no other medicines in them. Such is our confidence in the Thomsonian remedies that we are fully willing to trust them in all cases of sickness; and if you will say that you will undertake it for us we will furnish you with a set of books and you can use what medicines we have on hand while they last. By the time they are exhausted you will have a chance to procure more. You shall have the practice of the whole connection and we don't care whether you give a dose of steam medicine to any one else or not. Now say what you'll do."

I replied, "You are all my neighbors and particular friends. I would go a good way out of my usual course to aid or oblige any member of the family. But don't you think our good friends can sometimes require a little too much of us?"

"Shut your foolish mouth," said the old man. "You are struggling with a big family, and we want to help you. We don't want to mortify your feelings by making appropriations for your benefit. But we have a piece of work which we know you can do with benefit to us and credit to yourself, for which we are able and very willing to thoroughly remunerate you. Take these books and make yourself ready as soon as you can." I took the *Guide to Health,* and read it carefully in two days. I then went to the old man Pruett's to see the remedial agents. I found he had plenty of lobelia, cayenne, nervine, skunk cabbage, and bay berry. They were in loose papers, tin boxes, and all wasting. He had no preparations. I inquired how they got along without the preparations.

"Oh," said he, "they administer it all in the form of decoction or tea, and it cures every time." I told him that if I undertook to practice for him, I should like to have all the preparations and do the work according to the directions laid down in the book.

"That," said he, "is just what we want. You have bottles ready to put them in and can fix them scientifically. So take them all home with you and put them up." I called for some thread, and while I was carefully tying them and putting them into a box, the old man, who was observing me the while, remarked to some of the bystanders, "See those practiced fingers, how neatly and with what extraordinary facility they arrange and pack those papers. Just the manner he packs up them papers pleases me. It is a prophecy too that he will be sure to investigate the subject as he thinks how to enable him to serve us truthfully, but it will result finally in his making the grand discovery that the Thomsonian System, imperfect as it now is, is nevertheless vastly superior to the old school practice. And I make this prediction, that, as soon as he understands it, he will lay aside his poisons, and become a thorough botanic practioner; that he will become greatly distinguished as such and that he will make a fortune. Don't forget what I have said this day."

I remarked to him, "Well, father Pruett, if the play of my fingers in folding and binding up these papers inspires your prophetic spirit so highly, come up to my shop in fourteen days, when I shall have the No. 6, 3rd preparation, and all the tinctures filtered, bottled and neatly labeled. Then you will probably go into a prophetic trance, and I shall have to restore you by administering 'Wake robin,' and 'No. 6.'"

"Young man," said he, "it availeth nothing for you to make sport of my prediction. I repeat, you will be a steam doctor, widely known. You will throw away your poisons and become a great and notable advocate for the botanic system, when I shall rejoice, because I am the cause of it."

I carried the medicines home, compounded and made up all the preparations, put them in clear glass tincture bottles, put on fancy labels and set them up on some shelves I made for them. They looked very pretty and the taste and smell of them indicated that they were potent remedies. I had compounded and put into nice specie jars all the powdered preparations before the fourteen days were out. The old man Pruett came and was perfectly carried away with the appearance of the preparations; and said to his son-in-law, Dr. Bailey, who came up with him, "Why hadn't you made out such preparations, they are so nice?"

"Because they are just as good in their crude state," said the doctor. The old man looked at him a moment, and then turning to me said, "If I get sick, I shall send for you. You must be sure to come and bring with you some of these nice medicines. I am sure I shall prefer them to the lazy way we have been using them." I gave him specimens of the tinctures; he wanted to show them to the family.

They began to send for me before they had gone land hunting. I soon encountered two or three cases that were so violent that I was afraid to trust the new remedies in their treatment, and I said so. I was asked by the confident Kirk Pruett, whose Negro it was that was sick, if I understood the steam practice in such cases. On being answered affirmatively, he said, "Well, go ahead with the steam medicines. I will hold myself responsible for the result, for I know you'll cure him." Then I administered my first lobelia emetic. It was a bad case of fever. By the time the emetic had ceased to act, the patient seemed to be cured and wanted some broiled meat, which I ordered for him.

I had large saddlebags made, and I carried the Thomsonian medicines in one and the old school drugs in the other. There were a number of families in the community who had furnished themselves with Thomson's books, and they all encouraged me to go ahead in procuring plenty of medicines. They would employ me, if I would confine my practice in their families to the steam medicines; and I might administer my poisons to all else who desired it. All my old customers continued their patronage, and all the steam doctors far and near, when they had a bad case, sent for me; for my Pruett friends had taken pains to spread the news that I had made myself thoroughly acquainted with the system and that I had been performing miracles with the sick cases among them.

Some of my old school customers had been listening to the wonderful accounts given by the Pruetts of the cures I had performed, and when they had occasion for my services, desired me to practice the botanic system on them. It frequently occurred at houses where two were sick at the same time that one would require the steam practice while the other would say, "Give me the old school medicines, for I would rather die scientifically than be cured by quackery."

But the fact that the cases treated with the botanic agents recovered sooner every time and that under that treatment there were no deaths could not be concealed; and the people in my region of practice began to turn over to it in many families. They sent for me fifty miles or more, for which I often received $100. My business grew daily. I made so much money that year that I began to pay installments on my old $5,000 Mobile debt.

In the course of this year's practice I had, in hundreds of

cases, demonstrated the superiority of the botanic system, and I desired to discontinue the allopathic system altogether. Yet I knew many of my patrons still preferred the old medicines, and I did not wish to lay them aside. So I continued to carry the drugs with me, and wherever I could succeed in convincing them of the superiority of the other, I did so and gave it to them. About the middle of the second year of my double practice, I lost a two-year-old child under circumstances leaving me no ground to doubt the fact that the death was occasioned by the allopathic remedies. And, while I was gazing on the twitching muscles of the dying child, I made a solemn vow to myself that I would never administer another dose of the poisons of that system.

I started home, and after passing through the gate into the big road, I emptied the old school medicines from my saddle-bags and left them in a pile on the ground. It was at the heat of a summer day, and one of the vials containing sulphuric or nitric acid, bursting by the heat, flowed into a paper containing chloride of lime, when considerable effervescence took place. The people reported that it boiled and smoked there for two or three days and grew to a great heap. Many came to see it. The doctors, who by this time were beginning to say a good deal about my apostasy, made a great scandal out of the boiling mass I had thrown out at Malone's gate. But I turned the tables on them by telling the people that it was all old school medicines I had thrown out there, and that, if I kept my senses, I would never kill any more children with it, for I had vowed never to carry a particle of it with me again.

After this occurrence I carried none but botanical remedies with me. Now came *Howard's Improved System of Botanic Medicines*.[30] It was written in better style and spirit than Thomson's books were, and, after getting through with the perusal of it, I conceived the idea of combining my Indian medicines with it and trying to get up a Southern system of practice that would be more applicable to Southern disease. I studied hard all the time I was not actively employed. I very much needed a knowledge of systematic botany, and I studied it on horseback as I rode from place to place until I understood all that was known about it then.

About this time, I opened a correspondence with the Howards, and wrote an account of my conversion to the botanic system with a number of other articles describing cases and their treatment, which were considered very interesting and very highly spoken of by the editor of the journal who published them.[31]

CHAPTER SIX

Heading for Texas

---

^MAt this period [1834], people began to talk about what a fine country Texas was said to be. They had a great meeting on the subject and made up an emigrating company, which consisted of one hundred heads of families. This company included mechanics, school teachers, preachers and doctors. They bound themselves by signing an appropriate article to go all together to that country, if the exploring committee on their return should report favorably of it. The committee consisted of ten men, who were considered good judges of country, and whose veracity was reliable. They gave me the appointment of physician in the exploring party, and we were to be ready to set out on the 20th of November, 1834.

I went to work with all my might, putting my home and family in a condition to leave them and collecting funds to defray the expenses of the trip. The 20th of November came. The members of the committee were to assemble at my house and start from that point for the long journey. I was ready with my pack horse, a nice pack of choice medicines and a peck of sugared parched corn flour, a good rifle, powder, bullets, a butcher's knife, four pocket knives, fish hooks and lines, a good bowstring, a good big axe, a frying pan, coffee pot and tin cup. But the company did not come, not a man of them.

I intended to make the trip since I had put myself to the trouble of fixing for it, if no one else went. So I laid up the preparation carefully, for I was not quite ready to set out alone. I needed a little more money, if I had to go by myself. I turned out amongst my customers and in the course of eight or ten days had raised my traveling purse to $1050—$100 of it in specie and the balance in U.S. bank paper.

I was now ready, and gave notice that I intended to set out on the first day of January ensuing. A few days previous to that time, a good friend and neighbor[1] came to me and said that he hated to see me go off on such an expedition as that would be without company; that he had been thinking that if he could raise as much as $200 he would bear me company. This was talked of among the people, and on the 9th of January we set out, six men, eight horses and one dog.[2]

We crossed the Tombecbee River at Cotton Gin Port. [P]The ground was covered with snow. Our first camp was twenty-five miles from home, in the wild woods of the Chickasaw country; and except about fifty miles below the Choctaw country, and about twenty miles on the Bayou Rapides, in Louisiana, we saw no more neighborhood in six months.[3]

Our pack horses carried meal, a little bacon, a six-gallon brass kettle, coffee pot, tin pans, and a pint tin cup apiece. We had a good double tent, which we never set up except when it rained. We camped out all the time, did our own cooking, and slept in the open air. On our rifles we depended for our supplies of animal food, and on the pack horses for bread, coffee, sugar and soap. We fared abundantly better than we could have done at the hotels, had there been any in the country through which we journeyed. We ate but two meals a day—breakfast and supper. Our supper consisted of fried venison or turkey, corn bread and coffee. Supper over, the six-gallon kettle was hung on, containing a proper quantity of the grits sifted from our cornmeal (which we ground on a steel mill), salt, a little piece of bacon, and a venison ham or a turkey, and plenty of red pepper. As one or another of the company would be occasionally up during the night, the fire would be mended and the kettle kept boiling all the time. Being boiled all to shreds, the grits, as tender and much better than rice, with the holy glow of the cayenne regularly diffused through it, constituted one of the most digestible and healthy messes that could be made. We commenced on it at daybreak, and by sun-up breakfast was over and a good dog-bait left. We had a nice camp dog along.

The country through which we traveled, with the exception of only two days, was full of game—deer, turkeys, wild geese, mallard ducks. We very seldom struck camp without plenty for the company's consumption. The sixty-two-year old Methodist

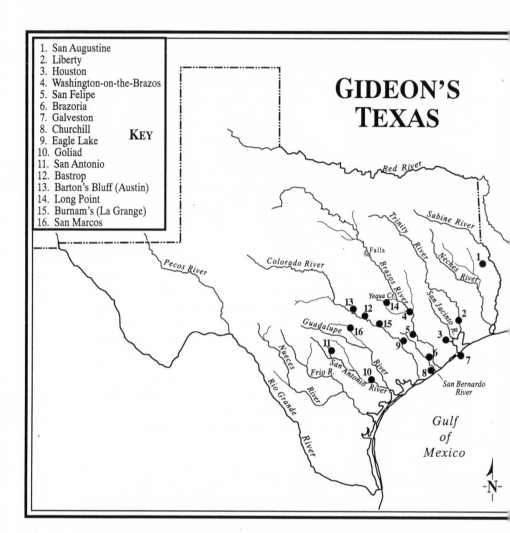

KEY

1. San Augustine
2. Liberty
3. Houston
4. Washington-on-the-Brazos
5. San Felipe
6. Brazoria
7. Galveston
8. Churchill
9. Eagle Lake
10. Goliad
11. San Antonio
12. Bastrop
13. Barton's Bluff (Austin)
14. Long Point
15. Burnam's (La Grange)
16. San Marcos

GIDEON'S
TEXAS

Red River

Pecos River

Colorado River

Falls

Trinity River

Sabine River

Neches River

Yegua Cr.

Brazos River

San Jacinto R.

Guadalupe

Nueces River

San Antonio River

Frio R.

Rio Grande River

San Bernardo River

Gulf
of
Mexico

1
2
3
4
5
6
7
8
9
10
11
12
13
14
15
16

-N-

preacher we had along, though he carried a good rifle and could shoot very well, did not seem to care about leaving the trace or path, so he rarely shot anything that did not come in his path. The four young men were poor hunters, very seldom making a successful shot. The reality of procuring meat for supper and breakfast devolved on me. Mine was a trained hunting horse—his name was Ned. One of the young men, when I would in the afternoon deviate from our course and flank along, would follow at a respectful distance, and when I would shoot anything, gallop up and take care of it. If it was a deer or big turkey, the hunting for that day would cease. But if the turkey was small, as they were generally very convenient in the trees around, I would take another. If it was a goose, since none of us liked them fried for supper (though in the boiled mess in the kettle they were a very savory, excellent food)—in that case I would continue hunting until I would get venison or a turkey.

After we got into Texas the game was very abundant, and I found but little difficulty in procuring plenty, more especially after getting into the wide-spread prairie country. Hundreds of deer were to be seen in all directions, and wild geese everywhere—thousands. When I wanted goose or a deer, I would ride towards them until they began to be suspicious. Then I would get down and push old Ned along between me and the game, as if I was going to one side of them, but getting nearer and nearer, until the game would be in range. Then stopping the horse and dropping on one knee, I could shoot under his neck. To kill the geese or the deer either on the prairie was easily effected, and we never failed to have plenty of nice venison or turkey for supper, and a kettle full of choice pieces hot for breakfast. On all the streams that pass through and drain the prairies, there are narrow belts of timber, and here we nearly always found flocks of turkeys. Then, west of [San] Augustine there were but few people seen. Once in forty miles you would perhaps find a family with a little corn patch and a log hut, with a cow or two. No Mexicans east of San Antonio, except at the mouth of the Brazos and La Bahia. No Indians, except a few straggling hunters west of the Brazos.

There was green winter grass (*Stipa setigera*)[4] in abundance for our horses west of the Colorado, and for our own consumption, all manner of good game, fish and honey. The range of country through which we circulated during February and March lay in latitude 29° and 30′ N. In perfect safety, with abundant supplies of food for ourselves and horses, we slept as soundly and more sweetly by our campfires in that balmy, dry climate than we would have done anywhere else in the world. It didn't rain on us in two months, and our horses had got to believe that our camp was their home, and seemed to be afraid to wander far from it.

While in this pleasant, dry region of country we had some nice little hunting occurrences. On a point of timber that terminated on a ridge that lay between two little creeks, at a mile or more distant, we thought we saw six big old bucks standing with their heads up in the edge of the timber. We divided the company, and each party turning slightly back, sank out of sight into the lower grounds of the two creeks. The movement was intended to make the deer think we were going away. But according to arrangement, as soon as we were out of sight of the deer, each party turned and made haste down the creeks until we were opposite the game; then deploying a little, we left our horses, and creeping up the hill, approached them stealthily from behind and on both sides. The underbrush was pretty thick, and we could not see them until we were quite near. It was quite curious to observe how much alike the action of the company was when we discovered that instead of six old bucks we found that many armed Indians. We all made ready and held our rifles at a poise until the Indians showed they had no fight at that meeting. They were standing erect with their heads turned towards the place where they had seen us last, and until we made a little noise in the dry leaves they had no idea of our near approach. They flashed their eyes around, and finding themselves nearly surrounded, their flight was as abrupt as that of a gang of quail. We being in the timber behind them, they ran straight into the prairie. They were armed with bows and arrows only, from which we supposed them to be a small hunting party of wild Indians who did not like the stealthy manner in which we had made our approach. By the time we had recovered our horses and assembled again on the prairie, we could barely distinguish them still running. They seemed to be veering towards a timbered region which was visible and lay far away to the right in the distance. We didn't kill anything that hunt.

Towards the last of February the turkeys were beginning to gobble in the early morning. I concluded to go out a little before day one morning and get one of them. I found a very nice place in a large hollow stump to hide myself in, and when it was light enough to see the sights of my gun, commenced yelping. An old gobbler answered very cleverly not far off, and seemed to be coming to me pretty fast. He had approached so near that I had cocked and placed my rifle in position, and had begun to peep through the brush for him; but contrary to my expectations he shied off. I couldn't imagine what was the cause of it. I had the leaf of a wild peach (*Cerasus caroliniana*),[5] a most excellent leaf to yelp with, and I had been admiring how well I was speaking turkey with it; had made no false or indifferent notes, and knew that on my part he had no grounds for suspicion.

I began to suspect that there might be somebody else about, and as I have known several casualties of that sort to occur in turkey hunting, feared I might yelp up an awkward hunter and get myself shot. So I sank down in the old hollow stump, ceasing my yelping, whilst the old gobbler went roaring off through the swamp.

After a reasonable time had elapsed, and I heard no noise, I peeped out through the slit in the stump where my gun lay. Soon I discovered the cause of the turkey's distaste to that vicinity. It was the first Texas leopard cat[6] I had ever seen. It was, with its legs greatly shortened, creeping towards me, working its mouth and face and eyes in a very singular manner. It sometimes appeared very amiable and lovely; and away back at the very end of his long tail, the black tip, elevated a little higher than any other portion of the animal, was moving and flitting about like it belonged to somebody else, appearing to be twice as far off as it really was. He was coming fast enough. I did not resume the yelp, but lay still, observing his very curious but not unpleasant grimaces. I thought to myself, "Come on old fellow, I know where you are; you can't make me think you are away out yonder where the antic flutter of the black tip of your tail looks so much like a butterfly. Come on, my dear; I am exceedingly glad to see you this fine morning." He moved with such extreme cautiousness, that though he was on a bed of dry leaves three or four inches thick, I could not hear the slightest rustle. When he approached within twenty feet of my hiding place, I concluded he was near enough. As there was no chance to shoot him but in the face, and it being so pretty I disliked to spoil it, I shot him in his left eye so carefully that I did not misplace a hair. I took his hide off very nicely, and preserved it entire, claws and all. It is the best formed and most beautiful of the cat family. The marking is so perfect, tadpole shape, black as jet, and thickly set on a dead-white ground. It was three and one-half feet in length, twelve inches high, and would weigh sixteen or seventeen pounds.

On another occasion, I had left the camp while the young men would have to spend a little time repairing a pack saddle, and I came to an open, clean space in the bottom, where the river, during a recent freshet, had deposited clean white sand over at least an acre. I had progressed to about the middle of it, when I heard a gobbler strut close by. There was not a bush nor anything on the sand behind which I could hide myself, and I dare not move a single step. There lay at my feet a small branch of a tree that had been blown there by the wind, not more than a yard long, having three or four locks of long moss (*Tillandsia usneoidis*)[7] hanging on it. This was my only chance. So I sank down in a sitting posture, balanced the little limb with the moss on top of my head, trying to look as much as I could like an old stump upon which the mossy limb had lodged, and with an elder leaf (*Sambucus rigum*)[8] I had in my hand, uttered one soft yelp. The old fellow roared out a big gobble, ran up within ten feet of where I was sitting, stood listening a moment, and then dropping his wings, jarred my very brains with his heavy strut. My gun lay across my lap, and he was so near that I daren't move a finger or even wink my eyes. He paid no attention to me, but in two or three of his half turns, when strutting, marked the sand with his jarring wings at least three feet nearer to me. He stamped and ranted and boasted of his gobblerhood: "I would like to see a gobbler that could stand before me." I was getting quite tired of the awkward posture he was holding me in, but consoled with the hope that he would go hunting the hen he had heard utter the low-soft yelp so recently. I had to let him go out of sight before I could change my position, fix my gun ready and call him back. As I expected, ere long he started off into the bushes. I was soon ready, and two low yelps brought him thundering back. Since in returning he came straight towards me, and wouldn't stop, I had to shoot him while in motion.

I had been married but a short time when I killed and carried home a very large gobbler. After the Negro cook had dressed it she brought it in to show how fat it was; and when I was expecting some flattering remark from my pretty young wife, she wrinkled up her little nose, and curling up her pretty lips said, "Oh! My, what a ghastly wound," pointing to the bullet hole in the turkey's breast. I was miffed, and I told the Negro to take it away. I told her if she ever got another of my killing to cook, she would see no ghastly wound in its body.

Ever after I shot the gobblers in the head, and during the fifty-three years we journeyed together (except the three or four years I lay sick), I don't think a single Spring passed that I didn't kill more or less gobblers. She never saw another that I killed with a ghastly wound in its body. I shot the one I yelped up on the sand in Texas in the head, but he had it tucked down in his bosom while strutting, and the ball passing through it, split his back open more than half-way to the root of his tail. I would never in all my life go hunting with a poor gun. I carefully studied the anatomy of the deer, and he could hardly stand in a position that I couldn't reach a vital part. Standing with the head from me, presenting the right side, I will cut the *vena portal*. In the same position, presenting the left side, I will place the ball an inch from the root of the left ear. When standing broadside I place it a little forward of the hip, three inches below the top of the back, and that cuts the descending branch of the aorta, right behind the kidneys. With my good eyes, steady nerves, and unerring rifle, if the deer was in range and standing perfectly still, it was a very rare thing for me to miss. If the deer was not still, and in range, I didn't shoot. Nothing could make me feel so much like a tacky, or bear so painfully on my sympathies, as the idea of going into nature's grand park and banging away at the biggest part of the first deer that presents itself, and perhaps wounding it, for it to run off and hide itself in some dense thicket, to lie and sigh and groan away its joyous, active life with its dying breath, with curses on the head of the senseless biped who inflicted the profitless injury. Very few of my deer, or any other game I shot, rotted in the woods; hence in my day-hunting I had but little use for a dog.

You will excuse this little egotistic digression, and return with me to our camp at Barton's Bluff on the south side of the Colorado.[9] We had found a bee tree, and while the young men were cutting out the honey, I went off to get a deer, preparatory to one of our grand venison and honey suppers. The big kettle and all our buckets were filled with nice, white honey-comb. I had selected, from a drove of twenty or thirty deer, a splendid forked-horn buck. We found a nice camping place, with plenty of good water and wood, and an abundance of green grass for the horses. Some cut green wood and made a good fire, while others sliced up the good lean parts of the venison into narrow strips; others collected some straight little prairie dogwood (*Viburnum dentatum*)[10] rods for broiling sticks, and pressed out each man's tin cup half-full of honey. Neither bread nor salt nor coffee is used at one of these feasts; and for its easy digestive qualities and agreeableness in eating it is most certainly not surpassed by any dish ever set before mankind.

Everything being in readiness, each man trimmed and sharpened at both ends two of the rods, and then running the small end three or four times through one of the slices of venison lengthwise, plants the other end in the ground at the proper distance from the fire, so as to place the meat over good, hot coals to broil. He spits another slice of venison on the other stick, and by turning and attending to it, soon has one of the slices thoroughly broiled. This he takes off the stick, and replacing it with another slice, sets it over the fire. By this time the piece taken off is sufficiently cool to begin to eat. The most approved plan for eating is to take the piece of meat in your left hand, your hunting knife in the right, plunge one end of the meat into your cup of honey, deep enough for a mouthful, thrust it between your teeth, and hold it fast while you saw it off with your knife. It is easy enough to see that by the time you consume the first slice the second will be ready, which is to be taken off and replaced with another, as in the first instance, and so on until you have supped up your half cup of honey. This is enough for any decent hunter to consume; a desire for more would indicate too much animal to be allowed the use of a gun—let him hunt with his nose, like his kind. I go into the woods occasionally yet, and if I can find a bee tree, kill a deer and have a feast. It's the only time I eat animal food. [M]I have often thought, at the time

I was so agreeably feasting in that way, that there could be no better preparation of food for man that is so suitable, so natural, so agreeable and so exactly suited to his constitutional requirements.

ᴾFrom Barton's Bluffs we continued our journey westward to where Austin now stands. Nobody lived near there then, and we found too many moccasin tracks to feel secure in regard to our horses. We stayed there but one night. We traveled over vast prairies southwardly; saw vast herds of wild horses, some buffalo, and countless deer. We did not attempt to shoot any till late in the afternoon, when one of the young men shot a little buck, took his hind quarters and the back straps (the dorsal muscles), carried them till we came to a pretty creek, when we pitched our camp. Here I saw my first prairie hen—a regular pinnated grouse[11]—and succeeded, after following near a mile, and when it was almost too dark to see the sights of my rifle, in killing one of them.

Our old Methodist preacher said it looked so much like a chicken it must be good, and if we would agree for him to do so, he would make a try of it for his own supper, and not join us in the venison and honey that time. We still had a kettle full of honey comb, and all went to work making a good fire, for it was blowing up one of those Texas Northers.[12] As soon as the fire was in proper condition, we were ready for broiling and sopping the venison in the honey, which continued perhaps an hour, and about the time we got through with our satisfactory feast, the old Preacher had set his pan of fried grouse off a little way from the fire and commenced his supper; he had made bread and coffee and promised himself a great repast. The old fellow was working away a long time; the boys had been out to see about the horses, had fixed their sleeping places and had scuffed and played a long time—9 o'clock—when the old man rose up from the frying pan, wiping his fingers on the long moss and saying, "Well, boys, you may all eat prairie chickens who like. That's the first one that ever I tasted, and I am determined it shall be the last."

"Why, papa," asked his son, "was it not well flavored?" "Oh, it tasted well enough," said the old man, "but it was so infernal tough. Why it's a wonder to me that Gid's rifle-ball penetrated the old tough carcass." His son proposed frying some venison for him to piece out his supper with; but the old man refused, on the grounds that he had worried himself down, gnawing and pulling at that old grouse, and he was sleepy.

We camped the next night after this on the head branch of the Navidad.[13] That day's journey passed us over the most delightful prairie country I had ever seen. As we passed over the dividing ridge, between the two tributaries of the Colorado and the Navidad and La Vaca, there was a vast, greatly undulating plain looking South, and the branches of the two above named little rivers, lay spread out before us, resembling a pair of enormous fans. The course of their branches were distinctly marked by the streaks of timber on the margins, presenting to our view a shade of darker green engraved in the face of the boundless plain of grass that slightly dipped away gulf-wards to the far-off smoky obstruction.

The deer were uncommonly plenty that day; but there was no timber in our course to creep behind, and we failed in getting one of them. The young men made the effort, and they could not make their horses go between them and the deer. Those four young men, together with the old saint, during their whole trip, with their choice rifles, positively did not kill so much meat as any one of them consumed. We always had plenty, however; but the old preacher in his even' service—and I always thought strange of it—thanked an absent Somebody for the venison and other game. When the sun was getting low, I could see the boys, who were all the time in plain view, would make a failure; so I galloped on ahead to the little streak of timber about a mile before us, and when I came there a large flock of turkeys flushed up from a fine pool of clear water where they were taking their evening drink, preparatory to flying up to roost. Being down at the water's edge, they were not apprised of my approach until I was quite near, so they were much frightened. And fluttering up in great confusion, they pitched on the first tree they came to. I soon secured a brace of them, and was returning to where old Ned was grazing around the pool of water, when I met the boys, who on hearing my gun came dashing to where I was. When I pointed to where the turkeys were in the trees, they rushed in and banged away until dark. They brought in one good one, but we had enough before.

They were good fat turkeys. We fried their breasts and had

a very comfortable supper, and for the first time in five or six nights, hung on the kettle. In it we placed, with plenty of nice grits, all the good pieces that remained of the three turkeys, some slips of fat bacon, and, of course, plenty of cayenne. Our watering place was the head spring of the little creek. An exceedingly clear pool of water, 25 or 30 feet in width and ten feet deep, it contained many blue catfish, some of them fifteen inches long. I got out a line, and baiting the hook with a portion of the liver of a turkey, threw it into the pool and very soon caught one that would weigh five or six pounds. The old preacher dressed and salted it, for a good fry in the morning. That was the most plentiful place [for game] I have ever found in any country. There were buffalo, bear, deer, turkeys, grouse, jack rabbits, fish, and (during the winter and until the first of April) the wild geese and many species of duck, in countless thousands. I haven't the least doubt, after I had made myself acquainted with the ways and haunts of game, that I could have procured a bountiful supply of meats to feed twenty men, and I would have used nothing but my rifle and fishing tackle. But I needn't brag about it. I was born in the woods, and lived many a day on my hunt with the blow-gun before I was seven years old. These boys slept in feather-beds.

We spent another day traveling over an exceedingly fine farming country, and turning our course more eastwardly, found ourselves at the edge of the Colorado bottom, twenty-five miles below where La Grange now stands. We pitched our camp when the sun was an hour high. At this camp, the old preacher asked me, "Well, Gid, I am satisfied with Texas; how do you feel on the subject?"

"I am not satisfied, Uncle Fred," said I. "It was to explore the country that I made my expensive outfit, left my family and came so far, and not having completed what I came for, I am not satisfied. Nor can I leave the country until I explore it far enough to be able to describe its geography, and its most prominent features as an agricultural and grazing country. We have seen the Trinity, San Jacinto and Brazos and Colorado; but there is a vast district S[outh] W[est] that we have not seen. I shall not be satisfied until I explore that region."

"Well," he replied, "We have all concluded to go home, and you have been the contractor, and paid from your own purse all the expenses of the trip. Get your book and let us attend to the money, for we intend to go."

The money was refunded, and for the two horses and equipage, we had a little auction. I bought one of the pack horses, the axe, and one tin bucket. All went quickly. We shook hands as affectionately as a set of good brothers would have done; and they left me sitting on a log, holding my horses, who were screaming and crying like two children, to follow the company.[14] Just beyond where I had shot [a] deer on the previous evening, the line of the timber curved to the right; around this corner the company turned, and were immediately out of sight. At this my horses became almost unmanageable. I did not succeed in pacifying them until I caressingly hugged old Ned around his neck and let him hug me, which he accomplished as he had done many times before (for I had camped out alone with him often in my hunting excursions during the past seven years) by throwing his jaws over on my back, and pressing about half his weight, with his neck on my shoulder. After my horses understood the meaning of the movement, they became quiet and reconciled to their condition, which they manifested by cropping the grass around where I sat.

And now I had time for reflection. I began to think of my situation, and to lay plans for future progress. It was the 10th of March; the grass was springing up, and the convenience for a good camp lay in grand profusion all around. At first I thought I would stake my horses on the grass, and lie up three or four days—for we had traveled without intermission from the day we left home. It would recruit my horses, and I could bogus about in the thick-timbered bottom and see what discoveries I might make. But recollecting that while we were on high ground the previous day we had seen far off in the north of our line of travel, and in the edge of the Colorado bottom, what we took to be a house—a settlement, I concluded to go there, and if the occupant of the place was a congenial spirit, I would rest a few days with him.[15]

The country over which we had been journeying during the past ten weeks presented no indications of its ever having been occupied by any people, not even Indians (only as a hunting ground), and if the supposed house we had seen in the distance the day before was really a house, it was the only one we had discovered in many days. I tightened up the gear of my pack horse, mounted old Ned, and set out. It was at least fifteen miles. I had progressed a little over half the distance, and was riding over a belt of timber that overspread the low grounds of a pretty little creek—the undergrowth being a bed of very thick-set switch cane, high as my horse's sides—when I came suddenly on an old she-panther and her two yearlings, lying in the thick cane. I was almost upon them before they saw me. They were very much alarmed and ran up the nearest trees. The old one ascended a large pin-oak (*Quercus catesby*) and the young ones went up a pecan tree (*Juglans olivæformis*).[16]

I concluded to shoot them, and tying my pack horse (with a long slack) to a sapling, dropped old Ned's bridle, and had to go off a little distance to shoot, for we were nearly under the trees they were in. I shot the young ones first. I brain shot them, and both fell speechless from the big limbs on which they lay, not far from my pack horse, but the cane was so thick he couldn't see them, and he did not get frightened. I walked around some distance to find a good place from which to shoot the old one. I intended to brain shoot her, for I knew if I wounded her she would be down amongst us before I could reload my rifle, and she was very capable of hurting some of us. She kept her face turned on me all the time and seemed to be deeply interested in trying to discover what I was crackling about in the cane for. She paid no attention to the horses. I was the fellow that engaged her attention. I could distinctly see the frown that wrinkled her skin betwixt her round eyes, and there I planted my lead. She whirled with all her limbs astrut and came very near falling on old Ned, who had moved along in picking the cane leaves to that point without my notice. She struck the ground with a heavy thump, and in rolling to one side, her left forefoot came in contact with one of his shoulders, and her sharp claws clung a little to the skin. Whereupon old Ned took a fit. He whirled and kicked the panther with such violence that he moved her eight or ten feet. The blow seemed to be force enough to have killed her, had she not been already dead. He threw off my saddle-bags and continued to kick and get further from the panther, until he got into the prairie, and then he dashed off with all his might. I ran out into the prairie and called to him, but he did not slacken his pace until he was a quarter of a mile. I called to him often, but he wouldn't come until I had to lie down in the grass, to assure him the danger was over. He came then, but I couldn't get him to enter the timber. I had to leave him there whilst I went and brought out the pack horse.

I pursued my course over the prairie until I came to the place we had seen from the distance. It was sure enough a house with a considerable family of motherless children, and their disconsolate, lonely father, who met me at the gate and welcomed me very warmly.[17] I related to him what had occurred between me and my traveling companions. He remarked that he was truly glad it had happened—that he had two big cribs full of corn and plenty in his house to eat, and that he should feel himself greatly obliged if I agreed to make his house my home, and remain with him for years.

I agreed to stop a while with him, until he got well enough acquainted with me, to enable him to ascertain whether he had not, in his cordial, fraternal welcome to me, made a mistake. "Light, sir, and let your horses go to the lot; I make no such mistakes; I have lived in the woods long enough to know that a man who can be so self-reliant as to suffer himself thrown off from his company, in an unoccupied prairie a thousand miles in extent, with no alternative for subsistence but a small-bored rifle, never finds himself in a fix that will force him to resort to a wrong action. I consider the circumstances that conspired to direct you to me to be a Providential interference, and declare you doubly welcome."[18]

His family consisted of four sons and two daughters, the eldest son and daughter nearly grown. They had been residing at that place twelve years; had one neighbor about two miles distant in the timber. Their mother had been dead but a few months. They all gathered around and were evidently greatly rejoiced at my presence. I remained with them, receiving their kind attentions and doing everything I could to reciprocate their kindness.

But my business was to explore the country and I was getting restless. Jesse Burnham, the owner of the place, was as good a man as any country or situation could produce, and when I explained to him the nature of my mission, he calmly said,

"Well, make this your home to return to and recruit when you are tired, or anything happens."

So, I concluded to leave my baggage and packhorse with him. ^MI began my excursion trips by staying out a week the first experiment, and found I could live well enough myself; and my horse could get a mouthful of nutritious food every step we traveled, if he desired it. Burnham did not like for me to make such extensive excursions alone. He said the Indians would find me and be sure to kill me, that he had been uneasy all the time I was gone by myself.

There was nobody to go with me, and I could not abstain from examining the country. So I told my friend Burnham there was not much danger of the Indians, with my cautiousness, and that go I must. To gratify him I remained with him five or six days, answering his questions. But the weather being fine, I set out on another trip. This time I journeyed coastwise, examining the mouths of the rivers from Brazos to Aransas bay. I was gone a fortnight this time. ^PTaking my two blankets and my saddle, my good five-pound axe under my saddle skirt, my medical saddle-bags, a tin cup, two lines and hooks, and my rifle and ammunition (of course), I crossed the Colorado and traveled in a northeast direction two days. Turned more eastwardly on the third morning and at noon came to the big Sand hills, in which heads, what I now know to be the Bernard,[19] a little river that makes its way alone through the vast grassy plains to the Gulf of Mexico.

I, without any instructions, fortunately decided to go down on the right hand side of the little river. I carried not a particle of any kind of provisions with me but found little difficulty in getting plenty of venison. I might have shot any amount of geese, ducks or turkeys. The turkeys were seen in every little streak of timber, and the geese and mallard ducks were spread out everywhere. But no kind of fowl, when cooked at the camp, eaten without bread or salt, is very palatable. I could make a blind of Old Ned, who understood the maneuver so well that *we* rarely failed getting meat. We didn't trouble the birds.

When I had progressed far enough down the head branch of the little river for it to form large, deep holes, I took up, in early evening one day, near one of these pools. There was timber on the low grounds, and by slipping along the edge of it I soon got a deer. I took its back straps and a piece of the liver, and returning to camp made a good fire, piling on a good chance of wood. While the wood was burning I got out one of my lines, baited the hook with a chunk of the liver, and threw it into the water. It had not sunk half-way down before it was grabbed, and pulling it up I found a large blue cat had it. He came up to the top of the water quite willingly, and there were two or three more whirling about in the scented water, but my fish finding it was no joke, turned and darted away with such force that he came near getting my line out of my hand. I checked him, however; at the full length of the line he shot upwards so swiftly, keeping the line twanging tight, that he threw himself a foot or two above the water. He cut up many antics and gyrations before he gave up, and I had to work my way around two or three trees that grew on the bank until I got to a shallow place at the lower end of the big hole, before I could get him out. Although I dragged him while he was tired, and until he was fairly grounded on the pebbly bottom of the little creek, which I could here leap across, it was with some difficulty that I got him out. I was afraid to trust my little line and made it fast to a snag nearby and left him panting, till I ran and got old Ned's lariat, made a running noose, threw it over his tail, and slipping it to his strong horns in the pectoral fin, drew it down close and then hauled him out and to my camp. I judged that he would weigh forty-four or -five pounds. He was a whopper, and dwelling as he had in very clear water, his skin was very blue above and white as the whitest paper beneath. Ned came up from his grazing to see what it was that I had dragged up from the water. He smelt of it, and when it flapped its tail, he jerked up his head and, turning away to his grass, made no remarks.

By the time I had broiled and ate one of the dorsal muscles of my little deer, I had a famous heap of coals and embers. Having such a fine opportunity for the experiment, I concluded to try if I could cook the fish so I could eat it without bread or salt. With the axe I chopped off the fish's head, and divided it lengthwise into equal halves. I then cut one of them in two, laid the raw parts together, and winding some long grass around it, opened a hole in the embers—down to the ground, laid in the fish and covered it over with a deep envelope of ashes. I then made a little scaffold over the fire, and placing the remaining half of the fish in small slices, with the venison I had on it, left them there to cure until morning.

And now when I had completed everything to my satisfaction, I spread down my pallet. I had been down but little time until old Ned walked up and took a stand near me. This was only the third night we had camped alone since we were left by our company, and the first night I had let him go footloose since. He behaved cleverly, and I never after put a rope on him of a night. When I awoke in the morning, I found my scaffold had dried the meat and fish almost to a bake, and if I had had a little pepper sauce and bread the fish was very nice. I drew out my fish from the embers, and found it still enveloped in the grass which was only scorched a little on the outside. But the fish was thoroughly done, and nearly as dry as good bread. It had absorbed a sufficient quantity of the alkaline principle from the ashes to answer in place of salt, and it was, to say the least of it, a very savory dish. I made a full breakfast from it, and it went very well. I called up my companion, and after packing up, we set out for another day's journey, leaving the nice dried meat and fish and ten or twelve pounds of excellently cooked fish on the ground, as I had no wallet or any way to carry any eatables along.

About an hour by sun I came to a good camping place. I turned old Ned loose, made a rousing fire, and went off half a mile to a grove, where I thought to get a deer. But they had been some way disturbed: they were all on the alert and running in every direction. It may have been a gang of wolves that had excited them so badly, or there might have been a party of Indians amongst them recently. I didn't succeed in getting any venison that evening. There were hundreds of turkeys in that fine oak grove, and I had to take one of them; it was a good fat hen. I put one-half of her, wrapped up in grass, in the embers, like I did the catfish. For my supper, I toasted, broiled and wallowed it in the ashes, but I couldn't make it compare with the venison. I was at no time that day, as I traveled in the far-reaching sea of grass, out of sight of droves of deer, and if I had thought it necessary, I had several good chances to have shot one. The scenery I passed over that day was wonderful to behold. Except when passing in a grove of timber, the view was rarely less than ten or twelve miles. There were four droves of mustangs. One drove had perhaps five hundred horses in it, and the horses were by a long way the wildest animals I saw that day. They would stampede before I got within a mile of them, and never stop till they had sunk to nothing in the far-off haze of the distance.

The deer were not so wild as the horses. I have been riding past a drove when some of them would lie down so near to me that I could distinctly see the action of their jaws while chewing their cud; I might have got one of them. Everywhere several species of geese were in large flocks, cropping the tender grass just springing up. A great many flocks of the sand-hill cranes were whooping out their loud warnings. There was another large white bird, with the pinion feathers all black. He is as large again as the crane, screams out the same note the crane does, and can be heard five miles.[20] In all the puddles and sloshes of water, ducks would fly in clouds. There were pinnated grouse, curlew, plover, sand-piper, and in the wet places, a good many snipe. Many of these birds, when flushed up, are very noisy, and my riding through their flocks all day kept up a continual uproar. I slept very well after the wolves quit trying to catch the geese. They were near enough three or four times for me to hear the sentinel distinctly when he warned the flock of the approach of the wolf. The word in the Canadian goose dialect is *hoank-lakiak*. I heard it often, and the wolf howled out his disappointment when he gave out trying any longer.

At the first peep of day, when the morning sparrow made his first low note, Old Ned, who had been standing a long time, sleeping with his forefeet on the edge of my pallet, on hearing the sparrow, pushed me with his nose. I was not asleep, but he didn't know that, and wanted me to get up. I arose, and opening the ashes, hauled out my roasted turkey. It was good, not very palatable, but its nutrient qualities supplied the demand of the digestive mill, and I felt quite comfortable after it.

This camp was at the upper border of a streak of timber, twelve miles wide. Pecan, pinoak, and the largest and tallest live oak (*Quercus virens*)[21] I ever saw anywhere else, with a thick set canebrake, vines, Bamboo briers (*Smilax lanceolata*) and scraggy shrubbery for undergrowth. It was a hard day's travel to get through it. I had to walk the greater part of the time and cut the vines that thwarted our course with my hunting knife. I saw plenty of bear and Mexican hog sign, but there was no chance to kill any of them because the cane was so thick. This wild hog is the peccary, a pachyderm, belonging to *Decotyles*.[22] I have forgotten his specific character. When you can skin out a quarter of one of them without touching the musk tumor on his back, it is equal to a half fat hog, pretty well tasted, and on a pinch, makes a satisfactory meal. I began to think towards evening that I should have to camp, and sleep in that thicket without anything to eat or drink—saw no water all day.

Then I succeeded in breaking through into the prairie which spread out south and southeast as far as I could see. I felt like a freedman—Ned was glad too. He stood gazing at a drove of mustangs away to the right, with a high head and dilated nostrils, until I began to fear he might take it into his head to go to them, and laid my hand on his bridle. Two or three miles to my left, I saw some cows; and supposing they had a home, I turned in that direction, intending if I found a house to try to get a little bag of salt, and then I could eat fowls or fish when I failed to get a deer.

It was evening, and before I got to the cows I saw a man come riding out from the Bernard timber towards them, and we met at the cattle. He instantly invited me to go and stay all night or a week with him, if I had time. I went with him. His name was Churchwell.[23] His dwelling was on the south bank of the Bernard; had resided there twelve years; had a lady wife and six children. Had a neighbor fifteen miles north—towards Brazoria, which was forty miles distant.[24] They treated me very kindly; the good lady made me a little pocket that held a pound and a half of salt, and gave it to me.

Morning came, and I asked for information for the purpose of steering clear of getting hemmed in among the lakes and bayous; he could give me none. Said it was eleven miles to the sea beach, but he had never been there in his life. Said he should be afraid of the Indians. I set out, found no difficulty or Indians; but fowls endless. There were a great many swans. I couldn't get near enough to shoot, but thousands were flying over me every few minutes, and I concluded to try one with my rifle. I let Ned go and waited a few minutes until a large flock came over, not exceeding forty yards high. I found I could hold my gun on one good enough; let fly, and he whirled down instantly. The balance of the flock turned, and circling round four or five times making such a fuss about it that I was sorry I had killed it. I was soon reloaded and could have killed another, but had no need for it. I took the dead one to a clump of timber, by the side of which ran a little drain of fresh water from the prairie. I stripped old Ned, dressed the swan; it was a young fat one. I prepared a low scaffold, and a big fire of green wood; salted a portion of the swan's breast in a little pile on the scaffold, and set out to explore the beach. There were to be seen in the lakes long ranges and banks of white pelicans. And yet the swans were most numerous and seemed to be gathering.

I went back to my camp, put some live coals under the scaffold, and started parts of my swan to cooking. It was drawing towards sunset when I observed the swans were settling in a line, extending parallel with the shore as far as I could see either up or down the beach, half a mile out to sea. By the time the sun had sank below the horizon, the entire host of them seemed to have pitched down and had formed a snow-white belt just outside the breakers for miles up and down the coast. There was no apparent commotion amongst them, no talking or noise going on. The white stripe formed by them on the water was half a mile or more wide, and was much broader at a point a mile or so below my position. It was the evening of the 5th of April, and it seemed like everything but myself knew what was to take place. All that quacking uproar of a thousand tribes of the feathered race was hushed up and perfect silence reigned.

I was engaged making my repast on the well-cooked swan, seasoned with salt. I thought it was flavored a little too much like mutton, and a little too greasy. It was, nevertheless, quite palatable, for it was the first mouthful I had tasted since early breakfast at Churchwell's. It was near seven o'clock—deep twilight; I was done eating, and was thinking about surprising those swans before day in the morning. At that moment the shrill note of a small tin trumpet sounded, down at the broad section in the drift of swans, waking sleeping echoes, breaking the dismal silence. At the sound of the second blast the note was repeated at measured distances, running along that vast belt of birds beyond the range of my earshot. At the same moment the threshing storm of wings commenced, which increasing every instant, soon surpassed the din and uproar of a rushing hurricane. They passed square over me at a height not exceeding thirty feet. They were five minutes or more in getting past. I could feel the concussion of their wings, and somehow or other they seemed to devitalize the air. My breathing was painfully oppressed while the living tornado passed over me. I felt like there wasn't air enough, as though the swans were using it all up to fly on.

When they were gone and out of hearing, the disagreeable silence returned, and I sank to the ground, feeling considerable exhaustion. I have witnessed the stampede of a thousand buffaloes; at another time, six or eight hundred mustangs. I had a million of wild pigeons pass over in a few minutes, but they all dwindle to insignificance when compared to that flight of the southern division of American swans, on the Texas gulf coast.[25]

I remained at that camp another day and night. Early in the morning of the second day, I ate some of my swan and proceeded down to the beach, taking my fish lines. I thought if I could get them I would try some salt water fish. When I came near the seashore, at the mouth of a bayou that was the outlet to a large lake,[26] I saw signs of many fish but found no bait that I could get. Lakewards, where the creek began to widen, there were many dark spots in the water that were really little clouds of small fish—roaches.[27] I could see the hawks and gulls picking them up. It was a long time before a gull would oblige me so far as to fly over the land with his fish. When one did, I fired at him, trying to kill him. I didn't do that, but my ball passed near enough to frighten him, so that he dropped the little silver-sided fish. I baited a hook with it, and casting it as far out in the creek as the line would reach, let it sink to the bottom. The banks of the creek were very low, and fringed with long grass that hung over in the water a yard or more. I let my hook lie some time, and not getting a bite I drew it ashore, intending to examine the bait and cast it out again.

But as the bait came up through the grass it was taken by a strong fish that darted away toward the lake until my line was all paid out. He was soon exhausted. I drew him forth and found it to be a large flounder—a five or six pounder; I said, another like that will be enough. I threw in the same bait, and this time it was taken as it was going down. I soon found it was a fish of a different character to the one I had caught. He put my small line to the twanging tension, and made it hiss through the water like a swift moving wire. I doubted its capacity to hold him for a while, but he played himself out ultimately, and I brought him ashore and landed him. It was a red fish, weighing about eight pounds. I put the other half of my roach on the hook, and soon got a sheepshead. I had enough for half a dozen men; so I strung them up and marched up to my camp. I tied the sheepshead, Indian fashion, between split sticks and barbecued it on the scaffold, making a good thing of it. I ate of this good fish several times before I slept. Before going to sleep I hurled the red-fish deep in the glowing embers, to have him ready for my breakfast. I could do nothing with the flounder. I made my pallet and lay down, feeling pretty lonely, as there was so little noise. The swans, pelicans, white-fronted geese, brants and many of the Canadian geese had disappeared. All at once it was a calm time.

After taking a very satisfactory breakfast off of my roasted redfish, I proceeded down the clean, hard beach about fifteen miles, and finding my path obstructed by the mouth of the Colorado, I turned to the right, and having seen enough of the sea coast, I concluded to beat back up the country. I saw some small, short-legged deer before I had made my way out from the lakes and marshy lands, and tried to get one of them but failed. I supposed that their diminished size was attributable to the poor pasturage they found there.

After I was clear of the marshes the prairie opened up before me. It was a sightly plain, narrowing towards and extending up the Colorado side. It had a heavy sprinkling of fine looking deer, mustangs and thousands of sand hill cranes, who on seeing me on horseback with my gun, kept up such an incessant whooping and shouting warning to their friends, that every other wild animal was constantly on the alert. Everything in a mile or two were looking at me as I rode along. There were plenty of deer on the prairie, and they seemed to be deeply interested in my movements. The cranes were evidently putting themselves to trouble to ensure a warning to the deer particularly. When they saw a gang of deer near the line of my travel, in advance of me, they would get up a big whooping and come flying over with all the noise they could make, and passing on go over the deer with such earnest, loud shouts that the deer, becoming alarmed, would be sure to run off. The cranes did that four times. It vexed me, and I said, "Mr. Crane, you are putting yourself to useless trouble; I have no desire to shoot your deer at this time of day; but if any of you come deafening my ears with your harsh whooping again, I'll make you afraid to try it a second time."

I hadn't traveled far until I saw right ahead, and distant not over a mile, a remarkably large drove of deer. They were grazing and were scattered across my path half a mile wide. At the same time, and more than a mile to the right, were to be seen ten or fifteen acres of cranes, busily engaged in digging bulbous roots. It is a species of lily[28] with which the coast prairie is thickly set, and at that season of the year when it is beginning to sprout the crane can find it easy. That perhaps is the cause of the appearance of such vast numbers of them on the coast prairies in April. As soon as they saw me and were sure that I was a man and had a gun, they raised the whoop, and there being so many of them, they filled the air with their discordant sounds. A party of them took upon themselves to come by where I was, screaming and shouting and showing me to the deer. As soon as I discovered that they intended to call on me, I jumped down, stepped off to a naked place, where I could stand firm, made ready and waited for them. They came so low that I could see their eyes. I covered the leader with my rifle, and at the moment when he checked an instant to make the turn towards the deer, I fired. He seemed to drop loose from his company, and whirling down, struck in twenty feet of me, with such force that it jarred the ground. Instantly the whole party turned, and with a loud *coor-r-ruck lak lak*, raised the whole flock. Meeting half-way, they all began to circle, every gyration of which came nearer to where I stood, and every one of them vociferating at the top of his voice *coor-r-ruck lak lak*. Soon they were turning, a heavy living cloud, in circles immediately above the dead one. I have been present in big battles, once in a devastating tornado, in a mast-snapping storm at sea, but I never heard that much noise before, and it was increasing rapidly, for I could see them collecting in flocks from every direction; besides there could be seen single cranes hurrying hither and thither on a higher sphere. These I took to be couriers, and were no doubt, if I could have heard them, yelling out the dread news. They were thickening up so fast and putting on such a threatening aspect, that it made my hair rise, and I confess that I couldn't avoid feeling a degree of alarm.

I had reloaded my rifle, but I was at a loss to know whether, if I shot another it would frighten or increase their resentment. They were, however, increasing to thousands, and it was very evident that I must do something. Appearances were momentarily growing, and if there was danger in the situation, procrastination would not result favorably. If I could have thought of it, and mounted Old Ned, it would have been right, and left them to examine the dead at their leisure.

I concluded to shoot another, hoping it would frighten and make them go further off. So I shot another, but in the confusion produced by a deafening uproar, I did not take sufficient pains, and broke his wing. He fell squalling to the ground. He struck about thirty yards from where I stood, and instantly fifty of them pitched down around the wounded one. I saw one of them walk a few steps towards me, and with his wide open mouth yell out something. The clamor was now becoming terrific. Old Ned came up to me looking like he was badly frightened, and fearing he might run off I mounted him. Before I could recover the bridle he dashed off and was running at full speed with me. He had taken the proper direction, and I let him have his own way. He continued to run at least a mile. The cranes were on the ground around the dead and wounded in thousands, and they were gathering to that point from all quarters; numbers were passing overhead in that direction. I continued to journey onwards until 4 o'clock, when I took up camp at a little creek of running water—cranes still flying over and hurrying down to the great gathering. I never expect to see another day as that was.

Setting forward again after breakfast, nearing the Colorado, I found myself before night in the canebrake between old Cany and the river. There was a good fresh-worn path there, or I should not have attempted to have made my way through the cane. I found it a good road, and traveling rapidly I was not many hours in reaching a farm in the midst of the thick cane, fifty-five or sixty miles from the coast. The people there told me that the road would continue to grow better, and that I should find several settlements before I got out of the cane. They invited me to tarry with them a few days, but I excused myself on the grounds of short time. The truth is, I did not like the appearance of those canebrake folks. I hurried onwards; my path was a wagon road now, and Old Ned made the miles pretty fast. Night brought me to the house of a man by the name of Heard,[29] and although I told him that I would prefer camping out, he said he could not permit me to do so; that there were Indians in the vicinity and, besides, he had a use for me. "So say no more about it, but alight; let the boy take your horse, walk in and let me introduce you to my family. Your name, sir?"

"Lincecum."

"What state?"

"Mississippi; but originally from Georgia."

We encountered his good lady at the door, and he introduced me as a man from "our" state but had forgot my name. I repeated it, and she rejoined, "Walk in, sir," with a very pleasant smile.

When we were seated she remarked, "I hope this is Dr. Lincecum of upper Mississippi. If so, I am almost acquainted with him. I have heard my dear father speak so often of him. Am I not correct in my surmise sir?"

"You are correct, ma'am, but who was your father?"

"Dr. Alexander."[30]

"Well, ma'am, you are, sure enough, very near acquainted with me. Your father and I were close friends a long time." I had to stay with these people several days and answer a thousand questions.

After washing up my shirts and mending the rents in my pants, they let me pass. Mr. Heard went out into the prairie a mile or so, and pointed out the tops of the timber growing around Eagle Lake, twelve miles distant. I got a late start, and the beauty of the scenery on that far extending plain almost paralyzed me. Ned, who had not been recently accustomed to it, had eaten a little too much corn, and he being a little sluggish I let him go his own gait whilst I was enjoying the delightful view. There was a big drove of mustangs bounding away on the far-off plain. All horses can't be brought to this high pitch of usefulness. For they, like men, are not all endowed with good self-preserving sense. I never use the word *instinct,* where the animal has brains. Here, I am speaking of a well developed, intellectual, educated horse, one possessing a high degree of enlightened selfishness. One like Old Ned, who seeing his master in a confused difficulty, discovers the best plan to pursue, runs up to him, presenting the saddle for him to mount, which his master accepts, and then dashes off with him on his back, proudly transporting him from the terrible din and clamor and threatening aspect of the million of cranes that were piling in from every side.

To return—on the route to Eagle Lake[31] I saw a great many deer, wild ducks, some Canadian geese, and but few cranes. I arrived about midway of the lake at one o'clock p.m. It is about six miles long and in some places four or five hundred yards wide, full of fish and alligators. It was such a pretty place I concluded not to leave it that day.

I selected a good sleeping place, stored away my saddle and things, and leaving Old Ned to take care of them, went off skirting the timber to try for a deer. I didn't begin to hunt soon enough. I came near walking into a lying-down gang of deer not more than a hundred yards from the horse. Such an oversight as that always vexed and caused me to grumble at myself for such carelessness. It was the time of day for them to be lying down, and I supposing they were all doing like those I had frightened away; they came into the edge of the timber from the prairie to obtain shade and cover. I went further into it, edging along very cautiously half a mile perhaps, when I came in sight of a single deer, lying down, ruminating very busily. I could see its head only. It was not exceeding thirty yards from me, and I had the advantage of the wind. So I stood perfectly still. It must be a rare thing, thought I, to find a single deer in these regions. I peeped and peered into every little opening in the brush, and presently a nice little yearling doe rose up about sixty yards from me, and stretching out one hind leg, showed that she had been lying there for some time. She was the right age and size for a good piece of venison, and I concluded to take her. She was standing squarely, broadside to me, and I aimed to cut the artery behind the kidneys. It was a flintlock, and that time missed fire. I did not move a finger even, for five minutes. There were at least forty rose up in sight, and they listened and gazed around with such severe scrutiny, that they forced me to keep my half-bent position until I was nearly ready to fall with fatigue. They relaxed their vigilance at last, and I cut down the pretty little doe. Splitting the skin on her back and peeling out the dorsal muscles, I turned them down to the last joint of the backbone, separated the loins from it and took both the hams with the backstraps to my camp.

I prepared a scaffold and a good fire near to it. About the time I had got a good bed of coals, and was about spreading out some pieces of venison on the scaffold, I thought I heard the sound of a human voice. I looked to see if Ned had heard anything. He was standing firm, on all his feet, with a high head, looking along the lake above, and now I discovered at a small distance towards the upper end of the lake, two Indians with rifles. They had seen me working about the fire and were approaching. It annoyed me some. My gun was close at hand, but she had missed fire that day. The Indians were seventy-five yards distant, advancing slowly, so I concluded I had best speak to them. I took up my gun and said in the Choctaw language, "If you are friends, you are welcome to my camp. If not, *yoma, hick, cahpanta* (stand where you are)!"

"We are peaceable friends," they replied without altering their pace.[32]

When they came to a tree thirty feet from where I stood, they set their rifles against it and advanced to shake hands. I put mine down and met them in the most approved Indian style. That over, one of them said they were not only friendly to the white people, but they were glad to find one that spoke their language so thoroughly.

"Where are your company?" they asked. I replied, "They haven't got in yet. I'll put the balance of the venison on the scaffold, and when it gets done we will all eat together."

"That is right," said they. The one who had been silent all the time now said, "Just as we came in sight of your smoke, we had found a bee tree. They were going into a hole near the ground; and from the quantity of wax they had spread around the hole where they enter, it is very likely a rich one. Seeing you have a good axe, I propose that my friend and I go and get some of it while you finish dressing the meat."

"And we'll have a great big venison and honey supper," said

I. I watched them as they went away. They left their guns, and as it would soon be dark they hastened away. In due time they returned, with a trough-like piece of the hollow tree piled up with nice honey-comb. They said there was plenty more in the tree and proposed that we stay here, kill deer, and eat it up and get fat. I consented and we commenced the feast at once. They ate on after I had finished.

One of them, as a kind of apology, said, "You don't eat much, or you are perhaps saving some for your absent companions."

"Well," said I, "Is that not right?" "Exactly right," said he, "and shows the true spirit of a good hunter. But I have been examining the signs around your camp and have discovered that your companions will not come in tonight." "Why not?" said I.

"For one of the best reasons in the world. There are none to come. You are a lone man." After the eating was over, we prepared to lie down. I offered one of my blankets, but they said, "No, we will do well enough." They gathered a bundle of long moss apiece and spreading it on the grass, lay down and seemed to be quite comfortable. They told me without my asking them that they resided on a little river east of the Trinity; that the tribe numbered two hundred and fifty; that they were farming successfully and their chief had sent them on a mission to a white settlement on Old Cany, who it was said were making sugar. If so, their chief had ordered them to carry home some seed of the cane to plant on their farms.

Then they asked where I resided—on what river in Texas? When I told them my home was a thousand miles towards the sunrise, they were surprised. And then came the question, "Where did you learn our language?" They had never heard of the Choctaw people, asked many questions about them. I left them talking when I went to sleep.

We were all up before day, ate what cooked venison we had on hand, made up to stay there another day and feast on the venison and honey. One of them said if he had a hook and line he would not eat any more venison that day. I got out a line for him. The other one, seeing me give him the line, said to him, "Now, do you go and bring in the balance of the honey, and our white friend and I will go out and get a good deer," and he appointed for me to go south whilst he would go north.

I pretended to be fixing and picking my flint until they were both gone. I wanted to put my money out of the pocket book into a secret pocket I had in my saddle pad. These Indians had been a good deal with the white people and might have learned some of their treacherous habits. So I left in my pocket-book a $5 bill on a badly broken bank, and three twenty-five cent pieces in silver. I left my coat hanging on a little tree, went to where I could hide myself, and waited for the man with the honey.

He was gone about an hour, and returning, brought back at least a bushel of splendid honeycomb on a kind of tray he had hewed out of part of the hollow tree. He set it down and was evidently smartly fatigued. Leaning against a tree to blow a little, he discovered my coat. It was a good cloth coat, and he went and took it down and examined the quilted collar, the lapels, weighed it in one hand, then hung it up and hastened off towards the honeytree. In the meantime I heard the hunter's gun. I waited a few minutes, until I saw the honey man coming with another load as large as the first. Going back, I met him at the camp. This time he had at least fifty pounds of comb, full of young bees as it could hold. They were all in the larvae stage, and white and fat as butter. He said that he had put all the young bees to themselves because he had always understood the white people didn't eat them. But as I was a hunter that could live in the wild woods on my gun, it might be that I was different in that respect, and he had brought them in to divide with me, if I liked them. I replied, "They are most excellent, healthy food; but when I eat venison I prefer the pure honey. I will give you my share of the bees this time."

The hunter came in with plenty of fat venison—all the good pieces of a big deer, tied up in the raw skin. He cut it into strings, and putting a little salt on it, left it on the skin until he had a good fire. He remarked that there was no scarcity of deer in this region, and he would put all that deer on the scaffold. He broiled some on sticks, so that by twelve o'clock he had some ready. We had eaten nothing only the few mouthfuls of cold meat in the early morning, and we were needing replenishing. The fisherman had got four large black bass and had rolled two of them carefully in the embers, without moving a scale on them. He dressed the other two, split them in halves and laid them on the scaffold over a slow fire.

I invited him to come and participate with us in the venison and honey. He replied, "No, my fish will soon be done, and I don't want to clog my appetite with venison when I have plenty of good fish."

By the time I got through with my dinner, he was taking his fish from the embers. He laid them on some long moss, and when they had cooled a little, he peeled the scales off with the skin from the upper side, and commenced eating the white flakes of the well-cooked fish with the young bees, which he bit off like bread from the edges of the pieces of comb.

I went off down the lake, leaving them both eating. I was gone three hours exploring the lake, and when I came back they were both asleep. I looked round and found the two roasted fish and noticed some of that on the scaffold had disappeared. I waked them up; they immediately put fire under the scaffold, and as soon as it was warmed up they ate again, both dining on the fish and young bees. After we had all lay down, I inquired, "What shall we do tomorrow?"

"Well, *Fulimatubbe* will go and catch more fish. We have venison enough, and you and I will hunt up another bee tree." "But have we not honey enough, too?" said I.

"Well, there may be enough for one day, but the *Foaooshe* (young bees) are all gone." I asked, "Did you eat all the *Foaooshe* yesterday?"

"Well, yes; we were both very hungry, having tasted but little since we left home, 150 miles, and the *Foaooshe* are at such a full ripe stage. In three days they will all take form, and then they are not good. I thought that as we have met and camped in this beautiful place, it wouldn't be a sign of good sense to go and leave it as long as the *Foaooshe* are good. We will do the hunting, and you can take *Suppoka* (Old Ned) and explore all around the lake if you like."

"Very well," said I, "be it as you say." They were such clever fellows, appeared to be so fond of me, and without my axe and fish hook they could neither procure one nor the other of what they liked so much. I made a substantial breakfast in the morning, cut out for a grand round of discoveries in the botany of

Texas, a great deal of which was new to me. I had progressed not exceeding three miles (it was about 8 o'clock a.m.), when I heard the merry laugh of a lady, and very soon there dashed up two carriages containing three ladies, as many gentlemen, and some children, with two out-riding Negroes. Who should it be but my friend Mr. Heard, with two of his neighbors and their families going to the very spring where I had my camp, to have a grand picnic. Heard and his good lady recognized me at once, and were greatly surprised to find me there. The balance of the party, who had been told all about the lone traveler—the wild man—seemed to be as familiar and as glad to meet me as did Heard and his good lady.

They inquired where I had started to now; I informed them, in as few words as possible, and that I intended to get back to that good spring and sleep one more night. "Turn right around and go back with us now; it will increase the pleasures of our picnic this beautiful day," said Mrs. Heard.

"A hundred per cent and more too," ejaculated one of the ladies, "I'm so glad we found you." I turned and went back with them. There was no one at the camp, and they were astonished at the big scaffold of meat and great pile of honey, and the fish scales and bones, and signs of so much eating for a single man.

I replied, "I am a very hearty man." It was all joy and high life with the delighted party and they were running everywhere! Already, one of the ladies, who complained that she had ate but little breakfast because they had started so early, was trying some of the nice barbecued meat—dipping it into my cup of honey as I instructed her, and using my hunting knife to saw it off at her pretty mouth. Mrs. Heard's children asked if they might have some of the honey.

I said, "Let them eat it all, if they want it, and the meat too. I can have a hundred-weight more honey and the scaffold loaded with choice venison and fish too; and this I will do if you will all agree to camp here to-night. It will make such a glorious chapter in my journal! What do you say?" The ladies voted unanimously to remain. The gentlemen did not oppose. The carriages were immediately unloaded, and the Negroes started back for a supply of blankets, more bread, coffee and so on. One of the younger men told the Negro to bring his violin—which was as much as to say, invite the neighborhood to come.

Carriages gone, and nearly the whole party engaged sawing away on the venison and honey, one of the men said, "Doctor, how the mischief are you going to replenish your camp with meat and honey, and you said fish, and it's now nearly 10 o'clock?" I didn't know the name of but one of my Indians. I called him up. He came up with a pleasing smile on his broad face, having six very fine black bass. I introduced him to the company and communicated my plan to him. He took the axe and his gun and set off in a high glee. I then told the ladies that to save the fish it would be best to dress and salt them soon, and spread them out on the scaffold with just fire enough to keep them pretty warm.

"Why, are they ours?" said the pretty lady. "Certainly," said I. "Oh well, then," said she, "we know what to do with them." The gentlemen went fishing and I remained at the camp, to be asked a thousand questions about the States (Texas was then a part of Mexico), and the people, the fashions, etc. About noon my Indians came in with the choice parts and pieces of three deer. For the season, the venison was very good. But the Indians said they shot none but the yearlings. They enlarged the scaffold, and spreading all the meat on it, cut wood for a big fire, so as to have coals enough, and they said they had found a bee tree, but it did not look very promising. If I would attend to the meat, they would go and cut it; and if it was not a good one they would hunt another. I remarked to him whose name I did not know, "That is right, and I am glad to find that you are such clever men. Now suppose we exert ourselves to feed all this people to their satisfaction here in the wild woods, and we shall excite the wonder and favorable sentiment, and they will have a tale to interest and amuse their children and friends for years to come. Now tell me your name, that I may introduce you to these fine ladies."

"It is," said he, "*Oka-noo-ah* (Walk-in-the-water); that is the name my mother gave me, my war name is different." So I introduced him to the ladies as "Mr. Walk-in-the-water," and they rushed up to shake hands, but he recoiled from it, saying, "There is blood on my hands, and in that condition I cannot touch the hands of such friendly and good looking people." I told him that the man that made the sugar was here, and that he could find out all about it, and how to proceed from him here. He was pleased, and hastened off into the woods. Not very long, and they came back with a fine supply of honey, and I suggested to them that if the people of the settlement heard of the big picnic we are having here, there will likely be twenty more here by sundown. Then he said, "We had better bring in some more venison and put on the scaffold, and we can fetch in the honey anytime; there is plenty in the last tree."

"That's a good thought," said I, and he hurried away. I and the pretty lady attended to the meat scaffold, and before very long the hunters came in with another good deer. *Okanooah* said, "*Fulimatubbe* will get some more fish, and I can attend the meat now, and you and these friendly people can do the eating." The handsome lady asked me what he had been saying? I told her, and she remarked, "He is a gentleman." I interpreted her remark, and he, looking much pleased, ejaculated, "*Yokoka,*" which corresponds with our "thank you."

The party were bringing in a good many fish, and now that *Fulimatubbe* had joined the fishers, our stock of food was rapidly growing larger. Then returned the carriages with the blankets and pillows, much bread, bacon, coffee, sugar, and a basket of wine, and twelve more of the people from the settlement, which for the first time, I heard them call Egypt.[33]

The returning ambulances had brought back supplies, with the wallets full, so that every newcomer had with him plenty to have feasted the whole party with no thanks to me and my Indians. They, however, didn't seem to care for their own preparations. The venison and honey, and fish, cooked Indian fashion, pleased them best. It was nearing suppertime, and I suggested to the ladies that they had basins and pans enough, and it would give the individual parties a fairer chance to press plenty of honey into them, than they could have in my old camp cup.

Everything was drawing to a point for the feast. The handsome lady came and said, "The whole party are going to sup on the fish and venison and honey. If you prefer it I will make some coffee for your supper?" I thanked her kindly, and said I preferred the honey and barbecued meat.

Seeing the violin case thrown out amongst their pots and blankets, and not having had one in my hands for months, I was hungry for music. I opened the case and found a splendid violin, in excellent condition. I took it out, and going near to two or three ladies, said, "Some of you were telling a newcomer what the wild man could do. With this good violin, I will furnish you with a little story that will bear telling as long as you live."

I performed "Washington's Grand March" so loud that I could distinctly hear the tune repeated as it returned from the echo on the opposite lake shore. I could feel that my very soul mingled with the sound of the instrument. At the time my emotions were about to make me become unfit for such a jovial company, the handsome lady ran up and, slapping me on the shoulder, exclaimed, "Good heavens, Doctor! Where are you going?"

I was startled, and turning up the violin, performed "Gen. Harrison's March," then "Hail Columbia" and then "The No. 1 Cotillion in the Beggar Set."[34] They all went to dancing. I quit.

Everything being in readiness for supper, Mrs. Heard beat a tumbler with the handle of a knife, and the fiesta commenced. They ate and bragged and laughed, until the darkness came and they had waked all the echoes of the old lake. Then they called up the Negro fiddler and tried to dance awhile, but the grass was too much for them. Then one of the ladies proposed that all should be seated and get the Doctor to treat them to a few pieces of his good music. While they were fixing the seats, *Okanooah* was expressing to me the delight he had experienced, and how glad he was that he had accidentally found me in his journey. These people had treated him so politely he should never forget it.

When the company were all seated, I inquired, "What style of music would you prefer; the lively or the grave?" The reply was, "Oh, give us your own musical taste; we don't want to hear anything we are accustomed to."

I was in high tune myself, and on that clear sounding instrument, before that gleeful company, I poured forth the wild, ringing, unwritten harmony, that is only heard and learned by the student of nature from her sweetest songsters, in the deep unhacked forest of Florida, and the jungle-enveloped coast lands of Mexico. I continued before that silent audience for at least an hour.

"Is it enough?" I said. "Oh, no; go on, go on," they all cried. I played on, till my musical appetite was satisfied. When the music ceased, preparations for sleep were made, and all lay down for the night. *Okanooah* brought his moss near to my pallet, and in a low tone said, "What's your plan for tomorrow?" I replied, "I have, for the enjoyment of your company, remained a day longer than I intended. I must pursue my explorations tomorrow; but so that you may have a fair understanding with the sugar man, I will call him and help you talk to him now." So I called Mr. Heard and told him the Indian's business. He willingly communicated all that was necessary, and informed him that he could come in November, and he would give him as much cane to plant as he would want.[35]

Okanooah said, "Then there is no use for me to go any further, I will travel tomorrow too." Accordingly, after a big breakfast in the morning, we all shook hands as affectionately as if we had been acquainted all our lives, and parted never to meet again.

CHAPTER SEVEN

An Observer of Nature
amidst the Wonders of Texas

PIn two days more, I reached the house of my friend Burnham Mand he was pretty smartly out with me. He said he expected me to stay with him and keep him company. Instead of that, he said, I preferred lying out in the woods. He never saw such a man. No one else had ever done so in Texas. "You must not try that again," said he. "It is the time of year for them to come down, and the prairies are already full of Comanches." I said I knew that. I had seen several squads of them in my travels. "What did you say to them?" he inquired.

"Say to them!" returned I. "Why, nothing. I did not let them see me. I don't allow Indians to see me when I am traveling in the prairie. I saw signs of them almost every day, and three times I saw them. Once at their camp broiling and eating meat, once running and heading off some buffalo from the main herd, and another time I saw ten or twelve of them sitting under a lone tree in the prairie. I could not discover that they had any enterprise on hand, though I did not feel sufficiently interested to enter into a close scrutiny."

"You are a strange man," said Burnham, "and you will get killed sure. You must stay with me. I can find amusement for you." PThe children were all glad to see me, as they were very uneasy for fear the Indians had got me. They had shot old Mr. Ally[1] full of arrows down at the corner of the field next to the river and killed him three days ago, and the Burnhams had been awfully afraid I had been killed. Mr. Burnham said there had been a few straggling Indians marauding in that vicinity. No one had seen them; and if old man Ally, who was dressing a deerskin down at the corner of the fence, had not been killed, it would not have been known that they were in that region. Burnham thought there were six of them, and the reason he had for thinking so was that the six arrows they had left sticking in the old man were all of a different style of workmanship. He thought they were gone.

I remained a week with Burnham and his children and narrated to them the big accidental picnic I had met with. They were greatly interested and wished they could get a violin, to hear me play. They said Mr. Creswell[2] had one, but they had never seen it, and they didn't know how a violin looked, or what it was like. ᴹWe hunted the deer twice and went to the ferry boat fishing three times. But I had in my mind planned an extensive trip. ᴾI was very desirous of making an excursion over the comparatively unexplored portions of Texas. These partially known and widely extended regions lay southwest and west over hundreds of miles of unoccupied country. The buffalo, the bear, the deer, the antelope, the peccary, the turkey, were all plentiful and were the only inhabitants of that vast domain, except in the upper portions of the water courses there were a few hairy beavers. I was very desirous of seeing it.

There came to Burnham's a man whose name was Keaton, and he said he had been all over this country; that he knew all about it. I asked him if he wouldn't like to explore it again. His answer was, "If I can get pay for it, I had as soon go as not." "What pay would you want?" I inquired. He said he would agree to go and show me the country, and ride his own horse, for a dollar a day. But I must feed him; his horse could find himself. I said, "It will be a trip of two or three months; we couldn't carry provisions that long."

"Oh, I know how we shall have to live; you find me plenty of venison, and I'll live well enough. I am no hunter, and could make out poorly on my own success in hunting." "It's a bargain," said I. "When can you be ready?"

"Any time after today," said he. "We'll set out day after tomorrow morning then; be with me early." We set out according to previous arrangement, and my pilot took the old San Antonio trail. Towards evening, he pointed to a black streak in the distance and said, "That is a grove of timber, and there we shall sleep tonight."

"Well," said I, "Do you go on, make up a fire and I'll try to get some venison for our supper." He went on, and about dark I came to the place he had selected and found him sitting at the root of a tree holding his horse. There were no fire or other signs of preparation for supper.

"Hello, Keaton," I said. "Are you sick?"

"No, I feel very well."

"Why didn't you make a fire?"

"Well, sir, that was not included in our bargain."

"I understand you now," I said. I went to work and made a fire, cut out some nice pieces of venison, broiled them nicely on some sticks, and sticking them in the ground, said, "Help yourself."

I broiled several other pieces and set them up convenient to him, until he had enough, and there was a steak or two left. And when he had quit eating, I asked him, "Have I come up to my bargain with you?"

"Oh yes," he said. "So far, I am content."

"You are, I find, a great stickler for men to come up to their contract with you."

"Well," he asked, "Is there anything wrong in that?"

"No, sir, in that respect you are perfectly correct; and if you are particular in complying with your part of a bargain, you are a Christian—doing unto others as you are willing to be done unto."

"That's my rule," said he.

"And do you think," said I, "that you are complying with your part of our contract, by taking me along these old trails?"

"I do," said he.

"My understanding of the contract is that you agreed to show me the southwest and west portions of unoccupied Texas. You can't show it to me while we travel along the roads and old pack horse trails, and besides, I do not need a pilot to show me how to go along a path."

"Well, sir," said he, "I can tell you once for all that I am not going out into the wide, pathless prairies to get lost and perish to death or to be butchered by the Indian." I made no reply, but resolved how I would manage the case without argument.

I was up before day, broiling and preparing meat for his breakfast and for myself too. I had it all ready by sunup, and called him to get up and eat. I wanted to be moving. He arose slowly, remarking at the same time with an oath, "You're an early riser."

"Ah! what time would you prefer rising, Keaton?"

"Oh, awhile after the dew has dried up from the grass."

"Well, get up and take your breakfast, for I shall be on my horse in thirty minutes." Nothing more was said.

When I had finished my breakfast I went out and brought both horses to camp, saddled up my own, and mounting said, "Keaton, I am going to travel—pointing with my gun W.S.W.— in that direction today," and moved off moderately.

I did not look back until I had progressed half a mile or more. When I did turn my head I observed Keaton was still standing at the camp with his horse ready. Half a mile further, I looked again, and he was following, but didn't seem to be in any hurry. Nor did he overtake me until about 12 o'clock, where I came to a plain horse track lying in a north and south direction on the interminable prairie.

As he came near, I observed, "You don't care for company, Keaton?"

"Well, yes," he answered, "Sometimes I do."

"Come up and tell me what track this is." He looked at it awhile, and then with another oath, said he didn't know.

"You told me," said I, "That you knew all this uninhabited country; but never mind, I think this is the track that leads from Bastrop to La Bahia, and that the best thing that you can do is to take the Bastrop end of it."

Said he (with some oaths), "I'm of your opinion on that subject, and if you'll tell me which end of the road goes there, I'll take it. How far do you think it is?"

"I can't tell you anything about distances, and I only guess that it goes to Bastrop; but it will take you there, or to some crossing place on the Colorado. Here is the money for the two days I had you with me."

He looked like he was going to refuse: "Here, take it," said I. "You may get hungry by the time you find a house."

I bid him farewell and left him sitting on his horse in the road. After I had proceeded perhaps a mile, I looked back just in time to see him sink down behind an elevation of ground that lay between us, and that's the last sight I ever had of him.

. . . [3]It was 1 o'clock p.m. The equinoctial storm was over, and the sky was blue as indigo. The weather prognostics indicated a good time for me, and I plunged into the far-reaching sea of grass and flowers, joyously and full of delight. I felt like I had escaped some heavy enthrallment, and my heart pulsated with goodness; my course lay W.S.W. and far away in the distance I could discover a dark line, which I took to be the nearest timber, and all in the bright expanse between me and it was dotted with flocks and horns of gamey fowls and quadrupeds of many species. Away four or five miles to the N.W. of my path was a large drove of mustangs which the distance had modified into a motley mass that seemed to be floating and rapidly diminishing as it receded from my sight. Many little bunches of prairie hens flushed up from the deep grass in short range as I broke through blooming prairie pea-vines and tangled grass and weeds that long afternoon.

It was getting towards evening and the timber was still far away. I pressed my heel to old Ned's side, and he reached his legs a few inches further and measured the ground with a quicker pace. I don't want it understood that I pricked the good old horse with a spur; for I didn't. I will here state once for all, that I never owned but one pair of spurs in my life, and after purchasing them I had not rode five miles before I pulled them off and hung them on a hickory bush that grew near the road. I found that I had inadvertently pricked the blood out of the side of the gentlemanly horse I was riding, and he was complaining at it hugely. I vowed that should never occur again, and to keep my vow, have never had another spur on.

One of my religious tenets is, when I have a sensible horse to take pains to convince him, in the first place, that I am his friend, and then patiently train him to the uses I have for a horse. After he has no more fears that I will hurt him, he will do everything I make him understand gladly. No, no, I didn't spur old Ned. He had been long trained that a gentle pressure with the heel to his girth meant go a little faster. I saw that night would overtake me before I could reach the timber, and I concluded to shoot a deer or an antelope the first good opportunity. The antelope are wilder and harder to get a shot at than the deer. I saw several little flocks of them, and tried to get a shot, but failed. When it was getting near sunset, there was a gang of them nearly right in front of me. When I came in half a mile of them and they were beginning to gaze at my movements, I tumbled suddenly down in the grass. Crawling under old Ned to the opposite side, I rose up and began guiding him along between myself and the game. I was making pretty good headway when the whole flock, not seeming to understand the nature and meaning of my maneuvering, came running right towards me. I made ready, took hold of Ned's bridle, squatted under his neck and waited for them. They dashed up within thirty paces of me before they stopped, and were scrutinizing me and my outfit very closely when I, having selected a very nice, small one, let fly. Not being steady in that squatting position, I made a bad shot, breaking its back a little forward of the hips. It fell, bawling so loud and constant that the flock turned back, and from the way their hair was all turned the wrong way, they were preparing for battle. But when they saw me separate from the horse, they understood the thing then and fled away over the wide scenery until the grass and the antelopes all looked alike.

I took its backstraps and the ribs from one side and hurried on to the timber. It was an hour after dark before I reached the timber. Ned and I were both tired and hungry. I turned him loose and he walked straight into the bushes. Soon I heard him stepping in the water, and it sounded like there was plenty of it. It was so dark that it was with difficulty that I kindled a fire. I got it going at last and broiled some of my antelope. It was the first I had ever tasted. I did not find it as pleasant food as the venison. With bread and salt it would be very palatable, but alone it is too greasy. In the morning I found I was in close proximity to a considerable creek. It was running flush then, but in the dry summer it would cease to run. I had no possible chance to know the names of the water courses I passed. The next day's travel brought me to a gushing little river, which I have since found out was the San Marcos.

The ground on the east side of the San Marcos Valley is considerably elevated, and when I had reached the top of the hill that overlooks the valley, a picture presented itself to my view that I thought was the most beautiful I had ever seen. From the top of that high hill the eye can take in the valley for twenty miles—ten above and as far below. It is in some places three or four miles wide, as level as water, and at that time was covered with a heavy coat of grass. The majority, or prevailing species, was that beautiful cow-fodder grass known to science as *Vilfa aspera* (Bebua).[4] There were some buffalo and several little herds of mustangs in sight. Deer were there too, but I was becoming so much accustomed to them that they were ceasing to excite attention. The nearest animal to where I stood was a she-wolf with seven half-grown whelps who were galloping away, not very hastily, towards the timber and brush that grew on the margin of the little river. I did not leave my point of observation in a long hour. I could not see what sort of a stream it was, it being entirely hidden by the brush.

To see the water and to taste of it was my first business, as I had been badly upset at one camp with the water that turned out to be bad. Let me digress and tell that tale here. After I saw a pool of more than ordinary clear water, I camped there. After I had broiled and ate my venison, when I went to the pool to slake my thirst, I found the water sour as diluted sulphuric acid and the same sort of tooth-sharpening taste. I called up Ned; when I took him to it, he smelt of it but wouldn't touch it. On this discovery my thirst increased greatly. It confused me so that I could think of nothing but water. Under the alarming influence of this dilemma, I saddled up old Ned, and dark as it was, set out in search of water. I concluded that straight ahead, in my daily direction, I would find water as soon as by any other course. Old Ned didn't show any signs that he was displeased at the idea of moving but nimbly tramped off through the narrow, dark streak of timber and into the brighter prairie. Though there was no moon, it was nevertheless light enough for me to distinguish dark-colored objects some distance. I could recognize the wild horses at the distance of fifty or sixty yards. In the night they are not so wild. They would, when I had the wind of them, suffer me to approach quite near them. I think they did not run till they smelt me. In that grayish, deerskin-colored starlight I could not distinguish the deer at all, and once I was right amongst them before they gave the signal snort and scampered off. I saw horses twice, and once a dark, single something slowly moving on the prairie. I rode towards it, and it soon disappeared behind the black curtain of the distance. I had progressed three or four miles from the sour water, when Ned began to bear on the bridle to turn more southerly. I could see by my guiding star that I was traversing my course correctly, and I straightened him up; but soon again, he was stealthily bearing more S.

"Well, old fellow," said I, "You have something in your head that interests you, and it may take us to something that will interest me too." Dropping the bridle on his neck, I said "Go ahead." He veered a few compass minutes more to the south and then went straight forward. I observed the stars, and selecting one that headed his course, found that he was going as straight as a line. It was a heavy bed of grass and prairie pea-vines we were passing over, and Ned being hungry, often bent down his head to get a mouthful of the delicious food. It was near midnight when I observed a long dark line in front. Not long and we were in the blinding shade of some large trees. Ned did not stop, but going freely into the obscurity, soon came to the water. I felt with a stick over the bank, and found that by lying down on my breast I could get water with my tin cup. It was not sour, but was evidently pretty thick with recently stirred up mud. I could hear Ned, who was unharnessed the first thing when he stopped, and who had found a place where he could get into the creek, forty or fifty yards lower down, pawing the water, showing that he didn't like it, and he was beating it up trying to make it better.

When it was light in the morning, I discovered that we had struck the not large creek at a considerable pool, fifty yards long and seven or eight yards wide. The pool was thick with mud, and my keeping quiet, not many minutes elapsed before two large alligators rose to the top of the turbid water. As is their custom when the water in the prairie creeks gets low, they were fishing out that creek and were that far on their way up. They devour fish, terrapins, snakes, frogs, and everything else found in those prairie drains. Even smaller alligators do not escape their voracious maw. I said to them, "Go on, old fellows, you are not in my way," and left them busy at their rapacious work.

But to return to my position on the elevated ground bordering the valley of the San Marcos. I followed the old she-wolf and her whelps until I came to the timber. I left Ned to amuse himself with the prairie grass, which he seemed to relish, until I made my way through the brush to the water. It was but a small distance until I was surprised by a rushing stream, thirty yards wide, of the clearest water I had ever met with in my life. It was five or six feet deep, and so perfectly transparent that I could see distinctly the moving particles of sand at the bottom. There were many fish, all so perfectly visible as the birds when flying in the air. I went to a place where I could reach the water, and taking up a cup full found it good cool spring water. I didn't know it then, but I do now, that it was but twelve miles to where the whole of that rushing column of transparent water gushes out at a single opening, at the foot of a big mountain. That spring is one of the wonders of Texas.[5]

The water being good, I ungeared my horse and told him to use his liberty as suited him best the remainder of that day, as I was going to examine this pretty river and its curiosities until evening. It was then in a perfectly natural condition. Not a hacked tree or other sign of human violence was to be encountered in any direction. The scar of civilization had never marred the beautiful face of that paradise valley with its ruinous tramp, nor had the supreme quiet of the birds and beasts ever been disturbed by the unholy clamor of the shouting saint.[6]

Because the wind was from the north-west, I went down the river south-east, so that I might not fail to kill something for my supper as I returned to my horse. I was perfectly overwhelmed with the blooming herbage, bending grass, and flowering trees. It was all new to me. I had never before observed the beautiful *Vilfa [Sporobolus] aspera,* that long wavy grass with its tops all bending northward, or the patches of tall white flowered *Argemone texana*[7] that dotted the wide area of grass. On closer investigation I found these circular beds of this prickly poppy invariably ornamenting an ant city. They were seen nowhere else in the valley and were doubtless put there by the ants themselves, not accidentally, but intentionally. When they locate a city in the edge of the timber, they plant grape vines (*Vitis texana*), Yopon (*Ilex vomitoria*), prickly ash (*Zanthoxylum fraxineum*), and a little scrubby tree producing a small quantity of gum elastic (*Bumelia lanuginosa*), staff vine (*Berchemia volubilia*), and hackberry (*Celtis occidentalis*).[8] All these trees and vines produce nut-like seeds, food for ants, and there can be no reasonable doubt that the seeds of these nut-bearing vegetables are intentionally planted and carefully nursed. Since I saw them in San Marcos Valley, I have bestowed twenty-five years close scrutiny on this species of ant, and know what I am talking about now [1874]. I have named this species the Horticultural ant.[9] Some of the entomologists (S. B. Buckley,[10] I think) call them *Echedoma Texana*. Mine is the appropriate name.

Some author has said, and all superstitionists believe it: "The faculty of reason belongs to man alone." Nothing can be farther from the truth. This unphilosophic idea is only entertained by those who do not put themselves to the trouble to examine nature. Why, positively I have seen enough of the intellectual action of this race of ants during the twenty-five years I had them under consideration, to fill a considerable volume. Their ornamental cities, shaded with fruit trees and grape vines; their governmental institutions, public works; tunnels under running watercourses thirty feet wide and ten feet deep to get into my son's garden and 450 yards under a heavy coat of prairie grass from their city to a blooming live oak, forming a subterranean passage through which to carry the tender leaves and filaments of the live oak, which they could not do over the ground through the close set grass. And this extensive tunnel (450 yards), the terminus of which vented in a yard at the base of the tree. There is no possible way for such a thing to be effected, except by the severest kind of engineering. Besides many other necessary works, every city has its well of water. I have seen six successful wells that were sunk in ant beds, two of them thirty-two feet to the water. They found the ants all the way to the water.

Their public works are executed by slave labor, which institution is very extensive. Pshaw! Man the only animal possessing the faculty of reason, indeed. The believers in the universal deluge may entertain such thoughts, but the serious investigator of natural history knows better. But enough has been said in this place. It does not belong to these sketches, and if the reader will consent to it we will return to where he left me, in the delightful valley of the San Marcos.

I continued to explore down the river until it was getting late in the day, when I commenced the return route. It was, I think, about four miles. I met with no opportunity to shoot a deer until I had approached within fifty yards of my horse, when I discovered, not far beyond him, three deer, who seemed to be gazing in amazement at Old Ned, while he was grazing around his saddle and spread-out blankets. I slipped into the edge of the bushes, and moving noiselessly through the trees and undergrowth till I was near enough, peeped out and found them still looking at the horse. They were all three big old bucks.

"At this season of the year you are poor venison," thought I, "But it's too late to hunt a better, so I must take one of you." They were holding high heads; I could see their large black eyes and great clumpy, velvety horns, which were several inches taller than their ears and pretty well widened at the top where the first long point was beginning to prong off. The one I chose was near, and being all ready I aimed at the center of the triangle that is formed by the eye, the root of the horn and the orifice of the ear. He fell, and on hearing the gun, Old Ned galloped up to see about it; he didn't know I was there. It turned out to be a very good deer. But in that abundant, almost evergreen pasture, it was hardly to be expected to find a poor deer at any season. I cut out and hung on the bushes meat enough for two or three days, so that if I remained longer than that night I should not have to take another life.

About the time I was finishing my repast of broiled venison, the wolves set up a loud cry, so near and there seemed to be so many of them, that I concluded to bring to camp some of the good pieces of meat I had left hanging on the bushes. It was not exceeding sixty yards from my pallet to where the dead deer lay, and numbers of the hungry wolves gathered there and fought and snapped and howled half the night. I buried a nice piece of meat in the hot embers, and hung the other pieces on the nearest snags to the fire. My pallet was twenty feet from the fire, under a little thick-top live oak, to shelter me from the dew and to be away from the heat of the fire. I was a little fatigued from my long afternoon walk, and must have slept very soundly. When I arose in the morning I found that it was well I had put some meat in the fire over night, for the wild dogs had got all that was hung up, and the old buck had been torn to pieces and his bones scattered, there was no telling where.

I ate breakfast about sun-up, from my roasted venison, which was very good, and saddling up, went a mile down the river to a place I had noticed the day before. Here I crossed the little clear stream, and taking my course, traveled onwards five or six miles, when I came to a plain traveled path which did not vary much from the course I was traveling. I had no idea of where it went or whither it came from. I didn't want to see anybody, or come in contact with any settlement, so I crossed the path, turning more to the south; saw cows and other signs that I was in the vicinity of inhabitants of some sort. I turned more south and after passing a pretty plain wagon road a mile or so, came to the low grounds of some considerable water course. By the drift-wood I saw lodged high up on the trees, I could see that it had heavy freshets sometimes. I had nothing to eat; it was too late to both examine the bottom and go hunting. Coming down from the hills was a little branch of clear water, and I pitched my camp there and went hunting. I could get nothing but one old fox-squirrel; had to roast him almost to a coal before I could get the dog odor out of it.

Having no breakfast to pester with the next morning, I made an early start, and going into the timber, which was large [cedar] elm (*Ulmus crassifolia*), pecan (*Juglans olivaeformis*),[11] and cottonwood (*Populus angulata [deltoides]*), came to a considerable river which was dashing its limpid waters swiftly. In taste and appearance it closely resembled the waters of the San Marcos.[12] I soon found a place to ford the rushing river, and being hungry and seeing but little sign of game about this stream, I somewhat hurriedly moved onwards. I did not succeed, though I saw many flock of deer, in getting anything to eat till near twelve o'clock. The deer didn't view Ned and me mixed up together with so much interest as they had done in other prairies. I made out to get one at last by pushing old Ned along between me and the gang of deer until they began to look suspicious, then let the horse go, fell down in the grass, and crawling quite low, succeeded in getting near enough. They were rather shying off, and the one nearest to me was standing quartering, with the head pointing away from me. I cut the portal vein, saw it hump up its back, walk a step or two, then faint. By the time I had reloaded my rifle it was up again; it gazed a moment after its retreating companions, turned as if to follow them, fainted again, and had expired before I got to where it lay.

I am obliged to have something to eat; yet I avoid these

death scenes as much as possible. I always shoot the head when they stand right, and then there is no fainting, sorrow-stricken death struggle in the case. When traveling alone in these wide, expansive prairies where the vision is only bounded by the blue mist of the distance, with nobody but old Ned (who never contradicts me) to talk to, where the vastness of the scenery affords me a pretty fair opportunity for making a comparison between my diminutive self—creeping ant-like—and the rest of creation, I become less morose, softened, and don't like to witness the suffering, the dying agony of sensitive beings.

I was now on the undulating prairies between (as I have since found out) the Guadalupe and San Antonio rivers; a beautiful country full of wolves and very wild deer—no mustangs or buffalo. I was inside of the hunting circle of several very ancient Mexican towns; San Antonio, the principal one, was not far to the right hand of the course I was now going. An hour and a half, by sun, I came to a very large prairie drain which was barely running but had frequent large deep pools full of fish. Its path was forty or fifty yards wide, and showed that it is sometimes a big river. Having brought some of the last deer I killed, tied to my saddle strings, I did not have to kill anything at that camp. I ungeared old Ned and spent an hour in the examination of a curious looking perpendicular cliff of black rock that cropped out abruptly from the end of a considerable hill, which terminated there, and overhung a deep pool of water sixty yards wide. I crossed the water path above the pool and reached the cliff at what had the appearance of the mouth of a cavern. I entered it, and found (turning to my left) a pretty good stairway. I ascended it until I reached its landing on a pretty floor of the same black rock. I made shift to climb higher on broken rocks and projecting crags until I was perhaps sixty feet above the water. Here I found a shelf seven feet wide, perfectly horizontal, projecting from the face of the cliff, forty yards long. Eight feet above, and parallel with the bench, was another projection twenty feet wide and as smooth on the underside as a slate. I think this last projection was the top of the rock and the adjoining hill overlapped it, and that it was covered with earth and vegetation, as the outer edge of the rock was wreathed with dewberry and other trailing vines. Altogether it suggested the idea that it had been torn and heaved up from below, and had left the main body of a large cavern in the depths of the earth.[13]

I should not have bored the reader with a description of this rock, but for the fact that when I had climbed high enough to see over the first bench or platform, I found it covered with turtle doves, perhaps a thousand, that fluttered away as I mounted the stage. The guano overlaying this bench was six inches or more thick. Except a cloud approaching from the north-east, with wind, no rain could ever reach this spot, it is so well protected by the overhanging rock. The guano was packed down smooth and level, and perfectly dry. The curiosity to me is in the fact that these birds seemed to have altogether a different course of action to any of that species I had found before. Thinking they might perhaps be a different species, I killed one of them to be certain. It was a true Columbia turtle, no mistake.[14]

I baited a fish-hook with part of it, threw it into the big pool, and before I had done broiling my meat for supper, I saw the little sapling to which I had fastened the line was violently shaking. It was a fish shaking it, which, after playing awhile, I drew out. It turned out to be about a nine-pound blue cat. It was full and plump, and looked healthy, but I had no salt with me that trip, so I set him free again. I have always found in uninhabited countries, the waters are crowded with fish. In populated countries, by being fished after at all seasons of the year, they are all destroyed. I have myself caught every perch, right at spawning time, for three or four miles of the creek, all full of eggs, in a single day. Hundreds of others were doing the same thing. Next year there were but few perch in that creek. I know now, that if we had let them alone until the spawning was over there would have been plenty of perch the next season. My experience in this matter clearly demonstrates to my mind that properly regulated game laws, strictly executed, would crowd the waters again with fish, thick as I have often found them in new countries, where the waters had not been fished at all. I came the next day to the narrow but deep, swift running river, with blue water. I did not know then what it was called; I know now it was the San Antonio river. Finding no place that I could ford it, I had to construct a raft.

I left Ned naked at the getting-in place, and at a few strokes paddled my raft of dry cottonwood poles, made secure with mustang grape vines, to the opposite shore, and carrying my saddle and blankets up to a good place for him to get out at, called him and spread the blankets on the saddle, like I always do when I take up camp. He kept his eye on me all the time I was fixing the blanket, and when I walked away from it he went into the water and swam over. He had performed that feat many times for me, but during this Texas trip no such occasion had occurred, and I had tied my raft, so that if he didn't swim over I could go back and ride him across. But he had not forgot it, and came to the saddle as formerly. He is so completely satisfied in believing that I am never far from the piled up saddle and camp things, that he would wait several days (where there is food and water), for me to return, perhaps longer. I have often left him at daylight, when on a camp hunt within eight or ten miles of home, and not returned till sundown, and oftener find him standing by the saddle, if it was after sundown, than any other place, and he would always utter a laughing sound and run to meet me, when I had to brace myself to receive one of his heavy, affectionate embraces. I don't like the word *whinny,* especially when applied to Ned. He never whinnied; it was always a grand horsy neigh or an affectionate glad laugh.

Ned was the only animal below the human that I ever saw mend up a burnt-out fire. I have many times seen him, where the gnats were bad and I had built him a smoke to keep them away from him, when it burnt down, scrape up the leaves and trash on it, press it down with his left fore-foot, making a good smoke; then get over it, and with a deep aspiration, or a kind of a satisfied sigh, drop his ears and look very wise.

But we must say, or "be damned" that "the faculty of reason belongs to man alone." Such profane sayings are never uttered by the intelligent experienced observer of nature. I have inquired of the advocates of the doctrine of instinct if they could show me the line of demarcation between the instinctive and the reasoning faculties. They failed to do it. If the hood of intellectual cowardice was not so tightly drawn over their mental vision, I could show it to them. They will not like to hear it and will splutter and utter confused sayings, but I will tell it, nevertheless.

The instinctive action ceases exactly at that point in the chain of progressive development where the brainy viscous—the organized brain structure begins. All above that point, be it copious or scant, great or small, much or little, is all clearly attributable to the varying degrees of the reasoning faculty, to the quantity and quality of organized brainy matter.

But let us leave this world-pestering topic, and return to where we left Ned dripping wet from having swam the San Antonio river. There was too much sign of the depredations of that destructive animal called man to make it a desirable region to me. The game was too scarce and wild for me to live well, and I was pretty sure I heard the report of a distant gun. Besides, I had recently crossed a well travelled road with some wagon tracks in it. As soon as Ned had dripped a little, I saddled up, and taking a south-west course, pressed my heels to the girth. Ned, reaching out longer steps, made speed until late in the evening. It was but two or three miles from the river till I came into the open prairie. When I had progressed ten or twelve miles, I noticed jack-rabbits, grouse, and deer were occurring at shorter intervals, but still too wild. I failed to get anything to eat that night, but Ned had good pasturage. I was quite hungry, and thought I must fix some plan to carry as much as would suffice for one meal at least.

At the first chirp of the daybreak sparrow, Old Ned, who was standing with his fore-feet on the edge of my pallet, pushed me with his nose, and I immediately went off in search of a deer or something else to eat. I was hungry. I saw many deer, but they were all up and very watchful. The bucks were at peace and were going in gangs, in which there were always some of them on the look-out. The does were found standing alone, not far from where their young fawns lay, and I could have shot one of them on two or three occasions, but I had two good reasons for not doing so. One was: the fawn being very young at that season, would be sure to starve to death; and the other was: a suckling doe is very poor diet. I walked and worried till near eight o'clock and had got nothing. The prairie hens all had young ones, and the cocks were too poor and tough. The jack-rabbits were blue and lean, and many were dropsical.

I began to think of resorting to my fish-hook and trying the little creek (or rather prairie drain) I was camped on. But in the midst of this dilemma of confusion and want I discovered, far away to the north, a large herd of bounding bucks that had been frightened, probably by some gunner from the settlements about San Antonio. They were at the time running on elevated prairie, and their forms so clearly outlined on the clear sky beyond that they appeared to my hunger-sharpened vision as large as elk. Their motion was very rapid and they were coming directly towards me. I sat down in the grass, examined my flint, set my gun-stick on the ground, and grasping it high enough for a rest, laid the gun on my clenched hand and sat waiting. I selected my victim as they came, and when they had arrived within forty yards I vociferated pretty distinctly, "Where are you all going?" They did not stop suddenly; some of them came almost to me, but being in position I did not have to move, and they did not seem to notice me. My victim stood right before me, not over twenty yards. Two seconds elapsed, and the poor little forked-horn fell with a broken neck. They could all see me then, and the wild, frantic leaping and scattering of the terror-stricken herd was remarkable.

I took one ham and the dorsal muscles and hurried back two or three miles to my camp. When I came there I was bathed in perspiration; but alimentiveness [hunger] was vehemently knocking at the door. Hastening to get a fire, I soon had some half-broiled meat for the ravenous development to gnaw at. I put all my meat on a low scaffold, and whilst I was attending to that I cast around to find something of which I could construct a contrivance to carry a little meat along with me. Near my smoking meat scaffold stood a broad-leaf elm sapling (*Ulmus americana*); I tried it and it peeled splendidly. "This'll do," thought I; and by the time my meat was thoroughly cooked I had made of the inner bark of that sapling, cut into strips of uniform width, a close, strong, cylindrical basket with a lid (capacity, a big quart) and filled it with meat. It was three o'clock p.m. I fixed up, and tying my basket on behind the saddle (it fit snug and I felt a pleasant glow of self reliance), I mounted, and Ned moved off in the proper direction, without instructions.

In the course of that evening's travel I discovered that the country was changing considerably. There were more mezquit [mesquite] trees (*Algarobia glandulosa*) trees, and the mezquit grass (*Stipa setigera*) was the prevailing pasturage.[15] I passed a very pretty little stream of clear water, and I was glad to see that there were no signs of people about it. I continued to beat on through the rank mezquit fields till near night, when I came to a streak of timber and good water, and as old Ned had been snapping at the heads of the good grass (the grains of which were as large and as full of farina as the oat grains) I stripped him and let him go to it. I hunted amongst the flowers for honey-bees, but there were none; they had not got that far out yet. I had about two pounds of cooked venison. I made up a little stick fire and warmed some of it; on which, with a tin-cupful of branch water, I satisfied the cravings of my appetite. Having meat enough left for breakfast, I spent the balance of the evening in oiling and cleaning up my gun, and put in a new flint. My gun had snapped [missed fire] but once since I left home.

Before sun-up next morning I was in the saddle, elated with the prospect ahead. I soon passed the narrow streak of timber in which I had slept; saw the majestic sun flame up amid the sparkling ocean of dewy grass, more glorious than a sunrise at sea. I was slowly entering the interminable plain, but Ned seemed to be waiting orders about the course. I touched his left shoulder with the tip of my finger lightly, and at the same time pressed my heels to the girth. He quickened his pace and veered three or four degrees south. My mind was employed incessantly with the botany, which was all new. I had never before that day seen the grand old *Opuntias,* with their heavily-armed thick leaves, as large as saddle-skirts. There were many varieties of the cactus family, besides the *Opuntia polyacantha.*[16] A great variety of flowering plants and herbs adorned the wide expanse, and brown wolves and daring coyotes were seen skulking in the distance, and deer all the time but very cautious. I was just crossing the threshold in the great entrance to one of nature's undisturbed, almost limitless parks, full of light and life and joy and butterflies. I dropped the bridle-reins on Ned's neck and he traveled rapidly into that wide field of nutritious grass and herbs.

I was passing the heads of the streams that drained the southern boundary of the great prairie about half-way between Goliad and San Antonio. At night I came to a pretty little river of clear water, but liable to go dry in summer. I reached the timber in time to roast some venison I had killed when I came in sight of the timber. During the afternoon of this day's travel the deer were not so wild as they had been the last day or two. The meat I brought to this camp was taken in the bald prairie, by maneuvering Ned along between myself and the deer. Sitting down on the ground with my ramrod for a rest, at a distance of fifty or sixty yards, I can be certain as fate. I don't want to wound them, and I rarely shoot over sixty yards, and though I shoot well off-hand, I never do it when alone. There was plenty of fish in this stream, and with little bits of the raw venison I caught half a dozen large red-bellied perch. Having no salt, I had to cook them to a crisp to make them eatable. The wolves howled gloriously that night in five or six directions. Some of them came near enough in the edge of the prairie for me to see their dark shadows (twenty yards), and I could have shot several times (though it was only a bright starlight night) with much certainty of hitting, but their outline was not sufficiently distinct for me to select a vital part. To kill would have been an accident; I don't care about wounding a wolf where there are so many.

In the morning I ate breakfast at daylight, packed my little basket, and left on my little scaffold enough to breakfast a coyote, of which he no doubt availed himself by the time the sound of my horse's feet was out of hearing. Half a mile above my camp, in the early morning, I found a much-used shallow ford. I got down to read the signs, and found the tracks of the wild beasts that inhabit the country and the moccasin tracks of four wild men. I was interested in reading these last named tracks correctly, and carefully examined the entrance to the ford on both sides of the river. I found they were all young men, going east, and were not being pursued. The prairie before me seemed to be shoreless, and I launched away, setting my course a few degrees north of that I had been traveling the day before. The moccasin tracks I had seen on the little river had excited my organs of watchfulness, and my observations for that day were extended to all parts of the far-off prairie. What a consoling help a good field-glass would have been to me that day. I, however, had no glass of any kind, nor compass; but I have never yet felt the need of a compass. The atmosphere was nearly calm and remarkably transparent; there was not a cloud to be seen, and the light was clear and steady. I could distinguish objects many miles away. Herds of buffalo and mustangs were visible at great distances, but I saw no signs of signal-smokes, nor anything else to indicate the proximity of Indians.

In that arid plain, water was getting a little scarce. It was sundown before I found any that was fit for use, and no wood. To kindle a little fire to warm my meat, I had to hunt up some old dead weeds that had flourished on the water's edge a year ago. It was dark before I got ready to kindle my fire, and as I did not desire to notify any Indian who might be in sight of my sleeping-place, by raising a beacon-light for him, I did not make a light. I know all about the red man; what he looks for, and his time for observation. It might have been nothing more than imagination, but I felt impressed with the idea that that was not the proper place for me to sleep that night. Those fresh moccasin tracks lingered on my mind. It might be they had discovered and dogged me all day to make an easy conquest of me while sleeping.

"Well," thought I, under this impression, "Whether there is any reason for it or not, I shouldn't rest well; and as the darkness of the night has hidden me from their observation, I had best keep out of it. It's no trouble to move from this place, and that will quiet my imaginary suspicions." I saddled up, and mounting old Ned, moved off, turning at least fifteen degrees more north than the direction of my course had been through the day. The clear night made it an easy matter to keep my course, and I found it abundantly more pleasant than in the hot sun. I continued onward ten or twelve miles, until I had left the ghosts of my morbid imagination far behind. My horse began to reach down and bite the grass, which he always does when wishing to show that he is fatigued. This time he was both tired and hungry. I had made a long day's journey, and I did not give him time to eat before I left my camp. I was beginning to feel dull myself, so I spread down my blankets on the dewy grass and let Ned get his supper. I ate my cold meat as I rode along, soon after I left the camp.

At daybreak Ned pushed me. I went to the little drain, washed my face and hands. Whilst Ned nipped some good grass along the margin of the drain, I took a seat on my saddle and ate my breakfast of jerked venison and water. I geared up and set out. It was a nice morning; only a slight mist hanging in the east produced a red glare to the flame of light that was looming up beyond. Away yonder in the east, in mid-prairie, the gleaming rays radiating from the same point, indicated the spot where the sun would soon appear. There, in the rear border of that pale, red flame, was distinctly seen a large drove of mustangs. Many of them were at play. It must have been two or three miles to where I was, and they had not observed me. Presently Old Sol peeped up, coming right out of the wet grass, and veiled in sufficient mist to prevent a glitter. I could see the first half inch of the sun's disc as it crept out from the center of the great plain. It continued to rise and widen as it came, and where it was a foot wide I saw the legs of a scampering horse blot it for an instant. At the moment when the sun had arose, until it seemed to be resting on the ground, standing on its lower edge in a halo of light, two horses in their play reared up and stood on their hind feet, heads high and rather drawn back, striking at each other with their forefeet, precisely in the center of the sun. They held their attitude a second or more, long enough to burn an impression of the picture on the nerves of my vision ineffaceably. The splendor, grandeur and majesty of the scene was so far beyond descriptive development that I shall not attempt it. "Alas!" I said, "What pity that some finely developed artist didn't see this—never again to appear—sunrise." A large, circular, golden frame, standing on the ground in the center of a vast halo of divergent rays of bright light, and pictured on a deep orange-colored background within the golden circle, a pair of finely-developed horses, black as jet, rearing up to their greatest height, standing face to face, on their hinder feet, and striking playfully at each other with their forefeet, and all in motion—it is a picture that has occurred but once to me during the eighty-odd years I have been making observations on the rising sun.

On account of my being too far down coastwise, I found good water but seldom, and the ground being so flat and level it was with much difficulty that I could procure sufficient food. The bad water was unpleasant (not to say unhealthy) to me and Ned both. So I turned more north, and two or three days carried me into an undulating country, where I could skulk along the gullies, the ravines and behind the little hills, and get my meat with much more certainty. In four days those little hills had increased to a range of pretty rough dimensions. Working my way as best I could into these piles of black rock for two days, I found the difficulty pretty fatiguing, both for myself and horse.

I climbed up to the top of a high peak to look out for a better way. It was impossible to judge from that mountaintop anything about which course was best. And I could not decide which direction I should take until I saw, away ten or twelve miles eastwardly, a signal-smoke loom up, and the answer to it rise more to the right. I decided then to go in the opposite direction. I got down again to my horse, and varying a little more west than I had been traveling in the forenoon, in the course of five miles of my winding path, came to a dashing little creek of good water. Here I concluded to spend the balance of the day, and if I failed to get a venison, I could probably get some fish.

It was a deep glen, the valley very narrow. I went off up the stream a mile or so, and found two yearling deer eating some kind of leaves on a little bench at least 65 yards above me. I could see no way to get nearer. I was in no hurry, for they had not discovered me. I got a good rest, and taking steady aim (nearly like shooting up a tree), shot one in the side, far enough forward to hit its heart. It sprang violently upward and came tumbling down the cliff to my feet. I concluded to bring my things up and camp there, which I did, and barbecued the greater portion of the little deer. I found them not very plenty in the mountains and intended to carry all I could of it along with me. I heard no wolves during the night. Was up warming up some meat for breakfast quite early, and packing up all I could carry. I made pretty good speed up the little creek as far as it went. Near its source I found a pretty plain buffalo trail, which evidently was very ancient. Crossing the creek I took the lefthand end of it, which went north-west by north, and with considerable labor succeeded in making my way through a rocky gap to the top of the mountains. There was an area of several acres of level ground, clothed in the common prairie grass, and if there had been water on it I should have spent the balance of the day there. There were eight or ten deer up there. They ran off on the ridge at the north end of the little prairie, and knowing they were acquainted with the best getting-down place, after I was satisfied with all the observations I could make in reference to the course to travel, I followed the direction the deer had taken. I found they had a little path which continued about two miles on top of the mountain, to where it traversed another small prairie, on which I again found the deer. At the far end of this second prairie their path went down the north side of the mountain. It was a much better road than the one I ascended the mountain in. It was late when I arrived at the base of the mountain. I found plenty of fresh bear and wolf signs but no signs to excite watchfulness—no moccasin tracks. A pretty creek of clear sweet water was there. I concluded to sleep there, and as I had plenty to eat, I did not have to go hunting. I spent my time in making observations on the natural history of the place.

Next morning I journeyed up the little creek; saw and followed a big flock of deer until they made their exit through a gap where there was a plain trail. I followed them further, and discovered that I was in their mountain path on which they passed northward from the south through that range of not very high but rocky upheaval. The deer were quite numerous, so were the turkeys. The bear sign seemed to be confined to certain districts, while the wolves were howling every night. They were at some of my camps pretty saucy, and I would have shot some of them, but couldn't tell how long I should remain in that difficult country to travel in and was afraid I might need the powder and bullets for other purposes. I continued to travel on that wild beast path three days, when I came to a rapid river, affording as much water as the Guadalupe, dashing its current in a southeasterly direction. Where I struck the river seemed to be an unfrequented region—no signs, old nor new, of human beings anywhere.

I could get a deer anytime I needed it, and had it been the proper season for it, I could have roasted a turkey every night. There was a black-dotted quail, very numerous, and it may be a little larger than bobwhite.[17] Where the valley would widen into a prairie of any size, there would be thousands of them. There were many other game birds, among them the chapparal cock, a species of the genus *Cuculus*.[18] Where valleys of any size occurred, they were bordered with bushes full of berries. They belong to the genus *Ribes*,[19] and would bear cultivation.

I crossed the pretty river and went a day's journey beyond; got out of the mountains; saw vast herds of quietly grazing buffalo, which indicated there were no Indians in that vicinity.

From that plain, or buffalo pasture, I concluded to turn my course homewards, and going N.E. by E., came upon the river again an hour by sun. I had passed through some rough rocks and high hills, but I had early in the day found the buffalo road and by that means found my way through the mountains to the river with little difficulty. I could cross it in that country of rocks very readily, and I got over and camped on the east bank of it. I had camped a hundred yards or more above the buffalo crossing to keep out of the way of passing animals. Towards midnight Ned came trotting up to where I lay, making his nasal signal, and I could hear some large thing wading in the water at the ford but did not discover what it was.

The high mountains were jammed down to the water where I slept, and I went back to the buffalo trail to find the best way out. It was a hard road to travel, gullies, hill-sides, and over rough declivities all day. I did not get out. Had to sleep among the rocks and also to listen at the most singular of all sounds— the long scream of the Mexican lion [probably *Felis concolor*, the cougar]. It resembles the sound of a middle size steam whistle nearer than anything else. My horse was tired and found but little to eat. I moved early, but like the day before, I was constantly in dread of meeting a gang of buffalo or wild horses. Had that happened, there was no chance of escape. That night I found a side valley to sleep in, where I was out of danger of being run over. At 12 o'clock next day I got out, and found myself on an elevated plain alive with various animals, all quiet. I saw no signs of Indians, and I was quiet too. I struck off nearly east. I needed water but found none that I could drink until I had passed the elevated tableland, which was at least twelve miles.

There was a good spring running out from among the rocks, just below the level of the place I had just crossed. I pitched my camp there, put Ned on the grass in the branch below, and made observations on the plain above to make sure there was no danger. I saw a few deer, two wolves, and (perhaps) five thousand buffalo.

In the morning I traveled along the edge of the plain for the purpose of getting around the numerous heads of small branches that dripped from the sides of that elevated ground. In doing so I was nearly South. But I came to a place in five or six miles, and I turned eastward again. I went down some quite rough declivities; saw some pretty cascades. Two days and a half I worked and worked among the creeks and rocks before I could get on to a reasonably decent country. I came out on a prairie country, and though it was many hundreds of feet lower than the table plain I crossed three days before, it was nevertheless a high, gently rolling region.

There was a sparkling little rivulet, and my meat being out I concluded to spend the evening in procuring supplies. I got a good deer in time to cook the nutritious portions of it, and what was left from my supper and breakfast, I made shift to pack in my little basket and tie to my saddle. I made two days' journey then before I shot another deer—till the evening of the third day. During these three days' travel I got along with only an occasional difficulty—never out of sight of deer, and was getting into the antelope range. Saw several prairie dog towns—graminivorous dogs with hare lips: food for rattlesnakes and owls that dwell in their burrows with them. Buffalo decreasing in numbers. Though this was not the kind of country for the large herds to frequent, I thought it would some day make a great sheep country.

The camp I was now at was on a small rivulet and a very pleasant place. I could get no venison; it was too late when I came to the water. Since I had some scraps of the jerked venison left, I didn't suffer much. I started early and had not progressed more than a mile when some deer came running up a hill; they were in thirty yards of me before they saw me. By the time they stopped, I had seen them coming, checked my horse, and was all ready for them. It was but a moment they had to survey me before the gun fired. It was a small deer, and I took it by its forelegs and dragged it fifty yards down the hill, to the branch that glided along at the foot of the hill. Almost everybody drags a deer by the hind legs; I prefer the easiest way.

By three o'clock p.m., I was on the route again and continued till near dark before I came to water. I saw very much game this day, and horses. I was off by light in the morning, making good headway until 12 o'clock, when I came to a nice little creek of very clear water, shaded by a streak of timber seventy yards wide, and the ground was clothed in the freshest, sweetest looking nimblewill grass [probably *Muhlenbergia Schreberi*]. Ned was pulling down the bridle so constant, and it was cool and shady that I got down, set my gun against the stump of a broken-down tree, within about a yard of where I seated myself with my back against the log. While Ned was cropping the grass, I was writing in my journal.[20] Whilst thus engaged, I felt the presence of somebody, and turned my eyes in the direction the impression came from. Near enough for me to have reached him stood a large, nearly naked Indian. Having my gun, he seemed to be curiously examining the lock. For a period I was shocked—fearfully shocked. I thought of six lone travellers that had been met and murdered at different points in Texas during the time I had been in the country. I felt quite lonely; I can't say how long that inactive period lasted. Presently, however, the confusion passed, like your breath evaporating from a highly polished razor blade, and it went off at the feet. The mental powers then played freer. The first thought was self-accusation for careless negligence; next, resentment at Old Ned for not warning me.

And then—how shall I manage the case?[21]

CHAPTER EIGHT

The Beautiful Maiden
and the Best Laid Plans

ᴾI knew from the start that the whole effort must be addressed to his superstitious fear; all else is useless. One thing, to begin with, was to avoid all show of anxiety, alarm or fear. An Indian, like a dog, will jump upon you at the slightest manifestations of timidity. My mental powers were rapidly returning to their duty now, and without changing my position, I addressed him calmly, but firmly, in the Choctaw language. [Once,] I had met with a Mexican, that I mistook for a Coshata Indian at San Felipe, at the Brazos, and spoke to him in Choctaw (which is the true language of the Coshatas),[1] and he answered me in good Choctaw. On my inquiry of him if he was a Coshata, he said "No, that he was a Mexican, but had been a prisoner with the Comanches many years—from his boyhood till he was twenty-seven years of age—and that he had learned that language from them. They called it the slave tongue, and that in every band or tribe of the wide-spread prairie Indians was always to be found some who could speak the slave tongue, by which the different tribes could and did communicate, and it becoming subject to all the tribes was the reason it was called the slave tongue."[2]

Thinking of what the intelligent Mexican had informed me, I used the Choctaw language to the naked wild Indian who stood so near to me with my gun in his hands. I said, "That gun has been doctored. It should not be handled by another until it has destroyed the enemy for which it was doctored." He immediately set the gun down in its place, and stepping off to a respectful distance, folded his arms and in deep mellow-toned Choctaw, said, "From what land came ye?"

"From three moons' journey towards the sun rise," I answered. "Are you going to the sunset?" he asked.

"I know not where I shall go to. I am hunting a white man who killed my brother while he was asleep. I traced him to the great prairie west of San Antonio. In that great waste I lost him; but if I live I shall find him yet. You remember I told you my gun is doctored?"

"Yes," said he, "And I hope you may find him. I know of one white man in the long-haired chief's band, but he has been there a good many winters."

I wrote out the unfinished sentence in my journal, and rising up from the sitting posture, discovered, at the distance of fifty yards, four more Indians. I asked where they came from?" He replied "We were all standing there when you rode up, and when you sat down against the log, I said I would go and see what you were after. When I came you seemed to be so busy making marks that you did not notice me; and seeing your gun, I thought I would look at it until you were done."

I spoke to them to come up, but he told me "They didn't understand you." He spoke to them in a language I had never heard before, and they came to us. After I asked them, through my first Indian, a few questions about their hunting exploits, they answered freely and seemed to be pleased with me. One of them came near and was about to take hold of my gun, when the linguist spoke sharply to him, communicating that the gun had been doctored, and what for; and then the man had respect for me.

I got into a big familiar confidential conversation, and to show them that I felt no uneasiness at all, told them that amongst the white people I was a great *Estahoola* (conjurer). To prove it to them, I went to my horse and got some oil of cloves, telling them I had some *bela* (oil) in that stone [vial], that if I would put the smallest quantity on their hands, it would make them strong and long-winded, and that they would smell it two days. They held out their hands, and barely wetting the tip of my finger at the mouth of the vial I rubbed it hard in the palms of their hands and told them to smell of it. They were greatly pleased, and said they could smell it all over the woods. I was beginning now to plan for making my escape. I wanted to conduct my farewell conversation so as to show that I did not entertain the slightest degree of suspicion as to their honesty and friendship, so I asked if they were on a hunting expedition, intending to leave the impression that after I made a big round in search of my man I should like to return and hunt with them half a moon. I foolishly asked, "*Cutemapillah che albanoa?*" (Where is your camp?).

The question had hardly escaped my lips before I thought how foolish it was. I might have been sure that the next word after telling me where their camp was would be an invitation to go to it and get something to eat. I saw at once that my plans for getting off creditably were blown up. To offer any excuse or apology to get off would show a want of confidence (fear), which would have ended further progress on my part in that expedition. They did as I expected; told me their camp was near and invited me to go and get something to eat. I mounted my horse and followed them slowly as they picked their way through the briers, not exceeding seventy-five yards, when we were out of the timber and in full view of their camp. It occupied about one hundred and fifty acres of the prairie. It was noon and they were all sleeping under the scattering live oaks that grew on the prairie, or I should have been apprised of their proximity.

There was but one tent set up. It was large and tall, made of dressed buffalo skins. They had arrived there that day and they were all lying down, seeming to be resting. At this new feature, and greatly increased apparent difficulty in my prospects, my mind was busily planning and scheming. I was waiting for something to turn up that would open a hole in the dark cloud that obscured my path. My Indians, whom I was following, went about midway into the encampment, and when we were passing near the big tent, I yelled out the Eagle-dance whoop as loud as I could scream (and that's remarkably loud). Jumping from my horse, I lay down on the grass in the broiling sunshine, letting Ned go. There was very little surprise or attention manifested amongst them. The five men who came with me did not stop nor even check their gait, but scattering as they advanced, were soon lost to my view.

Not long after, a woman came and took Ned to a shady live oak near, stripped him, and setting all my things carefully against the base of the tree, put a long raw-hide rope on his neck. She led him off to a good place of grass, fastened him to a little tree and left him. The care that the woman took with my things and my horse encouraged me greatly. A new thought came up. I will be very clever and ask them to let me live with them until I can find the man that murdered my brother. I will ask the men to aid me all they can. But before I had an opportunity to put any of the plans to the test, a very good-looking man (about 50 years of age) came and took a seat near me. Out of respect for his age, I raised to the sitting posture, and after he had surveyed my countenance for a moment, he asked: *"Cut le mansh miuta?"* (From whence came ye?)

I told him the same thing I had told the first Indian. "Where are the balance of your company?" asked he. I replied, "I have no company." He then said: "The chief told me to ascertain where they are, what's their business and their number."

"I have told you once that I have no company." He left me and went into the big tent. In a few minutes the chief himself came and took a seat near me and glared at me for a minute at least. I knew he wanted to make me quail; but I kept a steady gaze right back in his eye until he looked off himself, and casting his eyes on the ground, said: "I shall ask you some questions, and shall expect truthful answers." "Well," said I, "Put the questions properly and you will be sure to get the truth. My tongue is not forked."

"Where are the balance of the company to which you belong?" he inquired. "I belong to no company; I am alone," I said.

He asked, "What is the object of your traveling alone in these great plains?" I told about the murderer of my brother, etc. I could see he didn't believe me, and he left me without saying another word. Five minutes after, a very large, strong-looking Indian came and stood near me with a lance in his hand. I understood that. Directly I saw three men bring up their horses, saddle them, and ride rapidly off in the direction I came. Then came the good-looking old man, and told me to go to where the women had placed my saddle and things; that it was unhealthy to sit in the sunshine at that time of day. I followed him to the place, and found, sure enough, that the women had prepared the pleasantest kind of a lounge for me in the shade, with three or four ply of dressed buffalo robes spread on the grass. I seated myself on it, and invited the old gentleman to take a seat on it too, which he willingly did, and seemed to recognize the invitation as special good manners. He said, "I believe what you have told us, but the chief didn't, and has sent three men as spies on your back track, to search for your companions."

I said, "They will return and say they couldn't find them." He said he had told the chief that, but the chief said there was no harm in making sure. I had already become attached to the old man. His physiognomy, his prominent phrenologic developments, the tone of his voice, and his mode of speaking, all indicated an elevated type of intelligence and goodness. His organic developments were modified on that rare scale in the genus, that meets friends everywhere. I hastened to thank him for the friendly attentions already manifested towards me and hoped so to deport myself as to continue to merit his favor. He said he would do more. He was the chief's private adviser, and when I had made him thoroughly sure that my sentiments were true, he could prevail on the chief to be my friend too.

Then said I, "It's all well for me, for what I have stated will never have to be said another way." He said, "One of the men that came into camp with you today said you put something on their hands that smelt strong and pleasant; that you told them it would make them strong and you called it some kind of *bela*. What does all that mean?"

I replied "It means all I told them; and as I shall not be in a hurry to leave here, provided your chief will permit me to tarry, I shall have time to explain that and many other things to you that you will be glad to hear. *Alik-che Seah-ho* (I am a doctor)," I told him, "and the *bela* I rubbed on the hands of those men is some of my medicine. It gives strength and courage." He then informed me that he too was a doctor, and that he was proud of me. We soon became very good friends.

Probably an hour had passed since I was conducted to the pallet of buffalo robes when the old doctor called loudly in a language that I did not understand, nor know to whom he addressed it. Soon, however, a good-looking young woman made her appearance, with remarkably clean-washed skin, her abundant shining suit of hair clubbed on the nape of the neck, dressed (as I supposed) in her very best, which consisted of a string of odd-shapen white bone beads around her neck, an ample skirt ingeniously woven of some kind of bark and feathers, reaching three inches below the knee, and a very neatly-made pair of moccasins of reddish-brown deer-skin on a well formed foot. She brought with her a nicely cured buffalo tongue, and kneeling on the ground near where I sat, held out her hand towards the old doctor. He said, "She wants a knife." I handed my hunting knife, and as she took hold of it she looked at me very brightly and uttered a word of two syllables. I asked the doctor what she meant. "She said, it is well" he replied. She cut out about two inches of the thickest part of the tongue, smelt of it, and offered it with the knife to me. I accepted it and said in Choctaw, "*Yok-ko-ka.*" She looked at the old doctor; he told her that I thanked her for it, whereupon she sprang up and left.

It was not my time of day to eat, but I tasted a few mouthfuls of it and found it very sweet and juicy. Dried buffalo meat and tongue and raw liver was all I saw them eat while I was with them. Every hunter I saw come in brought with him a liver, which he would hang up, and immediately a gang of children of both sexes would be seen gathered around it, and dipping mouthfuls of the raw liver in the gall, so as to get two or three drops on it, ate it as if it was a great pleasure to them. The doctor said it was the food of the children; that it destroyed the worms, kept their bowels all right, and made them able to stand cold and fatigue longer. I tasted it; it is by no means unpleasant. For many forms of dyspepsia, in my opinion, it would be the proper diet, and it would be cleaner, nicer, and less liable to adulterations than the beef's paunch soup, called "pepsin," we find in the drug stores.

The old doctor spent most of his time with me. He had already begun to look upon me with a kind of superstitious veneration. I discovered this from the inquiries he made in reference to the *bela* I had rubbed on the hands of the men I saw first. My present position in regard to my connection with that tolerably imposing encampment of aboriginal Americans not being entirely satisfactory, my mind, in spite of all the friendly propositions made by the good old doctor, would cling to the subject of laying plans for a creditable escape. If I could increase his opinions of me without exciting his suspicion, I could in case of necessity use him as a gate through which to escape.

He was a doctor. And of all the superstitions in the world — that which excites hope most, deludes it most, holds more people in blindness, maims, cripples, kills and destroys more than any other—medical superstition is the greatest. If I could, by any adroit representation of the great powers of the strong concentrated oils, alkalis and acids I had in my saddle-bags, induce him, without committing an awkward blunder on my part, to believe these powerful medicines (*Itheish*) had been obtained through supernatural agency and that as fast as the nature of my confinement would permit me to communicate the grand secret and its method of procuring, he should have it—then I should be sure of his undying friendship. I commenced the subject with much caution.

First, in a low tone I informed him that, in my country, there were men who could compound medicines for various wonderful purposes. Some of these medicines were used to ensure the constancy and love of woman; others to restore health and children to barren women; medicines to keep off evil spirits, to bind your friends to you, to neutralize the plans of the tattler; and greatest of all, to render a warrior invincible on the battle field. I told him that I had some of these medicines with me; that I knew how to make them, and when the chief was satisfied that my tongue was not forked and would agree for me to stay for two or three moons, I would teach him the whole secret.

"You said you have some of those powerful medicines with you; would it be right for me to see them?" he asked. "Well, yes," I replied; "but we must be careful how we handle it."

I opened the end of my saddle bags and bade him look in it. There were thirty-seven vials. He did not know what a vial was, but said he was filled with wonder. He thought they were something that had been cut out of clear flint stones. But when I took the one having the clove of oil in it and handed it to him," he took it between his thumb and finger, remarking at the same time: "It is not what I thought it was. Is that some of the medicine you speak of?"

"That is the *Bela thlampco* (strong oil), one little drop of which I rubbed on the men's hands today at noon, and if they were here you could smell it yet." I then took out the cork, rubbed it on his hands and put a drop of it on his belt. He was delighted at the odor of it, and said he would go and let the chief smell of it. He was gone a good while. When he came back he said: "The chief has asked a great many questions about you. One was, 'Did he manifest any uneasiness when you told him what the three men were sent on his back track for?'" He said "I told him no, that you had remarked, 'When they come back, they will tell him the same story that he has already heard from me.'" He said the chief was delighted with the smell of the *bela,* and wanted a drop of it put on the sleeve of his fine, yellow dressed-deerskin hunting shirt.

I turned the vial to show him how to wet the cork, and let him go with it, telling him that he must wet the *estinka* (cork) but three times. He returned, and said the chief was thankful for the favor. Night was again approaching, and the old man called again to somebody. The same young lady that brought the buffalo tongue came, bringing some back straps resembling some badly tanned bridle reins. She presented a bundle of them to me. The old doctor said it was the nicely cured meat of a fat young buffalo cow for me to eat. Sun-cured with no salt, it was juicy and sweet, agreeable food, and I partook freely of it. I invited the doctor to eat with me, but he excused himself, saying he ate with the chief. I got my tin cup, and told the young lady to get one of those lads to run down to the branch and fetch me a cup of that clear, sweet water. The doctor told her what I said, and she bounced and fled with the speed of an antelope, and though it was three hundred yards she was back in half the time I expected her to make the trip; and she had scoured the cup, too. I told the doctor to say to her that I did not expect her to go for the water. She replied that she could go quicker than anyone else and bring the water better; and that when I wanted water at any time she was ready to get it for me. I said, "You are a good maiden," and getting out the clove oil, wet a small piece of paper with it, wrapped it securely up in another paper, and rubbing the cork on the palms of her hand, gave her the paper, saying: "This is all I have to reward you for your kindness to me." When the doctor told her my speech, she was delighted, and told me to let it be her that should hear my voice when I needed anything.

The doctor rose from his seat, saying he would soon return. It was nightfall before he came back. He said he had been detained in a long talk with the chief. I said, "It's night now, and I am suffering for water. How shall I manage to get it?" "Why didn't you call your young female friend," said he. "But it is night," said I.

"She don't care for night," and he called aloud. She came, and he told her what I wanted. She took the cup and was soon back with the water. "What had the chief to talk about so long?" I inquired.

"The hunters were not bringing in meat enough, and he was afraid this would not do long for a camp." I said, "You have been here but part of a day." "But the hunters have been three days in this region and have as yet brought in but little meat; and he talked about you some," he said.

"What was he saying?" I asked. "He said it was a very strange thing, if you have no company, that a lone man should be found so far out in these wide prairies," was his reply.

"Tell him that I was raised with the Muskogee Indians; that I can travel anywhere without difficulty; that I can live on what I can kill; that I speak many languages of the red people; that I never do harm to any people; and that I am not afraid, for I never expect to get amongst a nation of red warriors who are so low and cowardly that they would hurt a harmless traveler. No nation of people I was ever among made any attempt to do me an injury. Please tell him that much for me, and also tell him, when I get to sleep to relieve that poor fellow who guards me; that I never travel when I am sleeping." I lay down, and being tired was soon asleep.

I was up and saw the first gleam of light through the fractured rim of night on its eastern section. My guard was not on duty, but soon he resumed his lance. Ned saw me and laughed, at which all the Indians who were up said something, and laughed too. A woman went immediately and moved him to better grass. Soon the doctor came and said, "You are an early riser."

"Yes," said I. "I want to get all the daylight I can. It is very useful. I also want water enough to wash my face and hands. Tell my guard he is relieved until I go to the *boug vosha* (little creek) to have my morning bath." He told the man what I said, and he planted his spear in the ground and said he would go with us.

When we came back my female attendant brought me some nice dried tongue and some bridle reins, of which I made my breakfast. I made observation on the morning action of the women and children. I mentioned to my old friend that there were few men up yet. He informed me that all the men and a good many of the women had gone out to bring in the meat; that a runner had arrived in the night, reporting good success yesterday, and the chief had sent out all who were able to do anything to take care of the meat. "They went off," said he, "about the middle of the night."

I was surprised that the chief had not sent for me or come where I was. The doctor said he understood and spoke the slave tongue thoroughly. I inquired of the doctor about him, and if he was in bad health. He said, "No, he is only lazy." And now came the doctor's questions in reference to the potent *itheishe* (medicine). "You told me yesterday," said he, "that you had some of those powerful medicines, but you did not let me see them."

"Well, you shall see them now." I had a vial of very strong water of ammonia, and a vial of essence of peppermint. I held them up and said, "The vial in my right hand contains a medicine that will kill a man to smell of it, and this in my left will fetch him to life again, if you get it to his nose even in the last breath."

"How long does it to take to kill?" he inquired. "It does its work instantly," I replied. "I could let anyone take a slight breath of it, and as soon as I discovered its effects, apply the other, and prevent him from dying. But I wouldn't try it on a person that's easily scared, for fear he might get out of reach, and prevent me from applying the antidote."

I then got out my journal. In it I had placed some rare botanical specimens.[3] There were six of them. I asked him if he knew them. He replied, "In my own language I have a name for all of them, but only one of them is known as a medicine. Do you know them as a medicine?"

"Yes," I said. "They are, when properly compounded—with one other plant, which I have not found yet—the most wonderful and most powerful of all the plants. This compound medicine has power to protect a man from the bad spirits and live people, too. The vial in my right hand was made with only five of the seven charmed plants. When I find the other plant I shall make the strong, life-protecting medicine. You shall understand it, too."

"What kind of a plant is the one you lack," said he. I undertook to describe it, and drew it on paper, aiming to sketch out a plant that does not exist. He viewed it carefully, and when some time had elapsed, he said, pointing in the direction I came, "Half a day's travel in that direction, on the clean black soil, where a large dead oak had been consumed by fire last winter, are a number of plants of that sort that had sprung up since the other weeds and grass were killed."

I now, for the first time, saw my way to escape. I had no fears of being hurt there. I was certain I should be released as soon as the spies returned. But I had no surety, after I was set free, that for the sake of my good gun and horse, that there were not amongst the hunters and warriors of that large band of wild Indians, men to be found who would not scruple to follow me, and when at a proper distance from the encampment, overtake and murder me for such a prize. To elude all possible pursuit was my only chance in this multitude of untrained people. And this was the reason I was pleased when the old doctor pointed the weed on my back track. I could now show them, as I had several times told them, that I never was at a loss in the woods, and didn't care which way my course lay, so it would carry me to the object of my pursuits. And now I could see my way to safety and liberty. It set my mind at ease, and I could play off the big Indian in high style. I first got the old man to point the course exactly, and tell me how many water paths I would have to cross, and any other object of note, all of which I marked down on a blank leaf in my journal, which he admired very much, and said it was good. "But," said he, "I can get leave from the chief to go with you, and then we shall be sure to find it." I told him there would be no danger, now I had marked out the country, of a failure on my part. I thought if I took him with me there would be but one way to get clear of him, and I didn't like that.

And this all arranged, I held up two vials and said, "If you would like to try the power of these medicines, though they are not full preparations, I will exhibit them to you. I can administer it to you with such caution that there will be no danger in it, though for a moment you may think that it is killing you, but before it has injured you I can apply the antidote and restore you instantly. Such was his confidence in all I said that he consented without hesitation. I directed him to call up the people, let them see what the medicine can do, and hereafter when I am not with you and you have learned to make the medicine, they will know and believe in its power.

He called them—perhaps a hundred women, boys and girls, and a few men. I instructed him to inform them distinctly that I was a great medicine man, and that to show the wonderful powers of my medicine, he had consented for me to try some of them on him. I should put a medicine to his nose; he was to take one breath of it. It would instantly take his breath from him; but before he would have time to be clear dead, I would put a new breath in his nostrils, and he would be restored to life again as good as ever. I told him they must not stand so close around; if one of them should get a breath of the medicine, I should not be able to attend him until it would be too late. They all immediately drew back to a proper distance.

I fixed the old doctor in a sitting posture with his hands by his side, head erect; then I asked him, "Do you feel very well?" "Yes," he said.

"Are you hungry or thirsty?" "Neither," was his answer. I continued, "Are you all right everyway?" "Yes," he replied. "Then we are all ready," I said. Having loosened the corks, and standing on my knees, I opened the hartshorn and applied it fully to his nose. He slapped his hand to his forehead with much force and fell so far backwards that there was an awkward moment passed before I could get the mint hurriedly punched so as to spill a little against his nose and on his lips. All around was still as death, until the doctor spoke, and said, "I thought I was on the road to the *Yokneh owatta okchookemah* (good hunting ground). I am, however, as good as ever." He rose to his feet, at sight of which the whole crowd shouted loudly, and laughed that ugly, loose, throat laugh, that supervenes on fright.

I then told the doctor if any of the people present desired to be killed and made alive again, that I was ready; and rising to my feet I stood with the vials in my hands. He interpreted to them what I had said, and they fled wildly. The children who could not keep up, screamed with terror. My man with the lance had left it sticking in the ground and had fled. The doctor said they told him that my guard was the first one that got away. [B]He asked me for the vials that he might go and kill the chief. To this I would not consent, for said I, "If you kill him and fail to bring him to life, these people will kill me." But he called up a number of prominent men and women and explained that in case he failed to restore the chief, no responsibility should rest upon me. With this understanding I consented. So, taking the two vials and attending carefully to my instruction, he left, followed by the entire crowd but at a respectful distance, and entered the chief's tent. For a while all was silence, then a little bustle, followed by the biggest horse-laugh I ever heard. The commotion outside was indescribable. When the old man came back with the vials, he declared with enthusiasm that it was the greatest medicine in the world.[4]

[P]The doctor was greatly pleased, and asked me earnestly "if I would communicate the secret of making those wonderful medicines to him?" "Most assuredly," I replied, "and as soon as I return from getting that plant you have told me of, I will stay here, if the chief consents, until I learn you how to make them, and shall, by trying them, be satisfied that you do understand how to do it. I will go as soon as I have my liberty; and I can be back in two days. I shall then remain two or three moons, if there's no objections raised to it." I said, "You had better go and inform the chief that my protector has left me with nothing but his lance to keep the *shilloop* (spirits) off from me."

The old doctor went and had a talk with the chief a few minutes, and returning took his seat without any remarks. It was about noon, and my pleasant looking young squaw came with her bridle reins of buffalo meat and a good piece of tongue. It was small, and when she handed it to me she said something which the doctor interpreted, "I notice you do not eat much. The well cured tongue is at this day a little scarce. In a day or two I shall have plenty. Then I will bring you larger pieces."

I replied, "You are very kind to me. You bring me enough every time. But you can oblige me more than ever if you save me a whole tongue to give me when I start after a plant the doctor has told me of. I shall be gone two days. One good dry tongue will be enough." The doctor told her what I said. She asked, "When are you going?" "I think now I will start tomorrow evening," said I.

"I can have you a good tongue then," she replied. "That's a good gal," said I, "and when I get back I shall expect you to fetch my victuals to me again all the time." She said she would be glad, and snatching up my tin cup fled away to the branch as fleet as a fawn. She was soon back, and setting the cup near me hurried away like she had some other duty to perform. I told my old friend that I liked these people; they were so quiet. He said, "They are noisy enough sometimes."

"Would it be anything amiss to call up the boys and girls and let me talk to them?" I asked. "Oh, no," he replied, "They will be proud of it." Beckoning to a boy who was standing not far off, he told him to go around the camp and tell all the boys and girls as large as himself to come here directly. In the course of half an hour there had assembled seventy-five or perhaps a hundred boys and girls, all very nearly the same size. They were ten to twelve years of age, lively, good-looking children. The girls wore a small apron of plaited feathers. The boys were in a state of nudity.

I told them I was glad to see them; I intended to stay with them if they would let me, and I had sent for them to get acquainted with them. I was very fond of music and would be glad to hear them all sing together. They were timid about it, and I proposed to sing first myself, and then they must sing for me. I struck a merry Choctaw air that is very popular as their "tick dance" (*Hushoonte illa*). They seemed to enjoy it very much. The old man said it was a familiar tune with them.

I then stood up and said "Let us all sing together," and I commenced, tramping the time, and they, one or two at a time, joined in—girls first—and but little while passed till they were all singing the same Choctaw air. From merely tramping the tone of the music, I began to step and gyrate, making signs to them to do the same. Ten minutes had not elapsed till they were all dancing the true tick dance step of the Choctaw, performing the circular figure, and singing so clear and loud and harmoniously (Indian harmony) that they made me feel like I was back among the good old Choctaws again.

Then the dance was suspended for us to blow a little and

consult as to what dance shall come next. The girls and the by-standers, who were rapidly accumulating, called out for the same dance to be repeated. They wanted to hear me sing. I consented, and told them (through the doctor, of course) the order of the dance must be arranged in accordance with the Choctaw custom. The boys and girls are to be placed in the circle, the girls on the left side, holding on to the left arm of the male. I saw that the whole encampment were becoming highly interested in my movements. I also discovered that it pestered my old friend to interpret so much for me, and seeing the man that found me—*Neare*—I called to him and begged him to stay with me and interpret for me. The girls must all come out and stand around, a few paces outside of the circle I am forming of the boys, and when they are going round in the dance the girls must look at them; and when the one she likes best comes around she must go into the circle on his left side, break loose and dash away the hand that connects the circle on that side, cling to the arm of the one she has chosen, and join in the song and the dance.

The thing was soon arranged, and I, at the head of the circle, commenced singing and dancing the same tune we had just been performing. It was a new feature in a dance for the girls to choose their partners, and the deepest interest was manifested by the audience (principally women), to see how the children would manage it. The boys had danced two or three rounds when I sang out, "The time to choose partners has come; go in, only one or two at a time." They began immediately to pass in, chose their partners, and performed the scornful act of dashing away the left-hand boy admirably. The circle soon doubled its dimensions. I saw my pretty nurse instructing a little girl, who soon came running in, tore loose the boy on my left, disdainfully dashed him to one side, and then clung to my left arm like a little monkey as she was. To the outsiders (who were nearly all women), to see their little daughters thoughtfully selecting partners and the mortification of the slighted boys seemed to be highly amusing, and their merriment was beyond description.

The old man declared to me after it was all over that this people never had seen anybody that they thought so well of, nor anything so pretty or so full of amusement as the dances I had learned their children to perform that day. He said he told them that I had them under the influence of some of my medicines, and that he had no doubt that I could make a medicine that could set the whole encampment to dancing at once, and then earnestly asked, "Am I not right?"

"Yes," said I. "But would you like to see such an experiment?" I asked. "Why, yes," said he. "What harm could there be in it?" "Well, then," said I, "Tonight you shall see it."

I had danced and sung a full hour in the sun and was bathed in perspiration. My thoughtful attendant brought me a cup of water and said she would bring me some more directly. I had seated myself on my pallet of skins. My good friend, the doctor, who had waited for an invitation, was also seated and was expressing his wonder and astonishment at the very strange things he had witnessed this bright day. He said the powerful influence of the medicine I had thrown out when I was singing and dancing had affected everybody. He saw suckling women, with their babes on their backs, swaying and stepping. That he was ashamed to own it, but he barely made out to refrain from joining in the dance himself. I said to him, "You shall see more tonight."

We spent the afternoon in conversation—he asking and I answering questions most of the time. I asked him to describe again, if he pleased, the plant he had told me of, and point as near as he could the point-blank direction to it. He took great pains in doing so, but said: "I am sure I can get leave from the chief to go with you and then there will be no failure."

I thanked him very kindly, telling him at the same time that, with the instructions he had given me I should be very sure to find it. He should see the plant in my possession on the evening of the third day, after which, if everything went well, we would go to work and I would show him how to make not only the powerful medicines I had exhibited already to him but many more, and some of them a great deal more powerful. He had no doubt of what I told him.

Night came, and it looked like everybody in the encampment had come. I noticed some men and women too that I had not seen before. This was observable from the fact that they crowded closer in and their manifestations were of greater curiosity. I had instructed an old man to prepare a little drum by tying a piece of wet dressed deer-skin over the mouth of a small dirt-pot. Seating him to the center of a circle formed by the boys around him, and then stationing the girls in a circle outside, with proper instructions, I entered the circle of the boys. After I had sung and beat the time till the old man got the beat on his drum, we commenced moving round and keeping time with the drum. Then the dance began, and the boys gradually joined in the song; not long till the girls dropped in one by one, and choosing partners, swelled the dancing circle very rapidly. When all the girls had got in, and while we were waiting for the old musician to tighten and wet his drum-head, I exclaimed aloud, "We children would be proud of it if all the young men and women would join us in this grand tick dance." The old doctor repeated what I said in a language they understood. (I had previously thrown out, on little pieces of paper, and rubbed with my hands on the little girls' heads, nearly all the oil of peppermint I had.) The old man told me that he heard them say that they smelt the medicine, and that it had made them feel lively and fresh.

I immediately said aloud, "They have received the strength and the desire; tell them, old and young, to join in the dance instantly." And in ten minutes every one that had strength was stamping away in the immense circling crowd. I started the tunes, the old man beat his pot, and the intoxicated multitude took fire from the soul-inspiring melody and danced in a perfect frenzy of delight. At last, when I was getting tired of it, we made a failure in an attempt to perform the eagle dance. I told the old man to tell them the medicine having evaporated was the cause of their failure; that I had no more now that I could spare; but when I got back from my trip after the plant he had told me of, I would make plenty such good dancing medicine; that all those old crippled people, when they smell it, shall rise up and dance like the young people. And I dismissed them until I could have the materials to make more medicine. The crowd, highly pleased, dispersed, and in all my life I don't think I ever heard so many people talking at once as they went away.

My old friend met me, as I came puffing and sweating from this hot exercise, and said, "Can I ever be able to do the like of that?" I assured him he could, and more too. And now my good

maiden met me with a cup of cold water, which was very accept-
able. I lay down on my bed of skins, and was soon asleep. I had
triumphed with my plan to escape—good, confident, sound
sleeping went very much in my favor. The old man told me that
the chief had remarked in his presence that bad men, or cowardly men, never slept that sound amongst strangers.

I was up early, and my guard was as glad to get off to the
branch as I was. After a thorough bath, I returned to my skins,
leaving my protector behind. The old doctor was at my place
when I got back, and after inquiring for my health, told me,
"The chief said the three spies he had sent on my back track are
to return at noon today; and if he finds you have made a correct
statement, you will be free to go where you please."

"Then," said I, "I will set out just before sundown in search
of your plant, and when I get back we will compound all sorts
of medicines; and I have been thinking that if it will not be disagreeable to the chief, I will make my home with these kind
people, who appear to be so well pleased with me."

He said: "The chief will have no objections, but for your satisfaction I'll go and ask him now." He soon returned, and said:
"The chief will be glad for you to stay with us, and thinks I
should go with you to get the plant."

I remarked, "He is very kind, but he is not apprised of the
fact that that plant is one of the most powerful medicines, and
that when I get it, it is necessary for me to be alone. I should
make the trip to and from the place without being seen by anybody." "That is strange," said he, "But not more so than what I
have seen you do already."

"Tell the chief," said I, "I am very thankful to him; that I
shall not need any assistance in that excursion, and that when I
return I intend to try to be permitted to approach him, at least
as a subject."

Then came the pretty maiden with my breakfast. While I
was eating I told her, through the doctor, that I was going away
three days; would she not be glad to get clear of waiting on me
while I was gone. She replied, "No, I take pleasure in doing the
little things you require, and shall be glad when you return."

"Would you like for me to make my home in this camp?" I
asked. She smiled and said, "Yes, all the people, as well as myself,

would be glad for you to live with us," and she ran off laughing. I remarked to the old man, "She don't understand me." "Yes, she does," he replied.

"Has she got a husband?" I inquired. "No, she is free," said he.

I then got out the two vials, ammonia and peppermint, rolled them up carefully in a piece of dressed deer skin, which he procured for me, and gave him the package; telling him at the same time they were all I had of that kind of medicine, and if I was to accidentally break and spill it during my trip, I should have nothing to begin with to make more, and I wanted him to keep it safe till my return. He said the chief had a little box; he would get him to put the medicine in it, and there it would be safe. When he returned, after half an hour, from the chief's big tent, he told me that the chief was very glad that I had entrusted him with the strong medicine, and to tell me that in his box it is safe. I thanked him, and felt so much rejoiced at the success of my arrangement for a clear and uninterrupted escape, that fearing I should excite suspicion, I asked the old man rather anxiously to call my pretty waiter to come there, I wished to say a few words to her before the company came around.

Said he, "You love that girl, and I don't wonder; for she is so clever, we all love her," and he called her, *"Nilpe,"* and said something I didn't understand. She answered in a lengthy sentence, saying she would come before long, when she brought my meal. When she came with my dinner the old man said a good deal to her, and I could discover that she became more reserved and (I thought) shy. I asked, "Have you saved me a good dry buffalo tongue for my trip?"

She replied gladly, "There were some dry that smelt well, but I have two fresh ones in a hole now, cooking very nicely. They will be done soon, and will be more tender and better than dry ones." I replied, "Oh, yes, much better; and you are so good to me, I shall never forget it. I shall be very proud of those nice cooked tongues. My spirit will always love and thank you for them, and when I get back I shall be free and can wait on myself and you, too."

She rather modestly replied, "I shall always be willing to do what I can to oblige you," and left us. "That was a good word," said the old man. "She will love you when you come to stay with us."

"I shall be very glad," I said; and finding that I had placed the whole camp in utter darkness as to my designed escape, I was very happy. I said to myself: "Let me get once, good out of sight, and dear *Nilpe*, kind and good as she is, shall never hear of me any more. The sharp eyes and hound noses of your swift, vigilant hunters shall fail of tracing me to my hiding place. I know all their cunning plans and shifts and turns. To elude your plans is my business, and I feel confidence in myself that I shall not fail. So farewell, dear *Nilpe*."

While thus communing with myself I noticed a little stir and considerable talking amongst the people, and the old doctor said, "See the spies are coming in. They are all alive, and got no war locks with them." They rode directly to the big tent, alighted, dropped their ropes on the ground and went in. [B]My old friend ran to the back of the tent to eavesdrop.

[P]He soon came back smiling, and said, "All's well. I heard them tell the chief they had found three of your camps, and at each of them there was but one meat stick." Before he was done speaking, the man with the lance walked away.[5] The old man seemed delighted and, rising up, said, "Now they have left the chief, it is my duty to go and receive his commands."

He was gone half an hour, during which time, being a free man once more, I went to old Ned and moved him to a piece of good grass. The woman who had been attending to him saw me, and came and took the rope—for I had not tied it to anything— and seemed as if she intended to hold the horse to grass. I made signs to her, showing as good as I could, that the horse wouldn't go away. She didn't understand, and followed me to my little tree, where we met the doctor, who explained the matter to her. She said she was willing to hold the horse in the grass, or do anything else for me, if I would stay with them. The doctor told her what I was going to do, that I would soon be back, and make medicines that would make them all young again. She went off rejoicing, and telling every one she met what great things she had heard, and they all kept up a great chatter.

The doctor had a big talk with me, as follows: "The chief is highly pleased that you have come out all right. He is greatly attached to you, and when you return he intends offering a part of his tent, so that you may feel welcome, and dwell with him and his people." I desired the doctor to go right back, and tender to his chief my most sincere thanks; that I should accept of his hospitality with the greatest pleasure, and that I hoped that I should so demean myself as to make him feel that he had added a strong arm to his household. I added: "And just think, my good doctor, of the delight that will swell this lonely heart on my return from the search for this plant, when I am assured that I am returning to a worthy, strong friend, to a good home, and to a people who all love me. What more could I desire?"

He delivered my talk to the chief, who pronounced it good, and said, "It shall all be as he had said it when I got back." It was about 2 o'clock p.m., and I was so full of anxiety to put my grand, well conceived plan into action, that I feared I should make some blunder and spoil all. I remained seated on my skins, as calm as I could, talking with my old friend, rehearsing our plans for making strong, powerful medicines. He was full of hope and friendship for me, and made no effort to conceal his emotions—a thing I had never observed in an Indian before. He went so far as to say to me that he should think of no one else till he saw me again. I said, "It is the same with me, and that is a sign that we shall spend, now I am free, many useful days together."

And now the time had arrived for me to make preparations for my trip. I gathered up my saddle fixings, blankets, axe, cup and saddle bags and told the old man to call for my horse. Ned was soon brought, and I geared him up, with everything snugly in its place. "All aboard," was tempting, but the sun remained a little too high yet. The doctor asked me why it was not better to remain and make an early start in the morning?

I told him: "I have to have a night to myself to dream; in the camp I couldn't get an instructive dream. I shall sleep just outside the noise of the camps tonight, and to start soon enough to get out of the sound of it is all I want."

And now the trusting maiden brought the two tongues, nicely wrapped in grass, with good dressed leather strings just ready to tie to the cantle of my saddle. As she handed them to me she observed, "These are female cow tongues. You will find them much better than the coarse, big tongue of the male buffalo," and she looked so pleasant that I would have kissed her hand—but Indians don't know anything of that piece of deception. I caught her by the hand and held it until the doctor told her for me that when I came back it would be my turn to be the servant.

And now the sun being not over twenty minutes high, I shook hands with my old friend, with *Nilpe,* with the good little woman that cared for my horse, and mounting old Ned, I asked the doctor to say this to the multitude: "My heart shakes hands with you; when the sun is high as it is now, three days hence, you will see me again; and then I shall be ready to make stronger, better medicine than any I had exhibited. It will warm the hearts and bring into the dancing ring the oldest people in the encampment. I will dance, too, and we will have the big buffalo dance; it will make your hunters strong and lucky, and you shall hear your children cry for liver and gall no more."

He interpreted what I had said, and during the loud applauding shout of the mesmerized multitude, I rode slowly out of sight without looking back. I took the trail I came, which was very easy to follow, as it had been twice traversed by the three spies. When I arrived at the top of the hill on the opposite side of the branch, I peeped back under my arm, and was astonished to find myself in full view of the greater part of the encampment. I could see it over the top of the streak of timber that grew in the branch's low grounds, and I quarrelled at myself for going into such a trap, when it lay in such plain view.

I rode slowly onward, showing Ned that I wanted to keep on the trail, which he understood and learned to do before it was dark, so that when we could see it no longer he could follow it by the scent. I continued onward and knew, by the way Ned stooped his head down occasionally, that we were on the trail. When, after an hour's ride, we had come to some high, hard prairie with short grass, I got down and overhauled and arranged my baggage safely. Then I walked, leading my horse, squarely off a hundred paces or more towards a strip of timber on a branch to the left-hand (south) side of the trail. At this moment, the moon blazed up, seemingly from the prairie grass. It was light enough for my purpose before; but now it was so light that it alarmed me, and I stood still ten or fifteen minutes, sighting the prairie in all directions. I knew very well that there might be amongst the numerous bands of hunters that were coming in every night, some who on hearing of me and my good horse, fine gun and fixings, would think it a nice thing to track me up, scalp me, and be the owner of the rich outfit. But I didn't intend they should track me, and the brightness of the moon-light excited in me a greater degree of watchfulness.

I went some way further toward the timber, and then turned a half circle of twenty yards, still leading and going parallel with the trail I had just made. While leading my horse toward the timber, after crossing the main trail (which Ned told me of by putting down his head as we passed it) perhaps two hundred yards, I took another good survey of my surroundings; I could see nothing but the ocean of grass, which toward the moon was beginning to sparkle with the accumulating dew-drops. I muttered to myself, "I am safe once more. No one knows where I am now, and being three days in advance of any probable attempt to trace me, I shall be too far away by that time to be in danger of that band of Indians."

Mounting old Ned, I spoke to him, and, setting his head northward, said, "Well, Ned, you have some tall walking to do to-night." Starting him at the rate of about three-and-a-half miles an hour, I continued that course till about midnight, when I turned a little more east.

CHAPTER NINE

Shadows of the Texas Revolution

ᴾAt daybreak my course was northeast, which direction I followed all that day and night until the moon rose, when I turned five or six points more east. The ground over which I had urged my way had been very favorable. Some parts of it had been hilly and some places rocky, but I got along very well. The water-courses had been few and small—most of them dry. Ned began to want food; he did not complain, but when he was passing a big weed he would bite it low, or sometimes, when passing through low places, where there were bushes, he would snap off limbs as big as my fingers and crunch them up, as he kept his gait rapidly onward. When the sun rose the second morning, I turned in that direction, and I found myself rising constantly, till at noon I was on an elevated table-land extending far to the northeast. A great many buffalo were quietly grazing on the vast plain, which to me was an agreeable indication. Not far in a southeast direction the high table upon which I stood seemed to dip. I went there, and soon came to the brow of the high land, and far off to the southeast and south I could see timbers, indicating a considerable stream. I commenced the descent, found it pretty rugged, and had descended a mile and a half when I came to a kind of bench of level land fifty yards wide, clothed in luxuriant grass. There was plenty of water, and on the brink of it a thick hedge of a species of *Ilex* [the hollies]. From this elevated situation I could overlook a large portion of the country below. It was a suitable place for me to rest myself and my horse. I ungeared him ᴹand took him a little way down the stream, where he could get to the water. While he was slaking his thirst I poured many cups of water on his sweaty back. I turned him loose to graze, but he stood still while I ᴾfell down on my blankets, needing both sleep and rest. Towards evening I awoke much refreshed, to find that Ned, poor fellow, had slept as long. He seemed to have just commenced grazing, for he was not two steps from where I had left him when I fell asleep three hours before. I examined his back and found it all right; he, however, was pleased at my rubbing it. It was a good place for him, and as it would consume the remainder of the day for him to get his satisfaction, I determined to make a little excursion in the direction I should travel the next day.

After passing the little hedge of bushes that fringed the brow of the declivity, I could see from my still elevated position a vast district of the far-reaching plain below. Right ahead, not exceeding a mile below, and lying across the direction I intended to extend my evening walk, was a large drove of ᴹperhaps half a million buffaloes, which were quietly grazing on every part of that grand expanse. Hungry as I was, I did not think of shooting one of them, though I could easily have done so, for some of them were standing and chewing on the cud, in thirty yards of where I had crept up to the top of the high ground. I stood there overwhelmed in amazement while contemplating that countless herd of wild cows. ᴾThey were grazing and moving eastwardly. This circumstance changed my program. I did not want to stir up the quiet, feeding multitude, and have them bounding and snorting over the hills and valleys to attract the attention of any band of hunting Indians who might be skulking in that vicinity. I had just escaped from a three days' enthrallment and detention that had resulted from my own carelessness, and it made me more thoughtful and watchful. To avoid being seen by the buffalo, I turned and descended the rough declivity in a southwesterly direction and went down behind the quietly grazing herd. It was too late to go far, but I went far enough to reach the valley where flowed a creek of dashing clear water. I saw a flock of deer and a jack rabbit and thought about taking a sample of one of the deer. But recollecting that where my camp was there was no wood to make a fire to dress it, and that I had on hand one of the tongues that dear *Nilpe* had prepared for me, I told the deer to take care of itself till we met again.[1]

It was a lovely country for a hunting ground, and under

more favorable circumstances I should perhaps have lingered two or three days in that vicinity. The engravings on the stone leaves of the geological book were unusually interesting. The bottom of the creek was paved with slate, the lamine of which dipped perhaps 60% to the eastward, down the creek, and in the fissures between the upturned edges of the slate-plates was fine sand, amongst which I found numerous particles of gold. To the eye of the mineralist the rocks, the clay, the slate, all in that immediate district, bear unmistakable indications of a pretty heavy auriferous deposit. I had no means of ascertaining what the name of the creek was then, but I think it will be found by some industrious miner on one of the source branches of what is now known as the Concho river, a tributary of the Colorado of Texas. ᴮAt a distance of ten or twelve miles to the north I could see two mountain peaks. I wished to climb to their summits and examine them but feared exposing myself.

ᴾAfter discovering a pretty fair pass-way down the declivity for my descent the next morning, I returned to my camp about dark, where I found Ned standing near my saddle. He laughed, and looked like he had been sleeping. With a tin-cup of water I supped on part of my remaining buffalo tongue. I took to my pallet early, for the three hours' nap I had taken in the forepart of the afternoon had not compensated the loss of the two previous nights' sleep. Ned rested the greater part of the night.

We were on our journey early, and made a wide gap between the morning and evening of that bright day. I saw much game, a gang of wolves, a few antelopes, and many hares—all muley rabbits. We crossed one little prairie dog town, and I saw several rattlesnakes lying about the dog-burrows, and some owls. The dogs had discovered me in the distance, and, with two or three exceptions had gone in their holes. From the pile of pebble and sand that is brought out last from these burrows I am inclined to think that these little hare-lipped, grass-eating animals (they are no dog) extend their hole to the water. On top of the little mound of earth that is thrown out from them is always found water worn pebbles and white sand.

Knowing that it is a very rare thing for as large a herd of buffalo as I saw the previous evening to have no Indians hankering after them, my watchful developments had been excited to extreme vigilance all day. I had swept the far-off scenery with my telescopic eyes behind and in advance, to the right and to the left, and noted everything that moved in the vast area, which was only bounded by the bending blue ether. I saw some wild horses scouring the plains occasionally; no buffalo, but gangs of deer were constantly visible in many directions all day; flocks of prairie hens would be seen running swiftly from my path. Far away in the distance and right ahead loomed up a black streak which I knew to be timber. It was getting late in the afternoon, but that black streak must be reached or we would get no water. The evening was pleasant, my course was E.S.E., and the sweet south wind (the genuine sea-breeze) was sweeping diagonally across my path, moving the yielding grass in rolling waves like the sea. We reached the timber an hour after dark, found water and camped.

Not having stopped at noon, but traveled all day, myself and horse were both tired. Whilst I ate my piece of buffalo tongue with my cup of water, Ned stood where he stopped, and it was some time after I had made my pallet before he moved; he had traveled at least forty miles. I began to feel that my escape was a success, and the strain on my vigilance was relaxing considerably. We set out early next morning and soon crossed a big creek, where I saw much quiet, moving game. About 12 o'clock we came to a beautiful stream of clear, sweet water with a timbered bottom. I concluded to let my horse rest the balance of the day, and as I was getting tired of my stale buffalo tongue, I thought I would walk around a little and towards evening get me a piece of venison. I went up the stream, making but slow progress. Everything—the botany, the conchology, the geology—was new to me. The widely scattered specimens of natural history had never been disturbed or moved from the spot where the finger of Nature had dropped them. I had visited many unfrequented places, but never before had I found one at which I felt so clearly that I was the first that ever left a shoe-print on the white, clean sands of that clear dashing river. Properly circumstanced, I could have spent a month most delightfully there. I will not attempt a description of the records of the ages that lay so plainly printed on the rocks and stratified cliffs, the beds of fossiliferous oysters and casts of conches.

As I returned to my camp, near sunset, I discovered, a quarter of a mile distant on the prairie, six or seven deer that were coming towards the timber. If they continued their course, they would strike some distance below where I was. I hurried along through the timber and low undergrowth to the proper point and waited for them. When they came near enough I hailed them with, "Where are you all going this evening?" They halted, and remembering that my gun had not been fired in a week, I took very steady aim. She, however, went quick, and there was a broken neck twenty-seven paces from me.[2] I made haste to my camp with as much of the meat as I needed and got there in time to have my fire and cook my meal before dark. I had become too timid to run the risk of illuminating the leaves on the tree-tops after dark; it could be seen at a great distance on that level plain over which I had passed.

The next morning I roasted what was left of the venison in the embers of my little fire, ate it at daylight, and went by the beautifully written records that I had visited the previous day. I had my journal with me now, and I made many notes from the stone-book. But feeling at last that I had tarried in that region as long as was prudent, I set out directly east, traveled over a beautiful prairie full of grouse, jack rabbits, wolves and salamander.[3] Portions of the prairie were quite sandy, and in these sand-beds the little rows of sand piles were thickly dotted over the entire sandy district. Half a mile away in front of me, and lying on his belly right athwart the course of my line was a large, sooty colored wolf. His nose was near the ground, and he seemed to be intently gazing at something. He did not turn his head nor move a limb. I rode to within twenty-five paces of where he lay, and he paying no attention to me. I concluded I would wake him up and see what he was doing. So I dropped the bridle on Ned's withers, and at the same time gently pressed the reins with the tips of my fingers; he stopped, raised his head and holding his breath, gave me a chance to make a steady aim. The ball passed through the wolf's body behind the shoulders; he bounded up with a great dog cry and ran with all his might directly towards me, and before I could think what to do with my empty gun he tumbled in ten feet of me, dead. I went to the place where he had been so steadily and patiently watching and found a little pile of fresh sand that had been thrown up by a salamander, which explains the cause of the wolf's attitude. He was waiting for the salamander to come up with his load of sand, when he would nab him. I had many times seen these little sand hills torn up, but had not until today discovered how it had happened.

My first days were spent in the pine forests of Georgia where this sand flirting rodent was very abundant, and there (in my childhood) I learned to call them salamanders. They do not, however, belong to the batrachians [tailless amphibians—frogs and toads]. The pouched animal here alluded to is the Texas, or smaller, species of the two gophers. The full-grown Texas gopher will weigh half a pound. The gopher I found in Tuxpan, Mexico, when grown and fat, will weigh about two pounds. The dogs eat them greedily, and the Mexican native Indians told me they were delicious food for humanity. They are both injurious rodents belonging to *Diplostoma*.[4]

I did not travel over twelve miles this day till I came to another one of the pretty creeks with the transparent water. The quietly grazing antelopes and the big brown wolves, who would run off a hundred or two yards, and then sit down like a dog and watch my movements, assured me that they had not been disturbed lately. Consequently, I concluded to loiter away a little time on that pretty creek. Finding, by the size of the creek and deep-cut banks, that I was too near some main water-course (of which the creeks were tributary) for convenient traveling, I determined to ascend the beautiful stream I was now on until I found ground better suited to old Ned's abilities. The good old fellow was willing and would have traveled, obeying my signs for him to go faster or slower, until he fell dead without a single word of complaint. But I wanted to preserve his strength, and I didn't leave the rate of travel, or when to stop or start, to his judgment. In that far away, unpeopled desert, I viewed him as a very precious, useful companion.

We went inside the timber, and after traveling seven or eight miles, where the undulations became more abrupt, near the bank of the stream the hillsides were clothed with scraggy brushwood, and the bed of the creek was paved with ledges of coarse, gray limey sandstone. This was a delightful place. I stripped the horse and he went immediately to the water, lay down in it, rolled a little, and drank some of the water as he lay. This put me in mind of a bath, and, throwing off my clothes, I spent perhaps an hour in rubbing and scouring my dirty hide; after which I slept an hour, awaking about four o'clock. Recollecting there was nothing to eat in camp, I hurried off to find something. I had not proceeded half a mile before I found myself in the midst of a very large herd of deer. They were passing through the timber and crossing the creek. As yet I had not left the timber, and they were all around me the first thing I knew of it. I stood as still as the old elm stump near me, and from the way the deer looked at us I don't think they discovered any difference between the stump and me. A great many had passed before I discovered one for whose flesh I lusted. I took a ham and the back straps, and passing near the water as I returned, I saw some bees sucking the wet sand. I was too hungry then to hunt bees, but I didn't forget them. I had time to cook my venison good before night, and my supper was a good one.

Feeling pretty secure I slept soundly until day, and thinking of my honey bees, concluded to spend the day there and find them. It had been forty days since I had tasted toasted bread or salt. I was beginning to feel a desire for other food than broiled meat. I ate my breakfast and had enough meat left for another day. I told Ned, who was over demolishing a rich patch of prairie peas, to spend the day as suited him best, as I had determined to remain at that camp another day. Until 10 o'clock a.m. I employed myself making observations on the new (to me) beauties and instructive lessons to be found in undisturbed nature. Then I went to where I had seen the bees the evening before. There were two bees on the sand. One of them soon filled his pouch, and I got his course pretty correctly; the other bee soon went in the same direction. I set out tracing the course and examining the trees for holes, as far as the border of the prairie. No bees to be found; so I went back to the water where a great many were drinking and going off every minute. I watched four or five depart. They all went the same way I had been hunting. Three or four hundred yards out in the prairie stood a little post-oak grove, exactly in the course. I went there, and found one going in at a hole near the ground. I went to my camp, and for fear the sound I should make cutting into the hollow tree might alarm some of the skulking Indians, fixed up Ned with all my traps on him, so that if such a casualty should occur I might be able to make my escape by running.

Before I had struck a lick, I made a searching look over the widespread prairie. Everything was moving quietly. No signal-smokes, no rushing buffalo, no frantic mustangs beating the grass into dust with rapid feet. Some of the deer were standing, others carelessly ruminating, as they lay on the ground, while the big old brown wolf, looking very much like a shabby domestic dog, was slowly creeping about in the grass catching grasshoppers. "All alone once more," said I; and getting the axe, I found the tree a mere shell, not an inch thick. I had to strike it tenderly; it made no sound, being crammed full of combs. The combs were sealed up, and full of fine-flavored honey. I took out what honey I needed, with as little disturbance to the community I had robbed as possible; and then made myself sweat and pant carrying a big flat stone a quarter of a mile to place over the breach I had made, to prevent others from treating them as rascally as I had.

My meal that evening was very agreeable, surpassing anything found at the table of the wealthy. Good, fat, well-boiled venison, taken with pure honey, is as great an excitant of the power of the *sensorium commune* in the human species as a pure solution of sulph[uric] copper is to excite the power of a clean galvanic battery. No wonder the ancient hunters lived so long, when their children were raised on buffalo liver, ate raw with the gall, and the principal food of the adults was venison and honey. Longevity would be the reward of any people who would make that simple dietetic rule habitual.

Morning came again, and I had been long enough at that camp. Taking a breakfast of my last venison and honey, I left, keeping well out among the hills and small creeks. I saw immense numbers of deer, and the ground being hilly, I often came in short range of them before they saw me. I discovered that day a little trick in the deer, when they are suddenly frightened, that I had never observed before. I had climbed up a sharp little mountain, and immediately over its backbone lay half an acre of rich flat land, covered with a luxuriant growth of rank weeds and low hog-plum bushes, no portion of which was visible to me until I was on the very pinnacle of the ridge. To pass over this little sharp, spire-like elevation tumbled me rather hurriedly in amongst the plums and weeds and about forty deer, who seemed to be there on account of the ripe plums. At my sudden appearance amongst them, they were so badly frightened that they dashed frantically in every possible direction, bounding over the border of the little flat, and precipitately down the declivity beyond, with a rushing sound that could be heard for some time. Ned stopped, held himself steady, expecting me to shoot. The wild squandering of the deer was funny to me; I couldn't refrain from a good hearty laugh.

It was some minutes before I moved onward again, and I had not proceeded five steps until a deer that lay squatted in the thick weeds bounced up and fled away furiously down the mountain. Ned paused again, and on looking close, I could see another squatted in the bushes. Then I rode about over the little patch of thick weeds and jumped up six more, making eight in all that had squatted. They were all alike, cropped down on their brisket, with their necks stretched out at full length and their jaws lying flat on the ground, and this was the first time I had known them to resort to that species of deception.

I have known them to do it often since. In the season when their fawns are only a few hours old, I have seen the mother standing with a high head in the prairie, five or six hundred yards distant, watching my movements very closely, and when, for some cause my attention would be turned for a few moments in another direction, and I turned again to the deer, it would have disappeared. The prairie being many miles in extent, there was no possible chance for it to have got out of sight by running in that short time. I would go and see what went with it. I would be sure to find an old doe, dropped down on her brisket, legs doubled up under her, neck extended at full length, with her jaws flat on the ground. There is no doubt of the fact that they watch until you look in some other direction, when instantly they drop in the grass. I came to this conclusion from the fact that I have several times seen the mother doe standing on duty, on the prairie, and that she invariably disappeared when I was looking in another direction. Old bucks will do the same thing when they think you have not observed them. It has happened two or three times to me, when riding on the prairie, that I have discovered the head and horns of a big old buck in the high grass, not very far off; and if I turned my attention for a single moment, he would disappear. Then, riding out to the place, I would find him on his brisket with outstretched neck, like the doe.

There are many other instances of their squatting policy—some very interesting I could name, but deem what I have already said on that topic satisfactory. We will return to the little, rich, level patch of weeds and ripe plums on top of the mountain. They had been very abundant, and what few really ripe ones I found that had escaped the deer that day were excellent. I descended the mountain in an easterly direction, which, in the course of two or three hours, brought me into a more pleasant, wide-reaching valley country, and finally, towards evening, to a considerable stream of bright, dashing water. A few hours before reaching the little river, I had shot a nice little doe, and did not have to go hunting at that camp; I undressed myself and horse and we both went into the water and took a good washing.

So that my fire might not invite an unwelcome guest, I cooked my meat before night and put the fire out. I had noticed that Ned had been listening and scenting several times, but did not manifest any indications of alarm, or as I had several times before, I should have left the camp after dark. However, I had a quiet night's rest and was on the path next morning sooner than I could distinguish objects any great distance. About sunup the first thing attracting my attention was a little compact crowd of antelope not very far off. I fell off my horse and kicked up my heels in the most approved hunting style for a minute or two, and finding they were not coming to me concluded to peep and see what they were at. They were not there. Ned looked like he was laughing!

My course now was nearly east. The country was still broken and rocky, and the casts and fossiliferous remains of marine animals were remarkably profuse. Game was very abundant—deer, turkeys, antelope, wolves, and ravens. I shot a little deer in the afternoon, and, having tied my horse a hundred yards back in the edge of the timber, went after him. When I came to the deer again two ravens had possession of it, and they disputed my right to it with many loud threats and dips near my head while performing their gyrations above the place. I took my share, and had not gone forty yards before they were tearing the little deer to pieces again. I would have shot one of them, but I had already fired one gun in that vicinity, and I didn't like those ravens anyhow. They are always hanging about hunting parties, and I felt a little shy. I found a good, thick, wooded shelter for my cooking operations, and after dark, left it and traveled three or four miles into the prairie, where I found a lone live-oak, and made my pallet there. Ned found rich pasturage besides. From Ned's listening, scenting, and steady and long, thoughtful gazing into the far-off prairie, for the last two or three days, I was pretty well assured that he believed we were passing through a region that was infested by some grade of humanity. He indicated his suspicions so intelligently that he caused me to ply my telescopic eyes quite frequently.

The next morning Ned didn't come up early, and the grass was so wet I kept my pallet till the vast red source of light heaved up his broad, glowing face from the drenching grass. It was unusually beautiful this time. I made my breakfast from some of the last night's cooking. Ned came to camp, and we were soon contending with distance on the face of the vast prairie. About ten o'clock a.m. we came obliquely into a large, well beaten trail, and the ground was much trod up for thirty yards on each side of the main trail, showing that the movement had been a hurried one. The sign looked to be two or three days old, and from its direction would pass nearly over the country I had been moving in. This accounts for Ned's cautious scenting and sighting over the last two days. He examined and smelt of the trace very carefully, but he did not look round nor show any signs that he had made any discoveries. The large recent trail, and all the signs showing satisfactorily that the travel had been rapid, indicated that it had been made by a retreating war party; and that meant, except it be a straggling wounded man, there was no danger of meeting any Indians in the vicinity of that trail. Yet there was so much of it, I couldn't persuade myself to view it with the slightest degree of favor; instead, I became wild as the antelope—"go, whether there is danger or not."

So I crossed it at nearly right angles, and traveled rapidly north until dark. I had a good chance for an antelope, and twice for deer but I felt too wild, and I had a little scrap of meat. Night came after a thirty mile ride; then I felt more confidence. The country I had penetrated now was exceedingly rough, with pretty smart mountains, composed principally of piled up rocks. I found some water and camped. Ned was tired and the grass not very good; he stood around my pallet the greater part of the night. Before light next morning I climbed up to the ridge, at the base of which lay my camp, and stalked along on top of it until I came to the head of a ravine that made up and had indented itself in a little flat on top of the mountain. Here I seated myself on a rock and waited for day. It was not long, but before it came I had heard some slight rustling in the bushes, and once or twice a soft, faint snort, that put me in mind of a young goat. Light was flowing in now, and it was but a short time until, at the farther edge of the little flat, about thirty yards off, I could see something in motion. Slyly I crouched behind the rock I had been seated on. I was unaccustomed to the little noises I had heard, and could form no idea of what it might be. My suspense did not last long, for soon I could see there was a gang of something. It turned out to be a considerable herd of antelope, a few of which had reached the little flat, the rest of the flock grazing widespread on the side of the mountain and seemed to be ascending.

I could see now two nice little fellows parrying with their horns—half play and half earnest—and they were working round on the farther border of the little level to near the brink of the declivity. There was light enough, but they were constantly in motion, and I had to speak to them—"Hold still!" They both stood. I selected one and aimed to break his neck, but at the moment I touched the trigger the other one punched up his hind parts so suddenly that the bullet passed through his flanks. By this time, forty or fifty of the main flock had flowed over and filled up the little valley entirely. At the time the gun fired some of them were within ten feet of where I sat behind the rock. Of course they were frightened into the wildest disorder, and fled in all directions; three or four fell flat on the ground—squatted. But my attention was called to the one I had shot—all the rest turned back the way they came but the wounded one. He leaped with a flutter madly over the brim of the hillside, seeming to be badly hurt. I watched him closely as he fell and recovered on his way down the steep descent; but what was my astonishment when, not exceeding seventy-five yards distant, a very large mountain lion sprang up from amongst the rocks. Receiving my little frightened, tumbling antelope in his great outspread paws, he doubled and crushed it up as a cat would the smallest mouse. At the bend of the down-pressed head—the atlas —he tore out a big mouthful; one single contraction of the arms of the fierce beast completed the destruction of the antelope, and he sank down and seemed to be sucking the blood. But they were so buried among the broken rocks that I couldn't see distinctly what he was doing, and besides I was pretty busy keeping myself out of his sight and reloading my gun. This completed, I began to lay plans how to get a mess from my nice little antelope. The lion was lying quartering, with his left-side towards me. I could see his head very distinctly, and laying my gun on the rock behind which I stood, sighted at and behind the root of his left ear. The motion of his head in chewing was too great; I was afraid to wound him. I knew if he would hold his head steady five seconds I could from my position penetrate his atlas. I sighted again but thought there was too much shaking. After a while, when my excitement had subsided, I examined my flint, fixed my feet steady, and laying my gun in a good position, tried it all. Finding it properly adjusted, I cast my eye into the sights, and gave a low, rather prolonged whistle. He raised his head a little and looked far beyond for a single moment; the gun fired, he bowed down on his meat, and I hastened to reload my gun. After a few minutes I went cautiously down to the place. It was all over with him; he had struggled very little. He was a monster. I didn't examine him very nicely, for really he was looking so big and savage-like that I did not want to loiter about the place.

He would weigh, I think, four hundred pounds at least, and from tip to tip measured eleven feet. I concluded that with very little trouble there could be another lurking about those mountains, and taking the hams and back-straps of my game, left him. He had already devoured the head, neck and one shoulder of the antelope.

It was near 8 o'clock when I got back to the camp. Concluding to remain there that day, I built my fire and cooking-scaffold under a shelving rock, upon which I placed my nice fat meat and cooked it in good style. After my breakfast I took a round among the rocks and made many very instructive observations on Nature's grand piled-up rock series. There they lay, just as the fiery convulsion had heaped them. That portion of the earth's surface had not been defaced by the corroding tramp of ruthless civilization—everything lay in its place undisturbed.[5]

[M]I traveled eastwardly and crossed a beautiful little clear river. In the course of ten days' travel over various kinds of soil and country, I reached the Colorado river at Bastrop. My clothes were pretty well torn off, and it was with much difficulty that I succeeded in getting a shirt and pantaloons in the place (and they had been worn). I remained only one day in Bastrop. In three days more I was safely landed at my friend Burnham's, on the fifty-fifth day since I left him. He grumbled a little but was glad to see me, and so were his children. I remained with him three weeks, and it being pleasant weather, we rode to several of the neighboring settlements, which were to be found as near as twenty and thirty miles from his place. He also carried me to several very elegantly located leagues of land that he said could be had for twelve and a half cents an acre. He was very anxious that I should purchase a place, for he desired that I should fetch my family out and live neighbors to him.

I made one more trip of exploration, east of the Colorado. I examined the Little river country and continued up to the falls of the Brazos.[6] Thence on the return route through the Yegua country,[7] after examining the Long Point league two days I went to see Phelix Houston (who was S.F. Austin's agent), and tried to purchase the whole league.[8] He had been instructed to ask $5 an acre for it. I was not able to pay for it at that rate, but I marked it, as I intended to come back. I did go back thirteen years after and bought the same league at 75 cents an acre. From the Long Point tract I returned to my friend Burnham's and, after three or four days' rest, began to prepare for the homeward journey. It was thought to be a thousand miles to my residence in Monroe county, Miss. For that long a journey in the warm season, and the greater portion of the route a wild wilderness, I would require more luggage than my riding horse ought to carry. Having long ago sold my pack horse, I now had to get another but that was easy to do. I made a good pack saddle, packed my clothes, specimens, and cooking things on my new horse, and with many promises to come back, bade my friends an affecionate adieu and set my face homewards. I had promised to call at San Felipe and see Gale Bo[r]den, who had been a long time sick. I got there in the evening of the second day. Bo[r]den was very much gratified that I called on him.[9]

About that time Moseley Baker was beating up for volunteers to meet the invading Mexicans. All the men in San Felipe had already enrolled themselves. I thought pretty well of the chances it offered, and added my name to the list. But George Ewing (of Monroe county, Mississippi), Thomas Gay (of Georgia), Wm. Jack (of Alabama), and Travis (of Tuscaloosa, Ala.)— all old acquaintances of mine, opposed my joining them.[10] There was, however, quite a number of the company, including Captain Baker, very anxious for me to remain with them. Captain Baker assured me that as I had joined the first company of volunteers that had been raised in defense of the colony, and being fully competent to fill the office, there would be no opposition to my being surgeon-general to the forces that would occupy Texas west of the Brazos. He was going to the convention, and he intended to exert all his influence to obtain the appointment for me. He had no doubt of success.

I thought well of it myself, as I could very easily see, should the enterprise turn out a success, what permanent chaplets of wealth and glory would crown the performers. But those old friends I have named above, who were acquainted with my domestic condition, opposed my becoming a volunteer more vehemently than ever. George Ewing made a speech on the subject, in the course of which he remarked that Captain Baker no doubt thought it right, and that, as he did everything he laid his hands to, he would pursue it till his efforts were crowned with success. But Captain Baker was not, like him, apprised of the fact that in the State of Mississippi I had left an interesting family, a wife and nine children; and notwithstanding the fact that I might gain a high sounding reputation, it was nevertheless a perilous undertaking and it would be no advantage to my family for me to bleach my bones on the prairies of Texas. "It must not be," said he. "Dr. Lincecum must go home."

"But," said I, "My name is on the list and cannot be taken off."

"I have the list," said Gay, "and I will show you how it can be got off." Taking a pen, he erased the name from the list. Captain Baker was highly offended at what Gay had done, and they came very near having a serious difficulty about it. But when Ewing explained the case, with all its bearings to him, he too opposed my becoming a volunteer.

After attending one day to Gale Bo[r]den's case, I collected some meat and bread, packed up and left San Felipe, at 2 p.m., the fourth day after my arrival. I crossed the Brazos on the ferryboat, and went out about three or four miles to the edge of the prairie where I camped. It was a sad night for me, as I felt that it would have been better for me to remain.

I packed up and set forward, aiming for Gaines' ferry on the Sabine. I averaged about twenty-five miles a day. I had no path, and when I struck the Trinity river, I found it brimful and running swiftly. I gathered up some old dry logs, constructed a raft upon which I crossed the river with all my plunder, swam my horses over, and went several miles farther the same day. Continuing to travel every day, for it did not rain where I was from the time I left Burnham's—I struck the road that crosses at Hickman's ferry, seven miles below Gaines' ferry.[11] It was 12 o'clock when I struck the road, five miles from the Sabine river. The grass was good and I turned my horses on it to graze while I slept, for I had nothing to eat.

I had slept perhaps an hour, when I was awakened by a coarse voice, shouting, "Hello, traveler, are you asleep?"

It occurred to me that the sound of that voice was not friendly, and taking hold of my gun, which was sitting against the tree at my head, I rose up before I spoke. "Yes, I am traveling," said I, and I thought he looked like a robber.

"Which course are you going, east or west?" he asked. "I am going east," I replied. "That is my course," said he, "and I should like to join company with you."

I said, "Well, sir," and I wondered if I had said I was going west, if he would not have said that was his course. I resolved to watch him and let him get no advantage of me. He alighted, and let his horse graze awhile. The hour came for me to pack up, which I did, and we traveled on together. In about five miles we came to Hickman's ferry on the Sabine. I got bacon and bread there and we went on, I watching him all the time. He was very talkative. He proposed to join me, pay his part in the provisions and for the use of the pack horse and camp out with me. I agreed to all his propositions, for they were all fair. Near night we came to a good camping place, and he was so officious that he increased my suspicions very much. He would not allow me to do anything at all. He hobbled out the horses, made a fire and cooked supper, forbidding me all the time to do anything.

Supper over, he made down his pallet and after lying down was soon snoring—I thought a little too loud for a young man. I put my gun in good order, laid my big knife in a convenient place, and lay awake an hour. He snored on. After a while I called him. No answer. I called again and he did not cease snoring. I got up, having my knife ready. I took hold of the blanket upon which he lay; the long pine straw lay thick on the ground, making it an easy matter to drag him, which I did, carrying him off thirty yards or more. He did not seem to know anything had happened, and I left him in the enjoyment of his sound repose. I went to my pallet, satisfied that the man was what he said he was, and slept to near sunup. Soon after I had awakened, my companion also raised up. He looked around him and said "I should like to know how I came away out here."

We traveled onwards daily, and I found the young man as good a traveling companion as I had ever seen. His name was Mason Foley.[12] His home was on the Lavaca in Texas. After we had crossed Red river we got along better. We could get provisions and corn for our horses. At Alexandria, La., people were dying of the cholera rapidly.[13] We hurried through that place; and, though it was late when we got over the river, we went five or six miles into the pine forest before we took up camp. On the Wichita and San Louis rivers we heard nothing of cholera, but when we came to Mississippi and had to travel twenty miles along the levee among the rich farms on the banks of the river, the cholera was raging awfully. One man, who fell in company having his little son riding behind, told me that he had lost $400,000 worth of negroes; that his wife and all his children, except the one behind him, had died of cholera. I saw several houses along the river where all the inhabitants were dead, some unburied, and the dogs howling in the yard. We hurried onwards and crossed the great river at Rodney. I wrote a letter at Rodney, saying that I would be at home precisely at 12 o'clock on the 5th of August and mailed it to my wife.

Our road passed through Port Gibson, Clinton, etc. When we got into the Choctaw country, which was full of big hogs three or four years old, we had to be more careful at our camps. They were so troublesome that we decided to stop at the taverns along the remainder of the route, though the cost was four fold greater. When we came within thirty miles of Columbus, I stayed all night with my brother Grabel. It was the last time I ever saw him. He told me that a month before, my brother Rezin Bowie had died at Lexington, Ky., on his way to New York. He also informed me of the death of my friend John Pitchlynn, [Sr.,] who had died a few months before. We reached Columbus, Miss., the next day, and I stopped with my brother-in-law, Jo Bryan.[14] I married his sister, and he married my sister.

My clothes were pretty badly worn, and I went to Dr. A. Weir's store in Columbus and got an entire new suit.[15] Leaving my traveling companion, Mason Foley, I set out homewards next morning. I fell in company with G. W. Wall, who resided on the road 15 miles from my house, and I stayed all night with Wall, the following day being the one I had written from Rodney that I would be at home precisely at 12 o'clock. After breakfast I set out for home. When I came within half a mile of the house, it lacked half an hour of 12 o'clock. I got down and let my horses graze, while I finished up my journal. Old Ned, knowing that he was near home, would not eat, but kept punching me with his nose. The other did not know he was so near the end of his journey, and he took advantage of the chance for grazing.

Time, as it does in all other cases, soon ran out, and mounting old Ned, I rode up to the yard fence. The family were at dinner under the long shed that reached from the house to the well. They were so much engaged they did not see me for some minutes. I had time to count the children and see they were all there. Two of them, Leonora and Cassandra, whose heads were a yellowish brown when I went away, were black now, and that was about all the change I could discover. At length my old hunting dog, Hector, discovered me, and instantly ran and leaped up on the fence, then into my lap and very rudely jabbed his cold, wet nose into my mouth. The family then quit the table and did not finish their dinners.

I had been absent seven months, lacking four days. I counted what money I had left and found I had $37.37 ½ more than I started with (I had received for three cases of medical services $220). All was right at home.

CHAPTER TEN

G.T.T.: Gone to Texas, Gone to Tuxpan

[B]I resumed practice at once [1835]. [M]It was a sickly autumn, and I had to be on duty day and night. My success was as good as it could be, for I did not lose a single case of any description. [B]Because I had abandoned the allopathic system, the practice of poisons, the other doctors became highly offended and tried every way to break me down. They told the people that the botanic system in the hands of Science was a good thing, that they all understood it and practiced it when necessary; but administered by empyrics, it was very dangerous. As for steaming a sick person, it was truly preposterous, it was scandalous; they had known several people to die while being steamed. But this great clamor raised about me excited the attention of people far and near. [M]Those who resided too far off for me to visit came to see me, though I did very often visit the sick to the distance of fifty or sixty miles. So many cases of chronic diseases came to my house for treatment that I decided to prepare rooms for them. [B]So I erected a new office with rooms adjoining. Soon these were occupied and I had to build a house one hundred feet long, divided into rooms. The fame of this curative establishment was spread in all directions, and as a consequence, was turning my house into a tavern and subjecting my family to all the inconveniences of such an establishment. In response to the solicitations and encouragement of several prominent families of Columbus, I decided to move to that place, and purchased a house for my family and removed on 1st of January [1841].[1] [M]It took eleven wagons and a carriage to transport the things I had accumulated, and my big Mobile debt had been paid.

[B]My success there exceeded my expectations, although the opposition of the old school Doctors was even more pronounced and vindictive. Besides fraternity meetings and discussion for my special benefit there appeared at various times in the news-papers of the place scurrilous and malicious articles in derision of Steam Doctors.[2] As they were all anonymous, I allowed them to pass unnoticed for a time, but at the suggestion of friends and finally the Editor of the paper, I prepared and had published the following article, which shut them up as close as an oyster:

> Messrs. Editors: Having noticed in your papers, during the past six months, numerous articles of scurrilous stuff over the signatures of M.D.'s saying a great deal about a certain Steam Doctor, whom they call Esculapian. From those low pitched productions, I cannot discover what it is that they want. How-ever, to bring the matter at once to a focus: if any Gentleman desires to discuss before the public, over his true signature, the merits of the two systems of medical practice, he shall be accommodated, but I have no time to waste with the loafing slang-whangers and hangers-on of the profession. That class of poor fellows will please excuse me.
>
> signed,
Gideon Lincecum[3]

^MMy practice grew better every year after the removal. In my seventh year at Columbus I treated 2,236 cases, mostly fever. I lost no case of any kind of fever during the seven years I prac-ticed at Columbus. In my annual advertisements I stated that I would make no charge for a failure to cure fever of any kind.[4] During the seven years I booked $51,000, besides the cash fees. The last month I practiced amounted to $1,266. It was the month of September [1847].

[In anticipation of moving my family to Texas,] I quit the practice and spent all the time from then to the 30th of March, 1848, trying to collect. I got in possession of a considerable amount of money and still had outstanding $7,508 on solvent men that would have to be sued on, which would require eigh-teen months to make the money. I had no notion of remaining in Columbus that long. And I knew by experience that if I left it in the hands of any one to collect for me that I never should get any of it. So I tore up the notes and scattered them to the winds. I owed no man anything, and when I destroyed that bundle of notes no man owed me anything. I was even with the world every way and could go when and where I pleased. The people said I must not go away, but I had decided to go to Texas.

ᴮMy children were beginning to marry off and they seemed to think of nothing but frolicking. The boys drank and dressed extravagantly and the girls dressed and danced inimitably. They spent from three to five thousand dollars a year and seemed to act as though the source from which the money came was inexhaustable. I could not get them to set their minds on any kind of business. Parties and dancing schools,[5] shopping and "charge it to Poppa" was all they seemed to care for. The entire community of young people were similar in their habits. To remain and let them marry their equals, I could plainly see, would finally terminate in the most abject poverty and wretchedness. So, I determined to carry them to a country where the surroundings and conditions would be more promising.

This is the untold cause of my breaking up so abruptly the lucrative business in Columbus. ᴹI packed up all the medicines I had on hand and my furniture—all worth $5,000—sold my place, bought ten Negroes and ten fine horses. The horses I started immediately to Texas, in charge of two of my sons and one Negro man.[6]

On the morning of March 30, 1848, by nine o'clock we were all aboard the good steamboat New Era (Capt. Jo Estes).[7] It was not a very pretty day, but the citizens of Columbus nevertheless came out by hundreds, and by the time the boat was in motion the shores of the river were thickly set with ladies and gentlemen, whose waving hats and fluttering handkerchiefs testified that the parting hour was seriously and deeply felt.

ᴮMemory's pictures last longer than the objects that they picture. My letters from Columbus tell me that very few of the good people and friends that lined the shore the day we parted are now [1871] living, and now while I write, undying memory holds up in vivid colors all the lineaments portrayed in that final sad separation. ᴹAs the boat left the landing I looked back upon the fine dresses that lined the shore for hundreds of yards, and which were now, from the increasing distance, rapidly blending; and, while I gazed, the idea of what a number of precious friends I was leaving behind almost overwhelmed me. My heart throbbed heavily and I experienced emotions that have occurred to me but that one time in all my long life. ᴮWe reached Mobile on the third day and remained only long enough to have our plunder transferred to a New Orleans-bound steamship. By 1 o'clock we were steaming rapidly seaward. My mother and ten Negroes came with me, but meeting my brother Grant, in New Orleans, she went home with him to Catahoula Parish, La., where she died, on 28th of May. We came out of the Mississippi and went to Galveston on the steamship Palmetto, where we remained two days. Then taking a Buffalo Bayou boat we landed at Houston, Texas, on 11th of April, 1848. The second day after our arrival at Houston, the young men, my sons, Lycurgus and Lucullus, ᴹand the Negro arrived with my horses. We then made ready to go through the country to the place I had selected for our new home.[8]

ᴮHaving bought six road wagons, horses, harnesses, etc., we set out across the prairies in pretty good style. ᴹWe traveled leisurely, and at 10 a.m. the 22nd of April (my birthday), passed along the Long Point league, the tract of land I had selected thirteen years ago. It looked just as it did when I examined it in 1835. We moved into some very good houses, not more than a mile and a half farther, which I had rented from a man I met in Houston. ·

After examining a wide scope of country and finding no place that suited me as well as the Long Point tract, I decided to purchase. J. V. Matson paid for 2,000 acres and I took the rest of it. I paid seventy-five cents an acre for my part of it. Matson paid for his 2,000 acres one fitified Negro girl and the rest in Mexican ponies, at the same rate per acre that I paid.[9]

ᴮThere were no blacksmiths or other mechanics in many miles of Long Point and this was so inconvenient that I conceived the idea of building up a Mechanical Village. I offered to deed to any Mechanic a half acre lot of land, with all the rights and privileges thereunto belonging, except the right to sell or vend or traffic in ardent spirits or intoxicating liquors. Any business requiring industry was entitled to a lot. Many mechanics came and were well pleased with the place but the liquor clause backed them out. They said they would not sell their liberty for a league of the best land in Texas. They called Liquor, Liberty! But later, others accepted the terms, and my settlement developed into a thriving village. There were at one time four stores, a smith's shop, a wagon shop, cabinet shop, and a potter's shop at this place.

BNext came the preachers and wanted a lot upon which to erect a church. I readily consented, provided they would let me have a hand in locating it and a small item in its ornamentation, to which they agreed. After selecting the lot and deciding upon the size and style of house, we came to the question of ornament. In reply to a request for my views I said I would have an arch spanning the main entrance and upon it in letters eighteen inches long: FREE DISCUSSION. That broke the matter up and for the twenty years I remained, there was no church at Long Point. The idea of free discussion broke off all applications. I extended my farm and produced abundant crops for home consumption and much to sell.

[Editors' Note: Gideon recorded little about the years 1848–61 in his memoirs, but it was a busy and productive period for him. He devoted his enormous energies to the development of his farm and community and the avid pursuit of his scientific interests, while handing over most of his practice of medicine to several of his sons, especially Lucullus. He made many field trips to observe nature and to collect specimens and carried out a number of experiments. In the Lincecum Papers are almost 5,000 pages of typescripts of his correspondence, most of it from this period. He conducted a voluminous correspondence with other scientists and pseudo-scientists. His correspondence reflects interest in phrenology, spiritualism, genetics, and meteorology, and he even served as an official weather observer for the Smithsonian Institution. As the Civil War drew near, he strongly supported slavery, states rights, and Southern resistance to Northern domination and the hated abolitionists.]

MWhen the Civil War came we labored hard to perform our part in the struggle for liberty. I labored daily, making spinning wheels, looms, reels, spinning and carding machines, sleys, swifts—all the necessaries for making cloth. My wife and daughter spun and wove, knitted socks and did all they could to clothe as many soldiers as possible. We also fed, lodged and made music for all that called on us, and that was perhaps thousands.[10]

We lost our cause, and my wife was greatly mortified at it. She became ill about this time, and as the war left us nothing but our land, I proposed to her we send for the surveyor and have the land divided between our children, to which she consented.

It was not long before we buried her by the side of her oldest son, Lycurgus, at the Baptist Meeting House between Long Point and Union Hill.[11] I had nothing after her death to detain me at the lonely old Homestead. I put my ambulance in good order and with Wm. H. Lincecum and James Caldwell on their horses and little George Campbell in the ambulance, explored twenty-eight counties in upper and western Texas. We were three months out, camping all the time. I collected a great many subjects of natural history, among them two thousand butterflies, a number of mussel shells, fossil oysters, clams, conches, etc.[12] I was glad to be home again but was not contented. It did not seem like home. My sad soul missed the lost one.

On my return I found letters from two companies of people, who were on the road to Tuxpan, Mexico,[13] and wished to meet me at Goliad. There was another company headed by Wm. J. Russell of Rutersville, Texas,[14] who were going to the same place by water, but I was not ready and did not meet them. I wrote a great deal about this time, describing the natural history of Texas for the different academies.[15] I was also daily skinning birds and collecting subjects of natural science. Many of my letters had already been published in the Reports and Journals of the different academies of natural science, and I saw reprints and extracts from them in the Journals of Natural History of Europe. I corresponded with some of the great scientific men of Europe. To Sir Charles Darwin, author of "Origin of the Species," I am indebted for the most polite letter I ever received.[16]

I had been investigating the Texas Ants and other insects for twelve years and had learned much about them that had not been published. I was increasing my knowledge of them every day, but our Yankee masters began to bear too tight on me and I had to give it up. After much correspondence with the ship agents at Galveston and several disappointments,[17] I at last received a telegram that we must be in Galveston on 6th of June to get a schooner for Tuxpan, Mexico, to which place I had determined to go. We made ready as soon as possible, but the scene that occurred on parting with children, grandchildren, and friends was almost beyond my power to bear calmly. It was a very serious hour with me, but we reached Galveston on time and Captain Kried of the San Carlos informed me that the tickets to Tuxpan cost $25 per head, and there were nine of us.[18] But he made a reduction on the boys, which made it count only six, so our fare was $150 (with liberal baggage allowed). At 5 o'clock p.m. on June 9th we cut loose and turned our prow seaward. On 16th June at 10 a.m. we arrived in sight of Tuxpan. Could see the coast for twenty miles. Had a fair wind and sailed over the bar and into Tuxpan River without a pilot and landed at Morales Wharf.[19] The first thing that attracted my attention was the clean condition of the numerous laborers. At all the seaports I had ever seen, when a vessel landed with passengers, the bawling uproar among the laborers would be so great that a man could hear nothing else. Here it was very different. Their behavior was most respectful.

I was engaged most of the day in working my baggage through the Custom House. The officers were quite polite and allowed it to remain until I could make arrangements to remove it. I spent the next day trying to buy a house. There was some combinations amongst the Americans that I had to guard against. There was another thing that made against me—a fool tale that I had $20,000 in gold. Everybody wanted to borrow money, and I could get nothing at a fair price. Finally, I bought a place on the south side of the river, a thousand yards below the main street landing and moved to it. We had no mosquito bars and the mosquitoes kept us busy kicking and slapping all night, but we soon learned what to do for them. Our little field of two acres was planted and worked between showers, for it rained almost constantly. As soon as one crop was harvested, we planted another; and I continued to clear ground until I had seventeen acres: three acres in plantains and bananas, six in sugar cane and the balance in corn and small crops. My aim was to get a large cane field. I got a sugar-mill, furnace, and evaporator and commenced making sugar, but we were not strong enough to carry it on profitably. The boys were not big enough for the heavy work, so, I made haste to sell the farm and the growing crop included.[20]

I find this, both as to climate and people, a pleasant country to dwell in. I shall leave my mortal remains to be deposited here on the Tuxpan. There is much to admire and love here, but this is wholly attributable to the cerebral developments of the individual who is pleased or pained with any particular situation. Some specimens of organic development are satisfactorily situated in the solitary cells of a prison; other specimens, thus placed, would fret and die in a day. There are the two extremes and there is every shade of difference of character between them. Hence we find the world everywhere occupied, somebody pleased with every clime and country. Here we never have any sun-strokes or lightning strokes, no lock-jaw, no hydrophobia, nothing to hurt but four-nostril snakes and small-pox. Folks just die without help, when they are old enough, and in this climate it rarely occurs more than once in the same individual.

My Indian friend and guide came today and we sailed four miles down the river. We spent two hours digging in a shell bank and found plenty of signs of man. Very primitive but nothing important—bones, pottery and stone implements but no symbols. On this trip I saw some sea-nettles [probably Portuguese man-of-war] floating by. They are very numerous at this season and I am afraid of them. They are as large as a breakfast plate, with a star in the middle. They are composed of a transparent jelly-like substance, without feet, or fins, or mouth, or eyes or ears; and all the motion they are capable of, is the power to contract and expand the outer edge of their disc-like form. As they float they continue to contract and expand perpetually.

I am as well as common today but unable to work. To be deprived of this privilege, for a poor man, is a great loss. To capture a few butterflies, an occasional undescribed ant or a blooming botanic specimen is about the extent of my labors. When I don't feel well enough to sail my boat, I spend the time sitting under the shade of my mustang grapevine, studying the Stone Book of the history of the origin and progressive development of the earth's crust. Geology, though it makes some very creditable surmises, does not pretend to account for the origin of the Globe itself. Last night was high tide and this morning when I looked out of my window, I saw lying at my wharf a boat. Now the question is, what favor placed it there? It was controlled by a regular set of forces, as irresistible as the forces that landed this Globe in its present stationary predicaments and whirls it round its burning center.

It is too wet today for any outdoor labor and all are complaining, but that is in perfect accordance with our misdirected proclivities. The world with its natural phenomena don't quite suit us. Hence we complain and suffer and pray to the World-Maker to alter his universal program to suit our desires, go as it may with the desires and needs of our neighbors. If there is anything wrong it is the World-Maker's own fault and if he don't like the fix he has got it in, he will have to mend it himself.

Today about sunset the Bravo Ants[21] appeared in the hog-pen and soon after supper they came into my room. We were glad to see them and to keep them off the beds, we immediately tucked down all the mosquito bars. We then kept out of their way and observed their action. Their plan of invasion and success in capturing the insects that had taken winter quarters in the house was not only ingenious but extensive and wonderful to witness.

Great numbers of them were dispatched from the main Army into the house, where they were seen rapidly running over the walls in all directions and into the cracks and crevices and all the hiding places to be found, routing out every species of insects. It was amusing to see with what trepidation the insects fled from the approaching foe. While this was going on inside the house, the main body, in countless thousands, spread themselves on the ground outside like a carpet, in a belt three or four feet wide.

Soon the frightened roaches, ants, stinking pumpkin-bugs (which we could smell), spiders and many other creeping things were to be seen precipitately escaping from the invading foes that were scouring every part of the house. The ants inside did not capture many of the insects, for it seemed to be orders to drive them out to the devouring hosts, who were ready to sieze and devour eveything that came out. By daylight they had all disappeared.

I lay up all day reading Dr. Naphegy's "Days in the Great Sahara."[22] It is a well written book. He went without any European companion but traveling with an Arabic caravan from Morocco. His mishaps and adventures in crossing the Atlas Mountains are quite interesting. So is the whole book. I have commenced making collections of seed and looking out for plants for the accomplishment of an agreement made with the Agent of The Agricultural Society of New York.[23]

Damp, cloudy morning but it will be clear soon. The Chachalacas[24] say so, for they are sounding their coarse, rasping notes in all directions. Some of the vegetable kingdom are more reliable than I in foretelling changes in the weather. We have a great variety of Acacias here and Mimosas too. Some of them so delicate and sensitive that they will close up their leaves if you walk near them. I am making preparation today for an exploration trip to Tumilca,[25] a ruined city three leagues south of this place. The way through the thickets is difficult to find and it is hard to secure a guide, for it is said there are so many lions and tigers about the old ruins, that they are afraid to stay there all night. Tradition makes the lions kill several men, who had gone there in search of treasure. I shall take my gun and will be glad to meet a lion or tiger either.

The wind set right today and I concluded to sail down to the mouth of the river and examine again those shell banks. On the way we came to a bluff, portions of which (having been undermined by the slashing waves at the bottom) had recently slid into the river, leaving a new face to the bluff, which had not been exposed for many centuries. The entire bluff, four or five hundred yards in length and twenty-five to thirty feet in height, is an aqueous formation, composed of marine shells and pebbles and debris from the mountains and hills above.

The shell stratum is, at the water level, thirteen or fourteen inches thick, extending the entire length of the bluff. Then comes a stratum of charcoal and blackened debris of various descriptions: quantities of broken potware, bones and broken flint knives. One piece of pottery is an inch and a quarter thick, covered on one side with *Chapopote*. (*Chapopote* is the pitch of coal-tar, found here in great quantities in a natural state. We use it to make a leaky boat tight.) It is eight inches in diameter, nearly round and is evidently the bottom part of a strong pot that had been used for boiling *Chapopote*. The print, or marks, of the stick with which they scraped out the *Chapopote* from the bottom are plainly seen, showing that the end of the stick was an inch wide and had a gap in it and that the *Chapopote* was nearly cold when the marks were made.

In this blackened stratum we found shell ornaments curiously carved with holes in them, showing that they had been worn on the neck and breast. Also one well formed foot and entire leg from the hip down of a boy. It seemed to be the leg of a fat babe. On top of this stratum lay a human skeleton; the bones were large and lay folded together, arms on the thighs with the left hand on the hip. The evidences of their antiquity was found in the deposit that lay around them. The ornaments of carved shells, stone tools, flint knives, etc., show clearly that they were people belonging to the Stone Age, as did the great depth in which they are found beneath the surface. I must see that place again. There is more to be read there.

During an excursion the other day to some old ruins on the Zapatal, a pretty little river that discharges its waters into the Tuxpan in the south side, nine miles below town, I found the plants, specimens of which I enclose. These ruined cities, which are numerous and mostly large and extensive, are built of stone and clay, in the manner of a coarse concrete work and well done. Some extensive walls are still in a good state of preservation. One solid mass of stonework is one hundred feet square at the base, forty feet in heighth, shaped pyramidal.[26] There are many flights of stairs (still perfect) reaching to the top, which is solid and firm like the rest of the structure, and near the center on top is erected a small oblong room, open at the top about six feet wide and seven feet long and about the same in height. Worked in the wall inside of the superstructure on opposite sides are two seats or benches. No door or place of entrance has yet been discovered to this vast pile of well laid rocks. It is not even known that it is hollow, and no conjecture has as yet been proposed as to its use or for what purpose it was constructed in the very center of an immense city, the dilapidated houses of which, with its finely paved street lie closely scattered for miles around.

I happen to know well enough what it all means, for *Chahta-Immataha* communicated the history of these ruined cities to me long ago. These people were Sun-Worshippers. The great stone pile I have alluded to is a Temple of the Sun. The open terrace on the top was where they kept the perpetual fire of the Sun smoking and where they pushed up the golden image of that luminary for the people to gaze upon, on their festival days.[27]

I cannot write all the mighty thoughts that revolve in my old organization. There is too much for me to write. I sometimes feel lonely, with no one to express my thoughts to. It is a choking condition to be placed in. You have an idea which you would like to communicate, you look around upon your associates; you know them and you see plainly that it would be folly to express the thought. They could not hear it, they do not want it. It would bother their brains, which are not capacitated to receive and retain an idea that ranges above the animal developments. What would I care for the near proximity of the terminus of my route, if I had some one prepared to begin where I left off? It is not, however, my good fortune to occupy that agreeable position. I shall continue the daily record of my labors and the events that the times may bring forth. Our war has not terminated[28] but it is quieting down. There will be but little more of it, if outsiders will let us alone.

I will not pursue this narrative further. If it fails to interest you at the years of discretion, you may nevertheless find some hints that will instruct you on your life journey.

EDITORS' NOTE: Here, with the complimentary close "Your Grandfather, Gideon Lincecum," ended Gideon's letter to his "Bully Grandson," dated 3 November 1871. And here ends his autobiographical narrative. He remained in Tuxpan two more years, describing his life there in diary-like letters to his daughter, Sallie, by then married to William P. "Sioux" Doran. Sallie preserved these letters and they are to be found in the Lincecum Papers, but because Gideon did not write them as autobiography, they are not included here. They are, however, quite interesting and valuable as a history of the Tuxpan colony. For reasons that remain unclear, Gideon returned to Texas (and Long Point) in May, 1873. For the next fifteen months he carried on active correspondence with his scientific friends, and in mid-1874 he began his long series of autobiographical letters to the editor of *The American Sportsman*, which must have drained his remarkable energies. He weakened in the fall of 1874 and died at Long Point, 24 November. Upon learning of his death, the editor of *The American Sportsman*, Wilbur F. Parker, wrote a noble obituary for his readers, part of which reads as follows: "Born a frontiersman in 1793, brought up as he has told us among the Indians of the South, with whose usages, traditions, and languages he was intimately acquainted; endued with a splendid physique, a vigorous intellect and a strong will, he educated himself and amid all the difficulties of daily bread-winning for a very large family, raised himself to the position of an original thinker, a keen observer and an accomplished naturalist. He was a rare—a very rare—instance of a really self-taught man, who went to nature for his inspiration, and built up his knowledge upon the basis of personal observation. He was an industrious correspondent of many scientific journals . . . , while the lesson he taught to us was his broad inclusive sympathy for all God's creatures, great and small. From the ant to the buffalo, the lowly grass or the mighty forest tree, everything was good. He was gathered in ripe, by the reaper; yet though his years were many and he could not in the course of nature be expected to stay on this side of the river much longer, the old man was so bright and energetic that his call comes upon us with all the impressive force of sudden death. Our readers will miss an able contributor and a grand old sportsman."][29]

Notes

INTRODUCTION

1. *Monuments Erected by the State of Texas to Commemorate the Centenary of Texas Independence: The Report of the Commission of Control for Texas Centennial Celebrations,* Harold Schoen, comp., p. 163.

2. Samuel Wood Geiser, *Naturalists of the Frontier,* p. 214.

3. Samuel H. Kaye, Rufus Ward, Jr., and Carolyn B. Neault, *By the Flow of the Inland River: The Settlement of Columbus to 1825,* pp. 61, 80, 82–88, 92. Map of Township Plat T18-R19W, from Meridian of Huntsville, Alabama, surveyed by Charles M. Lawson in May-June, 1823, showing location of Gideon Lincecum's property near Peachland's Landing and Plymouth Bluff on the Tombigbee River at Columbus. Samuel Kaye, letter to Jerry B. Lincecum, 26 June 1992.

4. See Cheri Lynne Wolfe, "The Traditional History of the *Chahta* People: An Analysis of Gideon Lincecum's 19th Century Narrative." Ms. Wolfe has edited and annotated Gideon's manuscript in connection with her doctoral studies in American Civilization at the University of Texas.

5. Anna Lewis, *Chief Pushmataha, American Patriot: The Story of the Choctaws' Struggle for Survival.* For an assessment of her indebtedness to Gideon, see Clara Sue Kidwell and Charles Roberts, *The Choctaws: A Critical Bibliography,* p. 33.

6. Lois Wood Burkhalter, *Gideon Lincecum 1793–1874: A Biography,* p. 30.

7. James Oakes, *The Ruling Race: A History of American Slaveholders,* pp. 54–57.

8. Pat Ireland Nixon, *The Medical Story of Early Texas,* pp. 376–84.

9. Burkhalter, *Gideon Lincecum,* pp. 93–98.

10. This entire section on Gideon and "Killiecrankie" is paraphrased from Burkhalter, *Gideon Lincecum,* pp. 290–91, 298–99.

11. Ibid., p. 99n.

12. Ibid., p. 71.

CHAPTER ONE

1. Gideon's father, Hezekiah, was born c. 1770 in Warren County, Georgia, and died 4 March 1839 in Lowndes County, Mississippi. Mary H. Clay, "Gideon Lincecum, Southern Pioneer, 1793–1874," p. 3.

2. Gideon's mother, Sarah "Sally" Hickman, was born 5 March 1775, in Anson County, North Carolina, and died in Catahoula Parish, Louisiana, 28 May 1848. Burkhalter, *Gideon Lincecum*, pp. 12, 72.

3. For his genealogical facts, Gideon is relying not on records but on family tradition, especially that given him by his grandmother, Miriam Bowie Lincecum.

4. Almost all of the Saluda River is in South Carolina, but the village of Saluda is on the North Carolina side of the border. Since Gideon later confused the Saluda and Savannah Rivers, one cannot be confident he knew where his grandparents really settled.

5. If Hezekiah was born in 1770 and Miriam lived until 1813, she lived forty-three more years, not just forty-one.

6. There is little credible evidence that the British authorities paid for scalps of the rebellious colonists. It was reputed that the lieutenant governor of Canada, Gen. Henry Hamilton, paid red men for the white men's scalps, but this was never proved and his influence did not extend to Georgia, where the British governor, Sir James Wright, had a reputation for decency and moderation. John R. Alden, *The South in the American Revolution*, p. 280; and Kenneth Coleman, *American Revolution in Georgia, 1763–1789*, pp. 144, 277.

7. Augusta fell to the British on 29 January 1779. Efforts to verify the activities of Capt. Gideon Lincecum as claimed in family tradition have proved fruitless. However, it has been written: "Of Georgia's back-country war [in the Revolution] there are few written records, but it gave rise to a treasure trove of legends." Ronald G. Killion and Charles T. Waller, eds., *Georgia and the Revolution*, pp. 76–77.

8. Although "Nace" was probably the nickname of Capt. Ignatius Few, a prominent citizen of that part of Georgia, it is likely that Nace's brother, Col. Benjamin Few, or another brother, Lt. Col. William Few, Jr., was the person referred to here. Ignatius served as captain and brevet-major in the Continental Army, whereas the other two Few brothers commanded militia in this part of Georgia. Bernard Sutter, "Ignatius Alphonse Few," in *Men of Mark in Georgia*, ed. William F. Northen, 2:362; Kenneth Coleman, letter to Edward Hake Phillips, 12 Feb. 1992.

9. The editors have found no corroboration of William Higginbotham's account. Because the U.S. Census records for Georgia, 1790–1810, were destroyed when the British burned Washington in 1814, it is difficult to trace Georgians in this time period. A William Higginbotham does appear in the 1820 Census for Elbert County, which adjoined Warren County, and Jonathan Hagerthy's name appears sev-

eral times in the records of Warren County, but neither of their names (nor that of Captain Lincecum) appear in records of Revolutionary War veterans of Georgia. Allen D. Candler, compiler, *The Revolutionary Records of the State of Georgia;* Robert S. Davis, Jr., *Georgia Citizens and Soldiers of the American Revolution;* Effie T. McCall, *Roster of Revolutionary Soldiers in Georgia;* and Silas E. Lucas, Jr., ed., *Some Georgia County Records,* 1:187, 269, 323.

10. "David Creswell" (not "Criswell") appears in the Deed Records of Hancock County as a justice of the peace in 1792. Lucas, *Georgia County Records,* 1:82. Since the ambush of Captain Lincecum occurred near Sparta in Hancock County, this is probably Gideon's "Criswell."

11. The Edgefield District bordered the Savannah River, extending up river from near Augusta, Georgia, to the mouth of Little River. Gene Waddell, ed., *Mills' Atlas; Atlas of the State of South Carolina, 1825,* [pages unnumbered].

12. This family tradition regarding Edward and John Lincecum may be in considerable error. Records show that in April, 1779, both John and Edmund Lyncecum were court-martialed by a Patriot military court headed by Col. Matthew Singleton and Lt. Col. William Few. Both Lyncecums had been apprehended in the wake of the British retreat. John confessed "he was aiding and assisting in the taking and delivering Capt. David Robinson to the British forces," and Edmund confessed "that he was with the Indians in arms against the United States." Both men were said to be known by some members of the court to be "attrocious Villains" and were ordered to be kept in close confinement. Robert S. Davis, Jr., *The Wilkes County Papers, 1773–1833,* pp. 54–56. In October, 1778, a John Lincidum (the Lincecum name was frequently garbled by scribes) was paid £24 ($96) for twelve days' service as a spy by Col. William Candler of the Georgia Militia. Davis, *Georgia Citizens,* p. 34. John may have been working for both sides.

13. A "Clabon Newsom" is listed in the Warren County Tax Returns for 1794. He lived on "B[riar?] Creek, owned two slaves and 440 acres. Ruth Blair, ed., *Some Early Tax Digests of Georgia,* p. 183. "Claibourn Newsom" sold 180 acres on Big Briar Creek in Warren County in 1797. Lucas, *Georgia County Records,* 1:209, 227. Lucas cites many deeds in Warren County owned or transferred by Ignatius Few (see especially 1:230–34).

14. For a good treatment of the problems with the Muskogee Indians in Georgia in the 1780s, see Coleman, *American Revolution,* pp. 238–52. Gideon uses the name "Muskogee" to refer to the Creek Indians, whose language was Muskogean.

15. Records of the enlistment of Thomas Roberts and Hezekiah Lincecum could not be found, except that the names of both men appear as serving briefly in the Washington County militia in 1793. Up to that time Washington County embraced a large area adjoining Warren County and included present-day Hancock and Greene Counties, where Hezekiah was soon to live, if he was not there already. Murti

June Clark, *American Militia in the Frontier Wars, 1790–96,* pp. 210–11.

16. No Abram Brantley was found in the published tax records or in Marie De Lamar and Elizabeth Rothstein, *The Reconstructed Census of Georgia: Substitutes for Georgia's Lost 1790 Census,* but a number of Brantleys, including an Aaron Brantley, appear in the earliest surviving census of Washington County, Georgia, in 1820.

17. Stephen Camp's name does not appear in the 1820 Census of Georgia or the 1840 Census of Alabama. Camp was a fairly common name in Warren County, Georgia. A 1778 Wilkes (Warren) County deed of land adjoining "Widow Lansacum's" was witnessed by S.[Stephen?] Camp. Lucas, *Georgia County Records,* 1:238.

18. Apparently Sally Strange was the daughter of Isham Strange, who was living in Warren (Wilkes) County in 1787. As Sarah Lincecum, she is listed as a co-signer with Isham, Rachael, and Elizabeth Strange on a deed of conveyance of land in South Carolina to Andrew Kidd, 21 July 1787. Silas E. Lucas, Jr., ed., *Some South Carolina County Records,* 2:87. Isham Strange appears on the tax rolls of Warren County in 1794. Blair, *Tax Digests,* p. 165.

19. One enters a quagmire in trying to understand and verify Gideon's geography in this early period. He was not yet an eyewitness, so his facts are based on family tradition. County lines were undergoing considerable change, and surviving records are often confusing. Powell's Creek, to which he refers, is in Hancock County, which was carved out of Washington County in 1793. Hancock lies on the west side of the Ogeechee River, across from Warren County, which was formed from Wilkes County the same year, 1793. Records show that Miriam Bowie Lincecum had land on Powell's Creek in 1785, and in 1793 she is identified as being a citizen of Washington County, which embraced Hancock (but not Warren County) at that time. There is no indication in Gideon's narrative that Hezekiah (or Miriam) left Powell's Creek before Gideon was born, yet both Gideon and his biographer claim that Gideon was born in Warren County, which did not include Hancock County or Powell's Creek. Grace G. Davidson, *Early Records of Georgia,* 1:275; Lucas, *Georgia County Records,* 2:241; Blair, *Tax Digests,* pp. 35, 201; Burkhalter, *Gideon Lincecum,* p. 3.

20. Scull Shoals of the Oconee River was in Greene County, which lies just above Hancock County, but is now under the waters of Lake Sinclair. Supposedly it was named for skeletal remains found there from nearby Indian mounds, but a Daniel Scull is noted as living in Georgia in 1790, so the spelling may indicate another explanation. Kenneth K. Krakow, *Georgia Place Names,* p. 205; De Lamar and Rothstein, *Reconstructed Census of Georgia,* p. 52.

21. "Byrd Braswell" is listed in the 1794 Tax Returns for Warren County, and "Byrd Brazel" is listed in the 1820 census for Hancock County. Blair, *Tax Digests,* p. 185.

22. It is unlikely that Gideon saw Eli Whitney, who invented his first cotton gin on the Widow Greene's plantation near Savannah the

same year Gideon was born. Whitney soon improved the gin by utilizing circular saws, but long before Gideon reached the age of nine he was busy in his factory in Whitneyville, Connecticut. Constance McL. Green, *Eli Whitney and the Birth of Technology*, pp. 127-35.

23. Tyre Kelly was married to Hezekiah Lincecum's sister, Sally, and James and John Hickman were brothers of Hezekiah's wife Sally (the many Sallies—or Sarahs—in the Lincecum family lead easily to confusion).

24. Here Gideon has confused the Saluda River with the Savannah River, which separates Georgia from South Carolina. The town of Vienna, now under Clarks Hill Lake, was on the South Carolina side.

25. The fact that Asa Lincecum had his mother's maiden name suggests that his birth may have been illegitimate. There is confirmation that his surname was indeed Lincecum in sworn statements made in Lowndes County, Mississippi, on 14 May 1832, relating to the contested estate of Asa B. Lincecum. Asa died intestate in October, 1827 (exact date not recorded), and a lengthy court battle over his estate was finally settled after the executors journeyed to Mississippi and obtained depositions from Hezekiah Lincecum, Sarah Hickman Lincecum, and Gideon Lincecum. Copies of sworn statements obtained by B. J. Lincecum from Circuit Court of Cape Girardeau County, Missouri, and transmitted to Jerry B. Lincecum on 11 Nov. 1991.

26. According to the testimony of Sarah Hickman Lincecum in regard to the contested estate of Asa Lincecum (cited in note 25), "Parson Porter" was Alexander Porter, "a Preacher of the Gospel," who married Asa and Malinda in 1802. Porter is listed in the 1800 census for Abbeville District, and a deed was "Proved on oath of Revd. Alexdr. Porter" at the Clerk of Court Office in Abbeville in 1810. Silas E. Lucas, Jr., ed., *A Collection of Upper South Carolina Genealogical and Family Records*, 2:86.

27. Elva was the name given to Asa and Malinda's daughter. Later, a son, Harmon, was born. Asa and Malinda separated by mutual consent, and Asa moved to Missouri with Harmon. Elva remained with Malinda but died sometime before 1830. Malinda had two other children by a later marriage (or union). According to B. J. Lincecum, a present-day descendant of Asa's son Harmon, Asa had two other children, Resin B. and Isabella (Ibby), after his separation from Malinda, but he was apparently not legally married to their mother. The court battle over Asa's estate revolved around the question of who were his legal heirs, and the sworn statements by Hezekiah, Sarah, and Gideon proved to the satisfaction of the court that Asa and Malinda were legally married, making Harmon the only rightful and legal heir (his sister Elva having predeceased her father). Letter to Jerry B. Lincecum, 14 Nov. 1991.

28. The Choctaw (Muskogean) word "isunlash" (pronounced "is-oon-lush") means "tongue," and "Falakto" (pronounced "fil-lok-chee")

means "forked." Cyrus Byington, *A Dictionary of the Choctaw Language*, pp. 118, 199.

29. The Choctaw word for blowgun is "oski" (or "uski") "lumpa," in which the "l" is aspirated as a "thl." The printer may have misread or garbled Gideon's spelling of his Choctaw words. Ibid., pp. 307, 396.

30. Pendleton District, South Carolina, which lay along the upper Savannah River, later was carved into Oconee, Pickens, and Anderson Counties. Waddell, *Mills' Atlas*.

31. Pickensville was a small town about eighteen miles SSW of the present town of Pickens in Pickens County. Ibid.

32. Uncle Tyre may have been the same Tyre Kelly who married Elizabeth Jinkins in Morgan County, Georgia, 23 June 1808. Lucas, *Georgia County Records*, 2:83. Morgan County is just north of Putnam County, where the Lincecums were in 1808.

33. By the Treaty of New York, 1790, the Creek (Muskogee) Indians ceded their lands east of the Oconee River. In the period 1802–1805, they ceded more lands, including those between the Oconee and the Ogeechee Rivers. This was "the new purchase" to which Gideon refers. Wilcomb E. Washburn, ed., *The American Indian and the United States: A Documentary History*, 4:2288, 2324.

34. Young Gill does not appear in the 1820 Census; however, a "Gill" does appear in the tax returns of Hancock County in 1812, and a Thomas Y. Gill shows up in the Census of 1830 for Wilkes County. Blair, *Tax Digests*, p. 42.

35. Garland Lincecum, Gideon's oldest brother, was born in 1797 and died in Caldwell County, Texas, about 1856. Little is known about their sister Polly, and this is Gideon's only reference to her. No correspondence to or from her appears in the Lincecum papers, in contrast with a number of references or correspondence regarding his other sisters: Emily, who married Daniel Boone Moore; and Mary, who married Joseph Bryan. The Lincecums had a household slave named Polly (and later called "Aunt Polly"), who was just two years younger than Gideon; she lived with his family for about sixty years, and was almost like a sister to him, which raises the possibility that he had no sister named Polly. Curiously, Georgia records reveal that Gideon's grandmother, Miriam Bowie Lincecum, had a granddaughter named Linna (or Linda) Lincecum, whose relationship to Gideon is unclear. In the same document in which Miriam made provision for her "granddaughter Linna Lincecum," she deeded a slave ("one negro girl named Patt") to "my grandson Giddeon Berry" because of "the love and affection I have for my grandson." Lucas, *Georgia County Records*, 2:241. Since this document was dated 31 May 1793, less than six weeks after Gideon Lincecum's birth, it raises the possibility that he had an older sister (or half-sister—possibly a child of Sally Strange Lincecum). Linda could have been a cousin of Gideon's, but according to him, Miriam had lost all contact with Hezekiah's brothers' widows and their

offspring. A "Linda Lincecum" married Samuel Lord in Clarke County, Georgia, 12 September 1808. Blair, *Tax Digests*, p. 35.

36. In his "Personal Reminiscences," Gideon indicates he was thirteen (not fourteen) and says there were twenty-seven pupils in the school, including "three of my Indian playmates." He added, "The school operated as a drawback on our bow and arrow enjoyments." Gideon Lincecum, "Personal Reminiscences of an Octogenarian," *The American Sportsman* 4, no. 50 (12 Sept. 1874): 374.

37. Although the editors have been unable to identify the specific source of these lines of verse, there is abundant evidence that poetry of this type appeared regularly in late eighteenth-century editions of *The New England Primer* and other schoolbooks of that era. Verses by Isaac Watts, the eighteenth-century English poet and hymnwriter, were the most popular, and these lines are strikingly similar in style and theme to his work. Clifton Johnson confirms that Dilworth's speller was accepted almost universally until it was supplanted by Noah Webster's famous "blueback speller." Paul Leicester Ford, ed., *The New England Primer: A History of Its Origin and Development*, pp. 46–47; Clifton Johnson, *Old-Time Schools and School-books*, p. 186.

38. Georgia was the only state to distribute its public lands by a lottery. It held a series of lotteries, the first in 1805 and the second in 1807. "Registrants in the First Georgian Land Lottery," *The Georgia Genealogical Magazine* 1 (July 1961): 1–2.

39. Eatonton became the seat of Putnam County, which was created in 1807, just to the west of Hancock and Greene Counties.

40. Simon Holt is listed in Putnam County in the Census of 1820. At that time he had fifteen slaves. Fourth Census of the United States (1820), Georgia, Putnam County, Microcopy 33, Roll 9, Vol. 4.

41. William Wilkins is listed for "Eatonville" (Eatonton), Putnam County, in 1820 and had eighteen slaves. Ibid.

42. According to the 1820 Census for "Eatonville," Jeremiah Clark was single and had no slaves. Ibid.

43. John C. Mason's name appears in the 1820 Census for "Eatonville," and he had nineteen slaves. Ibid.

44. Mason Locke Weems (1759–1825), better known as "Parson Weems," was a popularizer of American history and was responsible for planting some of its famous myths, such as the fable of George Washington and the cherry tree. Emily E. F. Skeel, "Mason Locke Weems," in *The Dictionary of American Biography*, ed. Dumas Malone, Vol. 10, Pt. 1, 604–605.

45. Gideon's account of the impact education had on him is strikingly similar to that of a young man he later befriended in Mississippi, Peter Pitchlynn, who became one of the greatest principal chiefs of the Choctaw Nation. Pitchlynn credited Gideon as follows: "We dwelt in a remote wilderness where the light of Science and civilization had never shot a single ray. Twas then you came and took me by the hand and

led me by your council [*sic*] to the source of knowledge." Qtd. in W. David Baird, *Peter Pitchlynn: Chief of the Choctaws*, p. 20.

46. Although Ichabod Thompson's name does not appear in the 1820 Census for Georgia, a scrap preserved from the nearly totally destroyed Census of 1810 on Manufactures shows that Ichabod Thompson owned one of two cotton gins that were in Eatonton at that time. Robert S. Davis, Jr., *A Researcher's Library of Georgia History, Genealogy, and Record Sources*, p. 255.

47. Henry Branham is listed in the 1820 Census for "Eatonville," which shows he had eighteen slaves. Fourth Census of the United States (1820), Georgia.

48. Erasmus Darwin (1731–1802), the grandfather of Charles Darwin (1809–1882), published his two-volume work *Zoonomia, The Laws of Organic Life*, in 1794–1796. Gideon is in error in saying Erasmus was still alive in 1810. George C. Bouse, "Erasmus Darwin," in *The Dictionary of National Biography*, eds. Leslie Stephen and Sidney Lee, 5:536. Erasmus Darwin was offered the position of Royal Physician at London by George III, but he declined. Peter Brent, *Charles Darwin*, p. 13.

49. Erasmus Darwin's poetic work, *Botanic Garden*, was published in two parts, *The Loves of the Plants*, 1789, and *The Economy of Vegetation*, 1792. *The Temple of Nature* was published posthumously in 1803. Bouse, "Erasmus Darwin," p. 536.

50. Gideon is quite confused here. He was nine years old when Erasmus Darwin died. Perhaps he wrote to Robert Waring Darwin, the son of Erasmus and the father of Charles.

51. Gideon wrote his first letter to Charles Darwin, 29 December 1860, and a second letter, 4 March 1861, in reply to Darwin's letter to him, 27 January 1861. Regrettably, Darwin's letter is missing from the Lincecum papers in the Barker Texas History Center, University of Texas at Austin, but copies of Gideon's letters to Darwin are in his letter press, Vol. 2 (1859–1865), at the Barker Center. Gideon wrote to Darwin about his research on the agricultural ant of Texas, and Darwin read his letter to the Linnean Society of London in April 1861. Portions of it appeared in *Journal of the Linnean Society*, Zoology 6 (1862): 29–31, as "Agricultural Ant of Texas." Gideon's elaborate theories about a complex ant society led one eminent authority, Dr. August Forel, to comment: "These observations, although reported by Charles Darwin, inspire little confidence in me." Burkhalter, *Gideon Lincecum*, pp. 209–213. Today the agricultural ant is placed in the subfamily Myrmicinae and called *Pogonomyrmex molifaciens*.

52. This may have been the violin which was buried with Gideon (at his request) when he was laid to rest near Long Point, Texas, in 1874.

53. In an affidavit slip in the Lincecum Papers at the Barker History Center (Box 2E-364), Gideon affirms that he was mustered into service "about the 23rd of August 1812" in Capt. William Varner's Company, Colonel Freeman's Command, under Brigadier General

Floyd, in the Georgia Army against the Creek Indians. Perhaps Gideon's absence from home in military service accounts for his failure to mention a shocking incident that occurred in 1813 involving Hezekiah. While doing genealogical research in Georgia, B. J. Lincecum discovered the following record of the first criminal court proceeding for Putnam County:

"Jury	Sworn
1 Leon Moore	7 James Rockmoore
2 Joseph Smith	8 Micajah Gainey
3 Natl. Walker	9 John Robinson
4 Hezekiah Beefsey	10 William Robinson
5 Jesse Keeton	11 William Walker
6 James Walker	12 Elisha Trammel

Georgia
Putnam County } Ben a Negroe man slave, belonging to Robert McGough of Jones County Said State Stands Charged on the following Grounds towit: That the said Ben did on the thirtieth day of August in the year of our Lord one thousand eight hundred and thirteen, near the house of Hezekiah Lincecum, in the County aforesaid, in & upon the said Hezekiah Lincecum, in the peace of God & the Said State there being with force & arms, towit, an iron mattock, which he the said Ben then & there held with both his hands, upon the head of him the said Hezekiah inflicted a severe and grievous wound & crevice of the length of two inches & of the depth of half an inch penetrating to the skull of the said Hezekiah & scailing off a piece of the bone of the same, by which said grievous Wound & Bruise the said Hezekiah Lincecum was stuned & lay some time, towit, for the space of five minutes senseless, to the great damage of him the said Hezekiah Lincecum against the peace & dignity of said state to the evil and pernicious examples of all others in like case offending.

Hezekiah Lincecum
Prosecutor

We the Jury find the Prisoner guilty.

Wm. Walker, Foreman

Ben:
You will from hence be taken to the common Jail of this county where you will be Safely kept until Saturday the Eleventh Instant where you will be taken to the Place of execution and between the hours of Ten & Twelve O'Clock on that day be suspended between the heavens & the earth by the neck until you are dead dead dead & the Lord have Mercy on your soul.

Present their Honors,
W. Abercrombie
Jno. J. Smith
W. Roberts"

Photocopy of holograph original supplied to Jerry B. Lincecum by B. J. Lincecum, 14 Nov. 1991.

54. Gideon married Sarah (Sally) Bryan, 25 October 1814, in Putnam County, though the recorder spelled their names "Gidion Linsicum" and "Sally Bryand." Mary B. Warren, ed., *Georgia Marriages, 1811 through 1820*, p. 181.

CHAPTER TWO

1. Gideon is referring, of course, to Benjamin Franklin. In 1859, Gideon told a correspondent that he had encountered the writings of Franklin "by accident" at the age of seventeen, and Franklin "advised me to marry young, so that I might live to see my progeny grown up and thereby diminish the chances for leaving a batch of helpless orphans 'in this cold, unfriendly, god-made world.'" Gideon to Dr. R. P. Halleck, 21 March 1859, Letter Press, 1 (1859–1860), p. 4 (Lincecum Papers). In 1746, Franklin published a pamphlet, "Reflections on Courtship and Marriage: In Two Letters to a Friend," which promoted the virtues of procreating numerous offspring legitimately; however, modern scholars believe Franklin was merely the printer, not the author of this rather ribald essay. Leonard W. Labaree and Whitfield J. Bell, eds., *The Papers of Benjamin Franklin*, 3:74.

2. At the time Gideon was writing his "Personal Reminiscences," only nine of his thirteen children were living, if our evidence regarding the last child, Lucifer Hezekiah (1847–?) is correct. His first child, Lycurgus, born in 1815, died in 1849. The second, Lysander M., born in 1817, died in 1832, and the third child, Martha Anne Elizabeth, born in 1820, died in infancy in 1821. The only indication of Lucifer's death is a statement in a letter written in 1866 that "We have lost four children, Nos. 1, 2, 3, and 13 are dead. . . ." The other nine children were as follows: Leonidas L. (1821–1876), Leander William C. (1824–1883), Mary Elizabeth Catherine (1825–?), Lachaon Joseph (1827–1909), Lucullus Garland (1828–?), Leonora (1830–?), Cassandra (1832–1877), Sarah (Sallie) Matilda (1833–1919), and Lysander Rezin (1836–?). Burkhalter, *Gideon Lincecum*, p. 69.

3. According to Burkhalter, Gideon had six brothers: Garland, Rezin Bowie, Green, Grant, Thornton, and Grabel (mistakenly called Gabriel by Burkhalter). Very little is known of Green and Thornton, but Garland was, for years, Gideon's closest companion. Rezin Bowie died suddenly while traveling through Kentucky in 1835. Grant settled in Catahoula Parish, Louisiana, in 1840 (where his cousins Jim and Rezin Bowie had acquired land as early as 1802), and he and members of his family developed the small community of Lincecum Village near the town of Urania in present-day Grant Parish. Some of his descendants still live in or near Lincecum Village, where there is a Lincecum Baptist Church and Cemetery, which the editors have visited. Grant kept in contact with Gideon (though their relations became strained in the

1860s), and Gideon continued to write to Grant's son John after Grant's death in 1862. Grabel settled about thirty miles from Gideon in Mississippi but died there in 1836. Burkhalter, *Gideon Lincecum*, pp. 5, 21–22, 51, 72, 114, 270; Audrey Tracy, "Land Records Show Bowie Roots in Catahoula Parish," 22 Apr. 1979. Additional data from genealogical charts prepared by Douglas Hall, San Antonio, Texas, and Mabel Lincecum Sessions, Urania, Louisiana.

4. Gideon's attitudes toward blacks were ambivalent. Although he strongly defended the institution of slavery, he felt strong ties for some slaves like Dick. Another Lincecum slave, Lewis, was his boyhood companion and lifelong friend, as was "Aunt Polly." See Gideon, letter to Lewis Lincecum (also referred to as Lewis Shellhouse), 6 May 1868, and to "Bully Grandson" (Frank Doran), 4 Jan. 1873. Letter Press, 1867–68, and Box 2E-364, Lincecum Papers.

5. Gideon lived in Tuxpan, Mexico, from 1867 to 1873, as described later in this narrative.

6. Judge Christopher B. Strong is listed in the 1820 Census for "Eatonville," and is recorded as having a large family and eighteen slaves.

7. The Creek Indians had made the mistake of siding with the British in the War of 1812, and the tribe was severely defeated by Andrew Jackson at the Battle of Horseshoe Bend, 27 March 1814. Under the punitive terms of the Treaty of Fort Jackson, 9 August 1814, the Creeks were forced to cede most of their lands in Georgia, Alabama, and Mississippi. Thomas P. Abernethy, *The South in the New Nation, 1789–1819*, pp. 370–72.

8. No "M. Whitfield" appears in the 1820 Census, but James and Horatio Whitfield are listed as residents of "Eatonville." James Whitfield served with Gideon in the War of 1812 and, like Gideon, later moved to Mississippi, where, in time, he became governor of that state. Burkhalter, *Gideon Lincecum*, p. 124. There were several rifle makers named Gump or Gumpf at Lancaster, Pennsylvania, at this time. Christian Gump had a shop that made flintlock Kentucky rifles around 1800; from 1791–1842, flintlock and (later) percussion Kentucky rifles were made by Christopher Gumpf and his son Christopher, Jr. Around 1820, flintlock Kentucky rifles were also made in Lancaster by three other gunsmiths named Gumpf: Henry, Jacob, and John. Exactly who made Gideon, c. 1815, "the most completely finished rifle that I had ever seen up to that date," can only be conjecture. A. Merwyn Carey, *American Firearms Makers: When, Where, and What They Made From the Colonial Period to the End of the Nineteenth Century*, p. 48.

9. There were a number of "Mineral Springs" in Georgia. This one was near the Ocmulgee River, probably in Jasper County or Jones County. Other "Mineral Springs" are cited in Krakow, *Georgia Place-Names*, p. 150.

10. Elijah Saterwhite [*sic.*] married Rebecca Manning in Putnam County, 15 November 1819. Warren, *Georgia Marriages*, p. 260. His

name does not appear in the 1820 Georgia Census, but five other Sat-
terwhites are listed in that Census for Jones County, where Mineral
Springs likely was located.

11. This may have been the Stephen Heard who is listed in Morgan County in the Census of 1820. Morgan abutted Putnam and Jasper Counties. Burkhalter believed his name was Heard, not Herd.
Burkhalter, *Gideon Lincecum*, p. 20.

12. Green Wheeler is not listed in the 1820 Census of Georgia, but
a George R. Clayton is listed for Baldwin County, which adjoins Jones
and Putnam Counties.

13. Cat-ball, often called "cat," was a primitive form of baseball.
William A. Craigie and James R. Hulbert, eds., *A Dictionary of American
English on Historical Principles*, 1:444.

14. In his account in *The American Sportsman*, Gideon gives the date
of the Lincecums' departure as 27 December 1817, which may have
been the more accurate date. Lincecum, "Personal Reminiscences of
an Octogenerian," 4 (19 Sept. 1874): 390.

15. The name "Hightower" appears on several creeks in Georgia
but on no river, nor can it be found in Alabama.

16. If the Lincecums crossed Canoe Creek, they were considerably
north of the "Federal Road," on which two recent scholars said the
Lincecums traveled, as Canoe Creek is in northern Alabama. Henry
D. Southerland, Jr., and Jerry Elijah Brown, *The Federal Road Through
Georgia, the Creek Nation, and Alabama, 1806–36*, p. 105.

17. By 1820 the population of Tuscaloosa County was 8,229.
Thomas M. Owen, *History of Alabama and Dictionary of Alabama Biography*, 2:1337.

18. The Choctaw words for Black Warrior are "tashka" (warrior)
"lusa" (black), hence "Tuscaloosa" is a phonetic form. Byington, *Choctaw Language*, pp. 249, 395.

19. Dr. Jeptha V. Isbell was "probably the first physician" at Tuscaloosa and represented Tuscaloosa County in the Alabama Legislature,
1820–1821. Owen, *History of Alabama*, 2:1337.

20. The first census of Alabama was that of 1830. No John Weeks
appears in that census, but a Theophilus Weeks is listed in it as head of
a family in Tuscaloosa. In Gideon's 3 November 1871 autobiographical
letter to his "Bully Grandson," he refers to the man as John Weekly,
but that name does not appear in the 1830 Census either. Fifth Census
of the United States (1830), Alabama.

21. It is believed that the route the Lincecums took from the Black
Warrior to the Tombigbee was nearly the same as that of DeSoto's expedition in 1540. Martha M. Bigelow, "Conquistadores, Voyageurs,
and Mississippi," in *A History of Mississippi*, ed. Richard McLemore,
1:95–96.

22. The Eagle Hotel developed into a well known inn. In 1836, it
was advertised as "one of the best stands in [the] western country . . .
large and commodious and has attached to it all necessary out-

buildings, a barber shop, bath house, etc." *Columbus Democrat,* 6 Aug. 1836.

23. Map of Township Plat T18–R19W, from Meridian of Huntsville, Alabama, surveyed by Charles M. Lawson in May and June, 1823, showing location of Gideon Lincecum's field near Peachland's Landing and Plymouth Bluff on the Tombigbee River at Columbus. Samuel H. Kaye, letter to Jerry B. Lincecum, 26 June 1992.

24. The reference is to the young slave woman, Polly, who was with the Lincecums in Georgia, Mississippi, and Texas.

25. John Pitchlynn (c. 1756–1835) was born on a ship in the Caribbean, the son of a British trader, who died in the Choctaw country in 1774. John married into the prominent Folsom family of Choctaws. One of his sons, Peter P. Pitchlynn, became principal chief of the Choctaws in 1864. John was appointed Interpreter for the Choctaws by the United States in 1785 and served in that capacity for many years, participating in the War of 1812 and being present at the Treaty of Doak's Stand in 1820 and the Treaty of Washington in 1825. Along with Gideon Lincecum, he was a charter member of Masonic Lodge No. 5 in Columbus, Mississippi. He had eleven children, large herds of cattle and horses, at least forty slaves, and many acres of land. Baird, *Peter Pitchlynn,* pp. 6–18; Fifth U. S. Census (1830), Mississippi, Lowndes County, Reel M19-71, 85; Jennie H. Henry, ed., *Abstract of Annual Returns, Mississippi Free and Accepted Masons, 1819–1849,* pp. 33–35.

26. According to ornithologist Karl Haller of Austin College, what Gideon refers to here as "sea geese" were probably *Scoters* (of which there are three species). They are mostly coastal in winter but are often found inland as well.

27. Mr. Haller believes this duck to be the common Merganser (*Margus merganser*), which is a species with a great deal of white in its plumage.

28. This description completely stumped Mr. Haller, who credits Gideon with a discerning eye. Either the species died out before being recorded adequately, or Gideon's memory of it was garbled.

29. This was probably the *Trionyx* tortoise. Biologists do not take Gideon's theory of the "lefthandedness" of tortoises seriously, according to Dr. Howard McCarley, Professor of Biology, Emeritus, Austin College. Gideon's sample was far too small, statistically.

30. This so-called Military Road, which still bears that name in Columbus, Mississippi, today, should not be confused with the older, more westerly Natchez Trace, nor with the Gaines Trace, which was farther upstream at Cotton Gin Port. To further complicate matters, there was a network of trails known as "Gaines Old Trace," used by Edmund Gaines and others traveling from Pitchlynn's to the Natchez Trace as early as 1802. The Military Road, which opened in May, 1820, was soon superseded by the Robinson Road. Kaye et al., *By the Flow of the Inland River,* pp. 35–36; William A. Love, "Lowndes County, Its Antiquities and Pioneer Settlers," 359–61.

31. The 1830 Census lists a Joseph P. Caldwell in Tuscaloosa. Perhaps he was the man Gideon encountered here.

32. Gideon's house "was the first frame dwelling ever erected in the town" of Columbus. Moreover, "in this house on the first of January, 1821, the first mail that was ever brought to Columbus was opened by G. Lincecum, the first Postmaster." Kaye et al., *Inland River*, p. 87.

33. According to Kaye et al., "in 1820 the Alabama-Mississippi boundary line was surveyed and it was discovered that a tract of land lying along the east side of the Tombigbee which had been attached to Alabama was really in Mississippi. Mississippi Governor George Poindexter, in his messsage to the General Assembly on 3 January 1821, stated: 'It appears that a considerable population on the waters of the Tombigbee formerly attached to Alabama fall within the limits of this state.'" Monroe County, named for the incumbent President, James Monroe, was created by the Mississippi Legislature, in an act signed by the governor on February 9, 1821. Since Henry Greer's house in Columbus had served as the county seat of Marion County, Alabama, the act provided for an election to be held there, for the purpose of electing five county commissioners. "The next day, Feb. 10, 1821, the town of Columbus ... was chartered," and Gideon Lincecum was among those named by the legislature "as Commissioners to survey the town. This act also provided for the leasing of lots after the survey was made." The meeting to organize Monroe County was held on 4 April 1821, and Gideon Lincecum was elected one of the county commissioners. Kaye et al., *Inland River*, pp. 79–82.

34. The result was Franklin Academy (1821), which became the first free public school in Mississippi and is still in operation. John K. Bettersworth, *Mississippi: A History*, p. 565, and Noble H. Pace, Jr., "Franklin Academy," pp. 1–2. Kaye has made a drawing of the original Franklin Academy as reconstructed from its building specifications. See Kaye et al., *Inland River*, p. 84.

35. According to Dunbar Rowland, a list of the civil officers of Monroe County for 1821 "discloses the names of the following pioneers: Gideon Lincecum, Chief Justice of the Quorum, and Wiley Harbin, Ezekiel Nash, Stephen Harman, Frederick Weaver, Associate Justices; Bartlett Sims, Sheriff; Silas Brown, Assessor and Collector; Hezekiah Lincecum, Coroner. . . ." Dunbar Rowland, *History of Mississippi: The Heart of the South*, 2:793. Gideon had more help in these tasks than he indicates here, as some of them were shared with other commissioners. Kaye et al., *Inland River*, pp. 80–87.

36. John Pitchlynn, Jr., was the second of three sons the elder Pitchlynn had by his first wife, Rhoda Folsom. He was a true "prodigal son," but one who failed to repent of his ways. Baird, *Peter Pitchlynn*, pp. 6, 12; Burkhalter, *Gideon Lincecum*, p. 29.

37. There being no tribe with the name "Ooassashes," Gideon may be referring to the Ouachitas (Caddoan) or the Osages (Siouan), whose names were spelled phonetically in various ways. Frederick W. Hodge,

Handbook of American Indians North of Mexico, 2:156–61, 172, 1110–12. Perhaps this passage alludes to Gideon's shepherding the Choctaw ball players during the tour of the Southeast that he undertook as a moneymaking venture. It would be consistent with his humorous bent to look back on this failed commercial venture as "a failure to take scalps."

38. The wholesale firm of Dallas & Willcox (or Willcox & Dallas) of Philadelphia has proved elusive. The editors found some references to an early nineteenth-century Philadelphia merchant named Wilcocks, but no indication that he was in a partnership with anyone named Dallas (which was the name of a prominent family of attorneys in Philadelphia at that time).

CHAPTER THREE

1. H. B. Cushman, who served as a missionary to the Choctaws in Mississippi and was personally acquainted with Gideon, confirms that in 1820 the Choctaw Nation was divided into three districts, western, northeastern, and southern, and that these were ruled by (respectively) *Apushamataha [his spelling], Apukshinubi,* and *Mushulatubi.* Horatio B. Cushman, *A History of the Choctaw, Chickasaw, and Natchez Indians,* pp. 140–41.

2. In 1824, *Apukshinubi* met his death under suspicious circumstances at Maysville, Kentucky, on his way to participate in the controversial Treaty of Washington, a treaty he was expected to oppose. Angie Debo, *The Rise and Fall of the Choctaw Republic,* p. 49.3. Gideon kept a ferry on the Tombigbee opposite Columbus from 1822 to 1825. Clay, "Gideon Lincecum," p. 55.

3. Gideon kept a ferry on the Tombigbee opposite Columbus from 1822 to 1825. Clay, "Gideon Lincecum," p. 55.

4. Cushman records also that the Choctaws had a horror of death by hanging: "the soul of a Choctaw who had been executed by hanging was regarded as accursed—never being permitted to join his people in the happy hunting ground, but his spirit must forever haunt the place where he was hung." *History,* p. 218.

5. The 1820 Census for Mississippi lists a William Cocke as residing in Monroe County. Fourth Census of the United States (1820), Mississippi, Index, p. 214. A brief biography of Cocke makes it clear why Gideon referred to him as "the venerable Judge Cocke": Born in Virginia in 1747, he studied law there before migrating into western North Carolina, where he became associated with Daniel Boone and the settlement of Boonesboro on the Kentucky River. During the Revolutionary War he rose to the rank of brigadier general. During 1778 and 1779, he simultaneously represented Washington County in the Virginia Assembly and the North Carolina House of Burgesses. He served with distinction in law and politics as one of the first two senators from Tennessee. He eventually migrated to Mississippi and, after

a brief stint as a Chickasaw Indian Agent at Athens in Noxubee County (1816–1817), became instrumental (alongside Gideon) in the formation of the town of Columbus. On 4 June 1821, at the first meeting of the commissioners appointed by the Mississippi legislature for the laying out of the town, he was elected president, and he later served as the first President of the Board of Trustees of Franklin Academy. He died 22 August 1828. Kaye et al., *Inland River,* pp. 82–83, 107–108.

6. For a detailed account of *Pushmataha's* early life, see Gideon's colorful description in the latter part of his "Life of Apushimataha," pp. 434–85. Lewis's *Chief Pushmataha* drew heavily on Gideon's work.

CHAPTER FOUR

1. For a description and discussion of the prehistoric mounds in Mississippi, see Richard A. Marshall, "The Prehistory of Mississippi," in McLemore, *Mississippi,* 1:24–68.

2. The site of the former Choctaw village of *Bogue Toocolo Chito* is in Kemper County, Mississippi, about seven miles northwest of the county seat, DeKalb. Kenneth H. Carleton, "Eighteenth-Century Trails in the Choctaw Territory of Mississippi and Alabama," p. 117, and map in slip-case.

3. Efforts to establish a definitive translation of the name *"Chah-ta-im-ma-ta-hah"* have failed. *Chahta* is the Choctaws' name for themselves. A literal translation would be: "at the end of the Choctaw nation." Byington, *Choctaw Language,* pp. 190, 337, 440. Cheri Wolfe has found evidence that *"-Immataha"* meant "supporter" or "member of a warrior class" and occurred among Choctaw names listed in the French Dominion Records of the Mississippi Provincial Archives and was also recorded by John R. Swanton in *Source Material for the Social and Ceremonial Life of the Choctaw Indians.* Cheri Wolfe, letter to Jerry Lincecum, 22 Dec. 1992.

4. The resulting narrative of the traditional history of the Choctaws, which Gideon recorded and later (c. 1862) translated, has been preserved in the form of Gideon's translation, which is in the Lincecum Papers at the Barker History Center. The original manuscript in Choctaw was lost, along with other papers of Gideon, during the Civil War. His correspondence during the period 1861–1867 indicates that he believed his manuscript was potentially valuable, and feeling that the narrative should be translated in a more heroic style than he was capable of, he made efforts to secure the assistance of Prof. Edward Goodwin, an Alabama educator and novelist who was an expert in ancient languages. Goodwin died in 1863. Before leaving for Tuxpan in 1867, Gideon offered to sell the manuscript to Texas newspaper publisher Edward Hopkins Cushing for $1000 but was refused. In 1874, his friend Wilbur F. Parker, who was serializing Gideon's memoirs in his magazine, *The American Sportsman,* expressed interest in publishing the narrative (no money was mentioned), but Gideon

would not part with his only copy. Apparently he thought his children might be able to sell it after his death. With the manuscript in the Lincecum Papers is a four-page "Preface by Dr. Gideon Lincecum," written in pencil in what appears to be Gideon's hand, ending with his signature and dated 14 October 1874 (little more than six weeks before his death). It explains how he obtained the narrative originally and the circumstances under which it was subsequently translated. Gideon's manuscript has never been published in full, but excerpts can be found in Lincecum, "Choctaw Traditions about their Settlement in Mississippi and the Origin of their Mounds." Anthropologist T. N. Campbell has published three articles on Choctaw ethnography that draw heavily on this manuscript (see our Selected References). Currently the complete manuscript is being edited for publication by Cheri L. Wolfe at the University of Texas at Austin.

5. *Nanih-waya*, which in Choctaw means "the hill that brought (brings) forth," is a large mound, now considerably reduced in size, on the southern edge of Winston County, Mississippi, on Nanih Waya Creek. A good early description is in Henry S. Halbert, "Nanih Waiya, The Sacred Mound of the Choctaws." See also Calvin S. Brown, *Archeology of Mississippi*, pp. 24–28.

6. The Treaty of Hopewell, 3 January 1786, was one of several negotiated by American Commissioners with the Cherokees, Choctaws, and Chickasaws at Hopewell, South Carolina, in 1785–1786. Washburn, *History of Indian-White Relations*, p. 218.

7. The White Slue, though reduced in size, still exists. It is located a short distance from the Tombigbee River, across from Columbus, Mississippi.

8. *Anser canadensis* is, apparently, Gideon's own designation for the Canada goose. That species is generally designated *Branta canadensis* (not to be confused with the Brant, however). Roger T. Peterson, *A Field Guide to Western Birds*, pp. 17–18.

9. The scientific name of the Buffalo fish is *Ictiobus cyprinellus* (if a large-mouth sucker) or *I. bubalus* (if the small-mouth variety). Frank T. Knapp, *Fishes Found in the Freshwaters of Texas*, p. 43.

10. John Pitchlynn, Jr. (known familiarly as Jack), was murdered c. 1831, a victim of retaliation for killing his half-brother Silas in a drunken brawl. Burkhalter, *Gideon Lincecum*, p. 29n. Although Burkhalter seems to indicate that Garland Lincecum, Gideon's brother, attempted to protect Jack against retaliation, unpublished documents in the Columbus Public Library state there was speculation that Garland was hired as the assassin by Sophia Pitchlynn, the stepmother of Jack and the mother of Silas. Moina Evans, "Early Settlements West of the Tombigbee, and Sketch of the Pitchlyn Family," in "Pioneer Society Annals, Columbus, Mississippi, 1954–65," pp. 204–205.

11. The town of Cotton Gin Port developed on the east bank of the Tombigbee River, whereas the government's cotton gin had been erected among the Chickasaws on the west bank about 1801. In 1807–

1808, Gen. Edmund Pendleton Gaines surveyed a road, generally following an old Indian trail, from Muscle Shoals on the Tennessee River to Cotton Gin Port on the Tombigbee. This road became known as Gaines Trace and was well traveled. Jerry A. Harlow, et al., "Cotton Gin Port," *A History of Monroe County Mississippi*, pp. 50, 55; James W. Silver, *Edmund Pendleton Gaines, Frontier General*, pp. 19–20. Rev. Fred Weaver, who became a good friend of Gideon, led five families from Tennessee to settle the area on the east bank in 1816, and they became the nucleus of the town of Cotton Gin Port, which was officially organized 9 March 1825. W. A. Evans and W. B. Wilkes, *Mother Monroe: Pioneer Times in Monroe County*, pp. 40–42.

12. *Itewaumba* (*Itawamba*), whose Anglo name was Levi Colbert (1759–1834), was a leading chief of the Chickasaw Nation. For years he operated a ferry near Muscle Shoals, Alabama, at the Tennessee River end of Gaines Trace. In 1817, he moved to the other end of the Trace at Cotton Gin Port. He played a leading role in the treaties that provided for the cession of the Chickasaw lands east of the Mississippi. Returning from the Washington Treaty of 1834, he died at his former home in Colbert County, Alabama, leaving "for his family 1200 cattle, 500 horses, 40 slaves and numerous hogs and sheep." Don Martini, *Chickasaw Empire: The Story of the Colbert Family*, pp. 19, 43, 50–61.

13. Either Gideon or *Itawamba* has mixed up the history of the French fort. Celeron de Bienville did build a fort here in 1736, but the "massacre" took place at the Chickasaws' fortified town of Ackia, near present-day Tupelo, twenty-five miles north of Cotton Gin Port. There was no battle at the French fort. When the French abandoned the fort, they left many cannon and supplies behind because of the lowness of the river. Dunbar Rowland, ed., *Mississippi*, 1:22–23; Evans and Wilkes, *Mother Monroe*, p. 41; Harlow, "Cotton Gin Port," pp. 50–51.

14. Later Gideon became quite interested in the pseudoscience of phrenology, as his correspondence abundantly indicates.

15. The Choctaws did practice the custom of head-flattening of infants, a custom popularly thought to have been unique to the Flathead Indians of the Northwest. Hodge, *Handbook of American Indians*, 1:288.

16. Both a John Bickerstaff and a Johnson Bickerstaff are listed in the 1830 Census for Monroe County. Neither had any slaves. Fifth Census of the United States (1830), Mississippi, Monroe County, M19–71, pp. 127–28.

CHAPTER FIVE

1. Gideon's four children at that time (1824–1825) were Lycurgus, Lysander, Leonidas L., and Leander W. C. Martha Anne Elizabeth had died in 1821. Burkhalter, *Gideon Lincecum*, p. 69.

2. Gen. John Coffee, who had served under Gen. Andrew Jackson, was one of the Commissioners to mark the demarcation line between

the Indians and the Whites after the Treaty of Fort Jackson. So was Gen. Edmund P. Gaines, for whom Gaines Trace was named. Silver, *Edmund Pendleton Gaines*, pp. 54–59.

3. Paineyigaby (or Paneigby) Shoal has eluded efforts at identification, partly because of Gideon's (or the printer's) inconsistent spelling and partly because the area is now under the waters of the Tennessee-Tombigbee Waterway. The Chickasaw word for "ferry" is *peni*, which may give some clue to the origin of the name. Jesse Humes and Vinnie M. Humes, *A Chickasaw Dictionary*, p. 73.

4. *Aesculus rubra* seems to be Gideon's designation for the red Buckeye shrub, usually labeled *Aesculus pavia*, the fruit of which (when crushed) was "used to stupefy fish." Clair A. Brown, *Louisiana Trees and Shrubs*, p. 176. James Adair, the old Indian agent, describes the same method of catching fish with the buckeye root in 1775. Samuel C. Williams, ed., *Adair's History of the American Indians*, p. 432.

5. Neal Triplett, M.D., a Sherman, Texas, internist of long experience, opines that Gideon's illness was not a heart attack but heatstroke, which he survived because he covered himself in water almost immediately. Heart attacks among healthy young men like Gideon were extremely rare in those days. What made Gideon's illness so debilitating and so prolonged was the deplorable medical treatment to which he was subjected. Had he avoided the copious bleeding and the large doses of mercury, he would have recovered rather quickly. A. C. Greene, who wrote *Taking Heart* after making a detailed study of cardiovascular illness in order to recount his own experience as a heart transplant patient, agrees. Neal Triplett, M. D., letter to Edward Phillips, 27 Apr. 1992; A. C. Greene, letter to Jerry Lincecum, 16 May 1992.

6. Dr. John Hand was a prominent citizen of Columbus in the 1820s and 1830s, and his name appears in a number of documents from that era. For example, he was an early member of Masonic Lodge No. 5 in Columbus, which Gideon helped to found. "Source Material for Mississippi History: Lowndes County," Vol. 44, Pt. 2, p. 435.

7. While at Columbus Gideon wrote a letter to his wife reporting that he suddenly felt greatly improved and that his physician (Dr. Hand?) predicted his recovery. Gideon, letter to Sarah Lincecum, 19 May 1829, Lincecum Papers, Box 2E-363. The letter is reproduced in Burkhalter, *Gideon Lincecum*, p. 83.

8. The exact date of death of John Pitchlynn, Jr., has proved elusive, but a number of documents offer clues. For example, the Lowndes County Probate Book (1:106–107) records that on 3 September 1832, Letters of Administration for the Estate of John Pitchlynn, Jr., "late of Lowndes County (deceased)," were granted to Charles H. Abert, effective 10 September 1832. We know that he was killed in revenge for the murder of his half brother Silas, and a letter to Peter Pitchlynn (full brother of John, Jr., and half brother of Silas) indicates that news of the death of Silas was received at the Choctaw Factory by 25 June 1831. (Ben James, letter to Peter Pitchlynn, 25 June 1831,

xerox copy from Pitchlynn Collection, University of Oklahoma Library, Box 1, File 113.) In conjunction with a suit filed in the Circuit Court of Lowndes County (Cause # 22–1), records show that the county sheriff reported in April 1832 that he was unable to find John Pitchlynn, Jr., in Lowndes County. Thus it would appear that the death of Gideon's partner had definitely occurred by September, 1832, and possibly by April of that year.

9. The ball game played by the Choctaws was a type of lacrosse. Each player used two sticks rather than one, which is the custom today. George Catlin painted several Choctaw ballplayers as well as a scene of a game, which can be seen in his *Letters and Notes on the Manners, Customs, and Conditions of the North American Indians*, 2:124–27.

10. *Fulahooma* probably was the Choctaw named *"Falahooma,"* who is listed as receiving 160 acres of Mississippi land in *Mingo Mushalatubbee*'s district under the 1830 Treaty of Dancing Rabbit Creek, which provided for the removal of the Choctaws to the Indian Territory (Oklahoma). Document no. 1230, Walter Lowrie, Asbury Dickins, and John Forney, eds., *American State Papers: Public Lands*, 7:123.

11. On current maps, Oak Slush Creek enters the Tombigbee River from the west bank several miles upstream from present-day Columbus. In Gideon's writings the spelling of the name is ambiguous, and an earlier authority has persuasively argued that the creek's original name was *Okshash*, which means in Choctaw, "acorn mush." Love, "Lowndes County," pp. 352–53.

12. It is not known how far Gideon's tour with his ballplayers extended. One source says he found the Indians' drunkenness so annoying, he gave up in disgust around Huntsville, Alabama. Evans and Wilkes, *Mother Monroe*, pp. 23–24. He may have taken them as far as Washington, D.C., since he says he visited the grave of Pushmataha in the Congressional Cemetery.

13. William Wall was one of the trustees of the Cotton Gin Land Company that laid out the town in 1825. He is listed in the 1830 Census for Monroe County and is said to have twenty-eight slaves. Wall had a tanyard about ten miles northeast of Cotton Gin Port. A small community called Wall's Tanyard developed there, and Gideon lived nearby. Ibid., pp. 41–42, and Harlow et al., *History of Monroe County*, p. 77.

14. Robert Gordon was a very ambitious Scots-born merchant who traded with the Chickasaws, made a fortune, and later built a mansion in what became Aberdeen, which supplanted Cotton Gin Port as the leading town of Monroe County. Harlow et al., *History of Monroe County*, p. 53.

15. "Allopathy" was a term of derision given to the orthodox practitioners of early nineteenth-century medicine by the homeopathic leader, Dr. Samuel Hahnemann. John S. Haller, Jr., *American Medicine in Transition, 1840–1910*, p. 108; Norman Gevitz, ed., *Other Healers: Unorthodox Medicine in America*, p. 18. One authority labeled the allopath-

ists "the calomel-mercury-bleeding" doctors. R. Carlyle Buley, *The Old Northwest: Pioneer Period, 1815–1840*, 1:283.

16. By this time (c. 1831) Gideon and Sarah had eight children. Lucullus and Leonora were too young for school. Burkhalter, *Gideon Lincecum*, p. 69.

17. According to a deed dated 1 May 1831, Gideon sold ten lots or parcels in Cotton Gin Port for $430, perhaps to finance his children's schooling in Columbus. Monroe County Deed Book, No. 3, p. 87.

18. This house was to be Gideon's home until the family moved to Columbus in 1841. He became postmaster in 1838 and changed the name of the town from Wall's Tanyard to Electra, as one more fitting for the dawning age of electricity. He even found a use for electricity in treating some of his patients. In time Electra became Smithville and survives as such today. See "Smithville," in Harlow et al., *History of Monroe County*, p. 77.

19. Cholera first arrived in the United States in 1832, sixteen years after erupting first in India. It was particularly virulent in the Mississippi Valley in 1833 and resurfaced in June, 1835. Bernard DeVoto, *Across the Wide Missouri*, pp. 218–20.

20. "Six Towns," or *Okla Hannali* in Choctaw, was one of the main districts of the Choctaw Nation. It consisted of many towns but took its name from the dominant six towns that gained ascendency in the southeastern section of the Choctaw Nation in Mississippi, centered around Jasper County. Henry S. Halbert, "District Divisions of the Choctaw Nation," p. 381.

21. *"Eliccha chito"* is Gideon's garbled form of *"Alikchi chito,"* which is Choctaw for "great doctor." Byington, *Choctaw Language*, pp. 38, 107.

22. Pierre Juzon, whose name appears with various spellings, was a prominent Choctaw leader, who commanded a troop of Choctaws under Andrew Jackson at the Battle of New Orleans. He served as principal chief, 1838–1841, after the move to Oklahoma. He died in 1841. Kaye et al., *Inland River*, p. 58; Mary C. Park, comp., *Thumbnail Sketches of Choctaw Chiefs*, p. 70.

23. The Noxubee River is a considerable stream in East Central Mississippi. It runs diagonally through Noxubee County and enters the Tombigbee below the mouth of the Sipsey River in Sumter County, Alabama. Its name is derived from the Choctaw word *"nakshobi,"* which means "to stink." Byington, *Choctaw Language*, p. 284; *Soil Survey, Noxubee County, Mississippi*, U.S. Department of Agriculture, Soil Conservation Service, Oct. 1968, p. 2.

24. Unfortunately, the medical lore of the *"Eliccha chito of Okla hunale"* was never published except for some excerpts in Thomas N. Campbell, "Medicinal Plants Used by the Choctaw, Chickasaw, and Creek Indians in the Early Nineteenth Century"; Burkhalter, *Gideon Lincecum*, pp. 28, 330.

25. Yannubbee Town (or *Ayanabi*) was "a noted town" in the Northwestern District of the Choctaws in Mississippi. It was located on Yan-

nubbee Creek about eight miles southwest of present DeKalb. Hodge, *Handbook of American Indians,* 1:122; Halbert, "District Divisions of the Choctaws," p. 378.

26. Samuel Thomson (1769–1843) was a New England Yankee who established the Thomsonian system of medical treatment, which relied mainly on botanical medications. Like Gideon, he almost totally lacked a formal education and spent much of his time in the fields and woods, learning from nature. In 1822, he published his *New Guide to Health, or Botanic Family Physician,* which went through many editions. His system of herbal medicine sought to induce vomiting and/or sweating as a substitute for the conventional application of "bleeding, calomel and opium." Arthur N. Alling, "Samuel Thomson," *Dictionary of American Biography,* 9:488–89. See also William G. Rothstein, "The Botanical Movements and Orthodox Medicine," in Gevitz, *Other Healers,* pp. 42–46.

27. Thomson numbered his remedies, 1 to 6, and "No. 6" consisted of "draughts of brandy or wine mixed with botanicals," especially red pepper. Rothstein, "Botanical Movements," in Gevitz, *Other Healers,* pp. 42–43; Buley, *The Old Northwest,* 1:283–86; Burkhalter, *Gideon Lincecum,* p. 28n.

28. The term "steam doctors" was popularly and often derisively applied to practitioners of botanic medicine. The steaming came more from internal heat induced by the herbs than from external heat, such as steam baths. Buley, *The Old Northwest,* 1:284; Evans and Wilkes, *Mother Monroe,* p. 25.

29. The Pruetts or Prewitts (as their name appears in the 1830 Census) were a leading family in Monroe County. Abner Prewitt had forty-six slaves in the 1830 Census; Lemuel (Samuel?) Prewitt had thirty-one; Kirk Prewitt, fifteen; Dan Prewitt, twenty-four; Mary T. Prewitt, thirty-three; E. D. Prewitt, thirty-two; and John Kirk, who is listed with the Prewitts, had thirteen. Fifth Census, Mississippi, Monroe County, Reel M19–71, pp. 135–36, 142. It was said of Colonel Prewitt not only that he "owned a large amount of land and more than 100 negroes," but also that he "became President of the bank" of Cotton Gin Port and "was known as a man whose word could be relied on." Evans and Wilkes, *Mother Monroe,* pp. 26–27.

30. Horton Howard published *An Improved System of Botanic Medicine, Founded Upon Correct Physiological Principles* . . . (Columbus, OH: published for the author, 1832). It went through many editions in the next twenty-five years, even though Howard died in the cholera plague of 1832. Buley, *The Old Northwest,* 1:286. In the Lincecum Papers is an announcement, dated 3 March 1838, that Drs. M. Bailey and G. Lincecum were the legally appointed agents of the heirs of the late Horton Howard in the states of Mississippi and Alabama for the use of Howard's medicines. Burkhalter, *Gideon Lincecum,* p. 57n. At least one letter of Gideon's correspondence with the Howards has been preserved, and the Lincecum Papers include a document stating that

Gideon was an agent for selling Howard's book in his area. H. H. Howard, letter to Dr. Gideon Lincecum, 24 Jan. 1848, Lincecum Papers, Box 2E-363.

31. One scholar has identified the following journal articles by Gideon on this subject: *The Botanico-Medical Recorder* (later renamed *Healthside*), 8 (1839–1840): 66; 304–306; 9 (1840–1841): 81–85; 116–18; 130; 10 (1841–1842): 130; 12 (1844): 83–84; 13 (1844): 4–5. Clay, "Gideon Lincecum," p. 100. The editors have obtained photocopies of these articles, which took the form of "Letters to the Editor," some of them giving quite lengthy accounts of unusual cases and the treatments used, while others were brief comments on one or two points. Perhaps the most interesting was a lengthy account of the various treatments Gideon submitted himself to before recovering from his "heatstroke." Having been founded by Horton Howard, the journal was in these years edited by Dr. A[lva] Curtis, M.D.

CHAPTER SIX

1. This "good friend" was probably Rev. Fred Weaver, the pioneer settler of the area for whom Weaver's Creek is named. Evans and Wilkes, *Mother Monroe*, p. 41. Weaver had served with Gideon as one of the original commissioners to organize Monroe County. Kaye et al., *Inland River*, p. 80.

2. Gideon's original journal for this expedition has been preserved and is found in Box 2E-364, Lincecum Papers, Barker History Center. The journal was edited and published, with a map, by Gideon's great-grandson, A. L. Bradford, and Prof. T. N. Campbell as "Journal of Lincecum's Travels in Texas, 1835." Besides Gideon, the party included Fred Weaver and his son Calvin, Benjamin Nix, John Gavin, and possibly one other. Gideon, in all of his accounts of the expedition, says there were six in the party, but he never mentions the sixth member, unless the "G. Lincecum" he lists was not himself but one of his brothers, as Burkhalter suggests. Burkhalter, *Gideon Lincecum*, p. 35.

3. The party crossed Mississippi to Port Gibson, passed through Louisiana roughly eighteen miles north of Alexandria to Fort Jessup, and entered Texas east of San Augustine. From San Augustine they headed south to Liberty, then turned west to San Felipe on the Brazos, and then west-northwest to Bastrop. Their Texas route is traced on a map in Bradford and Campbell, "Journal of Lincecum's Travels," 184.

4. *Stipa setigera*, Gideon's name for green winter grass, has proven elusive. There are three possible plant species he may be referring to: *S. avenacea* (blackseed needle grass), *S. comata* (needle grass), and *S. leucotrichia* (Texas winter grass or spear grass). Donovan S. Correll and Marshall C. Johnston, *Manual of Vascular Plants of Texas*, pp. 121–23.

5. *Cerasus caroliniana* is now called *Prunus caroliniana* and is known as the laurel cherry or wild peach. J. C. Willis, *A Dictionary of the Flowering Plants and Ferns*, p. 225.

6. The "Texas leopard cat" is better known as the Ocelot (*Felis pardalis*). William B. Davis, *The Mammals of Texas*, pp. 108–109.

7. *Tillandsia usneoidis* is popularly known as "Spanish moss." Mary Motz Wills and Howard S. Irwin, *Roadside Flowers of Texas*, pp. 90–91.

8. Probably Gideon is referring here to the *Sambucus canadensis*, which is the American elder or elderberry. Brown, *Louisiana Trees and Shrubs*, p. 232.

9. Barton's Bluff, like Austin's hugely popular Barton Springs, is named for the early Texas pioneer, "Uncle Billy" Barton (1782–1840). "William Barton," in *The Handbook of Texas*, eds. Walter P. Webb and Eldon S. Branda, 1:118.

10. *Viburnum dentatum*, called arrow-wood, is a shrub with small white flowers and can grow to heights of twenty feet. Brown, *Louisiana Trees and Shrubs*, pp. 234–35.

11. The pinnated grouse is also known as the greater prairie chicken, *Tympanuchus cupido*. *Checklist of North American Birds*, p. 140.

12. The Texas Northers were, and still are, famed for their sudden arrival, with blustery winds and great chilling power. See Edward H. Phillips, "The Texas Norther." Gideon made many references to the Northers in his meteorological notebooks, Lincecum Papers.

13. The Navidad River, which is south of the Colorado River, has its headwaters in Fayette County about ten miles south of LaGrange. It joins the Lavaca River near Port Lavaca on the Gulf of Mexico.

14. At this point Gideon's journal ceases its daily entries. He summarized the next three months in one brief paragraph and then wrote a long essay on the geographical and natural features of Texas as a sort of guide to encourage immigration. It is possible that Gideon may have kept a second journal of his solo wanderings for the next three months, but if so it has been lost.

15. Perhaps for dramatic effect in writing this account for his readers in *The American Sportsman*, Gideon feigned ignorance regarding this house and its owner, even though he and his companions had camped there February 21 and again on March 3–4. Bradford and Campbell, "Journal of Lincecum's Travels," 189, 191.

16. What Gideon referred to as *Quercus Catesbaei*, or the Turkey Oak, is now called *Q. laevis*. Thomas Elias, *Complete Trees of North America*, pp. 364–65. For the pecan, Gideon listed the wrong genus. Although the pecan belongs to the walnut family (*Juglandaceae*), it is classified in the genus *Carya*. The species *olivaeformis is now called illinoensis*. Benjamin L. Robinson and Merrit L. Fernald, eds., *Gray's New Manual of Botany: A Handbook of the Flowering Plants and Ferns*, p. 331.

17. The "disconsolate, lonely father" was Jesse Burnam (1792–1883), whose name is often misspelled "Burnham." Like "Uncle Billy" Barton, Burnam was an early pioneer in the area, perhaps the earliest White settler on the upper Colorado River. His ferry and trading post were near present-day LaGrange in Fayette County. After losing his

first wife, he married again and had a total of sixteen children. Burkhalter notes that he and Gideon remained lifelong friends and Gideon visited him in 1867, when he lived on Doublehorn Creek in Burnet County, Texas. "Jesse Burnam," *Handbook of Texas*, 1:252; Burkhalter, *Gideon Lincecum*, p. 39n.

18. One must realize that Gideon, writing thirty-nine years later, could not possibly have recalled such conversations *verbatim*. He was a vivid, creative writer, who loved to entertain his medical patients with stories, especially ones based on this trip to Texas. Evans and Wilkes, *Mother Monroe*, p. 25.

19. The San Bernard River rises in Austin County in Central Texas. Running between the Brazos and Colorado Rivers, it empties into the Gulf of Mexico in Brazoria County.

20. Gideon is describing here the famous endangered Whooping Crane (*Grus americana*), whose present winter home, the Aransas National Wildlife Refuge, is about eighty miles down the coast. Peterson, *Field Guide to Western Birds*, p. 50.

21. The scientific designation of the great picturesque live oak is *Quercus virginiana*, not *Q. virens* (Gideon may have written an abbreviation which the printer misread). Ellwood S. Harrar and J. George Harrar, *Guide to Southern Trees*, p. 179. However, *Quercus virens* appears as the Bay live oak in Robert A. Vines, *Trees, Shrubs and Woody Vines of the Southwest*, pp. 170–71.

22. The peccary, more commonly called the javelina in Texas, belongs to the order *Artiodactyla* (cloven-hoofed mammals) and bears the Latin label *Dicotyles tajacu*, or *Pecari angulatus*, so "*Decotyles*" may have been another printer's error instead of Gideon's. William H. Burt and Richard P. Grossenheilder, *A Field Guide to Mammals*, p. 213.

23. The name "Churchwell" here raises problems of identification. The various census reports for early Brazoria County (and early Texas) fail to list a Churchwell. However, the name Churchill appears several times, including one "Stephen Churchill," who was a "pirate, pilot, and ferryman" on Galveston Island in the 1810s. Ernest W. Winkler, "Editorial Note," 203. More promising is Andrew Churchill of Brazoria County, who in 1847 bought a barrel of sugar from Peach Point Plantation near this area, where a community of Churchills took root on the west bank of the Brazos River. Abigail Curlee, "The History of a Texas Slave Plantation," p. 101. More intriguing is the possibility the man may have been Thomas T. Churchill, one of Fannin's men who was executed at Goliad on Palm Sunday, 1836. A scholar of the massacre has written, "There is substantial evidence . . . that Thomas T. Churchill should be 'Thomas T. Churchwell'. . . ." Herbert Davenport, "The Men of Goliad," pp. 33, 37.

24. Here Gideon's arithmetic or his geography is in error. Brazoria is only fifteen miles from the Gulf at the mouth of the San Bernard River.

25. Probably these were the Whistling Swans (also called Tundra Swans), *Cygnus columbianus,* or the Trumpeter Swans, *C. buccinator,* now very rare. Peterson, *Field Guide to Western Birds,* pp. 16–17.

26. Apparently this was Cedar Lake, which is a few miles down the coast from the San Bernard River. Farther down the coast, about fifteen miles, is Lake Austin, another possibility.

27. The roach is one of the names for the widely distributed golden shiner (*Notemigonus crysoleucas*). Francesca La Monte, *North American Game Fishes,* p. 158.

28. The Texas prairies have a number of varieties of wild lilies, but the Spider-lily (*Hymenocallis liriosme*) is especially common along the Gulf Coast. Wills and Irwin, *Roadside Flowers of Texas,* pp. 97–99.

29. Probably this was William Jones Eliot Heard (1803–1874), who in 1830 founded the community of Egypt (mentioned by Gideon later) and became a prominent citizen of this area, which in 1846 became Wharton County. In 1836, he commanded a company of Texas Volunteers at the Battle of San Jacinto, and in a Texas census of 1840 he is listed as having seventeen slaves and over five thousand acres of land. "William Jones Eliot Heard," *Handbook of Texas,* 1:549, 791; Gifford White, *1840 Citizens of Texas,* 2:27, 85. See also Samuel H. Dixon and Louis W. Kemp, *Heroes of San Jacinto,* p. 205, on Heard.

30. Burkhalter thinks this was Dr. S. A. Alexander, a "steam doctor" of Clinton, Mississippi. Burkhalter, *Gideon Lincecum,* p. 41n. The 1820 Census of Monroe County, Mississippi, lists an Archibald Alexander, and the 1830 Census lists both Samuel Alexander and Samuel Alexander, Sr., as residents in or near Cotton Gin Port. Fourth Census (1820), Monroe County, Mississippi, M33–58, p. 208; Fifth Census (1830), Monroe County, Mississippi, M19–71, p. 131. Gideon seems to be confused here, since Heard married twice, first to America Morton, the daughter of Rev. Quin Morton, and second to a "Miss Glass," which would seem to leave no room for a Miss Alexander. "William Jones Eliot Heard," *Handbook of Texas,* 1:549, 791; Annie L. Williams, *A History of Wharton County, 1846–1961,* pp. 294–97.

31. Eagle Lake, one of the few natural lakes in Texas, is in southeastern Colorado County, about twelve miles northwest of Heard's residence. The lake is still a great feeding range for waterfowl, especially in winter months.

32. Probably these were Alabama (*Alibamu*) or Coushatta (*Kosati*) Indians, a branch of the Creek Nation, whose language, Muskogean, was the same stock as that of the Choctaws. The Alabama-Coushatta had migrated into western Lousisiana and eastern Texas earlier in the nineteenth century. They still have a reservation in Polk County, Texas. Hodge, *Handbook of American Indians,* 1:43–44, 719–20; W. E. S. Dickerson, "Alabama-Coushatta Indians," *Handbook of Texas,* 1:20–21.

33. Egypt, which was founded by William J. E. Heard about 1830, is in Wharton County, approximately midway between Eagle Lake and the town of Wharton. "Egypt, Texas," *Handbook of Texas,* 1:549.

34. According to ethnomusicologist Christopher Goertzen, of the University of North Carolina at Chapel Hill, several pieces entitled "Washington's March" were common in print beginning in the mid-1780s. The most widely distributed of these was later retitled "Washington's Grand March." See, for example, Elias Howe, *Musician's Companion*, 1:26. If Gideon remembered exactly which tunes he played, his "General Harrison's March" may have been "The Battle of the Wabash," which appeared in 1814, honoring Harrison's victory over the Indians at Tippecanoe. Sigmund Spaeth, *A History of Popular Music in America*, p. 41. If, on the other hand, Gideon reconstructed more approximately, he may have been referring to "Harrison's Grand March," widely printed, beginning a few years later. Howe, *Musician's Companion*, 1:106. "Hail, Columbia," joined words composed by Joseph Hopkinson to Philip Phile's "The President's March" of 1798. The "No. 1 Cotillion in the Beggar Set" has proved elusive. Sets of cotillions, ubiquitous in print during the first half of the nineteenth century, gathered a handful of short dances (usually six; music and figures were printed together). This set's title probably refers to the first ballad opera, Christopher Pepusch and John Gay's *The Beggar's Opera;* though written in 1728, it remained popular during much of the nineteenth century. Christopher Goertzen, letter to Jerry Lincecum, 13 June 1992.

35. Elizabeth A. H. John has suggested that an entry in the Bexar Chronicles for 30 September 1835 may be connected with Gideon's indication here that he made arrangement for the Coushattas to return in the fall to obtain cane sprouts from Mr. Heard. The entry concerns two Coushatta Indians who fell victim to a Gonzales mob which was defying an attempt by the Mexican authorities to retrieve a cannon which had been lent to local citizens several years previously. Here is her translation of the pertinent paragraph: Francisco de Castatñeda to Francisco de Ugartechea, in sight of Gonzales, 30 September 1835. BA roll 166:886. "From a Cosataé Indian who presented himself to me this afternoon, fleeing because his companion had been killed after having been with them many days, [he] knows positively that they presently have 160 men and expect 300 more from San Felipe and Tenoxtitlán this afternoon." John suggests that because of the proximity of Gonzales to the settlement of Egypt, where Mr. Heard lived, it seems plausible that these two Coushattas, whose names are not recorded, might have been the same ones whom Gideon met at Eagle Lake in March 1835, since they planned to return to Egypt in the fall.

CHAPTER SEVEN

1. There are problems with this story of "Old Mr. Ally's" murder by Indians in 1835, as supporting evidence is lacking. The Alleys were early settlers in Austin's Colony, and John C. Alley was killed by Karankaway Indians in the lower Colorado River in 1822 or 1823. His

nephew, John Alley, received land on the upper Colorado River in Fayette County (near Burnam's) in 1827, but if he or any other Alley was killed by Indians in 1835, his relative, Abraham Alley, does not mention it in his recollections. J. H. Kuykendall, ed., "Reminiscences of Early Texas," p. 47. Burkhalter implies that William Alley was the massacre victim (Burkhalter, *Gideon Lincecum*, p. 43n), but Abraham Alley says his brother, William, was still living on the Colorado River in 1857. See also Lester G. Bugbee, "The Old Three Hundred," p. 110.

2. A "William Criswell" is listed in Burnam's area (Fayette County) in 1840, and "L. V. Criswell" is listed there in 1846. White, *1840 Citizens of Texas*, 2: 36; Marion D. Mullins, compiler, *Republic of Texas Poll Lists for 1846*, p. 38.

3. There appears to be an omission from Gideon's narrative here, but if so it was imposed by the editors of *The American Sportsman*.

4. The genus *Vilfa* is now called *Sporobolus*. *S. asper*, or tall dropseed, is found in east and southeast Texas. Willis, *Flowering Plants and Ferns*, p. 1211.

5. There are a number of copiously flowing springs at the base of the Edwards Plateau. Probably Gideon is describing here the springs that form the San Marcos River within today's town of San Marcos, where the Aquarena Springs are a major tourist attraction.

6. Gideon is in error here, for several Catholic missionaries visited the valley in the late seventeenth and early eighteenth centuries. They even had a mission here briefly in 1755–1756. Dudley Dobie, "San Marcos, Texas," *Handbook of Texas*, 1:559.

7. *Argemone texana*, also designated *Argemone albiflora*, is the Texas prickly-poppy, a wild white-flowered poppy with prickly leaves. Wills and Irwin, *Roadside Flowers of Texas*, p. 117.

8. *Vitis texana* is known today as *V. monticola* or the sweet mountain grape. It grows on limestone hills and ridges of the Edwards Plateau. Correll and Johnston, *Manual of Vascular Plants of Texas*, p. 1020. *Ilex vomitoria*, popularly known as yaupon, is a member of the holly family with red berries. Harrar and Harrar, *Guide to Southern Trees*, p. 448. *Zanthoxylum fraxineum* is the prickly ash or "toothache tree." It is also known as *Z. Clava-Herculis* and is frequent in forested areas of east and southeast Texas. Willis, *Flowering Plants and Ferns*, p. 1238; Correll and Johnston, *Vascular Plants of Texas*, p. 910. *Bumelia lanuginosa* is a tree called gum bumelia. It has flowers, berries, and thorns. Harrar and Harrar, *Guide to Southern Trees*, pp. 598–600. *Berchemia volubilia* is probably *B. scandens*, the supple-jack or rattan vine. Correll and Johnston, *Vascular Plants of Texas*, p. 1012. *Celtis occidentalis* is the common and prolific hackberry tree. Harrar and Harrar, *Guide to Southern Trees*, pp. 249–51.

9. Later authorities have generally doubted and even rejected Gideon's theory that the agricultural (or horticultural) ants intentionally planted the seeds around their mound "cities." Burkhalter, *Gideon Lincecum*, pp. 224–26. For an exception to this general view see the

opinion in Ralph A. Wooster, "With the Confederate Cavalry in the West: The Civil War Experiences of Isaac Dunbar Affleck," 25–26. Among Gideon's many articles on the agricultural or horticultural ant is one entitled "On the Agricultural Ant of Texas."

10. Samuel Botsford Buckley (1809–1883) was born and educated in the North but did most of his research in the South. He came to Texas in 1860 and later became Texas' state geologist. He and Gideon became active correspondents and friends, and Buckley accompanied Gideon on a research expedition in West Texas in 1867. "Samuel Botsford Buckley," *Handbook of Texas*, 1:238; Lincecum Papers. Gideon named a species of cutting ants after Buckley, as witnessed by his article, "On the Cutting Ants of Texas—*Oecodema texana buckley.*"

11. As noted in chap. 6, n.16, regarding the pecan, Gideon has the wrong genus.

12. Probably this was the Guadalupe River, which is joined by the San Marcos River near Gonzales and receives the San Antonio River just before it enters the Gulf.

13. Because of the number of cliffs and caverns in this part of Texas, the identification of this particular formation must await some enterprising rock-hound or spelunker. The editors are neither.

14. The "turtle dove" is a member of the *Columbidae* family, but Gideon's description is too limited to permit a precise identification of this particular species. Peterson, *Field Guide to Western Birds*, pp. 82–84.

15. *Algarobia* is now called *Prosopis*. *P. glandulosa* is the honey mesquite tree. Willis, *Flowering Plants and Ferns*, p. 40; Correll and Johnston, *Vascular Plants of Texas*, p. 784. Earlier Gideon referred to *Stipa setigera* as "green winter grass," but this "mesquite grass" may be the same prairie needle grass. Correll and Johnston, *Vascular Plants of Texas*, p. 121.

16. *Opuntia polyacantha,* the many-spined opuntia, is popularly referred to as prickly-pear cactus. Lauren Brown, *Grasslands*, pp. 386–87.

17. This may have been the Scaled ("Blue") Quail (*Callipepla squamata),* but other than the size, Gideon's description seems to fit better the smaller Mearns' Quail (*Cyrtonyx montezumae mearnsi).* Peterson, *Field Guide to Western Birds*, pp. 48–49.

18. The chapparal cock or roadrunner is a member of the cuckoo family (*Cuculidae),* but its Latin designation is *Geococcyx californianus.* Ibid., pp. 85–86.

19. The genus *Ribes* contains the gooseberries and currants. It is more likely that what he saw was blackberries (*Rubus trivialis),* and the printer may have misread his handwriting. Wills and Irwin, *Roadside Flowers of Texas*, pp. 123–24.

20. Gideon's original journal of 1835, or at least the only one that has survived, gives no indication of this interruption or encounter.

21. Gideon gives three accounts of the episode that follows. In his 3 November 1871 letter to "Bully Grandson" he covers the episode in

about 1,250 words. In the version published by the Mississippi Historical Society the account is limited to just 200 words, but in his account for readers of *The American Sportsman,* Gideon "pulled out all the stops." That version runs to about 8,400 words. Since he told the story to many of his patients as a form of therapy, the tale no doubt improved and expanded with the telling. Evans and Wilkes, *Mother Monroe,* p. 25. An authority on Indian captivity narratives, Dr. Michael Lynn Tate, of the University of Nebraska, Omaha, has serious doubts about some of the incidents described in Gideon's narrative, especially his use of medicine to overawe the Indians, a common device in romanticized frontier literature. Michael Tate, letter to Jerry Lincecum, 1 Nov. 1992.

CHAPTER EIGHT

1. In describing Choctaw as "the true language of the Coshatas," Gideon is referring to their common Muskogean root. Hodge, *Handbook of American Indians,* 1:719.

2. In his letter to "Bully Grandson," Gideon says it was the Indian that had just surprised him who explained the use of the term "slave tongue." The Indian said it was so-called because "'It is a slave to all the tribes.'" Gideon to "Bully Grandson," 3 Nov. 1871, p. 42. Probably the Indians who confronted Gideon here were Comanches.

3. This could be another indication that Gideon had a second journal.

4. It is strange that this very amusing and significant episode regarding the Indian doctor's experiment on the chief is lacking from Gideon's most extensive narrative, *The American Sportsman* version.

5. In his letter to "Bully Grandson," Gideon quotes the chief as telling his men to "'let that *hard eyed man* go.'"

CHAPTER NINE

1. In the *PMHS* version of his "Autobiography," Gideon says that he did shoot one of the deer, and he makes no mention whatever of "dear *Nilpe*." Professor Tate questions the authenticity of *Nilpe*, who, he says, "sounds too much like a Pocahontas character." Michael Tate, letter to Jerry Lincecum, 1 Nov. 1992.

2. Gideon's imaginative recall was working amazingly well to be able to place this deer at precisely "twenty-seven paces."

3. Gideon is not using the name "salamander" to refer to the common amphibian but rather to the plains pocket gopher (*Geomys bursarius*). Davis, *Mammals of Texas,* pp. 145–47. Probably the term "salamander" was a corruption of "sand mounder."

4. *Diplostoma,* meaning "double mouth," refers to the group of mammals having pockets or "mouths" in their cheeks for storing food.

5. Here Gideon's "Personal Reminiscences" ends, for he died (24 November 1874) before he could complete his extensive narrative relating to his escape from captivity in 1835. In the "Personal Reminiscences" he had reached the point where he was close to Bastrop on the Colorado River. The remainder of his Autobiography is based on his 1871 letter to "Bully Grandson" and the published version that appeared in *Publications of the Mississippi Historical Society* in 1903.

6. The falls of the Brazos are southeast of Waco, near present Marlin, in Falls County.

7. The Yegua Country is that part of Central Texas drained by the three branches of Yegua Creek in Lee, Milam, Burleson, Williamson, and Washington Counties. During 1962–1967 the creek's main course was dammed to form Lake Somerville. The Yegua empties into the Brazos River about ten miles west of Navasota. "Yegua Creek," *Handbook of Texas*, 2:943; "1976 Annual Report of the Chief of Engineers on Civil Works Activities," Department of the Army, 2:xvi, 17.

8. The Long Point League was part of the property owned by Stephen F. Austin in what is now Washington County. Gideon wrote: "Austin located it as No. 5 of his premium leagues as early as 1824." "History of the Discovery of Long Point, TX," an undated fragment in Gideon's hand, Lincecum Papers, Box 2E-363. Felix Huston (1800–1857), a prominent, swashbuckling Mississippian, did not come to Texas until 1836, so Gideon has mistaken the name of Austin's Agent. "Felix Huston," *Handbook of Texas*, 1:869; William R. Hogan, *The Texas Republic*, p. 281.

9. Although Gideon spelled the name "Boden," he was undoubtedly referring to Gail Borden (1801–1874), a remarkable, versatile pioneer, best known for his invention of the condensed milk process but also a major figure in the history of the Texas Republic. In the 1820s he resided in Mississippi and may have met Gideon at that time. Joe B. Frantz, *Gail Borden, Dairyman to the Nation*, 52–61, 76–77.

10. Moseley Baker (1802–1848) was another major figure of the Texas Republic. He distinguished himself in the military resistance to the Mexicans and later to the Indians. Not one with whom one could differ freely, he carried on a bitter quarrel with Sam Houston. "Moseley Baker," *Handbook of Texas*, 1:100–101. George Ewing arrived in Texas from Alabama in November, 1829, at the age of 38 and settled in Stephen Austin's Colony. Gifford White, *1830 Citizens of Texas*, p. 11. Thomas Gay was born in Georgia about 1805 and came to Austin's Colony in May, 1830. Gay Hill in Washington County was named for him (and for W. C. Hill). Ibid., p. 29; "Gay Hill," *Handbook of Texas*, 1:677. William Jack was from Wilkes County, Georgia, though he came to Texas from Alabama in June, 1830. Since he was born in 1806, he was still a boy when Gideon lived in Georgia and Alabama. White, *1830 Citizens of Texas*, p. 50; "William Houston Jack," *Handbook of Texas*, 1:899–900. William Barrett Travis (1809–1836), the heroic commander of the Alamo defense, was living in Alabama when Gideon was

there in 1818, but Travis was only a boy of nine then and lived far to the south of Tuscaloosa. Archie P. McDonald, *Travis*, pp. 27–51.

11. Gaines's Ferry on the Sabine was the entry point for many visitors and immigrants coming to Texas through Louisiana, and it connected with the Old Spanish Road (*El Camino Real*). It was named not for General Edmund Pendleton Gaines, who positioned his U.S. Army forces near there during the Runaway Scrape of 1836, but rather for his cousin, James Gaines, a pioneer settler and signer of the Texas Declaration of Independence, who owned the ferry and lived nearby. Lewis W. Kemp, *The Signers of the Texas Declaration of Independence*, pp. 127–34. Hickman's Ferry probably was named for Theophilus Hickman, a pioneer settler in northeastern Newton (Jasper) County below Gaines Ferry. "Hickman Creek," *Handbook of Texas*, 1:804–805; Mullins, *Poll Lists*, p. 77.

12. Mason B. Foley was a member of the prominent Foley family of Colorado (later Lavaca) County. In 1840, he is listed as owning 8 slaves, 100 cattle, and 1,796 acres in Colorado County. In the same tabulation, his father, Washington G. F. Foley, is credited with 41 slaves, 51 cattle, 1 stud, and 1737 acres. White, *1840 Citizens of Texas* 2:27; Burkhalter, *Gideon Lincecum*, p. 51n. Mason B. served with Ranger Capt. Jack Hays's Spy Company during the Mexican invasion of Texas in 1842. Paul C. Boethel, *On the Headwaters of the Lavaca and the Navidad*, pp. 23–24. In Gideon's surviving journal of 1835, he mentions that Foley had a companion, a "Mr. Cope," and implies that the three of them traveled together out of Texas, which casts doubt on the accuracy of Gideon's later autobiographical account. Bradford and Campbell, "Journal of Lincecum's Travels in Texas," p. 193.

13. Cholera resurfaced in the Mississippi Valley in June, 1835. DeVoto, *Across the Wide Missouri*, pp. 218–20.

14. Several recorders, including Burkhalter, have mistaken the name of this young brother of Gideon. His name was Grabel, not Gabriel, as proven by his own signature on a document relating to the estate of his brother, Rezin B. Lincecum. Estate File #88, Reason [*sic*] B. Lincecum Final Settlement, December Term 1837, Book A, Lowndes County (Mississippi) Records, pp. 320–21. Actually Rezin Bowie Lincecum, who carried the given name of his famous cousin (the brother of Jim), died several months earlier. Gideon shared equally in Rezin B.'s estate with his siblings: Garland, Grant, Grabel, Mary Bryan, and Emily Moore. John Pitchlynn, Sr., died in May, 1835. It is noteworthy that Gideon's brother-in-law, Joseph Bryan, had recently been boarding Hiram Pitchlynn (and, somewhat earlier, Thomas Pitchlynn), and he billed John Pitchlynn's estate for money owed for their board. John Pitchlynn File, No. 8, Item 70, Lowndes County Archives, Columbus Public Library.

15. Gideon had a good friend, Dr. Andrew Weir, who later followed him to Texas. He is listed in the 1830 Census for Lowndes

County and had two slaves. Burkhalter, *Gideon Lincecum,* p. 51n; Fifth Census, Mississippi, M19–71, p. 84.

CHAPTER TEN

1. On 20 February 1841, Gideon advertised his practice for the first time in the Columbus newspaper, saying he was "Late of Electra, Monroe [County]" and "has located himself permanently at Columbus Mi where he will attend to all cases in his profession." *Columbus Democrat,* 20 Feb. 1841, p. 1. Two years earlier, an ad appeared repeatedly in another local paper with the heading "Botanic Medicines" and the following text: "Greene Hill, at the Columbus Drug Store, has rec'd from the manufacturer a general assortment of the most approved Botanic medicines, comprising almost every article in the line. They were prepared and manufactured expressly for the Columbus demand, by Doctor Gideon Lincecum, and are warranted good and fresh. Those who use medicines of this description cannot apply too early." *Southern Argus,* 4 June 1839, p. 1. The same newspaper had a separate ad indicating that "Howard's Improved System of Botanic Medicines" was for sale "at the drug store of Greene Hill."

2. Examples of these attacks are numerous in the *Columbus Democrat* in 1841 until the paper changed ownership later that year and dropped coverage of the controversy. Writing in the 5 June 1841, issue (p. 2), "M.D." asks: "What think you, reader, of the innocent harmless reform Steam Doctor, who sweats you to prostration, and then strengthens your system with a purgative compound, as debilitating as I have shown the Bilious Physic to be?"

3. This letter of Gideon's could not be found in the *Columbus Democrat,* but the paper did print a long letter of his in defense of the botanic system of medicine. *Columbus Democrat,* 27 Feb. 1841, p. 1.

4. In a handbill which Gideon used to advertise his medical practice in Long Point, Texas, in 1850, he makes a similar guarantee regarding treatment of fever. The entire text of the handbill reads as follows:

DR. G. LINCECUM & SON, BOTANIC PHYSICIANS.

Will continue the practice of Medicine at the village of Long Point, and its vicinity, to any distance. Being well supplied with a full assortment of such Botanic Medicines as are needed in this climate—all fresh—they are ready day or night, to accommodate all those who may call for their professional services. With these advantages and many years experience in the diseases of the South, they flatter themselves, and they know, that they will be able, by close and prompt attention, to give general satisfaction. Their whole practice will be conducted on purely Botanic principles. They are no half way men. They have the temerity to take a bold and decided stand for progressive Medical reform. Such is their confidence in the supperiority [sic] and certainty of their remidies [sic], and their knowledge of disease, that they will make no charge for failure to cure any form of fever, where they are called during the first stage of the disease—have an efficient nurse, and the patient stricly [sic] following their prescription, and continuing to employ them throughout the case. They feel happy in assuring the community that they have prepared themselves for, and will be able to answer all reasonable expectation. And they are determined to give the public, particularly the friends of medical reform, by their superior skill and management an opportunity to remove from the Botanic System, the popular charge of ignorance and empyricism.

Long Point, Washington County, Texas.

5. In 1845, when Gideon's wife Sarah was visiting a spa (named "Gid's Springs") in Alabama, Gideon wrote her that he was "sending the girls to the Dancing School, and to the Singing School," so he was not blameless. Gideon, letter to Sarah Lincecum, 2 July 1845, Lincecum Papers, Box 2E-363.

6. There may have been other reasons for Gideon's rather sudden move to Texas, though there can be little doubt that his soul longed for the open country of the Texas prairies that he had enjoyed in 1835. Columbus was subject to frequent floods, including one in 1847. In that same year there was a lawsuit filed against one of his sons, in which Gideon was named a codefendant. Roderick B. Gary v. Leonidas L. Lincecum & Gideon Lincecum, Circuit Court, Lowndes County, Mississippi, March Term, 1848, File Civ. #7516, LCA, Columbus Public Library. Burkhalter says that Gideon's oldest son, Lycurgus, then thirty-two years of age, and another son, Leander (twenty-four), led the caravan to Texas and must have approximated their father's path of 1835. They started out in the spring of 1847, almost a year before Gideon and the rest of the family departed. In addition to household goods, the wagons contained Gideon's large collection of fossils and bones and $6,000 worth of medical supplies [Gideon said above the value was $5,000]. Burkhalter says the caravan included ten slaves and ten extra horses, as well as Lycurgus' wife Martha and their four children. They apparently arrived as early as July, 1847, since Leander married Miss S. J. Stone in Washington County on 20 July 1847. Further evidence that they arrived in 1847 is provided by documents indicating that Lycurgus enlisted in a Texas group of soldiers who fought in the Mexican War in August of that year, where he apparently contracted an illness which led to his death (at Long Point) in 1849. He is buried in an unmarked grave beside his mother in the family plot in Mt. Zion Cemetery, Washington County. Burkhalter, *Gideon Lincecum*, pp. 72, 78, 80.

7. The *New Era* was a 246-ton steamboat built about 1843. It had two captains, Lyles and Estes, the latter probably being Joseph H. Estes. John E. Rodabough, *Steamboats on the Upper Tombigbee*, p. 82.

8. There is a small journal in the Lincecum Papers, Box 2E-364, in which Gideon recorded the family's trip from Houston to Long Point, 12–22 April 1848. Gideon seems to imply here that Lucullus was the son who accompanied Lycurgus on the trip by land, but Burkhalter says it was Leander, and documents show he was the one who got married in Washington County in July, 1847. See note 6, above.

9. Gideon says he purchased the tract from Stephen Austin's nephew Moses Austin Bryan, who inherited it from his uncle upon the latter's death in 1836. Gideon's assertion had been doubted because Bryan was not included in Austin's will, but Burkhalter discovered there was a codicil to Austin's will in which he left Bryan an entire league, of which Gideon purchased 1,828 acres. "History of the Discovery of Long Point," Lincecum Papers; Burkhalter, *Gideon Lincecum*, pp. 72–73, note 1. James V. Matson, who bought 2,000 acres of the same Long Point league of land from which Gideon bought his acreage, married Gideon's daughter, Mary, on 5 October 1848, and he and Gideon were once partners in a grain mill. Unfortunately, the two men later had a complete falling out so bitter as to reflect no credit on either, and when Gideon divided his Long Point land among the children in 1867, Mary was left out. Burkhalter, *Gideon Lincecum*, pp. 79–80.

10. During the Civil War Gideon's fertile mind came up with many ideas to assist the Confederacy. He invented a machine to spin Spanish moss for the manufacture of bags and blankets, and he proposed the use of canisters of one-ounce balls to be fired onto the decks of enemy vessels or against charging infantrymen. Lincecum, letter to Col. S. D. Hay, 26 Oct. 1861, and to J[udah] P. Benjamin, 17 Dec. 1861, Lincecum Papers, Letter Press, Vol. 2, pp. 859, 906–908. Even after the fighting ended, Gideon's house was a refuge for ill or destitute returning veterans. In May, 1865, he wrote that his unmarried daughter, Sarah, "makes music for the soldiers that stop with us, and that's every night," and added "I help her." Lincecum, letter to Dr. A[ndrew] Weir, 20 May 1865, Lincecum Papers, Letter Press Vol. 5, p. 11.

11. Sarah Bryan Lincecum died 2 February 1867, and lies in an unmarked grave in the family plot in Mount Zion Cemetery, a few miles west of Long Point. Upon her death Gideon wrote: "She left the form" at ten minutes after 6 A.M., and he added, "The soul of my house it has fled. The loved one is gone, my incentive to action is dead. Oh! what shall I do whilst I lag here behind?" Lincecum Papers, Box 2E-363.

12. William H. Lincecum and George Campbell were grandsons of Gideon. James Caldwell was a young naturalist from Fort Jessup, Louisiana. Gideon kept a journal of the expedition and it is in the Lincecum Papers, Box 2R-79. The party left Long Point on 12 March

and returned on 3 June. They visited twenty-eight counties in west central Texas. The journal has never been published, except for excerpts which were widely circulated in Texas newspapers during the Texas Centennial of 1936; however, Burkhalter has summarized it well in *Gideon Lincecum*, pp. 231–37. Gideon collected a number of specimens on the trip which are catalogued in the journal. Despite his age and bereavement he could say, "I have stood the fatigue of travel and camp duties as well as any of the company." In this letter he mentions that they narrowly missed an encounter with marauding Indians. Gideon, letter to Mary Lincecum Matson, 2 May 1867, Lincecum Papers, Box 2E-363.

13. Tuxpan, which is located on the Gulf Coast of Mexico between Tampico and Vera Cruz, became a haven for die-hard ex-Confederates who could not bear to live under Yankee rule. A Texan, John Henry Brown, actively promoted the colonization of ex-Confederates in Mexico, especially favoring the Tuxpan River area, and his propaganda had its intended effect upon Gideon. Laurence F. Hill, "The Confederate Exodus to Latin America," pp. 323–26; Burkhalter, *Gideon Lincecum*, p. 241.

14. Apparently Gideon is referring to William Jarvis Russell (1802–1881), who actively participated in the Texas War for Independence, later settled in Fayette County, and became president of the board of Rutersville College, established near LaGrange in 1840. "William Jarvis Russell," *Handbook of Texas*, 2:520.

15. During the years 1866–68, Gideon carried on considerable correspondence with Northern scientists, especially Elias Durand and Joseph Leidy of the Academy of Natural Sciences, Spencer Baird of the Smithsonian Institution, and Alpheus Packard, editor of *The American Naturalist*. Lincecum Papers, Letter Press Vols. 5–7. Burkhalter lists most of Gideon's articles published at this time and has a fine chapter on his scientific work in *Gideon Lincecum*, pp. 172–227, 328–29.

16. See chap. 1, n.50 above. Despite Gideon's high esteem for Charles Darwin, he was not above criticizing him. Considering himself an expert in graphology (as well as phrenology), Gideon wrote: "From the indications displayed in his [Darwin's] autograf, I see, and he may not be co[g]nizant of it, that Charles occupies a plane above his nature. I could name others, who similarly placed by fortuitous circumstances, are addicted to airs and overpretensions." Gideon to Elias Durand, 21 Mar. 1861, Lincecum Papers, Letter Press Vol. 2, p. 553.

17. At first Gideon had planned to travel the 960 miles to Tuxpan by horse and wagon (his "ambulance"), but he was talked out of that. He then made arrangements to sail from Galveston on 15 May, but the ship became unavailable. Gideon, letters: to Elias Durand, 30 Oct. 1867; to Spencer Baird, 11 Dec. 1867; to Durand, 25 Apr. 1868. Ibid., Vol. 7, pp. 154, 220, 327.

18. Gideon was accompanied by his widowed daughter, Leonora

Campbell, and her seven children, one of whom died shortly after their arrival in Mexico. Burkhalter, *Gideon Lincecum*, pp. 253, 263.

19. In the Lincecum Papers is a map or sketch (perhaps drawn by Gideon), showing the mouth of the Tuxpan River. It indicates the jungle, with extensive groves of banyan trees, bordering the beaches and each shore of the river right up to the town of Tuxpan. Lincecum Papers, Box 2E-363.

20. In fact Gideon did not sell the farm. He continued to work arduously on it, save for a respite in 1871, when his new grandson-in-law briefly took charge. Burkhalter, *Gideon Lincecum*, pp. 272–79.

21. "Bravo" was Gideon's own name for these ants, which Burkhalter says were "probably a genera of the *Dorylinae* or army ants," in *Gideon Lincecum*, p. 274n.

22. Gabor Naphegyi (1824–1884) was a Hungarian resident of Mexico, who (according to Burkhalter) had "extraordinary control" over Santa Anna. Ibid., p. 273n. He wrote several books on Hungary and on Africa, including the one Gideon read: *Ghardaia; or Ninety Days among the B'ni Mozab: Adventures in the Oasis of the Desert of Sahara.*

23. Gideon also sent natural history specimens to the Smithsonian Institution from Tuxpan. Burkhalter, *Gideon Lincecum*, p. 257.

24. The chachalaca (*Ortalis vetula vetula*) is a large, brown, rather ugly bird that calls out its name raucously and monotonously every morning and before a rain. A few are found in the Texas Rio Grande Valley. Peterson, *Field Guide to Western Birds*, pp. 44–45.

25. Tumilco is a Totonac ruin near the coast south of Tuxpan. It is among "many mounds lacking any trace of stone construction" to be found in the Tuxpan basin. Jose G. Payan, "Archeology of Central Vera Cruz," in *Archeology of Northern Meso America*, eds. Gordon F. Eckholm and Ignacio Bernal, 2:512.

26. Gideon may be describing here the massive ruins of the ancient city of El Tajin, the most impressive archeological site in the State of Vera Cruz, about thirty-five miles south of Tuxpan. El Tajin was dominated by the great pyramid of the Niches, its stepped sides containing 364 niches, one for each day of the year (minus one). The fact that Gideon does not mention the niches may indicate that he did not actually visit the site himself. His narrative is ambiguous on that point. A good illustrated article on El Tajin is that by S. Jeffrey K. Wilkerson, "Man's Eighty Centuries in Vera Cruz." See also Payan, "Archeology of Central Vera Cruz," in *Archeology*, eds. Eckholm and Bernal, pp. 527, 541.

27. Gideon's interpretation of the lengthy traditional history of the Choctaws, which he took down from *Chahta-Immataha* in 1822 in the Choctaw language and translated into English almost 40 years later, included the idea that the tribe migrated from Mexico, where they had been part of a civilization that worshipped the sun. His observations of some ancient ruins near Tuxpan confirmed his belief. In a letter from

Tuxpan to Sallie Doran he wrote: "In the numerous piles of ruined cities . . . are found ample proof of what that old Indian, *Chahta-Immataha* told me." Burkhalter, *Gideon Lincecum*, p. 278.

28. Gideon is writing in late 1871 and is referring to the short-lived rebellion, largely inspired by Porfirio Diaz and his brother, that erupted shortly before and immediately after the re-election of Pres. Benito Juarez in October of that year. Ralph Roeder, *Juarez and His Mexico*, 2:719–20.

29. Wilbur F. Parker, "Dr. Gideon Lincecum," *The American Sportsman*, 4 (Dec. 12, 1874): 169.

Selected References

RECORDS AND DOCUMENTS

Deed and Court Records. Lowndes County Archives. Columbus Public Library, Columbus, Miss.

Fourth Census of the United States (1820). Georgia: Putnam County. Mississippi: Monroe County.

Fifth Census of the United States (1830). Alabama. Mississippi: Lowndes County, Monroe County.

Lincecum Papers. Barker Texas History Center, University of Texas at Austin, Texas.

Map of Township Plat T18-R19W, from Meridian of Huntsville, Ala., detail of acreage on Tombigbee River near Plymouth Bluff and Peachland's Crossing north of Columbus, Miss., surveyed by Charles M. Lawson in May and June, 1823.

"1976 Annual Report of the Chief of Engineers on Civil Works Activities," Department of the Army, Office of the Chief of Engineers. 2 vols.

Soil Survey, Noxubee County, Mississippi. U.S. Department of Agriculture. Soil Conservation Service. October, 1968.

BOOKS

Abernethy, Thomas P. *The South in the New Nation, 1789–1819.* Baton Rouge: Louisiana State University Press, 1961.

Alden, John R. *The South in the American Revolution.* Baton Rouge: Louisiana State University Press, 1957.

Baird, W. David. *Peter Pitchlynn: Chief of the Choctaws.* Norman: University of Oklahoma Press, 1972.

Bettersworth, John K. *Mississippi: A History.* Austin: Steck Co., 1959.

Blair, Ruth, ed. *Some Early Tax Digests of Georgia.* Atlanta: Georgia Department of Archives, 1926.

Boethel, Paul C. *On the Headwaters of the Lavaca and the Navidad.* Austin: Von Boeckman–Jones, 1967.

Brent, Peter. *Charles Darwin*. New York: Harper and Row, 1981.

Brown, Calvin S. *Archeology of Mississippi*. Oxford, Miss.: University of Mississippi Press, 1926.

Brown, Clair A. *Louisiana Trees and Shrubs*. Baton Rouge: Louisiana Forestry Commission, 1945.

Brown, Lauren. *Grasslands*. New York: Alfred A. Knopf, 1985.

Buley, R. Carlyle. *The Old Northwest: Pioneer Period, 1815–1840*. 2 vols. Bloomington: Indiana University Press, 1950.

Burkhalter, Lois Wood. *Gideon Lincecum, 1793–1874: A Biography*. Austin: University of Texas Press, 1965.

Burt, William H., and Richard P. Grossenheilder. *A Field Guide to Mammals*. 3rd ed. Boston: Houghton Mifflin, 1976.

Byington, Cyrus. *A Dictionary of the Choctaw Language*. Edited by John R. Swanton and Henry S. Halbert. Bureau of American Ethnology. Bulletin 46. Washington: Smithsonian Institution, 1915.

Candler, Allen D., ed. *The Revolutionary Records of the State of Georgia*. 3 vols. Atlanta: Franklin-Turner, 1908.

Carey, A. Merwyn. *American Firearms Makers: When, Where, and What They Made from the Colonial Period to the End of the Nineteenth Century*. New York: Thomas Y. Crowell Co., 1953.

Catlin, George. *Letters and Notes on the Manners, Customs, and Conditions of the North American Indians*. 2 vols. New York: Dover Publications, 1973.

Checklist of North American Birds. 6th ed. Lawrence, Kans.: American Ornithologists Union, 1983.

Clark, Murti June. *American Militia in the Frontier Wars, 1790–1796*. Baltimore: Genealogical Publishing Co., 1990.

Clark, Thomas D., and John D. W. Guice. *Frontiers in Conflict: The Old Southwest, 1795–1830*. Albuquerque: University of New Mexico Press, 1991.

Coleman, Kenneth. *American Revolution in Georgia, 1763–1789*. Athens: University of Georgia Press, 1958.

Correll, Donovan S., and Marshall C. Johnston. *Manual of Vascular Plants of Texas*. Renner, Tex.: Texas Research Foundation, 1970.

Craigie, William A., and James R. Hulbert, eds. *A Dictionary of American English on Historical Principles*. 4 vols. Chicago: University of Chicago Press, 1938.

Cushman, Horatio B. *A History of the Choctaw, Chickasaw, and Natchez Indians*. Greenville, Tex.: Headlight Printing House, 1899.

Davidson, Grace G. *Early Records of Georgia*. 2 vols. Vidalia, Ga.: Silas E. Lucas, Jr., 1968.

Davis, Robert S., Jr. *Georgia Citizens and Soldiers of the American Revolution*. Easley, S.C.: Southern Historical Press, 1979.

———. *A Researcher's Library of Georgia History, Genealogy, and Record Sources*. Easley, S.C.: Southern Historical Press, 1987.

———. *The Wilkes County Papers, 1773–1833*. Easley, S.C.: Southern Historical Press, 1979.

Davis, William B. *The Mammals of Texas.* Bulletin No. 41. Austin: Texas Game and Fish Commission, 1960.

Debo, Angie. *The Rise and Fall of the Choctaw Republic.* 2d ed. Norman: University of Oklahoma Press, 1961.

De Lamar, Marie, and Elizabeth Rothstein. *The Reconstructed Census of Georgia: Substitutes for Georgia's Lost 1790 Census.* Baltimore: Genealogical Publishing Co., 1985.

DeVoto, Bernard. *Across the Wide Missouri.* Boston: Houghton Mifflin, 1947.

Dixon, Samuel H., and Lewis W. Kemp. *Heroes of San Jacinto.* Houston: Anson Jones Press, 1932.

Eckholm, Gordon F., and Ignacio Bernald, eds. *Archeology of Northern Meso America.* 2 vols. Austin: University of Texas Press, 1971.

Elias, Thomas. *Complete Trees of North America.* New York: Van Nostrand, Reinhold Co., 1980.

Evans, W. A., and W. B. Wilkes. *Mother Monroe: Pioneer Times in Monroe County.* Aberdeen, Miss.: Mother Monroe Publishing Co., 1979.

Ford, Paul Leicester, ed. *The New England Primer: A History of Its Origin and Development.* New York: Teachers College Press, 1962.

Franklin, Benjamin. *The Papers of Benjamin Franklin.* Edited by Leonard W. Labaree and Whitfield J. Bell. 18 vols. New Haven: Yale University Press, 1959–74.

Frantz, Joe B. *Gail Borden, Dairyman to the Nation.* Austin: University of Texas Press, 1951.

Geiser, Samuel Wood. *Naturalists of the Frontier.* 2d ed. Dallas: Southern Methodist University Press, 1948.

Gevitz, Norman, ed. *Other Healers: Unorthodox Medicine in America.* Baltimore: Johns Hopkins University Press, 1988.

Gray's New Manual of Botany: A Handbook of the Flowering Plants and Ferns. Benjamin L. Robinson and Merrit L. Fernald, revs. 7th ed. New York: American Book Co., 1908.

Green, Constance McL. *Eli Whitney and the Birth of Technology.* Boston: Little, Brown and Co.: 1956.

Greene, A. C. *Taking Heart.* New York: Simon and Schuster, 1990.

Haller, John S., Jr. *American Medicine in Transition, 1840–1910.* Urbana: University of Illinois Press, 1981.

Harlow, Jerry A., et al. *A History of Monroe County, Mississippi.* Aberdeen, Miss.: Monroe County Book Committee, n.d.

Harrar, Ellwood S., and J. George Harrar. *Guide to Southern Trees.* 2d ed. New York: Dover Publications, 1962.

Henry, Jennie H., ed. *Abstract of Annual Returns, Mississippi Free and Accepted Masons, 1819–1849.* New Market, Ala.: Southern Genealogical Service, 1961.

Hodge, Frederick W. *Handbook of American Indians North of Mexico.* 2 vols. Washington: Smithsonian Institution, 1910.

Hogan, William R. *The Texas Republic.* Norman: University of Oklahoma Press, 1946.

Howe, Elias. *Musician's Companion.* Vol. 1. Boston: Howe, 1843.

Humes, Jesse, and Vinnie M. Humes. *A Chickasaw Dictionary.* Ada, Okla: Chickasaw Nation Publisher, 1973.

Johnson, Clifton. *Old-Time Schools and School-books.* New York: Dover Publications, 1963.

Kaye, Samuel H., Rufus Ward, Jr., and Carolyn B. Neault. *By the Flow of the Inland River: The Settlement of Columbus, Mississippi to 1825.* Columbus, Miss.: Snapping Turtle Press, 1992.

Kemp, Louis W. *The Signers of the Texas Declaration of Independence.* Salado, Tex.: Anson Jones Press, 1959.

Kidwell, Clara Sue, and Charles Roberts. *The Choctaws: A Critical Bibliography.* Bloomington: Indiana University Press, 1980.

Kilion, Ronald G., and Charles T. Waller, eds. *Georgia and the Revolution.* Atlanta: Cherokee Publishing Co., 1975.

Knapp, Frank T. *Fishes Found in the Freshwaters of Texas.* Brunswick, Ga.: Ragland Studio, 1953.

Krakow, Kenneth K. *Georgia Place-Names.* Macon: Winship Press, 1975.

La Monte, Francesca. *North American Game Fishes.* Garden City: Doubleday, 1988.

Lewis, Anna. *Chief Pushmataha, American Patriot: The Story of the Choctaws' Struggle for Survival.* New York: Exposition Press, 1959.

Lowrie, Walter, Asbury Dickins, and John Forney, eds. *American State Papers: Public Lands.* 8 vols. Washington: Gales and Seaton, 1834–61.

Lucas, Silas E., Jr., ed. *A Collection of Upper South Carolina Genealogical and Family Records.* 2 vols. Easley, S.C.: Southern Historical Press, 1981.

———. *Some Georgia County Records.* 5 vols. Easley, S.C.: Southern Historical Press, 1977–90.

———. *Some South Carolina County Records.* 2 vols. Easley, S.C.: Southern Historical Press, 1989.

McCall, Effie T. *Roster of Revolutionary Soldiers in Georgia.* 3 vols. Baltimore: Genealogical Publishing Co., 1969.

McDonald, Archie P. *Travis.* Austin: Jenkins Publishing Co., 1976.

McLemore, Richard, ed. *A History of Mississippi.* 2 vols. Hattiesburg: University and College Press of Mississippi, 1973.

Malone, Dumas, ed. *The Dictionary of American Biography.* 10 vols. New York: Charles Scribners, 1936.

Martini, Don. *Chickasaw Empire: The Story of the Colbert Family.* Ripley, Miss.: Don Martini, 1986.

Mullins, Marion D., comp. *Republic of Texas Poll Lists for 1846.* Baltimore: Genealogical Publishing Co., 1974.

Napheygi, Gabor. *Ghardaia; or Ninety Days among the B'ni Mozab: Adventures in the Oasis of the Desert of Sahara.* New York: G. Putnam, 1871.

Nixon, Pat Ireland. *The Medical Story of Early Texas.* Lancaster, Pa.: Lancaster Press Inc., 1946.

Northen, William F., ed. *Men of Mark in Georgia*. 7 vols. Atlanta: A. B. Caldwell, Publisher, 1910.

Oakes, James. *The Ruling Race: A History of American Slaveholders*. New York: Vintage Books, 1983.

Owen, Thomas M. *History of Alabama and Dictionary of Alabama Biography*. 4 vols. Spartanburg, S.C.: Reprint Company, 1978.

Park, Mary C., comp. *Thumbnail Sketches of Choctaw Chiefs*. Durant, Okla.: Three Valley Museum, 1987.

Peterson, Roger T. *A Field Guide to Western Birds*. 3d ed. Boston: Houghton Mifflin, 1990.

Rodabough, John E. *Steamboats on the Upper Tombigbee*. Ed. Helen M. Crawford. Hamilton, Miss.: Tombigbee Press, 1985.

Roeder, Ralph. *Juarez and His Mexico*. 2 vols. New York: Viking Press, 1947.

Rowland, Dunbar. *History of Mississippi: The Heart of the South*. 2 vols. Chicago: S. J. Clark Publishing Co., 1925.

Rowland, Dunbar, ed. *Mississippi*. 3 vols. Atlanta: Southern Historical Publishing Association, 1907.

Schoen, Harold, comp. *Monuments Erected by the State of Texas to Commemorate the Centenary of Texas Independence: The Report of the Commission of Control for Texas Centennial Celebrations*. Austin: Steck Company, 1939.

Silver, James W. *Edmund Pendleton Gaines, Frontier General*. Baton Rouge: Louisiana State University Press, 1949.

Southerland, Henry D., Jr., and Jerry Elijah Brown. *The Federal Road through Georgia, the Creek Nation, and Alabama, 1806–36*. Tuscaloosa: University of Alabama Press, 1989.

Spaeth, Sigmund. *A History of Popular Music in America*. New York: Random House, 1948.

Stephen, Leslie, and Sidney Lee, eds. *The Dictionary of National Biography*. 21 vols. London: Oxford University Press, 1960.

Swanton, John R. *Source Material for the Social and Ceremonial Life of the Choctaw Indians*. Bureau of Ethnology Bulletin, No. 103. Washington, D.C.: Government Printing Office, 1931.

Vexler, Robert I. *Chronology and Documentary Handbook of the State of Mississippi*. Dobbs Ferry, N.Y.: Oceana Publications, 1978.

Vines, Robert A. *Trees, Shrubs and Woody Vines of the Southwest*. Austin: University of Texas Press, 1960.

Waddell, Gene, ed. *Mills' Atlas: Atlas of the State of South Carolina, 1825*. Easley, S.C., Southern Historical Press, 1980.

Warren, Mary B., ed. *Georgia Marriages, 1811 through 1820*. Danielsville, Ga.: Heritage Papers, 1988.

Washburn, Wilcomb E., ed. *The American Indian and the United States: A Documentary History*. 4 vols. New York: Random House, 1973.

Washburn, Wilcomb E., ed. *History of Indian-White Relations*. (Vol. 4 of *Handbook of North American Indians*, William C. Sturtevant, gen. ed.) Washington: Smithsonian Institution, 1988.

Webb, Walter P., and Eldon W. Branda, eds. *The Handbook of Texas.* 3 vols. Austin: Texas State Historical Association, 1952, 1976.

White, Gifford. *1830 Citizens of Texas.* Austin: Eakin Press, 1983.

―――. *1840 Citizens of Texas.* 2 vols. St. Louis: Ingmire Publications, 1984.

Williams, Annie L. *A History of Wharton County, 1846–1961.* Austin: Von Boeckmann–Jones, 1964.

Williams, Samuel C., ed. *Adair's History of the American Indians.* New York: Promentery Press, 1986.

Willis, J. C. *A Dictionary of the Flowering Plants and Ferns.* 8th ed. Rev. by H. K. Airy Shaw. London: Cambridge University Press, 1973.

Wills, Mary Motz, and Howard S. Irwin. *Roadside Flowers of Texas.* Austin: University of Texas Press, 1961.

ARTICLES, PERIODICALS, AND MANUSCRIPTS

"Botanic Medicines" [Advertisement], *Southern Argus* (Columbus, Mo.), 4 June 1839.

Bradford, A. L., and T. N. Campbell. "Journal of Lincecum's Travels in Texas, 1835." *Southwestern Historical Quarterly* 53, no. 2 (1949): 180–201.

Bugbee, Lester G. "The Old Three Hundred." *Texas Historical Quarterly* 1, no. 2 (1897): 108–17.

Campbell, Thomas N. "The Choctaw Afterworld." *Journal of American Folklore* 72, no. 284 (1959): 146–54.

―――."Choctaw Subsistence: Ethnographic Notes from the Lincecum Manuscript." *Florida Anthropologist* 12 (1959): 9–24.

―――. "Medicinal Plants Used by the Choctaw, Chickasaw, and Creek Indians in the Early Nineteenth Century." *Journal of the Washington Academy of Sciences* 41 (1951): 285–90.

Carleton, Kenneth H. "Eighteenth-Century Trails in the Choctaw Territory of Mississippi and Alabama." Master's thesis. University of Georgia, 1989.

Clay, Mary H. "Gideon Lincecum, Southern Pioneer, 1793–1874." Master's thesis. Mississippi State University, 1953.

Columbus Democrat, 6 Aug. 1836; 20 and 27 Feb., and 5 June, 1841.

Curlee, Abigail. "The History of a Texas Slave Plantation." *Southwestern Historical Quarterly* 26, no. 2 (1922): 79–127.

Davenport, Herbert. "The Men of Goliad." *Southwestern Historical Quarterly* 48, no. 1 (1939): 1–41.

Halbert, Henry S. "District Divisions of the Choctaw Nation." *Miscellaneous Collections* (Alabama Historical Society) 1 (1901): 375–85.

―――. "Nanih Waiya, the Sacred Mound of the Choctaws." *Publications of the Mississippi Historical Society* 2 (1899): 223–34.

Hill, Laurence F. "The Confederate Exodus to Latin America." *Southwestern Historical Quarterly* 39, no. 3 (1936): 309–26.

Kuykendall, J. H., ed. "Reminiscences of Early Texas." *Texas Historical Association Quarterly* 2, no. 1 (1898): 29–64.

Lincecum, Gideon. "Agricultural Ant of Texas," *Journal of the Linnean Society,* Zoology 6 (1862): 29–31.

———. "Autobiography of Gideon Lincecum." *Publications of the Mississippi Historical Society* 8 (1904): 443–519.

———. "Choctaw Traditions about Their Settlement in Mississippi and the Origin of Their Mounds." *Publications of the Mississippi Historical Society* 8 (1904): 521–42.

———. "Life of Apushimataha." *Publications of the Mississippi Historical Society* 9 (1906): 415–85.

———. "On the Agricultural Ant of Texas." *Proceedings of the Academy of Natural Sciences* 18 (November 1866): 323–31.

———. "On the Cutting Ants of Texas—*Oecodema texana buckley.*" *Proceedings of the Academy of Natural Sciences* 19 (1867): 24–31.

———. "Personal Reminiscences of an Octogenarian." *The American Sportsman.* Issues of 12, 19, 26 September; 3, 10, 17, 24, 31 October; 7, 14, 21, 28 November; and 5, 12, 19, 26 December 1874; 2, 9, 16 January 1875.

Love, William A. "Lowndes County, Its Antiquities and Pioneer Settlers." *Publications of the Mississippi Historical Society* 7 (1903): 351–71.

Pace, Noble H., Jr. "Franklin Academy." Typescript from Mississippi State University. Manuscript Collection, Lowndes County Archives, Columbus (Miss.) Public Library.

[Parker, Wilbur F.] "Dr. Gideon Lincecum." *The American Sportsman* 4 (12 December 1874): 169.

Phillips, Edward H. "The Texas Norther." *Southwestern Historical Quarterly* 49, no. 1 (1955): 1–13.

"Pioneer Society Annals, Columbus, Mississippi, 1954–65." Typescript. Manuscript Collection, Lowndes County Archives, Columbus (Miss.) Public Library.

"Registrants in the First Georgian Land Lottery." *The Georgia Genealogical Magazine* 1 (July 1961): 1–16.

Tracy, Audrey. "Land Records Show Bowie Roots in Catahoula Parish." *Alexandria Daily Town Talk,* 22 April 1979: D-7.

Wilkerson, S. Jeffrey K. "Man's Eighty Centuries in Vera Cruz." *National Geographic* 118, no. 2 (1980): 203–31.

Winkler, Ernest W. "Editorial Note." *Southwestern Historical Quarterly* 22, no. 2 (1918): 202–203.

Wolfe, Cheri L. "The Traditional History of the *Chahta* People: An Analysis of Gideon Lincecum's Manuscript." Doctoral dissertation. University of Texas at Austin, 1993.

Wooster, Ralph A. "With the Confederate Cavalry in the West: The Civil War Experiences of Isaac Dunbar Affleck." *Southwestern Historical Quarterly* 83, no. 1 (1979): 1–28.

Index